Information Sources in Science and Technology

LIBRARY SCIENCE TEXT SERIES

Information Sources
in
Science and Technology

C. D. HURT
Director
Graduate Library School
University of Arizona
Tucson, Arizona

1988

LIBRARIES UNLIMITED, INC.
Englewood, Colorado

LIBRARIES UNLIMITED, INC.
P.O. Box 3988
Englewood, CO 80155-3988

Library of Congress Cataloging-in-Publication Data

Hurt, Charlie Deuel.
    Information sources in science and technology.

    (Library science text series)
    Includes index.
    1. Reference books--Science--Bibliography.
2. Reference books--Technology--Bibliography.
3. Science--Bibliography.   4. Technology--
Bibliography.   I. Title.   II. Series.
Z7401.H85   1988   [Q158.5]   016.5   88-22977
ISBN 0-87287-581-4
ISBN 0-87287-582-2 (pbk.)

For
Susan
for so many things

Contents

Introduction

Scientific and technical literature is more than a collection of sources. This book assumes the reader is aware that the proper use of sources has an antecedent—the proper understanding of the structure of the literature which supports the reference tool. The intent of this book is to give the reader an insight into the possible reference sources available in the wide area known as science and technology.

The provision of good reference service in science and technology, or any other area for that matter, hinges on the harmonious relationship of three basic elements: (1) knowledge of the user; (2) knowledge of the literature; and (3) knowledge of the sources. This book focuses on the last element.

At times, the literature of science and technology is discussed as if it were a thing in itself, somehow attaining the status of animate object. One purpose of this book is to allow the student of this literature to enter the maze of material without feeling unduly overwhelmed by the "literature monster." If the literature has grown, it is because the number of persons producing the literature has grown. In the heat of examination, it is all too easy to forget that science and technology literature is the output of scientific and technological experiment. Indeed, the best definition of scientific literature is just that: the tangible output of science.

A definition of technical literature is slightly more difficult, but is an analog to scientific literature. It can be considered the written communication as opposed to the artifact produced by technologists.

Derek Price, a student of scientific and technical literature all his life, once voiced the opinion that scientists are papyrocentric, while technology is papyrophobic, roughly speaking.[1] Price and others have argued that the intent of technology is *not* to publish, but to produce the artifact or process. Only after the claim can be made for the process or artifact in a legal manner will the technologist publish. The entire issue of proprietary information is a large issue in technology.

The scientist must publish in order to make the priority claim for the discovery. In point of fact, the scientist rarely produces an artifact. Even the processes developed by a scientist are not refined in the sense of ready for public use. In some sense it is the issue of public use which helps define the literature of science and technology.

Nan Lin devised a model of scientific and technical literature which suggests a hierarchical approach to the problem.[2] Lin suggests a "trickle down" process is at work. At the top of the hierarchy is the scientist. The scientist produces material for use by the technologist, who then provides a process or artifact for general consumption. Of note in Lin's model is lack of direct communication channels from the scientist to the public. This model alienates the scientist while at the same time placing the scientist on a pedestal of sorts.

Price and Lin have one major common thread—they both see science and technology as distinctly different. In the abstract, this is a reasonable approach. The actual practice of science suggests there are at least as many impediments to publication as there are in technology.

The scientist is quite careful about prepublication announcements and discussions of a potential discovery or even a particular research program for fear of being "scooped" by a colleague. Merton discussed the issue of priority as a part of the scientific literature process.[3] The thrust of Merton's work in this area is that priority to the scientist is the prime means of obtaining reward. The priority claim gives the scientist publicity for the present and a continued place in the pantheon of successful scientists, at least for the short term.

The reward model as proposed by Merton is especially important in understanding both the differences and similarities between scientific and technical literature.[4] If the scientist is to receive nothing but the recognition of peers as a result of scientific achievement, the importance of the literature and the quality of the literature is enhanced. At the time of Merton's writing, this was the normative structure of science.

Technology differs to some extent in that the reward for achievement is also the recognition of peers, but there can also be the potential for monetary remuneration. The obtaining of a patent or exclusive licensing arrangements is a large incentive or reward. Without question the issue of monetary reward as opposed to peer reward is a major difference in the two literatures.

Recent evidence suggests, however, that the differences, if they were truly present, have narrowed considerably. In a preliminary research venture, Narin and Carpenter suggest that science and technology are moving closer together.[5] The contemporary accounts of both science and technology suggest a melding of the two. Scientists are becoming more interested in the monetary rewards associated with their work. The use of patent literature by both scientists and technologists is increasing. All of this suggests a blurring of what were once considered clear distinctions between the two areas. In short, Price's general distinctions of the technologist as papyrophobic and the scientist as papyrocentric are less applicable now than they once were.

As a point of departure, let us make the assumption that the literature of science and the literature of technology are different literatures. What characteristics sustain the differences?

At the beginning, the major difference between science and technology literatures is the audience intended for each. In the case of the scientist, the audience is a select group of other scientists. A great deal of research has gone into the examination and delineation of "invisible colleges" in scientific disciplines and specialty areas.[6] To a great extent, the invisible college is a grouping concerned with informal communication rather than the formal communication as demonstrated by a journal article or monograph. Nonetheless, it is these people and those involved in the periphery of their influence who are the target audience. General science or even those in the same discipline are not usually the target.

The publication by a scientist is a number of things at once. The first is a staking of territory. The second is a priority claim. Finally, there is also the socializing factor of doing what is expected in science—publication of research findings. This is part of what Hagstrom means by normative science.[7] Indeed, it may be argued that the scientist who does not publish is not a scientist.[8] The point remains that the publication process for the scientist is a communication among a select group of like-minded scientists.

The technologist has a different reason for publication and a different audience. Publication for the technologist is a function of priority claim in the legalistic sense. An example of a priority claim in technology is a disclosure leading to a patent. The audience is ill defined in most cases. Consider the audience for a patent—basically anyone who wishes to search for and use the information contained in the patent. A second type of publication in technology is the technical report. The audience for the technical report is primarily a grant agency. The dissemination of the technical report is varied and inconsistent.

A second means of differentiating between the scientific and the technical literatures is in the form of publication. The case will be made later that this is perhaps the best distinction to delineate between the two. The technologist does not normally produce a journal article except in a house or professional organ. The preferred means of communication is via the technical report or at times the monograph.

The scientist is very much interested in publication of journal articles. Not only must they be journal articles, but they should be published in refereed journals. A substantial body of work has been done with the "gatekeeper" concept as it relates to scientific publication.[9] This gatekeeper or referee function introduces the potential for quality control in the literature. The necessity for insisting on the *potential* for quality control is evident in the number of cases of scientific fraud which have surfaced in recent years. This fraudulent research has been published via refereed journals. Nonetheless, the concept of papers being refereed by experts in the field prior to their publication has considerable virtue. The point here is less whether the process actually works, but that a procedure exists in the journal article publication mode that does not normally exist in the technical report mode.

One form of literature only briefly touched on previously is the monograph. In both science and technology, the monograph is the least desirable form of publication. The reasons for this are fairly straightforward. A monograph takes considerable effort and time to produce. This time and effort limits the amount of effort that can be expended at the research front. The longer a scientist or technologist spends away from the research front, the longer it will take to catch up. In some sense, the publication of a monograph may be a flag to the rest of the scientist's or technologist's peers that he or she have given up the research front to others.

In no way is this a suggestion that monographs are not important to either science or technology. Rather, they have a different function and their production carries a certain connotation for the author. The monograph is perhaps the one form of scientific and technical communication where there is some agreement both in terms of form and in terms of audience.

As the listing of source materials later indicates, there is a distinct difference in the format of the technological literature versus the scientific literature. Technical literature is less formal and formalized. This makes the technical literature somewhat more elusive in terms of bibliographic control. One mark of a technological versus a science library is a collection of technical reports.

This is not the specific place to enter into a prolonged discussion of the differences and similarities between and among science and technology. Close examination of the sources listed in the areas will help to point up the differences and similarities.

By no means are the sources listed here a complete listing of sources available. An effort was made to include the most important and useful items. This is a subjective judgment, likely to meet with some disapproval in certain cases. Comments concerning omissions or differences of opinion are welcomed.

In culling sources to be included, Ching-chih Chen's source book for science and technology was very helpful.[10] Much credit should also go to three graduate assistants, Ray Barker, Jerry McGovern, and Luan Knospe. Their work was instrumental in verifying and uncovering new material.

NOTES

[1]Derek Price, "Is Technology Historically Independent of Science? A Study in Statistical Historiography," *Technology and Culture* 6:553-568.

[2]Nan Lin, "A Comparison between the Scientific Communication Model and the Mass Communication Model: Implications for the Transfer and Utilization of Scientific Knowledge," *IEEE Transactions on Professional Communication* PC15:34-39 (1972).

[3]Robert K. Merton, "Priorities in Scientific Discovery," *American Sociological Review* 22:635-659 (1957).

[4]Robert K. Merton, *Social Theory and Social Structure* (New York: Free Press, 1968).

[5]Francis Narin and Mark Carpenter, "Are Technology and Science Becoming Indistinguishable?" *American Society for Information Science Proceedings* 21:199-203 (1984).

[6]As an example, see Diana Crane, *Invisible Colleges* (Chicago, IL: University of Chicago Press, 1972).

[7]Warren O. Hagstrom, *The Scientific Community* (New York: Basic Books, 1965).

[8]This presumes the freedom to publish. There are fields or areas of science which, for various reasons such as national security, preclude immediate publication.

[9]This concept was introduced first by Kurt Lewin, "Forces behind Food Habits and Methods of Change," *Bulletin of the National Research Council* 108:65 (1943).

[10]Ching-chih Chen, *Scientific and Technical Information Sources*, 2nd ed. (Cambridge, MA: MIT Press, 1987).

1 History of Science

History of science is a relatively new discipline. Its formal organization into the university system is only now firmly taking root. The antecedents of history of science can be seen in the efforts to understand science, particularly during the period following World War II.

Science and the efforts of technologists played an immense part in the war on all sides. Governmental and societal interest was piqued. Added to the scientific and technical efforts in the war was the scientific and technical race into space. The launching of *Sputnik* and the subsequent U.S. space effort focused even more attention on science and technology.

For all the attention they receive, scientists and technologists are, and remain, remarkably nonintrospective. A great deal of this behavior is learned in undergraduate and graduate education. It leaves the examination of the social fabric of science and technology to others, such as historians and sociologists.

A large, coherent body of literature exists in the history of science and technology. The material listed below is but a small part of the source and reference material allowing the user to enter that literature.

The areas are listed in the order in which overall source material appears later in the book. There is no attempt to create a hierarchy of disciplines or to suggest that one area springs from another. Rather, the focus of this historical section is to suggest a series of references in each of the areas examined which will meet the needs of the researcher and the general reader. However, by its nature, the historical section is predominantly composed of materials utilized more for research than for general reading.

The intent is to allow the reader the means by which to enter the historical analysis of a particular area, giving critical annotations to the source literature.

GENERAL

1. **Album of Science, Volume 1: Antiquity and the Middle Ages.** Murdoch, John E., ed. New York: Scribner, 1984. 403p.

A single volume of the *Album of Science* series, this includes brief narrative text, several hundred illustrations, annotated bibliographies, and well-prepared indexes. It is a must for all libraries with collections in science.

2. **Album of Science: From Leonardo to Lavoisier, 1450-1800.** Cohen, I. Bernard. New York: Scribner, 1980. 298p.

A detailed, pictorial history of science, this work contains illustrations taken from books and manuscripts, engravings, drawings, charts, maps, and paintings. A supplementary text accompanies the volume, and a bibliography is included. This is an invaluable reference for science historians.

3. **Album of Science: The Nineteenth Century.** Williams, L. Pearce. New York: Scribner, 1978. 413p.

Contains pictures, maps, photographs, and diagrams from the nineteenth century illustrating the development of science and technology. It is divided into sections, each with an informative introduction. Detailed indexing of illustration sources is provided. Highly recommended for high school, public, and academic libraries.

4. **Asimov's New Guide to Science.** rev. ed. Asimov, Isaac. New York: Hamondsworth, 1987. 880p.

Originally titled *Intelligent Man's Guide to Science*, revised editions of this volume were published in 1972, 1984, and 1985. Coverage includes the latest scientific developments. The guide's main audience will be laypersons.

5. **The Awakening Interest in Science during the First Century of Printing, 1450-1550: An Annotated Checklist of First Editions Viewed from the Angle of Their Subject Content.** Stillwell, Margaret B. New York: Bibliographical Society of America, University Press of Virginia, 1970. 399p.

This important two-part checklist approaches the study of first editions from a subject analysis mode as well as that of bibliographic interest. An author list of titles arranged under the categories of astronomy, mathematics, medicine, natural science, physics, and technology comprises the first part. In addition to the bibliographic information, there is also a list of references for each entry. The second part presents an analytical list of editors, places of publication, and names of printers and translators.

6. **Bibliography of Quantitative Studies on Science and Its History.** Hahn, Roger. Berkeley, CA: University of California, Office for History of Science and Technology, 1980. 84p.

A compilation from the International Symposium on Quantitative Methods in the History of Science, held at Berkeley in August of 1976, this covers broad topics such as methodology, bibliographic aids, manpower, input, and the like.

7. **Bibliography of the Philosophy of Science, 1945-1981.** Blackwell, Richard J., comp. Westport, CT: Greenwood Press, 1983. 585p.

A personal name index is included, but no subject index or annotations are provided. The lack of annotations dulls the utility of the work.

8. **Breakthroughs: A Chronology of Great Achievements in Science and Mathematics, 1200-1930.** Parkinson, Claire L. Boston: G. K. Hall, 1985. 576p.

A chronology of scientific discovery divided into subject areas within each year. The bibliography and name and subject indexes are helpful. Illustrations are provided where appropriate.

9. **Catalogue of Scientific Papers, 1800-1900.** Royal Society of London. London: Clay, 1867-1902; Cambridge, England: University Press, 1914-1925. 19v.

10. **Subject Index.** Cambridge, England: University Press, 1908-1914. 3v.

This comprehensive bibliography of the scientific literature of the last century covers periodical articles as well as the proceedings and transactions of societies published from 1800-1900. Arranged alphabetically by author, then chronologically under each author, each entry includes the author's name, complete title of article, periodical article, volume, date, and inclusive paging. All entries are given in the language of the paper without translation, except for titles in East European languages, which are usually translated into English, or French or German in some cases. Three separately published subject indexes cover pure mathematics, mechanics, and physics and provide brief title, author's name, periodical title, volume, date, and pagination. The classification used was that of the *International Catalogue of Scientific Literature* (see entry 21). Under the title *International Catalog of Scientific Literature*, the publication was continued into the present century for a time. Volume 1 contains sections on pure mathematics, while volumes 2 and 3 cover mechanics and physics.

11. **Critical Bibliography of the History of Science and Its Cultural Influence.** Berkeley, CA: University of California Press, 1913- .

This serial bibliography, arranged in a closely classified order, is a major tool. It has appeared annually in the History of Science Society's official journal as *ISIS, International Review Devoted to the History of Science and Its Cultural Influences* (Beltsville, MD: ISIS, 1913- . quarterly). A cumulation of the first 90 critical bibliographies was published in 1971 — *ISIS Cumulative Bibliography* (see entry 23).

12. **Dictionary of the History of Ideas: Studies of Selected Pivotal Ideas.** Wiener, Philip P., ed. New York: Scribner, 1980. 5v.

Pivotal ideas, central to the history of science, are discussed in this set. Such concepts include monism, dualism, matter, life (its uniqueness or its assimilability to matter), atomism, and primary qualities. The varied aspects of these concepts are unified in the separate index.

13. **Dictionary of the History of Science.** Bynum, W. F., E. J. Browne, and Roy Porter, eds. Princeton, NJ: Princeton University Press, 1985. 494p.

This dictionary concentrates on the development of Western post-medieval scientific thought. It also includes ancient, medieval, and non-Western theories that influenced Western science. It is helpful to students, specialists, and laypersons.

14. **Encyclopedia of Philosophy.** Edwards, Paul, ed. New York: Macmillan, 1972. 4v.

This encyclopedia illuminates the important contributions mathematicians, physicists, biologists, and chemists have made to the development of modern philosophical thought. With the *Dictionary of the History of Ideas* (see entry 12), it is essential to any history of science collection.

15. **Guide to the History of Science: A First Guide for the Study of the History of Science with Introductory Essays on Science and Tradition.** Sarton, George. Waltham, MA: Chronica Botanica, 1952. 316p.

A good general guide written by an authority, this is a classic in the field of history of science. It lays the groundwork for the study of science from a philosophical and sociological standpoint. Sarton was a giant in the field and the book is important for this reason alone.

16. **Historical Catalogue of Scientific Periodicals, 1665-1900, with a Survey of Their Development.** Gascoigne, Robert Mortimer. New York: Garland, 1985. 205p.

This is a companion to *Historical Catalogue of Scientists and Scientific Books* (see entry 17) by the same author. Contains a selected list of 900 periodicals arranged chronologically within a scientific field. It is particularly interesting for its retrospective coverage.

17. **Historical Catalogue of Scientists and Scientific Books: From the Earliest Times to the Close of the Nineteenth Century.** Gascoigne, Robert Mortimer, ed. New York: Garland, 1984. 1177p.

Contains bibliographical dictionary, chronological index to 13,300 people of scientific significance who can be found in reference works, and a reference to scientific works. Also serves as a catalog of the most widely available books written by persons in this list. This work can be used not only as an index, but as a bibliography to important works by important persons in science. Completely indexed, this is a useful tool for all research libraries.

18. **History of Science.** Sarton, George. Ann Arbor, MI: University Microfilms, 1975. 2v.

This is a reprint of the classic history published by Harvard University Press in 1952. Divided into two volumes, the first discusses scientific progress from ancient times through the Golden Age of Greece and the second includes Hellenistic science in the last three centuries B.C.

19. **History of Science and Technology in the United States: A Critical and Selective Bibliography.** Rothenberg, Marc. New York: Garland, 1982. 242p.

A bibliography of important secondary works published between 1940 and 1980, such as books, articles, dissertations, and a review essay. This covers a variety of fields such as women, government, science, and religion, but does not include medicine. A valuable tool for academic libraries.

20. **Information Sources in the History of Science and Medicine.** Corsi, Pietro, and Paul Weindling. London: Butterworths, 1983. 531p.

A four-part coverage of the historical development of science, medicine, and research methods, along with a description of the major libraries and archives. It includes technical issues, along with cultural and social aspects of science and medicine.

21. **International Catalogue of Scientific Literature, 1st-14th, 1901-1914.** London: published for the International Council by the Royal Society, 1902-1921; repr., New York: Johnson Reprint Corporation, 1975. 238v. in 32.

This is the most important science bibliography for this period. A continuation of the Royal Society's *Catalog* (see entry 9), it lists papers, monographs in serials, and independent works in the sciences, giving citations in a decimal classification order. Each issue is divided into 17 separate parts, each covering one subject: mathematics, mechanics, physics, chemistry, astronomy, meteorology, mineralogy, geology, geography (mathematical and physical), paleontology, general biology, botany, zoology, human anatomy, anthropology, physiology, and bacteriology. Each section includes schedules, indexes in four languages, author catalog, and subject catalog.

22. **Introduction to the History of Science.** Sarton, George. Baltimore, MD: Williams & Wilkins, 1927-1948; repr., Huntington, NY: Robert E. Krieger Publishing Co., 1975. 3v. in 5.

George Sarton was one of the giants in developing the history of science as a separate scholarly discipline. This work provides a narrative and a comprehensive bibliographic history of science for the period through the early 1900s. It is supplemented by *Scientific Thought* (see entry 33).

23.　**ISIS Cumulative Bibliography: A Bibliography of the History of Science Formed from ISIS Critical Bibliographies 1-90, 1913-1965.** Whitrow, Magda, ed. London: Mansell, in conjunction with the History of Science Society, 1971-80.

This work cumulates George Sarton's bibliographies that appeared in *ISIS* between 1913 and 1965. Volumes 1 and 2, part 1, cover reference works, monographs, pamphlets, and articles discussing the work and contributions of individual scientists. As appropriate, materials are grouped under the following categories: bibliographies, biographies, and collected editions. Volume 2, part 2, is arranged alphabetically by institutions with subdivisions. The work is formatted according to the LC rules of cataloging, filing, and transliteration. This exceptionally well-reviewed and well-organized tool is certainly the most important bibliography on the history of science ever published. For bibliographies after 1965, see *Critical Bibliography of the History of Science and Its Cultural Influence* (see entry 11).

24.　**ISIS Cumulative Bibliography 1966-1975: A Bibliography of the History of Science Formed from ISIS Critical Bibliographies 91-100 Indexing Literature Published from 1965 through 1974.** Neu, John, ed. London: Mansell, in conjunction with the History of Science Society, 1980- .

This is a supplement to *ISIS Cumulative Bibliography* (see entry 23) edited by Whitrow. It continues in the same vein and with the same careful selection of the best of the literature by an expert. The first volume deals with personalities and institutions. Other volumes are intended. This is a critical addition for any collection in the history of science.

25.　**ISIS Cumulative Index, 1953-1982.** Morley, Jane, et al., eds. Philadelphia: History of Science Society, 1985. 168p.

This is the cumulative index to what has become the most prestigious journal in the history of science area.

26.　**Lexikon der Geschichte der Naturwissenschaften: Biographien, Sachwörter und Bibliographien.** Vol. 1- . Mit einer Einfuhrung "Die Zeitalter der Naturforschung" und einer Übersichtstabelle von Josef Mayerhofer. Wien, Austria: Hollinek, 1959- .

This encyclopedia survey of the history of science through the end of the nineteenth century is a comprhensive bio-bibliography. Published to date are: Liferungen 1, *Introductory Articles and Aachen-Achord*; 2/3, *Achard-Bewegurg*; 4/5, *Bewegury-Daniel von Morley*; and 6, *Daniel von Morley-Dodel, Arnold*. Liferungen 1 through 6 compose Band I.

27.　**Reference Books for the Historian of Science.** Jayawardene, S. A., comp. London: Science Museum, 1982. 242p.

The work is divided into three parts: part 1, history and literature of science; part 2, history in general; and part 3, general reference books. Periodicals are included.

28.　**Repertorium Commentationum Societatibus Litterariis Editarum Secondum Disciplinarum Ordinem Digessit.** Reuss, Jeremias David. Gottingen, Federal Republic of Germany: Dieterich, 1801-1821; repr., New York: B. Franklin, 1962. 16v.

This multivolume work was the predecessor of the Royal Society's *Catalog of Scientific Papers* (see entry 9). Before 1800, it served as an index to Society publications. The volumes cover: (1) historia naturalis, generalis et zoologia; (2) botanica et mineralogia; (3) chemia et res metallica; (4) physica; (5) astronomia; (6) oeconomia; (7) mathesis, mechanica, hydrostatica, hydraulica, hydrotechnia, aerostatica, pneumatica technologia, architectura civilis, scientia navalis, scientia militaris; (8) historia; (9) philologia, linguae, scriptores graeci, scriptores latini, litterae elegantiores, poesis, rhetorica, ars antiqua, pictura, musica; volumes 10 through 16 cover scientia et ars medica et chirurgica.

29. **Science in America: A Documentary History, 1900-1939.** Reingold, Nathan, and Ida H. Reingold, eds. Chicago, IL: University of Chicago Press, 1981. 490p.

An overview of the issues, institutions, and individuals involved in science in the early twentieth century. The roles played by foundations and universities, as well as by individual scientists, are revealed through correspondence.

30. **Science in the Middle Ages.** Lindberg, David C., ed. Chicago, IL: University of Chicago Press, 1978. 549p.

Contributions from experts bring together a vast amount of history. Included are excellent bibliographies and a detailed source of historical reference.

31. **Scientific Books, Libraries, and Collectors: A Study of Bibliography and the Book Trade in Relation to Science.** 3rd ed. rev. Thornton, John L., and R. I. J. Tully. London: Library Association; distr., Detroit, MI: Gale Research, 1978. 508p.

This classic bibliographic history of science provides coverage of the production, distribution, and storage of scientific literature from early times to the present. Attention is devoted to scientific authors and their publications, the periodical literature, scientific societies, public and private scientific libraries, and scientific publishing and bookselling. In addition to a substantial bibliography, the volume contains a survey of guides to the literature, current and retrospective bibliographies, and other control tools.

32. **Scientific Societies in the United States.** 3rd ed. Bates, Ralph Samuel. Cambridge, MA: MIT Press, 1965. 326p.

Covers scientific societies in the United States from a historical perspective. Chapter titles include: "Scientific Societies in 18th Century America"; "National Growth, 1800-1865"; "The Triumph of Specialization, 1866-1918"; "American Scientific Societies and World Science, 1919-1944"; "The Increase and Diffusion of Knowledge"; "The Atomic Age, 1945-1955"; and "Scientific Societies in the Space Age." Numerous bibliographic references are provided.

33. **Scientific Thought, 1900-1960: A Selective Survey.** Harré, R., ed. Oxford, England: Clarendon Press, 1969. 277p.

Traces developments in the primary presuppositions of modern science since 1900. Twelve major topics are covered and include molecular biology, ecological genetics, and cell biophysics.

34. **Smithsonian Book of Invention.** 2nd ed. Staff of the Smithsonian Institution, comp. Washington, DC: Smithsonian Books, 1978. 256p.

This well-illustrated volume on inventions covers areas such as agriculture, industry, space, science, and medicine. Contains over 300 photographs, art works, and drawings.

35. **The Tradition of Science: Landmarks of Western Science in the Collections of the Library of Congress.** Bruno, Leonard C. Washington, DC: Superintendent of Documents, 1987. 364p.

This is not intended to be a survey, a descriptive guide, or a work of scientific history; instead, it is a blend of history and bibliography. Beginning with the time of the Greeks, 450 individual works are discussed including those by important and lesser known figures in the history of science. This is a general text of interest to undergraduate and general purpose collections.

36. **Women in the Scientific Search: An American Bio-bibliography, 1724-1979.** Siegel, Patricia Joan, and Kay Thomas Finley. Metuchen, NJ: Scarecrow Press, 1985. 399p.
An examination of the place of women in science in the United States, which places the considerable contributions of women in science into context within the history of science in the United States. This is an excellent source book for material related to women in science.

37. **Women Scientists from Antiquity to the Present: An Index.** Herzenberg, Caroline L. West Cornwall, CT: Locust Hill Press, 1986. 200p.
Covers approximately 2,500 women scientists and includes an index to 130 reference works. Listing is alphabetical with an additional list by field. This is a good starting point for information on specific women scientists.

HISTORY OF ASTRONOMY

38. **Astronomy of the Ancients.** Brecher, Kenneth, and Michael Feirtag, eds. Cambridge, MA: MIT Press, 1979. 206p.
An introduction to ancient astronomers through history, archaeology, technology, and mythology. Aspects covered include Indian medicine wheels, pictographs and petroglyphs, first scientific instruments, naked eye astronomy, Sirius enigmas, Stonehenge, Gorgon's eye, and language of archaic astronomy. All articles appeared originally in *Technology Review* (Boston: MIT, 1899- . quarterly).

39. **History of Modern Astronomy and Astrophysics: A Selected, Annotated** Z5/54 **Bibliography.** DeVorkin, David H. New York: Garland, 1982. 434p. .H57
A concise, well-written account of modern astronomy and astrophysics done from the D48 standpoint of a bibliography. The selections are good and the annotations informative. Sci

40. **Planets and Planetarians: A History of Theories of the Origin of Planetary Systems.** Jaki, Stanley L. Edinburgh, Scotland: Scottish Academic Press, 1978. 266p.
Traces the history of ideas in the formation of the solar system, concentrating on basic theories. Considered to be a good reference in history of science collections.

41. **Source Book in Astronomy: 1900-1950.** Shapley, Harlow. Cambridge, MA: Harvard University Press, 1960. 423p.
This source book contains excerpts from the classical works in astronomy from its beginnings to 1950. It is an excellent starting point for further exploration.

HISTORY OF BIOLOGICAL SCIENCE AND AGRICULTURE

42. **Agricultural Records in Britain, AD 200-1977.** Stratton, John M., and Jack H. Brown. Hamden, CT: Archon Books, 1979. 259p.

A compilation of agricultural records presented chronologically. Provides an overview of the effect of weather on crops, and includes general rainfall tables and a table of agricultural prices back to 1257.

43. **Agriculture in America, 1622-1860: Printed Works in the Collections of the American Philosophical Society, the Historical Society of Pennsylvania, the Library Company of Philadelphia.** Tucher, Andrea J., comp. New York: Garland, 1984. 2v.

An alphabetical bibliography of the printed works on agriculture issued before 1861. This is highly recommended for libraries interested in the history of agriculture.

44. **The Art of Natural History: Animal Illustrators and Their Work.** Dance, S. Peter. Woodstock, NY: Overlook Press, 1978. 224p.

Contains examples of zoological illustrations from paleolithic cave paintings through the nineteenth century. High quality reproduction is provided throughout, and the information is accurate. Highly recommended for almost any library.

45. **A Bio-Bibliography for the History of the Biochemical Sciences since 1800.** Fruton, Joseph S. Philadelphia: American Philosophical Society, 1982.

An alphabetical listing of names with dates of birth and death, followed by a listing of biographical and bibliographical reference work. A valuable work for historians of science, although some may object to the editor's selection of names. Supplemented in 1985.

46. **British Natural History Books, 1495-1900: A Handlist.** Freeman, Richard B. Hamden, CT: Archon Books, 1980. 437p.

A listing of all books about wild animals and plants of the British Isles and all books about wild animals and plants in general, published or printed in the British Isles, or published abroad by British authors. Arrangement is by main entry.

47. **A Century of DNA: A History of the Discovery of the Structure and Function of the Genetic Substance.** Portugal, Franklin H., and Jack S. Cohen. Cambridge, MA: MIT Press, 1977. 384p.

An excellent explanatory source on the history of DNA; covers the 100-year period from 1809 forward, in the isolation of DNA and the genetic code. Discusses all major researchers involved: Franklin, Chargaff, Watson, and Crick. Also contains detailed explanations of morphological structure of the molecule as well as other facts of microbiology.

48. **The Eighth Day of Creation: The Makers of the Revolution in Biology.** Judson, H. F. New York: Simon & Schuster, 1980. 686p.

A documentary history of the discovery of DNA. In three sections; the first describes events leading up to the discovery of DNA; the second details the state-of-the-art in molecular biology; and the third deals with protein crystallography. Thorough, interesting, and well-referenced. For a wide audience. A fascinating history.

49. **Evolutionary History of the Primates.** Szalay, Frederick S., and Eric Delson. New York: Academic Press, 1979. 580p.

A valuable reference work on various aspects of the taxonomy and evolutionary history of primate species. It lists fossil primate deposits in alphabetical and chronological order and contains figures and an excellent extensive bibliography. This is a worthy text for graduate or upper level undergraduate students, as well as for all primatologists.

50. **Guide to the Literature of Botany: Being a Classified Selection of Botanical Works Including Nearly 6,000 Titles Not Given in Pritzel's "Thesaurus."** Jackson, Benjamin Dayden. London: Longman's Green & Co., 1881. 626p.

This is an outstanding bibliographic guide that lists works covering the early botanical literature. It is of great value in the historical analysis of botanical literature.

51. **History of American Ecology: An Original Anthology.** 3rd ed. Egerton, Frank N. Salem, NH: Ayer Company Publications, Inc., 1984. 1v. (various paging).

Discusses eighteenth and nineteenth century developments in the four disciplines of ecology: limnology, oceanography, plant ecology, and animal ecology. Includes primary essays on Lamarckian and Darwinian thought. Illustrations and graphs are provided.

52. **History of Biology: An Annotated Bibliography.** Overmier, Judith. New York: Garland, 1984. 350p.

A good, comprehensive source for information on biology. Annotations are clear and to the point.

53. **History of Fishes.** 2nd ed. Norman, J. R., and P. H. Greenwood. New York: Halsted Press, 1977. 467p.

A natural history of fishes, clearly written and illustrated. Contains an analytical index.

54. **History of Life Science.** 3rd ed. Gardner, Eldon J. Minneapolis, MN: Burgess, 1972. 464p.

The only general history of the total field that provides adequate coverage of the developments since circa 1930.

55. **History of the Life Sciences: An Annotated Bibliography.** Smit, Pieter. New York: Hafner, 1974. 1071p.

Originated as part of the life sciences section of Sarton's *Guide to the History of Science* (see entry 15). Over 4,000 entries emphasizing historical aspects of the life sciences, for scholarly research in biology and medicine. Includes works published through 1971.

56. **Human and Mammalian Cytogenetics: An Historical Perspective.** Hsu, T. C. New York: Springer-Verlag, 1979. 186p.

Discusses the important discoveries of DNA, chromosomal structure, and other aspects of cytogenetics while providing biographical information on key researchers. This is an interesting scientific history.

57. **An Illustrated History of the Herbals.** Anderson, Frank J. New York: Columbia University Press, 1977. 270p.

A scholarly history of herbal medicine containing much botanical and biographical information. Includes reproductions of woodcuts and engravings. A wealth of information concerning ancient herbal medicine is discussed making this a valuable addition to college and botanical libraries.

58. **An Introduction to the History of Virology.** Waterson, A. P., and Lise Wilkinson. London: Cambridge University Press, 1978. 237p.

Examines the evolution of the study of viruses while emphasizing the conceptual study of viruses, including animal, bacteriophages, scrapie, and others. Contains important historical information and is well referenced.

59. **Natural Science Books in English: 1600-1900.** Knight, David M. New York: Praeger, 1972. 262p.

A bibliographic essay on scientific development in Great Britain over three centuries. It does not include full bibliographic data for many entries. Should be of use to both bibliographers and bibliophiles.

60. **North American Forest History: A Guide to Archives and Manuscripts in the United States and Canada.** Davis, Richard C., comp. Santa Barbara, CA: ABC-Clio Books, 1977. 376p.

A useful record of manuscript groups in repositories including some oral history and photography on North American forestry.

61. **Old Farm Tools and Machinery: An Illustrated History.** Blanford, Percy W. Fort Lauderdale, FL: Gale Research, 1976. 188p.

Details the development of agricultural tools from animals to steam to tractors. Illustrations of types of machinery include ploughs, harvesting, and feeding. An excellent addition for history of technology collections.

62. **The Story of the Royal Horticultural Society, 1804-1968.** Fletcher, Harold R. London: Oxford University Press, 1969. 564p.

This is a history of the society. The appendices include a calendar of events for the society from 1804 to 1968, the original charter of the society, and a list of the past and present holders of the Victoria Medal of Honor. This is a history of the foremost horticultural society in the world. As such, it will find a place in any horticultural research collection.

63. **Studies in the History of Biology.** Coleman, William, and Camille Limoges, eds. Baltimore, MD: Johns Hopkins University Press, 1977- . annual.

Contains scholarly contributions on the history of biology and is a major addition to the literature. It discusses aspects of evolution, genetics, and Darwinian thought. This is an excellent source for contemporary review articles in biological history.

64. **The Virus: A History of the Concept.** Hughes, Sally S. London: Heinemann Educational Books, 1977. 140p.

A survey that concentrates on virus research up to the turn of the century. Highly recommended to microbiologists and historians, it is invaluable as a background against which to view current virology.

HISTORY OF CHEMISTRY

65. **A Century of Chemistry. The Role of Chemists and the American Chemical Society.** Skolnik, Herman, and Kenneth M. Reese, eds. Washington, DC: American Chemical Society, 1976. 468p.

The book traces the development of chemical science and technology in the framework of the 27 technical divisions of the Society. It includes 100-year records of ACS people and events.

66. **Chemical, Medical, and Pharmaceutical Books Printed before 1800, in the Collection of the University of Wisconsin Libraries.** Neu, John, ed. Madison, WI: University of Wisconsin Press, 1965.

Includes the D. I. Duveen collection in chemistry and alchemy. An excellent checklist for major collections.

67. **Discovery of the Elements.** 7th ed. rev. Weeks, Mary Elviva. Ann Arbor, MI: Books on Demand, University Microfilms, Inc., 1980. 896p.

Accurately covers the individual discovery of elements through lawrencium.

68. **Evolution of Chemistry: A History of Its Ideas, Methods, and Materials.** 2nd ed. Farber, Eduard. New York: Ronald Press, 1969. 437p.

This volume surveys the historical development of chemistry from its origins. It is a good tool for short vignettes.

69. **A History of Analytical Chemistry.** Laitenen, Herbert A., and G. W. Ewing. Washington, DC: American Chemical Society, Division of Analytical Chemistry, 1977. 358p.

A valuable source for analytic chemists and for students in all disciplines of science. Particularly valuable for the history of technology.

70. **History of Biochemistry.** Florkin, Marcel, ed. New York: American Elsevier, 1972- . [presently in 5 parts].

Part 1 is titled "Proto-Biochemistry," 1972; part 2, "From Proto-Biochemistry to Biochemistry," 1972; part 3, "A History of the Identification of the Sources of Free Energy in Organisms"; and parts 4 and 5, "The Unravelling of Biosynthetic Pathways."

71. **History of Chemistry.** Partington, James Riddick. London: Macmillan, 1961-1970. 4v.

A detailed history of chemistry that is well documented and exhaustive through the late 1960s.

72. **Select Bibliography of Chemistry, 1492-1902.** Bolton, Henry Carrington. Washington, DC: Smithsonian Institution, 1893-1904; repr., Millwood, NY: Kraus Reprint, 1973. 4v.

A bibliography covering 18,000 chemical books published in Europe and America from 1492 to 1902. Volume I covers 1492-1892 and is divided into seven sections: Section 1, bibliographies; section 2, dictionaries; section 3, history; section 4, biography; section 5, chemistry, pure and applied; section 6, alchemy; and section 7, periodicals. More extensive coverage is provided in the supplements and the eighth section, which was published later, covers the academic dissertations with emphasis on France, Germany, Russia, and the United States.

73. **Source Book in Chemistry, 1400-1900.** Leicester, Henry Marshall. Cambridge, MA: Harvard University Press, 1963. 554p.

74. **Source Book in Chemistry, 1900-1950.** Leicester, Henry Marshall. Cambridge, MA: Harvard University Press, 1968. 408p.

Contains excerpts from the works of noted chemists, from 1400 through 1950. A bibliography of biographies is provided.

HISTORY OF GEOSCIENCE

75. **American Environmental History: The Exploitation and Conservation of Natural Resources.** Petulla, Joseph M. San Francisco: Boyd & Fraser, 1977. 399p.

Provides a basic history of the U.S. environmental resources from a conservationist and anticorporate viewpoint. It is well illustrated. Recommended for agricultural and engineering libraries.

76. **Birth and Development of the Geological Sciences.** Adams, Frank Dawson. New York: Dover, 1954. 506p.

This is an excellent general history on geology. Geological ideas from the time of the ancient Greeks to modern day science are covered. Each chapter deals with specific topics, including the origin of mountains, earthquakes, and origin of springs and rivers. Of particular note is the historical treatment of the continental drift theory.

77. **A Century of Weather Service: A History of the Birth and Growth of the National Weather Service, 1870-1970.** Hughes, P. New York: Gordon & Breach, 1970. 212p.

Besides the text and photographs, an appendix lists chronologically the meteorological milestones of the American Weather Service, 1644-1970. Important because of its basic historical orientation without being overly technical.

78. **Exploring the Ocean World: A History of Oceanography.** Idyll, Clarence P., ed. New York: Thomas Y. Crowell, 1972. 296p.

Covers the history of oceanography, including the science of the sea, underwater landscape, biology of the sea, physics of the sea, chemistry of the sea, food from the sea, farming the sea, mineral resources and power, underwater archaeology, marine ecology and pollution, and man beneath the sea. Each chapter is by a different author.

79. **Images of the Earth: Essays in the History of the Environmental Sciences.** Jordanova, L. J., and R. S. Porter, eds. Chalfont St. Giles, England: British Society for the History of Science, 1979. 282p.

Contains individual perspectives on the history of geology, covering a broad scope of the field. This reference is important because of the breadth of the expertise of the authors involved. Environmental science is seen from several perspectives, giving a much more balanced view than other histories.

80. **Into the Deep: The History of Man's Underwater Exploration.** Marx, Robert F. New York: Van Nostrand Reinhold, 1978. 198p.

Traces the history of deep-sea diving from early Greek times. An interesting source of references. Not a scholarly book, but readable with references to more scholarly material.

81. **Mapmakers of America: From the Age of Discovery to the Space Era.** Hirsch, S. Carl. New York: Viking, 1970. 176p.

A useful, compact history of map making, and one of the few books covering the topic. This book is not comprehensive but covers the history of map making better than others.

82. **Scripps Institute of Oceanography: Probing the Oceans, 1936 to 1976.** Shor, Elizabeth N. San Diego, CA: Tofua, 1978. 502p.

A clear and accurate history of oceanographic research completed by the Scripps Institute. It is important for its historical as well as enumerative listing of research.

83. **Source Book in Geology, 1900-1950.** Mather, Kirtley Fletcher. Cambridge, MA: Harvard University Press, 1967. 435p.

Gathers together in a collection of excerpts material from the progenitors of geology.

84. **Thermal Theory of Cyclones: A History of Meteorological Thought in the Nineteenth Century.** Kutzbach, Gisela. Boston: American Meteorological Society, 1979. 255p.

Examines thermal studies of cyclone developments in the nineteenth century. Excellent illustrations included. Mainly for university libraries, meteorologists, and science historians.

85. **Two Hundred Years of Geology in America: Proceedings of the New Hampshire Bicentennial Conference.** Schneer, Cecil J., ed. Hanover, NH: University Press of New England, 1979.

A welcome addition to all geology and history of science collections. Based on a compendium of 27 papers presented at a bicentennial symposium at the University of New Hampshire.

HISTORY OF MATHEMATICS

86. **Bibliography and Research Manual of the History of Mathematics.** May, Kenneth O. Buffalo, NY: University of Toronto Press, 1973. 818p.

This manual is divided into two parts, with the first part covering retrieval, storage, and analysis of information. Part 2 is a bibliography on the history of mathematics and "focuses on utility for information retrieval rather than on matters of antiquarian interest." Entries are arranged under the headings of "Biography," "Mathematical Topics," "Epimathematical Topics," "Historical Classifications," and "Information Retrieval." Sufficient bibliographic information is provided, though it does not provide title of articles or contents of books.

87. **History of Mathematics.** 4th ed. rev. Cajori, Florian. New York: Chelsea, 1985. 524p.

A history useful to math historians, covering the basic tenets and discoveries in the realm of mathematics.

88. **History of Mathematics, from Antiquity to the Beginning of the 19th Century.** 2nd ed. Scott, Joseph F. London: Taylor & Francis, 1960; repr., New York: Barnes & Noble, 1969. 266p.

Outlines the chronological development of basic mathematical ideas over the past 2,000 years. Provides excellent appended biographical notes. It is directed toward those with a reasonably high degree of prior knowledge or a highly structured interest in the field.

89. **Mathematical Papers of Isaac Newton.** Whiteside, Derek T., ed. Cambridge, England: Cambridge University Press, 1967-81. 8v.

Each volume covers the years indicated: volume 1, 1664-1666; volume 2, 1667-1669; volume 3, 1670-1673; volume 4, 1667-1684; volume 5, 1683-1684; volume 6, 1684-1691; volume 7, 1691-1695; and volume 8, 1697-1722. A major work of clear importance to academic libraries.

90. **On the History of Statistics and Probability.** Owen, Donald B., ed. New York: Marcel Dekker, 1976. 466p.

Papers covering a wide range of topics on the development of statistical theory. This book is both comprehensive and readable. Intended for more academically directed readers, it is not a layperson's guide to probability and statistics.

91. **Source Book in Mathematics, 1200-1800.** Struik, Dirk Jan, ed. Princeton, NJ: Princeton University Press, 1986. 427p.

Covering the thirteenth century to the end of the eighteenth century, this source book is a collection of excerpts from the works of Western mathematicians. Includes only pure mathematics and fields of applied mathematics that have influenced the development of pure mathematics. This is a reprint of the 1969 edition.

92. **Studies in the History of Statistics and Probability.** Kendall, M. G., and R. L. Plackett, eds. London: Griffin, 1978. 2v.

Covers the origins of statistics from 1710 through 1973. It is important because of its clear and concise treatment of the major statistical breakthroughs.

HISTORY OF PHYSICS

93. **Applications of Energy: Nineteenth Century.** Lindsay, Robert B., ed. Stroudsburg, PA: Dowden, Hutchinson, and Ross, 1976.

This collection of papers from the second half of the nineteenth century presents that period's concepts of energy. It is well annotated. These are benchmark papers on energy.

94. **Bibliographical History of Electricity and Magnetism.** Mottelay, Paul F., comp. London: Griffin, 1922; repr., New York: Arno Press, 1975. 673p.

The chronological bibliographic history spans the time from 2637 B.C. to December 25, 1821. The book is exhaustively documented.

95. **Birth of Particle Physics: Proceedings of the International Symposium on the History of Particle Physics, May 1980.** Brown, Laurie M., and Lillian Hoddeson, eds. Cambridge, England: Cambridge University Press, 1983. 412p.

The results presented at the International Symposium on the History of Particle Physics in May 1980. Included are two panel discussions and additional papers from remarks made from the floor and physicists not present at the conference.

96. **Collected Papers of Albert Einstein.** Stachel, John, ed. Princeton, NJ: Princeton University Press, 1987- . irregular.

The first volume of this work is titled *The Early Years, 1879-1902*. Projected to be 40 volumes, it is intended to be a compilation of the complete papers of Einstein with over 14,000 documents drawn from the Einstein Archive as well as newly discovered documents. The papers range from his work on special and general relativity to his concerns with civil liberties. This is a major compilation of Einstein's papers and is a necessity for any research library. Following the publication of volume 1, the papers will be divided into two series, with the documents in each volume in chronological order. One series, the *Writings*, will include published and unpublished articles, lecture notes, patent applications, and accounts of his lectures and interviews. The second series, the *Correspondence*, will include all available letters written by and received by Einstein. The two series are planned to be cross-referenced. Translations of the first volume are available and are planned for the two series.

97. **Electricity from Glass: The History of the Frictional Electrical Machines, 1600-1850.** Hackman, W. D. Alphen aan den Rijen, Netherlands: Sijthoff-Hoordhoff, 1978. 310p.

Classifies and describes the evolution of electrical machines to the beginnings of the industrial revolution. Presents the beginning of a systematic catalog of electrical inventions. Includes illustrations and is helpful in understanding the origins of electrical experimentation.

98. **Energy: Historical Development of the Concept.** Lindsay, Robert B., ed. Stroudsburg, PA: Dowden, Hutchinson, and Ross, 1975. 369p.

An historical reference on the history of energy. Covers papers written from antiquity through the mid-nineteenth century. Important because of the scope of the book and the care with which prior theory is explained.

99. **From X-rays to Quarks: Modern Physicists and Their Discoveries.** Segre, Emilio. San Francisco: W. H. Freeman, 1980. 337p.

A clear and readable explanation of important physics research done in the last 100 years. Covers the discovery of X-rays, relativity, radioactivity, and the formulation of modern quantum theory. Provides excellent photographs and personal anecdotes about such personalities as Marie Curie and Max Planck. Some background knowledge of chemistry and algebra is assumed. A bibliography is included. This is a worthwhile text for all students and professors.

100. **General Relativity: An Einstein Centenary Survey.** Hawking, Stephen W., and W. Israel. Cambridge, England: Cambridge University Press, 1979. 919p.

Contains essays on the progress of the theory of relativity, marked by the 100th anniversary of the birth of Albert Einstein. This is a well-arranged volume, covering progress by the decade.

101. **General Relativity and Gravitation: One Hundred Years after the Birth of Albert Einstein.** Held, A., ed. New York: Plenum, 1980. 2v.

Contains review and research articles on general relativity and gravitation. Contributions are made by international experts. This is a recommended reference source in the history of physics.

102. **History of Modern Physics 1800-1950.** Holton, Gerald, and Katherine R. Sopka. Los Angeles: Tomash Publications, 1983. 4v.

Volume 1, *ALSOS* by Samuel Goudsmit; volume 2, *Project Y: The Los Alamos Story*—with part 1, *Toward Trinity* by D. Hawkins and part 2, *Beyond Trinity* by E. C. Truslow and R. C. Smith; volume 3, *American Physics in Transition: A History of Conceptual Change in the Late Nineteenth Century*; volume 4, *The Question of Atoms: From the Karlsruhe Congress to the First Solvay Conference.* A major contribution in the history of modern physics, this is well documented, readable, and good in details.

103. **History of Physics.** Weart, Spencer, and Melba Phillips, eds. New York: American Institute of Physics, 1985. 375p.

A valuable library reference, a useful supplementary text for college courses, and stimulating reading for both physicists and informed public on the history of physics. Written by accomplished physicists including seven Nobel Prize winners, this is well documented and contains over 300 photographs and illustrations.

104. **History of the Quantum Theory.** Hund, Friedrich. trans. by Gordon Reece. New York: Barnes & Noble, 1974. 260p.

Translated from the German edition published in Mannheim, West Germany in 1967. This is really the history of *old* Quantum Theory. It traces the development of quantum mechanics from Planck to the mathematical conundrums presented by the theory. An excellent history by an active participant in developing the theory.

105. **Literature on the History of Physics in the Twentieth Century.** Heilbron, J. L., and Bruce R. Wheaton. Berkeley, CA: University of California, Office for History of Science and Technology, 1981. 485p.

A comprehensive bibliography of twentieth-century physics literature. It is arranged by subject, except for three chapters dealing with histories, biography, and institutions. Numerous cross-references and an index to authors are provided. Necessary for collections on history of science or physics.

106. **Masers and Lasers: An Historical Approach.** Bertolotti, Mario. Bristol, England: Adam Hilger, 1983. 268p.

An informative and authoritative account of the history of quantum electronics and quantum optics. For second- or third-year students of physics at the college level.

107. **The National Physical Laboratory—A History.** Pyatt, Edward. Bristol, England: Adam Hilger, 1983. 270p.

A complete chronological overview of the origins of the National Physics Laboratory. Contains six appendices with biographies of principal characters, a calendar of events, and highlights of the history of standards, as well as diagrams, tables, historical records, and many photographs.

108. **Neils Bohr, Collected Works.** Amsterdam, Netherlands: North-Holland, 1972- .

Volume 1, *Early Work (1905-1911)*, 1972; volume 2, *Work on Atomic Physics (1912-1917)*, 1977; volume 3, *The Correspondence Principle (1918-1923)*, 1972; volume 4, *The Periodic System (1920-1923)*, 1976.

109. **Origins in Acoustics: The Science of Sound from Antiquity to the Age of Newton.** Hunt, Frederick V. New Haven, CT: Yale University Press, 1978. 196p.

Filled with extensive references from the seventeenth century forward, this source contributes to the understanding of the origins of acoustics. It is detailed and highly recommended.

110. **The Physicists: The History of a Scientific Community in Modern America.** Kevles, Daniel J. Cambridge, MA: Harvard University Press, 1987. 512p.

A primary reference source for scholars and educators in physics history. The vantage points taken by this work allow the physics community to be viewed from several perspectives. This is a well-rounded examination of the physics community.

111. **Revolution in Miniature: The History and Impact of Semiconductor Electronics Re-Explored.** 2nd ed. Braun, Ernest, and Stuart MacDonald. New York: Cambridge University Press, 1982. 247p.

Documents the beginning of the semiconductor industry in a careful, accurate manner. A must for history of science collections.

112. **Rutherford and Physics at the Turn of the Century.** Bunge, Mario, and William R. Shea, eds. New York: Science History Publications, 1979. 184p.

Describes the state of physics at the turn of the century, focusing on such luminaries as Einstein, Rutherford, Chamberlain, Wilson, and Freud. This is a lively and interesting volume for history of science collections.

113. **Sourcebook on Atomic Energy.** 3rd ed. Glasstone, Samuel. Huntington, NY: Krieger, 1979. 883p.

Covers significant developments in the fields of science falling under the general heading of "atomic energy."

114. **Thirty Years of Fusion. Fusion: Science, Politics, and the Invention of a New Energy Source.** Bromberg, Joan Lisa. Cambridge, MA: MIT Press, 1982.

The basic story of magnetic fusion as described by the 30-year-old U.S. program to confine and control the fusion process with macroscopic electromagnetic fields.

HISTORY OF TECHNOLOGY

115. **Aeronautics and Astronautics: An American Chronology of Science and Technology in the Exploration of Space, 1915-1960.** Washington, DC: U.S. National Aeronautics and Space Administration, 1961. 240p.

A listing, by day and year, of important events in aeronautics. Contains a subject and name index. Important for historical reasons.

116. **Airplanes of the World, 1490-1976.** 4th ed. rev. Rolfe, Douglas. New York: Simon & Schuster, 1978. 482p.

A 12-part reference that details aviation history from the fifteenth century to the present. For each aircraft, an introduction, drawing, and full description are provided. Manufacturer, nomenclature, and aircraft nickname indexes are included. Of interest to all library collections.

117. **An Annotated Bibliography on the History of Data Processing.** Cortada, James W., comp. Westport, CT: Greenwood Press, 1983. 215p.

Focuses on the contributions, rather than the documentation, in hardware and computing concepts made by institutions as well as individuals. Concentrates on the evolutionary eras from before 1800, 1800-1939, 1939-1955, and 1955-1982 which have been periods of major growth in the computer industry.

118. **Bibliography of the History of Electronics.** Shiers, George. Metuchen, NJ: Scarecrow Press, 1972. 323p.

A collection of descriptive annotations of books, articles, and reports on the history of electronics and telecommunications from the 1860s to the 1950s. Emphasizes the historical aspects of electronics and telecommunications since 1860. For everyone from the electronics buff to the science historian.

119. **A Centennial History of the American Society of Mechanical Engineers, 1880-1980.** Sinclair, Bruce. Toronto: University of Toronto Press, 1980. 256p.

A history of the American Society of Mechanical Engineers in both the sphere of social economy and the sphere of technology. It deals with how the society serves its members and the public, and the standards it sets. Good reading for members. A major contribution to the history of engineering.

120.   **The Early Years of Modern Civil Engineering.** Kirby, Richard Shelton. New Haven, CT: Yale University Press, 1932. 324p.

Composed of insights on the history of civil engineering during the eighteenth and early nineteenth centuries. Topics covered include roads and pavements, railroads, bridges, sewers, and biographical entries on practitioners are provided. Bibliographies appear at the end of each chapter.

121.   **Electrical and Electronic Technologies: A Chronology of Events and Inventors to 1900.** Davis, Henry B. O. Metuchen, NJ: Scarecrow Press, 1981. 213p.

The volume has six sections, each describing a particular era, from before Christ through the nineteenth century. Each has an introduction and a chronological sequence of entries specified by the individual responsible for the innovation. Index is topically arranged.

122.   **Electronic Inventions and Discoveries: Electronics from Its Earliest Beginnings to the Present Day.** 3rd ed. rev. Dummer, Geoffrey W. A. Oxford, England: Pergamon, 1983. 233p.

Covers inventions from Europe and the United States. Inventions are arranged in chronological order from 1642 forward. Serves as a valuable source in history of technology collections.

123.   **From Dits to Bits: A Personal History of Electronic Computers.** Lukoff, Herman. Portland, OR: Robotics Press, 1979. 219p.

An entertaining account of the development of the computer. For public libraries and history of science collections. Written by a leader in the field of computers and computer design.

124.   **Helicopters of the World.** 3rd ed. Taylor, Michael J. H. London: Allan, 1981. 112p.

Traces the history of the helicopter around the world. Arranged alphabetically, it provides detailed descriptions and serves as a basic source for information on helicopters, particularly older models.

125.   **History and Philosophy of Technology.** Bugliarello, George, and D. B. Doner. Urbana, IL: University of Illinois Press, 1979. 384p.

Based on 24 papers from the Symposium on the History and Philosophy of Technology, Chicago, 1973, this book contains a varied collection of papers on the history and philosophy of technology. An excellent overview of the problems presented in addressing technology from a philosophical viewpoint.

126.   **History of Building Types.** Pevsner, Nikolaus. Princeton, NJ: Princeton University Press, 1976. 352p.

Surveys the history of architecture from the Middle Ages to the modern times. Contains a good bibliography and illustrations. A valuable reference.

127.   **History of Computing in the Twentieth Century.** Metropolis, N., J. Howlett, and Gian-Carlo Rota, eds. New York: Academic Press, 1986. 693p.

A multi-authored book on the history of computing that offers material by pioneers in the field. Of interest to computer scientists, mathematicians, and electrical engineers.

128.   **History of Control Engineering: 1800-1930.** Bennett, Stuart. London: Peregrinus, 1986. 220p.

This history of engineering covers a broad range of concepts. It is detailed and well referenced. For theorists, engineers, and students.

129.   **History of Engineering and Science in the Bell System: The Early Years (1875-1925).** Fagen, M. D., ed. Murray Hill, NJ: Bell Telephone Laboratories, 1975. 1073p.

The most comprehensive account of the technical evolution of a major industrial corporation. The volume is organized by technical categories, each covered chronologically from 1875 onward.

130.   **History of Man-Powered Flight.** Reay, David A. New York: Pergamon, 1977. 355p.

Describes hundreds of man-powered flight vehicles. Discusses Daedalus and Leonardo da Vinci. A well-done reference which includes technical details.

131.   **History of Microtechnique.** Bracegirdle, Brian. Ithaca, NY: Cornell University Press, 1978. 359p.

This book comprises a history of the microscope and its uses in scientific research beginning in the eighteenth century. There are numerous illustrations and a descriptive bibliography of works published before 1910. This is an impressive, scholarly work that contains much noteworthy information.

132.   **History of Programming Languages.** Wexelblat, Richard L., ed. New York: Academic Press, 1981. 758p.

Constitutes the proceedings of an ACM SIGPLAN Conference held in June 1978. It is a record of the early history of 13 languages that have set the tone of most of today's programming.

133.   **History of Public Works in the United States, 1776-1976.** American Public Works Association. Chicago, IL: American Public Works Association, 1976. 736p.

Comprehensive discussions on the provisions of water power, waste disposal, and transportation to the general public. Emphasizes the nation's efforts to improve the human environment. This is a valuable collection of information recommended for all research and public libraries.

134.   **History of Technology.** Singer, Charles Joseph, et al. Oxford, England: Clarendon Press, 1954-1958. 5v.

Titles of the volumes are: volume 1, *From Early Times to the Fall of the Ancient Empires*; volume 2, *Mediterranean Civilizations and the Middle Ages*; volume 3, *From Renaissance to the Industrial Revolution*; volume 4, *Industrial Revolution*; and volume 5, *The Late 19th Century.* An outstanding history of technology containing full bibliographies, tables, maps, and illustrations.

135.   **History of Technology,** Volumes 6 and 7. Williams, Trevor I., ed. Oxford, England: Clarendon Press, 1978.

Volume 6, *The Twentieth Century, c. 1900 to c. 1950*, part 1; volume 7, *The Twentieth Century, c. 1900 to c. 1950*, part 2. A multi-volume treatise on the history of technology up to the twentieth century. Covers all areas of technology. This is a scholarly and well-researched work.

136.   **History of Technology and Invention: Progress through the Ages.** Daumas, Maurice, ed. trans. by Eileen B. Hennessy. London: J. Murray, 1980- . 3v. irregular.

An excellent, three-volume set on the history of technology; each chapter is written by leading experts in their fields. Covers transportation and communication, textile industries, and military techniques. Essential source for all libraries.

137. **History of the British Petroleum Company: The Developing Years, 1901-1932, Volume 1.** Ferrier, R. W. New York: Cambridge University Press, 1982. 696p.

Presents the detailed history of the Anglo-Iranian Oil Co., now known as British Petroleum, in its actions with the Middle East. Its thorough format will prove to be a useful source for the serious student of the Middle East.

138. **History of Theory of Structures in the Nineteenth Century.** Charlton, T. M. New York: Cambridge University Press, 1982. 194p.

A unique, comprehensive account of a century of the development of the theory of structures with a detailed and critical account of the development and application of those principles.

139. **History of Tribology.** Dowson, D. London: Longman, 1979. 677p.

Discusses the chronological development of tribology, including biographical information on people who founded this new science. An excellent firsthand source for information on and about the founders of tribology as well as the area itself.

140. **The Rocket: The History and Development of Rocket and Missile Technology.** Baker, David. London: New Cavendish Books, 1978. 276p.

Traces the development of rocketry from the Sung dynasty through the nineteenth century. Presents synthesized data otherwise available in many different sources.

141. **The Science of Mechanics in the Middle Ages.** Clagett, Marshall. Madison, WI: University of Wisconsin Press, 1959. 2v. 711p.

A historical study covering the modification of Aristotelian mechanics during the thirteenth through fifteenth centuries. Highly recommended for historical collections.

142. **Scientific Instruments.** Wynter, Harriet, and Anthony Turner. New York: Scribner, 1975. 239p.

A collectors' book on commonly used instruments from 1550 to 1850, including astrolabes, quadrants, spheres, orreries, compasses, navigational gear, chronometers, sundials, perpetual calendars, gnomons, surveying rods, theodolites, alidades and levels, spectables, telescopes, pocket globes, microscopes, and backstaffs.

143. **Two Hundred Years of Flight in America: A Bicentennial Survey.** Emme, Eugene M., ed. San Diego, CA: Univelt, 1977. 310p.

Culls papers presented at a symposium which covered dirigibles, airplanes, and space flight. Includes charts, graphs, and illustrations. A good source for general information.

HISTORY OF MEDICINE

144. **A Biographical History of Medicine, Excerpts and Essays on the Men and Their Work.** Talbott, John H. New York: Grune & Stratton, 1970. 1211p.

A compilation of biographical essays on those who contributed greatly to the medical sciences from 2250 B.C. to the first half of the twentieth century. Entries are illustrated by a photograph or composite illustration of the biographee, and information on the subject's life and contributions is provided along with excerpts from his or her writings.

145. **Garrison and Morton's Medical Bibliography: An Annotated Checklist of Texts Illustrating the History of Medicine.** 4th ed. Morton, Leslie. Philadelphia: Lippincott, 1983. 1000p.

This bibliography is an attempt to bring together in convenient form references to the most important contributions to the literature of medicine and ancillary sciences, and, by means of annotations, to show the significance of individual contributions in the history and development of the medical sciences. Entries are chronologically arranged by medical category and include full name of author with dates, titles, publisher or journal citation, and in most cases, a brief annotation.

146. **History of Medical Illustrations from Antiquity to A.D. 1600.** Herrlinger, Robert. London: Pitman Medical, 1970. 178p.

A translation of *Geschichte der medizinischen Abbildung*, this is an excellent book on medical illustrations.

147. **History of Medicine.** Major, Ralph Herman. Springfield, IL: Charles C. Thomas, 1954. 2v.

Directed toward the medical student and practitioner, this book provides a "continuous account of the stream of medical history" and includes names and some biographies of eminent physicians. Each section is concluded with a biographical addendum on those only mentioned in the text.

148. **History of Medicine.** Sigerist, H. E. New York: Oxford University Press, 1967. 2v.

Volume 1 covers primitive and archaic medicine and contains exhaustive bibliographies. Volume 2 was reprinted in 1987 and is devoted to early Greek, Hindu, and Persian medicine.

149. **Nursing: An Historical Bibliography.** Bullough, Bonnie, Vern L. Bullough, and Barrett Elcani. New York: Garland, 1981. 408p.

Coverage is through 1978. Arranged by broad subject area, this is an important work for pulling together otherwise ephemeral material.

150. **Source Book of Medical History.** Clendening, Logan. New York: Dover, 1960. (c.1942). 685p.

Composed of original contributions in the field of medicine, this collection is arranged in chronological order from the *Kuhun Papyrus* of 1900 B.C. to Wilhelm Conrad Roentgen, *On a New Kind of Rays* (1895). A critical book for historical collections.

2 Multidisciplinary Sources of Information

A great deal of science and technology is inter- and multidisciplinary. The sources of material found in this section have a broad use in science and technology and can fall into one or more sections elsewhere in the book. The size of this section is another indicator that science and technology are becoming more interdependent on techniques and methodologies from other disciplines.

This section also begins with material on literature and librarianship. To be complete, a book of this sort must include some materials on how to handle the literature and the questions asked of the librarian.

A plethora of information is provided in this section. It is perhaps the most important of all the sections in the book because it gives some background and theoretical underpinnings on which to hang the provision of information in science and technology. Not all the theory is consonant, but any theory of how science and technology operates should not be expected to be fully consonant. Science, particularly, is predicated on the interplay between competing theories. With the above in mind, this section should be used as a basis for further research.

GUIDES TO THE LITERATURE

Q158.5
.W64
1986
Sci
Ref

151. **AAAS Science Book List 1978-86.** Wolff, Kathryn, Susan O'Connell, and Valerie J. Montenegro, comps. and eds. Washington, DC: American Association for the Advancement of Science, 1987. 600p.

Compiled from *Science Books & Films* (American Association for the Advancement of Science, 1975-), this new edition replaces all previous editions and supplements covering over 2,000 science books for junior and senior high school students, junior college students, and general audiences. Bibliographic information and annotations are clear and readable, and all books selected for inclusion have been evaluated by science experts— science teachers, scientists, and other professionals. Arranged under the Dewey Decimal System, every listing includes publisher information, grade level designations, and annotations presented in an easy-to-read, nontechnical format.

Q225.5
H47
1980
Sci Ref

152. **Brief Guide to Sources of Scientific and Technical Information.** 2nd ed. Herner, Saul. Washington, DC: Information Resources Press, 1980. 160p.

This guide to major sources of information covers directories, ongoing research and development, current or recent research and development results, significant American research collections, organization of personal index files, computer-generated information, machine readable databases, and others. Arrangement is by period, and general information as well as specific reference tools are discussed. Although somewhat dated, this is still a good source to consult for an overview of the field of interest.

153. **European Sources of Scientific and Technical Information.** 6th ed. Harvey, Anthony P., and Ann Pernet, eds. Essex, England: Longman Group; distr., Detroit, MI: Gale Research, 1985. 504p.

T10.65
.E8
E8
1993
Sci
Ref

Formerly titled *Guide to European Sources of Technical Information*, this geographical arrangement of sources concerns pure sciences and applied technology information. An attempt is made to identify key national centers of information. This is a very useful tool for particular information requests.

154. **Finding Answers in Science and Technology.** Primack, Alice Lefler. New York: Van Nostrand Reinhold, 1984. 364p.

Q158.5
.P75
1984
Sci
Ref

A general overview of and introduction to the location of information and the formulation of a search strategy. Chapters on specific information sources are included. Serves the undergraduate science student and the nonscientist librarian or teacher as well as all science libraries.

155. **Guide to U.S. Government Scientific and Technical Resources.** Aluri, Rao, and Judith Robinson. Littleton, CO: Libraries Unlimited, 1983. 259p.

Q224.3
.U6
A43
1983
Sci

A helpful guide to accessing federal, scientific, and technical information used in the flow of scientific and technical communication. Major sources of information are described for each category.

156. **Information Sources in Science and Technology.** 2nd ed. Parker, C. C., and R. V. Turley. London: Butterworth, 1986. 328p.

Directed toward those using materials published in Britain, the main part of the book covers people, organization, literature, and information services and libraries. This is a good overview of the types and variations of scientific literature and their intended uses.

157. **On Documentation of Scientific Literature.** Loosjes, T. P. London: Butterworth, 1973. 187p.

Z699
.L583
1973
Main

Emphasizes theoretical problems of bibliographic control and information retrieval covering monographs and serials, bibliographic aids, machine translations, as well as general design of retrieval systems. This work is important because the theoretical concepts it discusses are still as valid today as in 1973.

158. **Science and Technology: An Introduction to the Literature.** 4th ed. Grogan, Denis. London: Clive Bingley, 1982. 400p.

Q225.5
.G75
1982
Sci

An effective text for library schools in Great Britain, this work covers the various literatures of the sciences and technology. The slant is distinctly British, making this piece important for its international flavor.

159. **Science and Technology in Latin America.** Latin American Newsletters Limited. Roper, Christopher, and Jorge Silva, eds. London: Longman; distr., Detroit, MI: Gale Research, 1983. 363p.

Q127.13
L3
1983
Sci
Ref

Describes science and technology research country by country for those in Latin America. Very detailed, it is a virtual one-of-a-kind book that deals with a geographical region often overlooked by many.

Q127.NI5
S263
1982
Sci
Ref

160.　Science and Technology in the Middle East: A Guide to Issues, Organizations, and Institutions. Sardor, Ziauddin, ed. London: Longman, 1982. 324p.

　　A description of scientific and technological developments in the Middle East since 1975 begins the text and is followed by a description of five major regional science and technology organizations with their origins and projects. An account is given of the organization and administration of science and technology, and government and academic research institutions are listed with their research projects. Approximately 200 major establishments are provided with addresses.

161.　Scientific and Technical Information Resources. Subramanyam, Krishna. New York: Dekker, 1981. 416p.

　　This is a combined reference of several publications with a narrative description of each. It is most helpful to those information professionals working with the science and technology collections, and as a textbook to those in library schools.

Q158.5
C53
1987
Sci
Ref

162.　Scientific and Technical Information Sources. 2nd ed. Chen, Ching-chih. Cambridge, MA: MIT Press, 1987. 824p.

　　A completely updated edition that covers information sources in all fields of science and technology, mostly published after 1977. Grouped by type of publication then subdivided into discipline, over 4,000 entries are included under 23 categories. All entries under each chapter are grouped by subject first, then alphabetically by title. In addition to full bibliographic information, both critical and descriptive annotations are given whenever possible. Most annotations are descriptive rather than critical, and review sources are provided. Complete indexes are available.

Z675.T3
S8
1972
Main

163.　Scientific and Technical Libraries: Their Organization and Administration. 2nd ed. Strauss, Lucille J., Irene M. Shreve, and Alberta L. Brown. New York: Becker & Hayes, 1972. 450p.

　　This manual discusses scientific library practice in the areas of scientific and technical libraries, budgets, staffs, buildings, materials, services, processes, and acquisitions. While somewhat dated, it serves as general orientation to library school students, beginning special librarians, administrators, and library consultants.

T11
.S39
1986
Sci
Ref

164.　Scientific Writing for Graduate Students. Woodfors, F. Peter, ed. Bethesda, MD: Council of Biology Editors, 1986. 187p.

　　A collection of widely scattered source materials and references necessary for the preparation of a course. Also provides a framework of instruction from which to work with a minimum of preparation. Compiled by perhaps the most respected editorial group in science.

Q223
.C48
1983
Sci

165.　Sociology of Science: An Annotated Bibliography on Invisible Colleges, 1972-1981. Chubin, Daryl E. New York: Garland, 1983. 202p.

　　Invisible colleges, which are informal groups of scientists engaged in the exchange of information about their research, have been a major factor in the advancement of various fields of science. This is a review and collection of their findings presented in a most authoritative format.

Z7914
A22
S87
Main

166.　Standards and Specifications; Information Sources: A Guide to Literature and to Public and Private Agencies Concerned with Technological Uniformities. 6th ed. Struglia, Erasmus J. New York: Bowker, 1985.

Lists sources of information for all types of standards and specifications. Information is divided into general sources and directories, bibliographies and indexes to periodicals, catalogs and indexes of standards and specifications, government sources, associations and societies, international standardization, and periodicals. Most book and periodical entries are annotated.

167. **Subject Collections.** 6th ed. Ash, Lee, and William Miller, comp. New York: Bowker, 1985.

Z731
A78
1985
Main
Ref

Contains entries covering a myriad of subject headings. Serves as a guide to the special collections of universities, public and special libraries, and museums.

168. **University Science and Engineering Libraries.** 2nd ed. Mount, Ellis. Westport, CT: Greenwood Press, 1985. 303p.

Z675.
U5
M68
main

A good text providing a general overview of major issues faced by most academic libraries having departmental units or special collections.

169. **Yearbook of Science and the Future.** Chicago, IL: Encyclopaedia Britannica, 1969- . annual.

Q9
.B78
Sci

This nontechnical yearbook presents the past year's developments in science, dealing with all subjects, ranging from evolution of the stars to ship design. Articles on topics of contemporary interest are followed by a review of the scientific year, honors and awards, and obituaries. Well-written, it is arranged with a detailed index and excellent illustrations.

ABSTRACTS, INDEXES, AND BIBLIOGRAPHIES

170. **Abstracting Scientific and Technical Literature.** Maizell, Robert E., Julian F. Smith, and T. E. R. Singer. Huntington, NY: Krieger, 1979. 297p.

T10.8
M35
Sci

This introductory guide and text for scientists, abstractors, and indexers clearly lays out the ground rules for writing a good abstract. It is a no-nonsense book on an important topic in science and technology.

171. **Abstracts and Indexes in Science and Technology: A Descriptive Guide.** 2nd ed. Owen, Dolores B. Metuchen, NJ: Scarecrow Press, 1985. 235p.

Q158.5
.09
1985
Sci
Ref

Provides a comprehensive listing of indexing tools in scientific and technical subjects. Entries, described in outline form, are arranged under the areas of general, mathematics, statistics, computer science, astronomy, chemistry and physics, nuclear science and space science, earth sciences, archaeology, anthropology, engineering, technology, energy and environment, biological sciences, health sciences, and agricultural sciences. Databases in each area are now covered.

172. **American Library Resources: A Bibliographical Guide (Supplement) 1971-1980.** Downs, Robert B. Chicago, IL: American Library Association, 1981. 209p.

Z1002
.D6
Main

A bibliographic guide to bibliographies listing resources in American libraries. The term *bibliography* in this context covers union lists, surveys, checklists, and catalogs of particular libraries and special collections within them. Since the basic arrangement is by DDC, science librarians should check those sections of the basic volume and the supplements that contain the 500 and 600 classes. It is fully indexed by author and subject.

Z1035.1
A55
Main
Ref.

173. American Reference Books Annual. Wynar, Bohdan S., ed. Littleton, CO: Libraries Unlimited, 1970- . annual.

Now in its nineteenth edition, *ARBA* is the most comprehensive review source for reference books published or distributed in the United States. Beginning with the 1987 volume, *ARBA* incorporates Canadian reference publications as well. Reviews have an average length of 250 words and are written by subject specialists and the staff of *ARBA*. In addition to critical annotations, citations to reviews in major library journals are appended. Science and technology reference sources are to be found in part 4, "Science and Technology," covering the following areas: science and technology in general, agricultural and resource sciences, biological sciences, engineering, health sciences, high technology, physical sciences and mathematics, and transportation. About 350 reference books in the science and technology section are reviewed in each volume. An essential resource for all types of libraries. An abridged edition, *Recommended Reference Books for Small and Medium-Sized Libraries and Media Centers*, published since 1981, offers an excellent selection for smaller libraries and media centers.

174. ASLIB Book List: A Monthly List of Recommended Scientific and Technical Tools, with Annotations. London: ASLIB, 1935- . monthly.

A broad subject index arranged by UDC categories, this monthly publication offers brief critical annotations. The import of this work is that it acts as a checklist for English-language and foreign materials.

Z1002
.B594
Main
Ref.

175. Bibliographic Index: A Cumulative Bibliography of Bibliographies. New York: H. W. Wilson, 1938- . biannual with annual cumulations.

A classified listing of separately published and concealed bibliographies including the sciences. The coverage of the sciences varies, but the information obtained is exceptional.

Z7405
.D5
R42
Main

176. Bibliography of Scientific, Technical, and Specialized Dictionaries, Polyglot, Bi-Lingual, Uni-Lingual. Rechenback, C. W., and E. R. Garnett. Washington, DC: Catholic University of America Press, 1969. 158p.

This guide identifies specialized foreign-language science dictionaries. Though entries need to be checked for later editions, it is included here because of its critical examination of dictionaries in science and technology.

Z7403
.F7
Sci

177. Bulletin Signaletique. Paris: Centre National de la Recherche Scientifique, 1948- . monthly; some sections are quarterly. Title varies; formerly called *Bulletin Analytique*.

A well-executed, comprehensive abstracting service covering most fields of science and technology. Each section covers a specific subject or topic and can be purchased separately. All foreign titles are translated into French with a notation of the original language of the title. Complete citations and description abstracts are provided. There is some overlapping with other major indexing and abstracting services, but the currency of *Bulletin Signaletique* makes it a worthwhile purchase for most larger collections. The following numbered sections pertain to the sciences:

101. Sciences de l'Information, documentation.
110. Informascience.
120. Geophysique Externe. Astronomie et Astrophysique.
130. Physique Mathematique, Optique, Acoustique, Mechanique.
140. Electrotechnique.
145. Electronique.
160. Physique de l'etat condense.

161. Structure de l'etat condense. Cristallographie.
165. Atomes et molecules. Plasmas.
170. Chimie.
220. Mineralogie, geochimie, geologie extraterrestre.
221. Gisements metalliques et non metalliques.
222. Roches cristallines.
223. Roches sedimentaires, geologie marine.
224. Stratigraphie, geologie regionale et general.
225. Tectonique.
226. Hydrologie, geologie de l'ingenieur, formations.
227. Paleontologie.
310. Genie biomedical. Informatique biomedicale.
330. Sciences pharmacologiques. Toxicologie.
340. Microbiologie. Virologie – Immunologie.
346. Ophtalmologie.
347. Oto-rhino-laryngologie, stomatologie, pathologie cervicofaciale.
348. Dermatologie – Venereologie.
349. Anesthesie. Reanimation.
351. Revue bibliographique cancer.
352. Maladies de l'appareil respiratoire de coeur et des vaisseaux – Chirurgie thoracique et vasculaire.
354. Maladies de l'appareil digestif – Chirurgie abdominale.
355. Maladies des reins et des voies urinaires – Chirurgie de l'appareil urinaire.
356. Maladies du systeme nerveux myopathies – neurochirurgie.
357. Maladies des os et des articulations – Chirurgie orthopedique – Traumatologie.
359. Maladies du sang.
360. Biologie animale. Physiologie et pathologie des protozoaires et des invertebres. Ecologie.
361. Endocrinologie et reproduction. Gynecologie. Obstetrique. Embryologie.
362. Diabete. Maladies metaboliques.
363. Genetique.
365. Zoologie des vertebres. Ecologie Animale. Physiologie Appliquee Humaine.
370. Biologie et physiologie vegetables.
380. Agronomie-Zootechnie-Phytopathologie-Industries alimentaires.
390. Psychologie-Psychopathologie-Psychiatrie.
522. Histoire des sciences et des techniques.
730. Combustibles-Energie.
740. Metaux-Metallurgie.
761. Microscopie electronique-Diffraction electronique.
780. Polymeres. Peintures. Bois. Cuirs.
880. Genie chimique. Industries chimique et parachimique.
885. Nuisances.
890. Industries mecaniques-Batiment-Travaux public-Transports.

178. **Core List of Books and Journals in Science and Technology.** Powell, Russell H., and James R. Powell, Jr. Phoenix, AZ: Oryx Press, 1987. 134p.

This is an example of what core lists should not emulate. Its inclusion here is justified on the grounds that inferior material often has a positive contribution, usually unintended by the authors. In this case, it makes all other similar works shine by comparison. The major strike against this book is that the work is based only on materials in the respective author's libraries. Other shortcomings are that no online services are covered and no annotations are given for journal materials. Those who know even a modicum about literature use by scientists and technologists understand the heaviest use is journal and online services, the area in which this work is weakest. Not recommended for any collection.

179. **Current Contents.** Philadelphia: Institute for Scientific Information, 1961- . various sections. weekly.

This is not an index but a listing of the contents of the current issues of many leading journals in the sciences. It is available in the following sections: *Life Sciences; Physical, Chemical and Earth Sciences; Engineering, Technology, and Applied Sciences; Clinical Practice; Agricultural, Biology, and Environmental Sciences;* and *Arts and Humanities.*

180. **Dictionaries of English and Foreign Languages: A Bibliographic Guide to Both General and Technical Dictionaries with Historical and Explanatory Notes and References.** 2nd ed. Collison, Robert L. New York: Hafner, 1971. 303p.

An obsolete but reliable listing for older standard dictionaries.

181. **Dissertation Abstracts Online.** 1980- . monthly.

An online guide to American dissertations accepted at accredited institutions since 1861. Available from DIALOG.

182. **Federal Research in Progress.** 1983- .

A current database giving access to information about ongoing federally funded research projects in the fields of physical science, engineering, and life science. Available from DIALOG.

183. **Guide to Microforms in Print: Author, Title: Incorporating International Microforms in Print.** Westport, CT: Meckler, 1978- . annual.

This is a cumulative, annual listing of books, journals, newspapers, government publications, archival material and collections, but not of theses or dissertations. Each entry gives the following information: author, title, volumes, date, price, publisher code, and type of microform code. For subject access to this listing, there is *Guide to Microforms in Print: Subject* (Westport, CT: Meckler, 1978-).

184. **Guide to Reprints.** Kent, CT: Guide to Reprints, 1986. 975p.

A list of books, journals, and other materials available in reprint (full size, hardbound) from publishers in the United States and some foreign countries. A directory of publishers represented in the guide is provided. It is supplemented by *Announced Reprints* which frequently does not include prices and announces titles which fail to materialize.

185. **Handbooks and Tables in Science and Technology.** 2nd ed. Powell, Russell H., ed. Phoenix, AZ: Oryx Press, 1983. 297p.

This is a bibliography of handbooks and tables in the science and technology field. They are listed alphabetically by title with separate sections for medical handbooks and National Bureau of Standards publications. Subject and author indexes are included.

186. **Index to Scientific and Technical Proceedings.** Philadelphia: Institute for Scientific Information, 1978- . monthly with semiannual cumulations.

An annual index to proceedings contents, this comprehensive index is the only indexing service covering this subject matter. Annually 3,000 volumes of proceedings are covered and material is accessed in five different ways: author's name, conference sponsor, subject category, title words, and author's organization.

187. **Index to Scientific Reviews.** Philadelphia: Institute for Scientific Information, 1974- . semiannual.

    A comprehensive international, interdisciplinary index covering over 30,000 reviews each year from over 3,400 journals and review publications. Covers literature of science, medicine, agriculture, technology and certain aspects of behavioral sciences. Four inter-related indexes provide a variety of access points to the review literature: author, title word, author affiliation, and specialty name.

Z7403
I42
Sci
Ref

188. **Index to U.S. Government Periodicals.** Walters, Ivan A., Jr., ed. Chicago, IL: Informdata International, 1984- . quarterly (4th issue is cumulative).

    A significant contribution to the access of journal articles published by the U.S. government. Dating from 1970, 176 journals are indexed, only 50 of which are included by standard indexing sources. Author and subject indexes are also available. This is a must for all libraries interested in government publications.

189. **Information Science Abstracts.** New York: Plenum, 1966- . quarterly.

    Continuing *Documentation Abstracts*, this source covers "information" in the broad sense, including its generation, publication, collection, and documentation. Six hundred articles are abstracted from over 350 journals covering material in documentation and related fields. In classified arrangement, this work can be accessed by the author and an-nual subject indexes. Available from DIALOG as an online database.

Z699
A1
D6
Main
Ref

190. **International Bibliography of Directories/Internationale Bibliographie der Fachadressbuecher.** 6th ed. Lengenfelder, Helga, ed. New York: Saur, 1978. 473p.

    A listing of directories previously published throughout the world in the fields of science, business, sports, the arts, libraries, health services, and many more. It is written in both English and German, though only geographical names in the list of directories are German. A valuable addition to large research and business library collections.

191. **New Technical Books: A Selective List of Descriptive Annotations.** New York: New York Public Library, 1915- . 10/yr.

    Useful as a current bibliography of scientific and technical books, the entries are arranged by subject with annual author and subject indexes. Full tables of contents fol-lowed by brief descriptive notes are included in most annotations. Dewey Decimal Classification used.

Z5854
N542
Sci

192. **Pure and Applied Science Books: 1876-1982.** New York: Bowker, 1982. 6v.

    This bibliography contains more than 220,000 titles in all the physical and biological sciences, and all the technologies, published in the last 107 years. Entries are listed under 56,000 LC subject headings with author and title indexes.

Z7401
P89
1982
Sci
Ref

193. **Referativnyi Zhurnal.** Moscow: Akademiia Nauk SSSR, 1953- . monthly.

    This is the principal Soviet abstracting service covering all subject areas including science and technology. At the present time, the journal is published in 69 sections, each devoted to a separate discipline or aspect of a discipline. The coverage is international with approximately 30 percent of abstracts from literature published in the Soviet Union and satellite countries. The abstracts are descriptive, occasionally providing direct quotes from other abstracting services including the United States. All sections contain author indexes in Cyrillic and Latin alphabets, and occasionally subject indexes are issued at a later date.

Following are the *Zhurnal* sections that pertain to the sciences:

Astronomiya (Astronomy).
Aviatsionnye i raketnye dvigateli (Aircraft & rocket engines).
Avtomatika i vychislitel'naya tekhnika (Automation …).
Avtomobil'nye dorogi (Motor roads).
Avtomobil'nyi i gorodskoi transport (Motor & municipal transport).
Biofizika (Biophysics).
Biologiya (Biology).
Dvigateli vnutrennego sgoraniya (Internal combustion engine).
Ekonomika promyshlennosti (Industrial economics).
Electronika (Electronics).
Elekrosvyaz' (Electric communication).
Farmakologiya … (Pharmacology).
Fizika (Physics).
Geodeziya i aeros'emka (Geodesy & aerial surveying).
Geofizika (Geophysics).
Geografiya (Geography).
Geologiya (Geology).
Gornoe delo (Mining).
Gornoe i neftepromyslovoe mashinostroenie (Mining & oil industry machines).
Informatika (Informatics).
Issledovanie kosmicheskogo prostranstva (Space research).
Khimicheskoe, neftepererabatyvayushchee i polimernoe mashinostroenie (Chemical, oil-refining, & polymer machinery).
Khimiya (Chemistry).
Kibernetika (Cybernetics).
Korroziya i zashchita ot korrozii (Corrosion …).
Kotlostroenie (Boiler-making).
Legkaya promyshlennost' (Light industry).
Lesovedenie i lesovodstvo (Forestry).
Mashinostroitel'nye materialy (Engineering materials …).
Matematika (Mathematics).
Meditsinskaya geografiya (Medical geography).
Mekhanika (Mechanics).
Metallurgiya (Metallurgy).
Metrologiya i izmeritel'naya tekhnika (Metrology & measuring instruments).
Nasosostroenie … (Pumps).
Oborudovanie pishchevoi promyshlennosti (Food industry machines).
Obshchie voprosy patologicheskoi anatomii (Pathological anatomy).
Okhrana prirody i vosproizvodstvo prirodnykh resutsov (Protection of environment and natural resources).
Onkologiya (Oncology).
Organizatsiya upravleniya promyshlennost'yu (Industrial management & organization).
Pochvovedenie i agrokhimiya (Soil science & agricultural chemistry).
Pozharnaya okhrana (Fire protection).
Promyshlennyi transport (Industrial transport).
Radiatsionnaya biologiya (Radiation biology).
Radiotekhnika (Radio engineering).
Raketostroenie i kosmicheskaya technika (Rocket engineering).

Rastenievodstvo (Plant breeding).
Stroitel'nye i dorozhnye mashiny (Building & road machines).
Svarka (Welding).
Tekhnologiya mashinostroeniya (Mechanical engineering).
Teploenergetika (Thermal power engineering).
Truboprovodnyi transport (Pipelines).
Turbostroenie (Turbine engineering).
Veterinariya (Animal husbandry & veterinary science).
Vodnyi transport (Water transport).
Voprosy tekhnicheskogo progressa i organizatsii proizvodstva mashinostroenii (Problems of machine building industry).
Vozdushnyi transport (Air transport).
Vzaimodeistvie raznykh vidov transporta (Coordination of transport).
Yadernye reaktory (Nuclear reactors).
Zheleznodorozhnyi transport (Rail transport).

194. **Science Books: A Quarterly Review.** Washington, DC: American Association for the Advancement of Science, 1965- . annual.

Q181 .A1
A67
Sci

This annotated classified list of new books in the pure and applied sciences is a good source for current titles.

195. **Science Citation Index.** Philadelphia: Institute for Scientific Information, 1961- . quarterly with annual cumulations; now bimonthly.

Q1
S68
Sci
Ref

The only index with extensive coverage of the international literature of science including life sciences, physical sciences, chemistry, earth sciences, agriculture, environmental sciences, clinical medicine, engineering, and technology and applied sciences. Contains over 600,000 items indexed each year from over 3,000 journals in many languages. Each issue is made up of four separate indexes: an author index, title word index, author's affiliation index, and the unique *Citation Index*. The *Citation Index* identifies in alphabetical order all current items listed by the author as well as all of the cited or referenced works in a given year. This manner of indexing cuts across disciplinary boundaries and differences in vocabulary as they are presented in individual disciplines. About 85 percent of the citations are from periodicals, the balance are from patents, government reports, books, dissertations, contracts and personal communications. The *Source Index* is a bibliographical listing of all the works containing the footnotes or bibliographies cited in the *Citation Index*. Its arrangement is alphabetical by author with listing of co-author, full title, publications source volumes, issue, pages, year, type of item, and the number of references in the bibliography. It also provides a corporate and anonymous source listing. The *Permuterm Subject Index* is an alphabetical keyword index referring the user to the works listed in the *Source Index*. The *Science Citation Index* is published in six bimonthly softcover issues, and in an annual hardcover accumulation as well as multiyear accumulations. Annual accumulations are available from 1961. Four five-year accumulations are available for 1965-69, 1970-74, 1975-79, and 1980-84.

196. **Scientific and Technical Books and Serials in Print.** New York: Bowker, 1972- . annual.

Z7401
SS73
Q158.5
Sci
Ref

Formerly published under the title *Scientific and Technical Books in Print*, this byproduct of *Books in Print* and *Subject Guide to Books in Print*, lists approximately 115,000 books and 18,000 serials available from 2,000 publishers. Using LC subject headings, entries provide the following bibliographic information: author, co-author, or editor, if any; title; price; imprint; and year of publication.

T45
K93
1984
Sci

197. **Scientific, Engineering, and Medical Societies Publications in Print.** 5th ed. Kyed, James M., and James M. Matarazzo. New York: Bowker, 1983. biennial.

This book is intended to provide some bibliographic control and sales information for material not normally covered in standard publication-finding tools. The 365 organizations that submitted publications lists (513 were contacted) are listed in alphabetical order. Under the name of each society, publications are listed in one of three categories—books, periodicals, and nonprint materials. Book titles are listed alphabetically under subject headings supplied by the society (an exception is monographic series, which are listed in numerical order). Where applicable, author, edition, publication date, order number, and price are listed. Periodicals and nonprint materials are also listed alphabetically by title. Author, subject, and periodical indexes complete the volume.

198. **Soviet Science and Technology.** 1975- . monthly.

Database offering access to scientific and technical literature from Soviet bloc countries. Available from DIALOG.

Z7913
T36
Sci

199. **Technical Book Review Index.** New York: Special Libraries Association, 1935- . monthly.

Contains printed excerpts from reviews appearing in scientific and trade publications. The time lag is often up to nine months. Author indexes are provided.

200. **World Bibliography of Bibliographies and of Bibliographical Catalogues, Calendars, Abstracts, Digests, Indices, and the Like.** 4th ed. rev. Besterman, Theodore. Lausanne, Switzerland: Societas Bibliographica, 1965-1966. 5v.

One of the most important bibliographies of separately published bibliographies in all fields. Some 117,000 items are arranged under 16,000 headings and subheadings in the first four volumes. The last volume serves as an index, listing in one alphabet authors, editors, translators, titles, etc. *A World Bibliography of Bibliographies 1964-1974*, by Alice F. Toomey, was compiled as a supplement to this edition and lists works represented by Library of Congress printed cards.

ENCYCLOPEDIAS AND TREATISES

T10.8
.M35
Sci

201. **Abstracting Scientific and Technical Literature: An Introductory Guide and Text for Scientists, Abstractors, and Management.** Maizell, Robert, Julian F. Smith, and T. E. R. Singer. New York: Wiley-Interscience, 1979. 297p.

Instructing in the techniques of abstracting, this book introduces users to the composition and standards of the *Official Gazette* of the U.S. Patent Office, *Chemical Abstracts*, *Biological Abstracts, Metals Abstracts*, and the NTIS services. The section on organization and administration of small business abstracting services with or without computers is supplemented by flow charts. Actual abstracts and reprints of guidelines are included.

202. **Encyclopedia of Modern Technology.** Blackburn, David, and Geoffrey Holister, eds. Boston: G. K. Hall, 1987. 248p.

This encyclopedia is composed of 34 chapters grouped around nine very broad categories. For each chapter a brief historical survey of the field is provided with a discussion of its current significance. The strength of the book is its illustrations. The use of these illustrations, some of which were commissioned, is outstanding. The arrangement and indexing are not conducive to ready reference. This is, however, excellent background reading and is recommended for general collections.

203. **Encyclopedia of Physical Science and Technology.** Meyers, Robert A., ed. Orlando, FL: Academic Press, 1987- . 15v.

Q123
E497
1992
Sci
Ref

A scholarly encyclopedia containing signed articles. The information included is duplicated in both the Van Nostrand Reinhold (see entry 212) and McGraw-Hill (see entry 207) encyclopedias. The decision to purchase needs to be made on the basis of expected user group. This is an excellent competitor in a crowded race.

204. **Information Retrieval, British and American, 1876-1976.** Metcalfe, John. Metuchen, NJ: Scarecrow Press, 1976. 243p.

In this source information retrieval is covered in chronological order beginning with 3000 B.C.

205. **Information Storage and Retrieval Systems for Individual Researchers.** Jahoda, Gerald. New York: Wiley, 1970. 135p.

Addressing the important aspects of indexing, keyword-from-title indexes, citation indexes and others, this reference work also includes a chapter on planning, design and evaluation of personal indexes. Serves as a useful tool for librarians or researchers working to start or improve an index to a documents collection.

206. **Information Systems.** Vickery, B. C. Hamden, CT: Archon Books, 1973. 350p.

Z699
V494
Main

Consists of 12 chapters discussing basic channels of information exchange, components of information systems, reference retrieval, conceptual mathematical models, retrieval language models, and the design of the system.

207. **McGraw-Hill Encyclopedia of Science and Technology.** 5th ed. New York: McGraw-Hill, 1987. 20v.

Q121
M3
1987
Main
Ref
+
1977
Sci

This one-of-a-kind encyclopedia for high school and undergraduate students provides general coverage of all areas of science and technology. It is also useful for advanced researchers who need information topics outside of their areas of expertise. This edition contains some 7,800 articles written by more than 2,500 scientists and engineers. All major articles are signed. Most longer articles begin with a definition of the subject, followed by a detailed discussion of certain aspects of a given topic, with a brief bibliography appended. There are many helpful cross-references in the text, but pronunciation of scientific terms is not indicated. This encyclopedia is an authoritative and up-to-date work for libraries of all types. It is supplemented by *McGraw-Hill Yearbook of Science and Technology* (see entry 208).

208. **McGraw-Hill Yearbook of Science and Technology.** New York: McGraw-Hill, 1972- . annual.

Q121
M31
Sci
Ref

Containing signed articles in a superb format, this is one of the most authoritative encyclopedia yearbooks on science and technology. A comprehensive reference, it covers key advances, discoveries, and developments in science and technology annually. Significant review articles are also included. Supplements *McGraw-Hill Encyclopedia of Science and Technology* (see entry 207).

209. **On Documentation of Scientific Literature.** 2nd ed. Loosjes, Thomas P. London: Butterworth; distr., Hamden, CT: Archon Books, 1973. 187p.

Z699
L583
1973
Main

Discusses in theory the problems of bibliographic control and information retrieval in such areas as general design of retrieval systems and bibliographic control of articles in periodicals. Bibliographic aids and their uses are covered, as well as the problems of machine translation.

501.49
U43t
Sci

210. **Technical Reporting.** 3rd ed. Ulman, Joseph N., and Jay R. Gould. New York: Holt, Rinehart & Winston, 1972. 419p.

Serves as an excellent guide for writing formal and informal reports, laboratory reports, theses, instructions, proposals, technical papers, and articles. Provides style requirements, instructions on tables and other visual presentations, and rules of grammar and punctuation.

Z669.8
D65
Main

211. **Understanding Scientific Literature: A Bibliometric Approach.** Donohue, Joseph C. Cambridge, MA: MIT Press, 1974. 101p.

This book provides descriptions of bibliometric techniques and their application to definite subject literature. Bradford's law of scattering and Zipf and Booth's relationships on word frequency, bibliographic coupling, citation tracing, and epidemic theory are included.

Q121
V3
1983
Sci

212. **Van Nostrand's Scientific Encyclopedia.** New York: Van Nostrand Reinhold, 1983. 3067p.

One of the best encyclopedias of science and technology, it is authoritative and well edited. Definitions are given first in simple terms, followed by more detailed and technical explanations. Over 2,450 line drawings and small diagrams illustrate the text. Science in this work includes earth and space sciences, life sciences, mathematics and information sciences, energy technology, materials sciences, and physics and chemistry. In the area of energy, terms associated with the topical subjects of chemical fuels, fossil fuels, geothermal energy, hydropower, nuclear energy, solar energy, and tidal and wind energy are covered. A good source for references to named laws and effects. Within definitions, words that are defined elsewhere in the book appear in boldface. There are frequent cross-references, but no biographies.

DICTIONARIES

PE1693
D4
1992
Main
Ref

213. **Abbreviations Dictionary.** 7th ed. De Sola, Ralph. New York: Elsevier, 1986. 1240p.

This compact volume of over 160,000 entries includes alphabet abbreviations, acronyms, anonyms, eponyms, appellations, contractions, geographical equivalents, historical and mythological characters, initials, nicknames, short forms, slang shortcuts, signs, and symbols, with corresponding full identification.

PE1693
A2
Main
Ref +
Sci
Ref

214. **Acronyms, Initialisms, and Abbreviations Dictionary.** 12th ed. Towell, Julie E., and Helen E. Sheppard, eds. Detroit, MI: Gale Research, 1987- . 3v.

Volume 1, *Acronyms, Initialisms, and Abbreviations Dictionary*, contains over 420,000 entries for alphabetical designations, contractions, acronyms, initialisms, and similar condensed appellations. All are listed alphabetically by acronym.

Volume 2, *New Acronyms, Initialisms, and Abbreviations*, supplements volume 1 and provides about 20,000 new entries arranged by acronym and by meaning. All entries in the first supplement are cumulated in the second.

Volume 3, *Reverse Acronyms, Initialisms, and Abbreviations Dictionary*, contains 420,000 entries arranged alphabetically by complete word, with the acronym as definition. Covers hundreds of fields and allows the user to find the accepted short form for organizational names and technical terms.

QH83
A94
Sci Ref

215. **Bioscientific Terminology: Words from Latin and Greek Stems.** Ayers, Donald M. Tucson, AZ: University of Arizona Press, 1972. 325p.

This book is divided into two sections covering bioscientific words derived from Greek and Latin. Hundreds of examples with definitions are provided, and interesting topics, such as the derivation of words from what we now know are erroneous scientific theories, are covered. It is helpful to the student not as a dictionary, but as a presentation in the use of Greek and Latin in scientific terminology.

216. **Cambridge Illustrated Thesaurus of Science and Technology.** Goodman, Arthur, and Ronald Denney. Cambridge, England: Cambridge University Press, 1985.

Q121
G64
1985
Sci Ref

Most suitable for high school libraries or lower, this thesaurus is very nontechnical and oriented to the layperson.

217. **Chambers Dictionary of Science and Technology.** Edinburgh, Scotland: W & R Chambers, 1974. 1328p.

Q123
D53
Sci

Acknowledged as one of the most comprehensive single-volume dictionaries of its kind, this is a completely revised and expanded edition covering dozens of new fields. The terms are arranged in alphabetical order with most compound and modified words grouped under the first component. The definitions are labeled to indicate the field, and if a term is used in more than one field the definitions are arranged alphabetically by the label.

218. **Dictionnaire des Abbreviations et Acronymes scientifiques, techniques, économiques: Dictionary of Scientific, Technical, and Economic Abbreviations and Acronyms.** Murith, Jean. Paris: Lavoisier, 1984. 407p.

Lists 33,000 abbreviations in fields of science, technology, and economics. Abbreviations and acronyms are alphabetical with the complete name or title listed beneath. Areas from all appropriate languages are included.

219. **Dictionary of New Information Technology Acronyms.** 2nd ed. Gordon, Michael, Alan Singleton, and Clarence Rickards. London: Kogan Page, 1986. 250p.

QA76.15
G67
1986
Sci
Ref

An alphabetical listing of over 10,000 acronyms used in such disciplines of information technology as telecommunications, dataprocessing, and microelectronics. Each entry is expanded and annotated if necessary. Those in the field of information technology will find this useful.

220. **Dictionary of Physical Sciences.** Daintith, John, ed. New York: Pica Press; distr., New York: Universe Books, 1977. 333p.

Q123
D22
Sci

Commonly used scientific terms in physics, chemistry, and astronomy are listed alphabetically with cross-references. The main branches of physics, chemistry, and astronomy and relevant terms from related fields such as electronics, computer science, and mathematics are covered.

221. **Dictionary of Science and Technology, English-French.** Dorian, A. F., comp. New York and Amsterdam: Elsevier Scientific Publishing, 1980. 1085p.

Q123
D672
Sci
Ref

A comprehensive dictionary covering some 150,000 terms from over 100 fields. Fields to which the term belongs are indicated with the French equivalent. Definitions are not provided unless they are necessary for clarity.

222. **Dictionary of Science and Technology, English-German.** 2nd ed. rev. Dorian, A. F., comp. New York and Amsterdam: Elsevier Scientific Publishing, 1978. 1401p.

Q123
D67
1978
Sci
Ref

This dictionary is composed of the definitions of terms from the branches of science and technology, mathematics, and medicine. The field associated with each term is indicated by abbreviations, and gender is provided.

QC82
J4
1986
Sci Ref

223. **Dictionary of Scientific Units, Including Dimensionless Numbers and Scales.** 5th ed. Jerrard, H. G., and D. B. McNeill. London: Chapman & Hall, 1986. 222p.

This alphabetical listing contains over 400 units with concise definitions, appropriate historical references, and additional sources of information. In this specialized dictionary one will find a number of lesser known units; better known units will be found in most general scientific dictionaries.

T9
C885
1970
Sci
Ref

224. **Dictionary of Technical Terms.** 11th ed. rev. Crispin, Frederic Swing. New York: Bruce Publishing Co., 1970. 455p.

Intended primarily for public and high school libraries, this dictionary contains over 10,000 clear, precise definitions. More specialized terms are classified into one or more of 89 categories, ranging from advertising to mechanics to woodworking. Of greatest value, however, is the dictionary's provision of accent, syllable division, hyphenation, and capitalization for each vocabulary entry.

PE1596
E6
Main
Ref
Sci
Ref

225. **Eponyms Dictionary Index: A Reference Guide to Persons, Both Real and Imaginary, and the Terms Derived from Their Names.** Ruffner, James A., ed. Detroit, MI: Gale Research, 1984- . with supplements.

An index containing entries covering over 20,000 eponyms, together with the 13,000 personal names upon which they are based. Each eponym entry provides the word or phrase, the person's name on which the eponym is based, one of 60 subject categories, and source citations. Arrangement of biographical entries is in the same alphabetic sequence, with names, dates of birth and death, nationality, occupation, citations giving biographical details and eponym(s) based on the person's name. Categories excluded are trade names, legal cases, geographical features, buildings, streets, and astronomical bodies and features.

Q123
D37
1976
Sci
Ref

226. **French-English Science and Technology Dictionary.** 4th ed. de Vries, Louis. New York: McGraw-Hill, 1976. 683p.

Revised to include some 4,500 terms, this is a good language dictionary with terms derived from the fields of aeronautics, agronomy, astronautics, astronomy, astrophysics, botany, chemistry, data processing, electronics, entomology, genetics, geology, geophysics, horticulture, mathematics, nuclear science, oceanography, physics, radar, radio, television, and zoology.

Q123
D4
1978
Sci
Ref

227. **German-English Science Dictionary.** 4th ed. de Vries, Louis. Updated and expanded by Leon Jacolev. New York: McGraw-Hill, 1978. 628p.

Includes recently specialized terminology from the fields of nuclear science and engineering, computer science and dataprocessing, solid-state physics, molecular biology, genetics, automation, soil and environmental sciences, electronics, chemistry, physics, biology, and agriculture.

PE1693
I5
SciRef
MainRef

228. **International Acronyms, Initialisms, and Abbreviations Dictionary: A Guide to International Acronyms, Initialisms, Abbreviations, Alphabetic Symbols, Contractions, and Similar Condensed Appellations in All Fields.** Crowley, Ellen T., ed. Detroit, MI: Gale Research, 1987.

Containing several thousand entries covering the gamut in terms of science and technology, this is a potentially invaluable source.

Q123
M15
1978
SciRef

229. **McGraw-Hill Dictionary of Scientific and Technical Terms.** 3rd ed. Parker, Sybil P., ed. New York: McGraw-Hill, 1984. 1781p.

A comprehensive, sci-tech dictionary, the new edition includes 7,500 new entries and is made up of some 98,500 terms and 115,000 definitions. Illustrations are provided, and the terms defined cover 100 fields, general and specialized. Biographical entries are included on over 1,000 individuals associated with the defined laws, reactions, and phenomena contained within. The appendix includes a periodic table of elements, a table of fundamental constants, and a list of specialized abbreviations and acronyms.

230.   **New Trade Names Dictionary: A Guide to Newly Noted Trade Names, Brand Names, Product Names, Coined Names, Model Names, and Design Names, with Addresses of Their Manufacturers, Importers, Marketers, or Distributors.** Wood, Donna, ed. Detroit, MI: Gale Research, 1987. 371p.

T223
V4
A22

This is a compilation of trade names, brand names, and company names arranged in one alphabet and covering apparel, appliances, automobiles, beverages, candy, cosmetics, decorative accessories, drugs, fabrics, food, furniture, games, glass products, hardware, jewelry, paper products, pet supplies, tobacco products, toys, and other consumer-oriented items. Each entry includes a brief description of the product; name of the company that manufactures, imports, or distributes it; and a code indicating the directory from which the information was taken. Company listings give the company's name and address.

231.   **Ocran's Acronyms: A Dictionary of Abbreviations and Acronyms Used in Scientific and Technical Writing.** Ocran, Emanuel Benjamin. London: Routledge and Kegan Paul, 1978. 262p.

Q179
024
Sci
Ref
D

A collection of abbreviations and acronyms used in scientific and technical writing. Entries are subdivided and listed by 47 subject areas in the sciences, engineering, and related technical areas. Foreign abbreviations and acronyms are not included, nor are those for governmental bodies, associations, and institutions.

232.   **The Penguin Dictionary of Science.** 6th ed. Uvarov, E. B., and D. R. Chapman, eds. revised by Alan Isaacs. New York: Schocken Books, 1986. 468p.

Q123
U88
1986

An alphabetical, word-by-word listing of approximately 5,000 entries in the fields of astronomy, biology, biochemistry, cosmology, mathematics, physics, and, in response to contemporary demands, the space sciences. Entries average two or three lines. Cross-references are provided, and italicized words in a definition denote those which are defined in the dictionary. There are occasional figures and tables. The material is directed to the student, rather than the specialist.

233.   **Pugh's Dictionary of Acronyms and Abbreviations.** Pugh, Eric, comp. London: Library Association, 1987 ed. 366p.

T8
P79
1986

The new edition has been expanded to include over 5,000 new entries with a total of 27,000 acronyms and abbreviations used in the fields of management, technology, and information science. Listed alphabetically, it includes acronyms and abbreviations from western and non-western languages.

234.   **Russian-English Dictionary of Scientific and Technical Usage.** Kuznetsov, B. V. Elmsford, NY: Pergamon, 1986. 655p.

Q123
K793
1985
Sci Ref

Incorporating lexigraphical principles first used in the author's *Russian-English Polytechnical Dictionary* (Pergamon, 1980), this excellent dictionary is limited to terms "that cause most trouble in translating because of a multiplicity of meanings associated with them." It assists in overcoming the problem of a grammatically correct translation becoming awkward in the target language. This work will be used by the novice as well as the seasoned translator. As such, it will be indispensable for any translator of scientific and technical Russian language material.

235. **Russian-English Scientific and Technical Dictionary.** Alford, M. H. T., and V. L. Alford. rev. ed. Oxford, England: Pergamon, 1981. 2v. 1423p.

Composed of some 100,000 entries encompassing terminology from 94 specialized fields, this is one of the most comprehensive dictionaries in this important area. It also includes instructions for learning large vocabularies, and for the usage of dictionaries.

236. **Russian-English Translator's Dictionary: A Guide to Scientific and Technical Usage.** 2nd ed. Zimmerman, Mikhail. New York: Wiley, 1984. 544p.

This work emphasizes more recent developments of laser techniques and space research with examples of usage taken from the latest English books and journals in several areas of science and technology.

237. **Scientific Words: Their Structure and Meaning.** Flood, Walter Edgar. Westport, CT: Greenwood Press, 1974. 220p.

An alphabetical listing of word roots, prefixes, and suffixes elemental in the formation of scientific terms. A definition of each element is provided along with an illustration of the use of that element in a word. Current to 1960.

238. **Thesaurus of Information Science Terminology.** rev. ed. Schultz, Claire K. Metuchen, NJ: Scarecrow Press, 1978. 288p.

Contains an alphabetic list of terms, a hierarchical arrangement, and an index to multiword terms. Thesaurus building and use is covered in seven chapters.

239. **Vocabulary of Science.** Hogben, Lancelot Thomas. New York: Stein & Day, 1970. 184p.

Designed to aid the librarian engaging in scientific word building or dissection, this book is devoted exclusively to the field of science and lists English-Greek and English-Latin vocabulary by parts of speech and categories of nouns.

240. **World Guide to Abbreviations of Organizations.** 7th ed. Buttress, F. A. Detroit, MI: Gale Research, 1984. 731p.

Contains approximately 18,000 abbreviations with almost 5,000 of the entries relating to the European Economic Community.

HANDBOOKS

241. **Handbook of Chemistry and Physics: A Ready-Reference Book of Chemical and Physical Data.** Cleveland, OH: Chemical Rubber Co., 1913- . annual.

Revised annually, this invaluable source incorporates the latest verified discoveries in physics and chemistry. Tabular data in these fields is provided with sections covering the elements, atomic weights, organic compounds, and physical constants.

242. **Handbook of Data Processing for Libraries.** 2nd ed. Hayes, Robert M., and Joseph Becker. Sponsored by the Council on Library Resources. Los Angeles: Melville, 1974. 688p.

This handbook on the application of data processing techniques to library operations is broken up into four sections: introduction, management of library data processing, data processing technology, and library subsystems. The chapter on mechanized information services, in its survey of representative operational systems of mechanized bibliographic retrieval, provides a number of models that are pertinent to a variety of situations.

243. **Handbook of Technical Writing Practices.** Jordan, Stello, ed. New York: Wiley, 1971. 2v.
    This comprehensive handbook includes an extensive glossary and covers in four parts various documents and publications produced by the technical writer, such as equipment instruction manuals, parts catalogs, management reports, proposals, sales literature, etc.; support activities, such as editing, illustrating, and data processing; the management of technical writing; and guides and references, including style manuals and data sources.

244. **International Critical Tables of Numerical Data, Physics, Chemistry, and Technology.** National Research Council. New York: McGraw-Hill, 1933. 7v.
    This older work is still useful as a compilation of chemical and physical tables. It is considered to be a classic source for tabular information.

245. **Tables of Physical and Chemical Constants, and Some Mathematical Functions.** 15th ed. Kaye, G. W. C., ed. London: Longman, 1986. 477p.
    An excellent listing of pertinent tables arranged in three main sections: physics, chemistry, and mathematical functions.

SERIALS

246. **Abstracts and Indexes in Science and Technology: A Descriptive Guide.** 2nd ed. Owen, Dolores B., and Marguerite M. Hanchey. Metuchen, NJ: Scarecrow Press, 1985. 235p.
    Provides a description of the materials one would encounter in conducting a literature search in scientific and technological subjects. The abstracts and indexes are listed under the following headings: general, mathematics and statistics, astronomy, chemistry and physics, nuclear science and space science, earth sciences, engineering and technology, geological sciences, agricultural sciences, health sciences, and environment. Each title is described in outline form, with the following topics covered: arrangement, coverage, scope, locating material, abstracts, indexes, other material, and periodicals scanned.

247. **Directory of Published Proceedings, Series SEMT – Science/Engineering/Medicine/Technology.** White Plains, NY: InterDok Corp., 1965- . annual.
    "A bibliographic directory of preprints and published proceedings of congresses, conferences, symposia, meetings, seminars, and summer schools which have been held worldwide from 1964 to date" (verso of title page). Arrangement is chronological; entries provide place, name of meeting, principal sponsors, publisher or distributor, address, order numbers, price, plus, if necessary, title and series or journal of publication, editor, and pagination. Sponsor and subject indexes provided.

248. **Guide to Magazine and Serial Agents.** Katz, Bill, and Peter Gellatly. New York: Bowker, 1975. 239p.
    This somewhat dated guide is designed to help librarians determine the best periodicals or serials subscription agent for their particular library by "giving enough background information concerning serials and their management to provide an understanding of the agent-library relationship and by providing facts, details, and descriptions of the services and procedures of the major and selected smaller domestic and foreign serials subscription agents" (page xi). The first three parts of this guide describe the essentials of ordering serials publications, record maintenance, agency services, selecting an agent, claims, and claiming. The final section includes a helpful checklist of the typical agency services and a well-annotated list of 172 agencies that handle serials.

HF5351
684
1985

Main Ref
Sci Ref

249. Guide to Special Issues and Indexes of Periodicals. 3rd ed. Uhlan, Miriam, ed. New York: Special Libraries Association, 1985. 160p.

This guide provides easy access to the specialized contents of selected American and Canadian trade, technical, and consumer journals. Arranged in alphabetical order by periodical title, the main text contains a descriptive listing of annual special issues, features, supplementary issues, and/or sections appearing on a recurring basis, as well as information on editorial and advertiser indexes. A comprehensive subject index aids in locating the contents of the specials.

505.09
K93
Sci

250. History of Scientific and Technical Periodicals: The Origins and Development of the Scientific and Technical Press, 1665-1790. 2nd ed. Kronick, David A. Metuchen, NJ: Scarecrow Press, 1976. 336p.

Covers the history of the origins and developments of the scientific journals. Information on definitions and history of the scientific periodical is provided along with discussions on substantive journals, society proceedings, abstract and review journals, collections, almanacs and annuals, etc. The volume concludes with selected bibliography and subject, name, and title indexes.

Z6941
I48
Sci
Ref

251. International Serials Catalogue. Paris: International Council of Scientific Unions, Abstracting Board, 1978. 2v.

An alphabetical listing of serial applications abstracted by ICSUAB. Includes full bibliographic information.

Z5063.A2
PT
Sci
Ref

252. Proceedings in Print. Arlington, MA: Proceedings in Print, 1964- . bimonthly.

Originally devoted to the aerospace industry, it enlarged its scope covering several fields of science, technology, and medicine. Entries provide full bibliographic citations for proceedings covered and each issue is in two parts: entries for proceedings published in the last two years and proceedings published previously. Indexed by corporate authors, agencies, editors, and keyword or subject headings.

Q1
H57
Sci,
Main

253. Scientific Periodicals: Their Historical Development, Characteristics, and Control. Houghton, Bernard. Hamden, CT: Linnet Books, 1975. 135p.

This small book is an adequate history of the scientific periodicals. It also contains selective lists of science periodicals, as well as an analysis of abstracting and indexing services.

254. Serial Titles Held by the Academy of Natural Sciences of Philadelphia, June 1987. 2nd ed. Philadelphia: Academy of Natural Sciences, 1987. 682p.

Because the Academy of Natural Sciences of Philadelphia's collection is so rich in subjects it covers, a list of the titles it possesses is a valuable tool for interlibrary loan, verification, and collection building. If a library is interested in using the checklist approach, this is one excellent list to use.

Z7403
W92
1963
Sci
Ref

255. World List of Scientific Periodicals Published in the Years 1900-1960. 4th ed. London: Butterworth, 1963-1965. 3v.

This is a union list of more than 60,000 titles in the British libraries concerned with natural sciences plus some additional titles. The emphasis is on the years 1951-1960 which amount to 25 percent of the total coverage. Ten thousand titles incorporated in the third edition have been omitted since they cover social sciences. Arrangement is alphabetical by title indicating location in the library, dates of publication, standard abbreviations, etc. Despite its location of files in British libraries, this work is essential for American science libraries, for it is the only comprehensive source for the period. Recommended for retrospective use only.

256.   **Yearbook of International Congress Proceedings.** Brussels: Union of International Associations, 1969-70. 2v.

    This yearbook consists of proceedings, reports, symposia, and other documents produced by international congresses. It is indexed by keyword and author. For older information consult the following: *International Congresses and Conferences, 1840-1937: A Union List of Their Publications Available in Libraries of the United States and Canada* (New York: H. W. Wilson, 1938).

JX 1904
44
Main

DIRECTORIES

257.   **Annual Register of Grant Support: A Guide to Grant Support Programs of Government Agencies, Foundations, and Business and Professional Organizations.** Los Angeles: Academic Media, 1969- . annual.

    Arranged in four main categories with one devoted to science. Entries provide brief information on grant programs, monetary allocations, plus information about eligibility requirements. Subject, organizational, and geographic indexes are included. Supersedes *Grant Data Quarterly* (1967-1968).

LB 2336
A5
Main
Ref

258.   **Computer-Readable Data Bases: A Directory and Data Sourcebook.** Williams, Martha E., ed. Chicago, IL: American Library Association, 1985- . 2v.

    Volume 1 is titled *Science, Technology, Medicine*; volume 2, *Business, Law, Humanities, Social Sciences*. Covers over 2,805 databases worldwide. The information provided for each database includes: acronym and full name; issuance; correspondence with printed source; producer, distributor, and/or generator; subject matter and scope; indexing; availability in batch or online mode; tape specifications; database services; producer user services, if offered, and the address and telephone number of the contact person for further information. There is also a listing of outmoded databases that have been replaced by more current ones, or whose existence cannot be verified. Indexes are included for broad subject categories, database name, producer, and processor. The directory is compiled from the database on databases maintained at the University of Illinois Information Retrieval Research Laboratory.

Z 699.2
C 66
1985
Sci
Ref

259.   **Current Contents Address Directory — Science and Technology.** Philadelphia: Institute for Scientific Information, 1984- . annual. 4v.

    Over one million authors are represented in this directory. Access is by author name, organization, and geographic location. This information is derived from the ISI publications.

Q 145
C 86
Sci
(up to 1987)

260.   **DataBase Directory.** White Plains, NY: Knowledge Industry Publications, 1985- . semi-annual updates.

    Containing about 2,400 entries, this is an alphabetical listing of databases accessible online in North America. Yearly subscription includes spring and fall issues. The directory covers more than 2,000 databases and database systems including full text, textual and numeric, numeric, property, bibliographic, and referral databases in all subject areas. Each entry gives the subject, a general description of content and scope, corresponding printed sources, subject access, producer and producer services, time coverage and file data, language used, restrictions and conditions, how accessed, and vendor and price. It is indexed by subject, producer/vendor, and alternate name of database.

QA 76.9
D3
D295
Sci

261. **Directory of American Research and Technology.** 21st ed. Jaques Cattell Press, ed. New York: Bowker, 1987. 744p.

This directory is limited to nongovernmental laboratories devoted to fundamental and applied research, including development of products and processes. The information, based on a questionnaire, provides all the essential facts about each company, its subsidiary laboratories, its chief administrative and research executives, its personnel, and a brief statement of its chief research and development activities. Alphabetically arranged, it concludes with three indexes: personnel, geographical, and subject.

262. **Directory of Directories.** 4th ed. Marlow, Cecilia Ann, and Robert C. Thomas, eds. Detroit, MI: Gale Research, 1986. 2v.

Similar in format to the *Encyclopedia of Associations* (see entry 269), entries provide accurate titles and subtitles, full publisher addresses, description of coverage, analysis of information in a typical entry, arrangement, type of index, number of pages, frequency, editor's name, former title, price, and whether the database is machine-readable. It updates and revises the entries found in the inter-edition supplements, *Directory of Information Service*, and adds detailed entries on directories not covered in the supplements. Nearly 9,600 detailed subject headings with numerous cross-references structure the work.

263. **Directory of Information Management Software for Libraries, Information Centers, Record Centers.** Cibbarelli, Pamela, and Edward J. Kazlauskas. Studio City, CA: Pacific Information, 1985/86. 239p.

The directory and its supplement provide descriptions of 65 currently available software packages useful to libraries and information centers.

264. **Directory of Online Databases.** Santa Monica, CA: Cuadra Associates, 1979- . quarterly.

Updated quarterly, this directory of online databases is international in coverage. Information is provided on type of database, subject producer, content, coverage, online service, and updating. Producers and addresses are listed, and subject, service, producer, and database name indexes are included.

265. **Directory of Publishing Sources: The Researcher's Guide to Journals in Engineering and Technology.** Balachandran, Sarojini. New York: Wiley-Interscience, 1982. 343p.

This directory of almost 300 technical journals has a detailed subject keyword index to help locate specific subject areas. It serves engineers and scientists who wish to publish their articles.

266. **Directory of Research Grants.** Phoenix, AZ: Oryx Press, 1987. 981p.

Arranged by 84 academic disciplines, this is a directory of research grants awarded to academic departments. Each entry includes a brief description of the grant, the amount, application date, and sponsor. Indexes cover grant names, sponsoring organizations, and sponsoring organizations by type.

267. **Directory of Scientific Directories: A World Bibliographic Guide to Medical, Agricultural, Industrial, and Natural Science Directories.** 4th ed. Harvey, Anthony P., comp. Essex, England: Longman, 1986. 232p.

Lists about 1,800 directories published from 1950 to 1971 and includes those published separately as well as in periodicals. Arrangement is by continent, then by country, and within each country by subject.

268. **Directory of Special Libraries and Information Centers.** 10th ed. Darnay, Brigitte T., ed. Detroit, MI: Gale Research, 1987. 2v.

This directory covers all types of special libraries in the broadest sense of the word. Special collections in university or public libraries, governmental libraries, company libraries, specialized libraries of associations, and institutions are covered. Volume 1 provides an alphabetical approach to over 14,000 special libraries. Each listing contains the name of sponsoring organization, name of library, address and telephone number, name of person in charge, founding date, size of staff, important subjects in the collection, special collections, size and composition of holdings, number of regularly received serials, services available to outside inquirers, publications of the library, special catalogs and indexes maintained, and names of supervisory staff plus automated library operations and memberships in networks and/or consortia. A subject index concludes the volume. Volume 2 serves as a geographic-personnel index. The geographic section lists by state or province all the institutions included in the first volume. The second section provides an alphabetical listing of the names of library personnel with professional title and affiliation. Volume 3 is an inter-edition supplement called *New Special Libraries* that keeps subscribers up to date on new libraries or important changes.

269. **Encyclopedia of Associations.** 22nd ed. Detroit, MI: Gale Research, 1987. 1v. in 3. 2666p.

Strives to cover all national, nonprofit membership organizations, foreign groups, international groups, some local and regional groups, and citizen action groups. Each entry is listed under one of 17 broad categories. Information given includes: name, acronym, keyword, address, telephone number, chief official and title, founding date, number of members, staff, state and local groups, description, committees, sections and divisions, publications, affiliated organizations, mergers and changes of names, and conventions/ meetings. Volume 1 includes an alphabetical keyword index and the listings of the national organizations of the United States; the geographic-executive index makes up volume 2. Volume 3 contains periodic issues of *New Associations and Projects*, which keeps the encyclopedia updated between editions.

270. **Encyclopedia of Information Systems and Services.** 6th ed. Schmittroth, John, ed. Ann Arbor, MI: Gale Research, 1985- . irregular.

Provides information on organizations concerned with new forms, new media, and new methods for providing information services. Among these organizations are publishers, computer software and time-sharing companies, micrographic firms, libraries, information centers, government agencies, clearinghouses, research centers, professional associations, and consultants. Not covered are printed and legal services, traditional academic and special libraries, public information offices, hardware manufacturers and distributors in the computer and micrographics field, conventional indexing and abstracting services, and most library automation programs, which are limited to such housekeeping functions as circulation, serials control, and acquisitions. The information was obtained by questionnaire or other means. The first of two sections contains one-page listings for each major organization; the second provides a more condensed description for organizations of lesser importance or for entities that failed to supply all needed information. Each entry provides name, date established, executive and equivalent full-time staff, description of system or service, input, holdings, publications, and microform applications and services. Among the 13 supplementary indexes are a geographic index and indexes of commercially available databases, micrographic associations, and serials publications.

Q180
E9
E88
1985
Sci Ref

271. European Research Centres: A Directory of Organizations in Science, Technology, Agriculture, and Medicine. 6th ed. Williams, Trevor I., ed. Essex, England: Longman; distr., Detroit, MI: Gale Research, 1986. 2v. 2453p.

This directory contains profiles of approximately 20,000 laboratories and the like. It is indexed by name and subject area.

Q180
E9
E88
1982
Sci

272. European Research Index. 4th ed. Williams, Colin H., ed. St. Peter Port, England: Francis Hodgson Ltd., 1977. 2v.

First published in 1965, this directory covers establishments in Europe, including Eastern Europe. Government and independent establishments, university research departments and research laboratories of industrial firms are covered as well as all international science bodies with European headquarters. Information includes name of executive, address, parent body (if any), and a brief description of research activities. Country and title indexes are provided.

T10.65
E8
E9
1984
Sci
Ref

273. European Sources of Scientific and Technical Information. 7th ed. Harvey, Anthony P., ed. Harlow, England: Longman, 1986. 356p.

First published in Paris under the title *Guide to European Sources of Technical Information*, this directory makes no claim to being exhaustive; rather, it attempts to supply a contact point within each European country for each subject area. Emphasized in this edition are fee-based services. The major drawback to this publication is its cost, presently $190.00.

QA76.9
D32
F4
Main Ref
Sci Ref

274. Federal Data Base Finder: A Directory of Free and Fee-Based Data Bases and Files Available from the Federal Government. 2nd ed. Zarozny, Sharon, and Monica Horner. Chevy Chase, MD: Information USA, 1987. 368p.

A directory of 3,000 databases and files available from the federal government. Most of the entries included in each database are either government technical reports or government documents.

Z675
G7
B46
Main

275. Federal Library Resources: A User's Guide to Research Collections. 2nd ed. Benton, Mildred, comp. New York: Science Associates/International, 1984. 103p.

The following information is provided for 163 libraries: name and address, person in charge, agency affiliation, business hours, description of services, and brief information on resources. Appended is a subject index to library collections, an index to names of administrative personnel, and a list of libraries to which questionnaires were sent, with indication of changes and nonrespondents.

AS911
A2
F65
Main Ref
Sci

276. Foundation Directory. 10th ed. New York: The Foundation Center; distr., New York: Columbia University Press, 1985. 885p.

Included are foundations that possessed assets of $1 million or more, or made total contributions of $100,000 or more in the year of record. The foundations must be "nonprofit, with funds and program managed by its own trustees or directors, and established to maintain or aid social, educational, charitable, religious, or other activities serving the common welfare, primarily through the making of grants." The arrangement is by state, with the following data provided: address, founding date, purpose and activities, financial data (including assets and expenditures), and a list of officers. Four indexes are included: index to field of interest; cities within states; donors, trustees, and administrators; and foundation name. Available from DIALOG as an online database.

277. **Government Research Directory.** 4th ed. Gill, Kay, and Susan E. Tufts, eds. Detroit, MI: Gale Research, 1987.

Containing over 2,900 entries, this is a comprehensive descriptive inventory of the research programs of the U.S. government.

Q179.98
G68
Sci

278. **Guide to U.S. Government Directories.** Larson, Donna Rae. Phoenix, AZ: Oryx Press, 1981. 208p.

This listing of directories published by the U.S. government contains factual data on coverage of the directory, information available, types of indexes used, and ordering information. A complete subject index is provided.

279. **ISI's Who Is Publishing in Science: An International Directory of Scientists and Scholars in the Life, Physical, Social, and Applied Sciences.** Philadelphia: Institute for Scientific Information, 1971- . annual.

Q145
J56
Sci

to 1978

Continuing the annual *International Directory of Research and Development Scientists* (ISI, 1968-1970), this incorporates the addresses and organizational affiliations of authors of articles published in journals covered by the *Science Citation Index* (see entry 195).

280. **Libraries, Information Centers, and Databases in Science and Technology: A World Guide.** Lengenfelder, Helga, ed. New York: Saur, 1984.

An international directory of special libraries of more than 3,000 volumes in over 150 countries, 350 information and documentation centers, and 360 online databases from nearly 200 producers. It is indexed by general name and English keyword, and is arranged by country.

281. **National Directory of Newsletters and Reporting Services.** Detroit, MI: Gale Research, 1978- . annual.

Z6941
N3
Main

Covered are newsletters issued by businesses, associations, societies, clubs, government agencies, etc. Entries include title, name and address of the sponsoring organization, editor, description of scope and purpose, frequency, subscription price, circulation, former or alternative titles, and advertising information. Title, publisher, and subject indexes are provided.

282. **National Trade and Professional Associations of the United States.** Russell, John J., ed. Washington, DC: Columbia Books, 1966- . annual.

HD2425
DS3
Sci

Provides address, name of executive, number of members, information on staff, telephone, publications (if any), annual budget, and information on meetings.

283. **Online Bibliographic Databases: A Directory and Sourcebook.** 3rd ed. Hall, James L. London: ASLIB, 1986. 509p.

Z699.22
H34
1986
Sci Ref

Slightly dated, this is a directory of online bibliographic databases accessible through online services suppliers throughout the world. Alphabetically arranged, each entry contains information on name and acronym of database, supplier's name and address, subject field, printed versions (if any), file details, charge, and more.

284. **Research Centers Directory.** 11th ed. Palmer, Archie M., ed. Detroit, MI: Gale Research, 1986. 2v.

AS25
D5
Main Ref
Sci Ref

The material is arranged in 15 broad subject categories from agriculture, home economics, and nutrition to social sciences, humanities, and religion. The volume concludes with three indexes: institution index, alphabetic index of research centers, and subject index. Information provided for each research center includes: name, address, director's name, year founded, sources of support, size and type of staff, annual budget, principal fields of activity, research facilities, publications, and library facilities. All scientific research centers of consequence are thoroughly covered.

285. **Science and Technology Libraries.** 10th ed. Darnay, B. T., ed. Detroit, MI: Gale Research, 1987. 563p.

This is a subject index to the entries in the *Directory of Special Libraries and Information Centers* (see entry 268). The volumes cover: v.1, business and law libraries, including military and transportation libraries; v.2, education and information science libraries, including audiovisual, picture, publishing, rare book, and recreational libraries; v.3, health sciences libraries, including all aspects of basic and applied medical sciences; v.4, social sciences and humanities libraries, including area/ethnic, art, geography/map, history, music, religion/theology, theater, and urban/regional planning libraries; v.5, science and technology libraries, including agriculture, environment/conservation, and food sciences libraries.

286. **Scientific and Technical Organizations and Agencies Directory.** Young, M. L., ed. Detroit, MI: Gale Research, 1987. 2v.

A guide to approximately 12,000 new and established organizations and agencies concerned with the physical sciences, engineering, and technology. It is presented by type of organization and includes master name and keyword index.

287. **Scientific, Technical, and Related Societies of the United States.** Washington, DC: National Academy of Sciences, 1971- . annual.

Deals exclusively with membership societies concentrating on a particular scientific, engineering, or other technical disciplines. Entries are listed alphabetically by association name. Included in each entry are name of association, address, executive officers, a brief paragraph on history and organization, statement of purpose, membership, meetings, professional activities, and publications.

288. **The Software Encyclopedia 1986.** New York: Bowker, 1986- . annual. 2v.

Over 25,000 programs from 3,000 producers and vendors are listed along with descriptions and availability. Simple listings and an index are provided.

289. **Technical Abstract Bulletin.** Defense Documentation Center, Defense Supply Agency. Springfield, VA: Clearinghouse for Federal Scientific and Technical Information, 1953-1967. semimonthly.

Covering classified scientific research, this source has limited utility. Includes four indexes: corporate-monitoring agency, subject, personal author, contract.

290. **World Guide to Scientific Associations and Learned Societies.** 4th ed. New York: Saur, 1984. 947p.

A thoroughly revised and expanded edition that includes about 22,000 international, national, and regional associations from 150 countries in every area of science, culture, and technology. Over 12,000 periodicals and bulletins of these associations are also included with a special index of official association abbreviations. A subject index of activities, organized by country is available. Arrangement is by country, abbreviated form of name, and area of specialization.

291. **World Guide to Technical Information and Documentation Services. Guide mondial des centres de documentation et d'information techniques.** 2nd ed. Paris: UNESCO; distr., New York: UNIPUB, 1975.

Provides information on 476 centers in 93 countries and territories. Entries include history, address and telephone, staff, subject specialists, library collection, and bibliographic, abstracting, reprographic, and translating services. The emphasis is on agriculture, architecture, building, chemical engineering, chemistry, electrical engineering, forestry, geology, industrial management, mechanical engineering, metallurgy, nuclear physics and chemistry, nutrition, physics, textiles, and water. This somewhat dated directory still allows access to information on some less well known centers.

BIOGRAPHICAL DIRECTORIES

292. **American Men and Women of Science. Physical and Biological Sciences.** 16th ed. Jaques Cattell Press, ed. New York: Bowker, 1986. 8v.

Q141
.A47
Sci

An outstanding biographical directory whose criteria for inclusion are: (1) achievement, by reason of experience and learning, of a stature in scientific work equivalent to that required for a doctoral degree, coupled with currently ongoing activity in scientific research; or (2) research activity of high quality in sciences as evidenced by publications in reputable journals; or, for those whose work cannot be published because of government or industrial security, research activity of high quality in science as evidenced by the judgment of the person's peers; or (3) attainment of a position of substantial responsibility requiring scientific training and experience to the extent described for (1) or (2). Gives name, birth date and place, marital status, degrees, major field of interest, positions held, memberships, and address of each of 130,500 scientists representing 79 broad disciplines. The last volume serves as an index to the set and contains a discipline index and geographical index. Each section is now on a three-year revision cycle.

293. **Asimov's Biographical Encyclopedia of Science and Technology: The Lives and Achievements of 1,510 Great Scientists from Ancient Times to the Present, Chronologically Arranged.** 2nd ed. Asimov, Isaac. Garden City, NY: Doubleday, 1982. 941p.

Q141
.A74
Sci
Ref

This is a reprint of the edition published in 1972. Its purpose is to provide a history of science through a chronology of biographies of great scientists. Although it contains many entries, there are omissions.

294. **Biographical Dictionary of American Science: The Seventeenth through the Nineteenth Centuries.** Elliot, Clark A. Westport, CT: Greenwood Press, 1979. 360p.

Q141
.E37
Sci
Ref

A retrospective companion to *American Men and Women of Science* (see entry 292), this work contains sketches on some 600 scientists. Appendices on birthyear, birthplace, education, occupation, and fields of science are included.

295. **Biographical Dictionary of Scientists.** 3rd ed. Williams, Trevor I., ed. New York: Wiley, 1982. 674p.

Q141
.W62
1982
Sci
Ref

Contains biographical sketches of varying length on deceased scientists, technologists, inventors, and explorers. At the end of each sketch, bibliographical references are provided.

296. **Biographical Encyclopedia of Scientists.** Daintith, John, Sarah Mitchell, and Elizabeth Tootill, eds. New York: Facts on File, 1981. 2v. 935p.

Q141
.B53
Sci
Ref

Containing biographies of almost 2,000 scientists of yesterday and today, this reference concentrates on the traditional sciences. A chronological listing of scientific achievement, discovery, and publications is included.

297. **Biographical Memoirs.** National Academy of Sciences. Washington, DC: National Academy of Sciences, 1877/79- . annual.

An annual providing biographical sketches, portraits, lists of publications, and chronology of events of deceased members of the Academy.

298. **Biographical Memoirs of Fellows of the Royal Society.** London: The Royal Society of London, 1955- .

Contains portraits and biographies of recently deceased members, including a complete biobibliography of the member's papers. For obituary notices prior to 1932, consult the *Proceedings of the Royal Society*.

299. **Biographisch-Literarisches Handwörterbuch zur Geschichte der exacten Wissenschaften.** 2nd ed. Poggendorff, Johoun Christine. Berlin: Akademie Verlag, 1863- . Publisher varies. Leipzig: Barth, 1863-1904; Leipzig: Verlag Chemie, 1925-1940. Series resumed in 1953 with Band 7a.

A German-language handbook on the lives and published works of mathematicians, physicists, chemists, mineralogists, and other physical science scientists, including those from other countries. Each entry includes full name, academic and honorary degrees, positions held, dates and places of birth and death, principal articles about the scientist including obituary notices and principal publications.

300. **Dictionary of Scientific Biography.** Gillispie, Charles Coulston, ed. New York: Scribner, 1970-1981. 16v.

The set comprises fourteen basic volumes, a supplement, and the index. Edited under the auspices of the American Council of Learned Societies, it is a comprehensive reference work in the history of science. Some 5,000 biographies of mathematicians and natural scientists cover all regions and historical periods, including such topics as Japanese, Egyptian, Mesopotamian, Indian, and pre-Columbian sciences. The biographies, ranging in length from five hundred to twenty thousand words, were written by fifteen hundred authors from ninety countries. All articles were specially commissioned and cover scientists from antiquity to the mid-twentieth century. Well-documented biographical sketches of scientists no longer living are provided and the selection criteria are influenced by "contributions to science ... sufficiently distinctive to make an identifiable difference to the profession or community of knowledge." The scope is international, but, as indicated in the preface, some countries (India, China, Japan) will not be as well represented as Western scientists. The work is completed by an index which contains over seventy-five thousand entries. Periodicals, societies, universities, museums, medals, lectureships, and prizes are accessed.

301. **Directory of Experts and Consultants in Science and Engineering.** 2nd ed. Woodbridge, CT: Research Publications, 1987. 2v.

Volume 1 contains biographical entries arranged in a subject classification. Volume 2 contains a name and expertise index. Curiously, no geographic index is provided. To some extent this title is misnamed, because the primary focus is on technology only. The work is derived from *Directory of Experts and Consultants in Science and Engineering* (Woodbridge, CT: Research Publications, 1985). This last title is, in turn, derived from *Who's Who in Technology* (Woodbridge, CT: Research Publications, 1986). Some loss in translation can be detected. This is recommended only if the two larger works are not available.

302. **Index to Biographical Fragments in Unspecialized Scientific Journals.** Barr, E. Scott. University, AL: University of Alabama Press, 1974. 294p.

Covering the years 1798-1933, this is an index to biographical information in seven English-language journals of general science, including *American Journal of Science* (1819-1920); *Nature* (1869-1918); *Philosophical Magazine* (1798-1902); *Popular Science Monthly* (1872-1915); *Royal Society of Edinburgh. Proceedings* (1832-1920); *Royal Society of London. Proceedings* (1800-1933); and *Science* (1883-1919). There are approximately 15,000 citations to 7,700 scientists and non-scientists, including references to about 1,500 portraits. Each entry provides journal citations, the full name of each person, pertinent dates, nationality, and specialties. Tables at the end of the book show the year(s) that correspond to each volume of each journal indexed.

303. **Index to Scientists of the World from Ancient to Modern Times: Biographies and Portraits.** Ireland, Norma Olin. Boston: Faxon, 1962. 662p.

An index to collected and composite works of biographical reference.

Q141
.I73
1962
Sci
Ref

304. **McGraw-Hill Modern Scientists and Engineers.** New York: McGraw-Hill, 1980. 3v.

This is a revised and expanded edition of *McGraw-Hill Modern Men of Science* (1980), which supplements the *McGraw-Hill Encyclopedia of Science and Technology* (see entry 207). Three hundred new sketches are included, for a total of 1,140 biographies of the leading figures in science and engineering from 1920-1978 "... selected by the editor from recipients of major awards and prizes given by the leading societies, organizations, and institutions of the world." The autobiographies or biographies are written by subject specialists, and each sketch is accompanied by a portrait. Date of birth, education, contributions and research, awards, a short bibliography, and cross-references are included. Field and analytical indexes are provided. Some articles are written in highly technical language, but the volume serves as a valuable reference for use by science and engineering students, historians, and educators.

Q141
.M15
1980
Sci
Ref

305. **Prominent Scientists: An Index to Collective Biographies.** 2nd ed. Pelletier, Paul A., ed. New York: Neal-Schuman, 1985. 356p.

Covering biographies of 12,211 scientists in various fields of science, the indexes include one alphabetized by surname and one by the scientist's associated field. The primary emphasis is on books published between 1960-1983. Recommended to all public and academic libraries.

Q141
.P398
1985
Sci
Ref

306. **Scientists and Inventors.** Feldman, Anthony, and Peter Ford. New York: Facts on File, 1979. 336p.

Includes over 150 scientists and inventors whose entries are presented in chronological order. Two pages are devoted to each entry which includes a portrait, a picture or diagram of the scientific principle or the equipment or product discovered or invented, and in some cases a photograph of a contemporary application.

Juven.
T39
.F37
1979

307. **Who Was Who in American History—Science and Technology.** Chicago, IL: Marquis Who's Who, 1976. 688p.

A selective biographical reference work comprising abbreviated sketches of 10,000 engineers, inventors, and scientists now deceased whose contributions to the advancement of science and/or technology during the past 350 years are considered notable. Data consist of facts on birth and death, parentage, education, marriage and offspring, academic/business positions and accomplishments, major publications, honors, and awards.

Q141
.W56
1976
Sci
Ref

Q141
.W6
Sci Ref

308. **Who's Who in Frontier Science and Technology.** Chicago, IL: Marquis Who's Who, 1985. 800p.

Approximately 16,500 people working in North America are listed with standard "who's who" information. Scientists are cross-referenced by specialty.

Q141
.W589
1978
Sci

309. **Who's Who in Science in Europe: A Reference Guide to European Scientists.** 5th ed. Essex, England: Longman, 1987. 3v.

Scientists from Eastern and Western Europe working in the biological, physical, medical, and agricultural sciences are listed with typical "who's who" information.

Q145
.D498
Sci

310. **Who's Who of British Scientists, 1980-1981.** 3rd ed. Dorking, England: Simon, 1980. 589p.

In addition to biographical information, this source provides a list of scientific societies and their journals, a list of independent or commercially-produced scientific journals, research establishments, and a classified index by area of specialization. Its purpose is to list the "top 10,000 of British men and women in the biological and physical sciences or who are enjoying careers of distinction after basic training in a scientific discipline."

Q141
.O34
1986
Sci

311. **Women in Science: Antiquity through the Nineteenth Century: A Biographical Dictionary with Annotated Bibliography.** Ogilvie, Marilyn B. Cambridge, MA: MIT Press, 1986. 254p.

A selected biographical reference work containing 186 biographical sketches, primarily limited to Western scientists. Arranged alphabetically by last name, entries range from one paragraph to over eight pages, depending on the person's impact and available written information. Suitable for academic and some school and public libraries.

CATALOGS

312. **Catalog of the John Crerar Library, Chicago.** Boston: G. K. Hall, 1967. 78v.

The catalog is divided into four component subsections: *Author/Title Catalog*, 35v.; *Classified Subject Catalog*, 42v.; *Subject Index to the Classified Subject Catalog*, 610p. Ranked among the greatest scientific and technical libraries in the world, Crerar holds a collection in excess of 1.1 million volumes. This catalog is a printing in book form of the actual catalog cards. The collections include holdings of the Illinois Institute of Technology and are of research strength in the basic sciences, including physics, chemistry and biology; medicine, including anatomy, physiology, biochemistry, and pharmacology; agriculture, especially agricultural engineering and chemicals; and technology, including all branches of engineering.

313. **Catalog of the Library of the Academy of Natural Sciences of Philadelphia.** Boston: G. K. Hall, 1972. 16v.

This dictionary catalog contains many analytic entries in the fields of systematics, paleontology, and stratigraphic geology for 150,000 volumes.

Z881
.C512
Main
Oversize

314. **Center for Research Libraries Catalogue: Monographs.** Chicago, IL: Center for Research Libraries, 1969-1970. 5v.

A main entry catalog of monographs held by the center, it omits such categories of materials as archival materials; children's books; Chinese books; foreign, state, and federal government documents; and dissertations.

315. **Center for Research Libraries Catalogue: Serials.** Chicago, IL: Center for Research Libraries, 1972- . 2v. irregular.
    This set consists of two volumes which list by main entry those items that were formerly listed in *Rarely-Held Scientific Serials* (Chicago, IL: Center for Research Libraries, 1964). The center is known for its holdings of serials.

*Z881
.C514
Main
Oversize*

316. **Published Library Catalogs: An Introduction to Their Contents and Use.** Collison, Robert. London: Mansell Information; distr., New York: Bowker, 1973.
    Limited to the "English-speaking world," this volume contains about 600 library catalogs and narrates through survey chapters 11 areas that they cover. The areas are general catalogs, auction sale catalogs, book industries, philosophy and religion, social sciences, science and technology, arts and architecture, literature, history and biography, music, and geography.

*Z695.87
.C6
Main*

317. **Research Catalog of the Library of the American Museum of Natural History: Authors.** American Museum of Natural History Library, New York. Boston: G. K. Hall, 1977. 13v.
    Including bibliographic and journal citations, this catalog is accessed through personal, corporate, and joint author; compiler, editor, and illustrator indexes.

*Z7409
.A44
Sci
Ref*

318. **Research Catalog of the Library of the American Museum of Natural History: Classed Catalog.** American Museum of Natural History Library, New York. Boston: G. K. Hall, 1978. 12v.
    Lists over 325,000 volumes that deal with a variety of natural science fields, including geology, zoology, anthropology, entomology, mineralogy, and paleontology. Also includes a listing of 17,000 serial titles.

*Z7409
.A47
1978
Sci
Ref*

THESES AND DISSERTATIONS

319. **American Doctoral Dissertations.** Ann Arbor, MI: University Microfilms, 1964- . annual.
    Complete listing of all doctoral dissertations accepted by American and Canadian universities.

*Z5055
.U49
A62
Main +
Sci Ref*

320. **Comprehensive Dissertation Index, 1861-1972.** Ann Arbor, MI: University Microfilms International, 1973. 37v.
    Containing 417,000 entries, this comprehensive inventory of doctoral dissertations provides a listing of the output of graduate schools in the United States and some foreign universities. The computer-generated index is by keywords and authors. This is an expanded version of its predecessor, *Dissertation Abstracts International Retrospective Index*, published by University Microfilms in 1970. Other University Microfilms sources were used, along with the Library of Congress' list of *American Doctoral Dissertations Printed in 1912-1932* and H. W. Wilson's *Doctoral Dissertations Accepted by American Universities 1933/34-1954-55*. Dissertations not found on those lists, however, may be found in this index. This volume is kept current by annual supplements.

*Z5053
.D574
Main Ref
+
Sci*

321. **Dissertation Abstracts International. B: The Sciences and Engineering.** Ann Arbor, MI: University Microfilms International, 1969- . monthly.
    A compilation of abstracts of dissertations available from University Microfilms either on microfilm or as xerographic reproductions. Institutions have increasingly begun to

*Z5053
.D572
Main
Ref*

require dissertations to be sent to University Microfilms, increasing the need for *DAI*. The main list is arranged alphabetically by subject field and by university. Each listing includes title, order number, author's name, university, date, name of supervisor, abstract, and number of pages. *DAI* first appeared as *Microfilm Abstracts* (vols. 1-11, 1935-1951) and later as *Dissertation Abstracts* (vols. 12-29, 1952-1969). *DA* has appeared in two sections since 1966: A: *The Humanities*; and B: *The Sciences and Engineering*. Section C: *European Abstracts* was added in 1977. A number of European institutions are now represented. Keyword, title and author indexes appear monthly. Available as an online database from DIALOG, this same information is available directly from University Microfilms as a CD-ROM product. The CD-ROM version contains dissertations from 1861 to the present and is updated monthly. On two discs, updates will be available from University Microfilms.

322. Guide to Theses and Dissertations: An Annotated, International Bibliography of Bibliographies. Reynolds, Michael M. Detroit, MI: Gale Research, 1975. 599p.

A classified bibliography of completed dissertations, master's theses, and announcements of those in progress. The first two sections are divided into universal and national. National listings are arranged by country, listing all general bibliographies with broad national inclusions. Subject lists arranged by discipline comprise the rest of the book, including lists of both completed dissertations and dissertations in progress or preparation. Restricted to separately published lists only. Consult the *Bibliographic Index* (New York: H. W. Wilson, 1937-) for concealed lists of dissertations in progress.

323. Index to Theses Accepted for Higher Degrees in the Universities of Great Britain and Ireland. London: ASLIB, 1950/51- . annual.

Dissertations and theses produced by science departments of universities in the United Kingdom of Great Britain and the Republic of Ireland are well represented in this significant annual series. Arrangement is by degree-awarding school, then by discipline, and by author. An author index is provided.

324. Masters Abstracts. Ann Arbor, MI: University Microfilms International, 1962- . semiannual.

Restricted to selected universities, this reference contains published abstracts of theses on microfilm. Cumulative author and subject index is provided. Useful in the bibliographic handling of master's theses.

325. Masters Theses in the Pure and Applied Sciences Accepted by Colleges and Universities of the United States and Canada. New York: Plenum, 1974- . annual.

Master's theses from nearly 250 U.S. and Canadian universities are covered and are listed alphabetically by author within study disciplines. Mathematics and the life sciences are excluded.

MEETINGS

326. Forthcoming International Scientific and Technical Conferences. London: ASLIB, 1971- . annual with quarterly supplements.

Conferences are listed in chronological order with date, title, location, and address. Includes subject, location, and sponsoring organization indexes.

327. **International Congress Calendar.** Brussels: Union of International Associations, *AS7*
1961- . annual. *.I57*
  Consists of a listing of projected meetings of international congresses over a period of *Main*
about five years prepared by the Congress Department of the Union of International
Associations from primary sources of information. A geographical and chronological list
are provided with an international organizations index and an analytical index. Monthly
supplements appear in the magazine *Transnational Associations* (1977-).

328. **MInd: The Meetings Index.** 1984- . bimonthly. Science/Engineering/Medicine/ *Q158.5*
Technology (SEMT) Series. *.M635*
  Accessed by keyword, location, date, and sponsoring organization, this classifies and *Sci*
indexes forthcoming meetings to be held on a worldwide basis.

329. **Scientific Meetings.** New York: Special Libraries Association, 1957- . *Q101 S63*
  Arranged alphabetically by association, university, or society, this is a listing of scien- *Sci*
tific, technical, medical, health, engineering, and management organizations and univer- *Ref*
sities and colleges that sponsor future national, international, and regional meetings, symposia, colloquia, and institutes. A chronological record of all meetings listed is provided,
along with a subject index. Publisher and frequency varies.

330. **World Meetings: United States and Canada.** Newton Centre, MA: Technical *Q11.T2*
Meetings Information Service, 1963- . quarterly. *Sci Ref*

331. **World Meetings: Outside USA and Canada.** Newton Centre, MA: Technical Meet- *Q101*
ings Information Service, 1968- . quarterly. *.W65*
  Both series provide sponsor, source of general information, technical sections or brief *Sci*
meeting description, number of papers to be presented, languages and translation facilities, *Ref*
projected attendance, availability of abstracts or papers, and information on exhibits for
future medical, scientific, and technical meetings. Covers the two-year period following the
publication date.

TRANSLATIONS

332. **Consolidated Index of Translations into English.** Compiled by the National Trans- *Q158.5*
lations Center, the John Crerar Library. New York: Special Libraries Association, 1969. *C67*
948p. *1969*
  A compilation of information on the availability of translations which have appeared *Sci*
in a number of different lists issued by different agencies. Restricted to translations in *Ref*
English of serially published originals. Divided into two sections: the serial citation index
and the patent citation index. Translation bibliographies, selective translation journals,
and collections of translations are included.

333. **Consolidated Index of Translations into English—II.** Chicago, IL: National *Q158.5*
Translations Center, 1986. 3v. *C672*
  Supplement to *Consolidated Index of Translations into English* (see entry 332). *1986*
Sci Ref

334. **Guide to Scientific and Technical Journals in Translation.** 2nd ed. Himmelsbach,
Carl J., and Grace E. Brociner, comps. New York: Special Libraries Association, 1972.
  Lists some 278 "Cover-to-Cover Translation Journals" and 53 "Selections, Collec-
tions, and Other 'Translation Journals'," predominantly from the Soviet Union, which

have been transliterated and arranged alphabetically. Cross-references from translated titles to original titles are given in part 3. The last three sections provide "Some Frequently Encountered Russian Abbreviations of Soviet Journals and Their Full Titles," and the "Russian Alphabet and Transliteration." The compilers have made every effort to identify each journal precisely, indicating availability, merges, name changes or publication cessation, and order information.

335. **Index Translationum.** New York: UNIPUB, 1948- . annual.
Covering translated works published in over 60 countries, the information in this reference aid is arranged by country and includes author, original and translated title, subject, translator, and place of publication. Classified by the Universal Decimal Code.

336. **Transdex. An Index to Translations Issued by the US Joint Publications Research Service.** Wooster, OH: Bell & Howell, 1970- . monthly.
Contains a significant number of translations, depending on specific region, issued by the Joint Publications Research Service.

337. **Translation and Translators: An International Directory and Guide.** 2nd ed. Kaiser, Frances E. New York: Special Libraries Association, 1984. 214p.
The register of translators and interpreters is arranged in two categories: literary and industrial, and scientific and technical. An index by language is provided for easy access to the right person. There is also a list of translation associations and centers, and training programs and guidelines for translators. A good reference source for any scientific library that has to handle much foreign materials.

338. **Translations Register-Index.** New York: National Translations Center, 1967- . twice monthly.
A direct successor to *Technical Translations* (Washington, DC: U.S. Department of Commerce, Office of Technical Services, 1959-1967), which in turn superseded *Translation Monthly* (Chicago, IL: Special Libraries Association, 1955-1958), this index lists all new translations added to the National Translations Center, and provides references to translations available from the National Technical Information Service (formerly the Clearinghouse for Federal Scientific and Technical Information) and commercial sources.

COPYRIGHTS AND PATENTS

339. **Central Patents Index—CPI.** London: Derwent Publications Ltd., 1970- . weekly.
One of the most significant of this publisher's computer-based current awareness services, this patent alerting system is issued in several forms. The database comprises basic patent specifications from 24 countries with about 12,000 added weekly. Four printed sections are published, each containing six index approaches. Sections are titled: "General," "Electrical," "Mechanical," and "Chemical." The *General Patents Index* consists of three printed abstracts journals (P—*General*; Q—*Mechanical*; R—*Electrical*) and is also issued as 19 sets of cards and as 100 feet of 16mm microfilm in nine- to ten-week intervals. *Central Patent Index* contains two alerting bulletins each with its own patent number index, CPI class index, patentee index, and basic number or patent concordance index. The bulletins are arranged by country and by systematic classification.

340. **Complete Guide to the New Copyright Law.** New York Law School Law Review. New York: The School, 1977. 448p.

A guide for librarians and educators covering aspects of the proposed legislation that did not change and commentaries on the law as passed. Topics covered include: duration of copyright, notice, deposit, and registration; analysis of infringement sections; fair use; CATV copyright; sound recordings; termination of transfers and licensing; and international copyright.

341.　**Copyright Handbook.** 2nd ed. Johnston, Donald F. New York: Bowker, 1983. 381p.

This handbook is the publisher's book-length version of how the law should be interpreted. It covers user rights; copyrightable material; copyright notice; deposit copies; registration; ownership, transfer, and licenses; exclusive rights; infringement remedies; duration; international considerations; fair use; library reproduction; limits on exclusive performance and display rights; and compulsory licenses. The appendices include the full text of both the 1909 and the 1976 laws, the CONTU guidelines, and examples of many of the copyright forms.

342.　**Foreign Patents: A Guide to Official Patent Literature.** Kase, Francis J. Dobbs Ferry, NY: Oceana, 1973. 358p.

This book is very specific with respect to foreign patents and is particularly directed to patent attorneys and agents who must consult patent literature. The author notes "it is intended as an introduction to the foreign official patent literature, such as printed patent specifications and patent journals. It is essentially a guide to the meaning of the dates and numbers on patent specifications and abstracts, and should assist the searcher in ascertaining the state of prior knowledge." Arranged alphabetically by country, entries contain: (1) the name and address of the patent office or body that handles industrial rights grants; (2) an English translation of any existing printed specifications; (3) a description of the official patent journals and other relevant publications excluding monographs, and collections of patent laws and regulations; and (4) the patent duration. Also of value for the explanation of British patents is F. Newby's *How to Find Out about Patents* (London: Pergamon, 1967).

343.　**Index to Classification.** U.S. Patent Office. Washington, DC: U.S. Government Printing Office, 1956- . irregular.

An index to classification by subject descriptor, this is an important source for libraries and information centers handling technology and technology transfer.

344.　**Index to Patents Issued from the United States Patent and Trademark Office.** U.S. Patent Office. Washington, DC: U.S. Government Printing Office, 1920- . annual.

345.　**Official Gazette of the United States Patent and Trademark Office.** Patents. Washington, DC: U.S. Government Printing Office, 1872- . weekly.

Divided into two parts, this index contains an alphabetical list of persons or companies with new or reissued patents and an index of inventions arranged by Patent Office classification. Patents are divided into general and mechanical, chemical, electrical, and design groups. The first three groups above are numbered consecutively. A separate numbering system is used for design patents. Also included is a geographic index of inventors.

346.　**Index to the U.S. Patent Classification.** U.S. Patent and Trademark Office. Washington, DC: U.S. Patent and Trademark Office, 1987. 236p.

Consists of an alphabetical list of subject headings referring to specific classes and subclasses of the patent classification system.

347. **Index of Trademarks Issued from the United States Patent Office.** U.S. Patent Office. Washington, DC: U.S. Government Printing Office, 1927- . annual.
Contains information on trademarks registered with the Patent Office.

348. **Inventor's Patent Handbook.** rev. ed. Jones, Stacy V. New York: Dial Press, 1969. 229p.
A handbook to patents and procedures for application. Additional information may be found in Terrence W. Fenner's *Inventor's Handbook* (New York: Chemical Publishing Co., 1969).

349. **Manual of Classification.** U.S. Patent and Trademark Office. Washington, DC: Patent and Trademark Office, 1979- . A looseleaf, continually revised service.
Numbers and descriptive titles of all the classes and subclasses are provided. Having identified a field of interest by a precise class and subclass number, one can monitor new developments in the weekly issues of the *Official Gazette* (see entry 345).

350. **Manual of Patent Examining Procedures.** U.S. Patent Office. Washington, DC: U.S. Government Printing Office, 1949- . irregular.
An important source for technologically oriented libraries, this manual covers material pertaining to all practices and procedures used by examiners at the Patent Office.

GOVERNMENT DOCUMENTS AND TECHNICAL REPORTS

351. **Correlation Index: Document Series and PB Reports.** Special Libraries Council of Philadelphia and Vicinity. New York: Special Libraries Association, 1953. 271p.
A listing in alphanumeric arrangement of technical report numbers and the corresponding PB (Publication Board) accession number. Location of report abstracts in the early issues of the *U.S. Government Research and Development Reports*, then known as the *Bibliography of Technical Reports*, is accomplished through use of the PB number.

352. **Government Publications: A Guide to Bibliographic Tools.** 4th ed. Palic, Vladimir M. Washington, DC: Library of Congress, 1975.
Intended as a practical guide for the researcher, student, and reference librarian, this book outlines "bibliographic aids in the field of official publications issued by the United States, foreign countries, and international governmental organizations." Included in the guide are catalogs, indexes, bibliographies, checklists and other bibliographic aids that did not originate from government agencies. Full bibliographic information, LC classification numbers, and annotations are provided in each entry. The guide is divided into three parts: part 1, "United States of America: Federal, State, and Local"; part 2, "International Governmental Organizations: General, UN, League of Nations, Other"; and part 3, "Foreign Countries: General, Western Hemisphere, Europe, Africa, Near East, and Asia."

353. **Government Reference Books: A Biennial Guide to U.S. Government Publications.** Littleton, CO: Libraries Unlimited, 1970- . biennial.

An indispensable tool for identifying and assessing key information resources from the printed matter issued yearly by U.S. government agencies. The ninth biennial volume lists and describes hundreds of reference documents published during 1984 and 1985. Arranged in four main sections—"General Reference," "Social Science," "Science and Technology," and "Humanities"—the guide includes atlases, bibliographies, catalogs, compendiums, dictionaries, directories, guides, handbooks, indexes, and other reference aids issued by the government. Complete bibliographic descriptions are given including LC card numbers, S/Ns, ISBNs, ISSNs, and SuDocs classification numbers. Indexed by personal author, title, subject, and corporate author.

354. **Government Reports Announcement and Index.** Vol. 75- , no. 7- . Washington, DC: National Technical Information Services, April 4, 1975- . biweekly.

Previously published under the titles *U.S. Government Research and Development Reports* and *Government Reports Announcement*, this biweekly listing contains available reports from NTIS and is arranged in 22 subject fields. Fields covered include aeronautics; agriculture; astronomy and astrophysics; atmospheric sciences; behavioral and social sciences; biological and medical sciences; chemistry; earth sciences and oceanography; electronics and electrical engineering; energy conversion; materials; mathematical sciences; mechanical, industrial, civil, and marine engineering; methods and equipment; military sciences; missile technology; navigation, communications, detection, and counter-measures; nuclear science and technology; ordnance; physics; propulsion and fuels; and space technology.

355. **Government Wide Index to Federal Research and Development Reports.** Washington, DC: Clearinghouse for Federal Scientific and Technical Information, 1965-1971. 71v.

A subject, personal author, corporate author, report number, and accession number index to the *U.S. Government Research and Development Reports* (1946-71), *Technical Abstract Bulletin* (1958-62), *Scientific and Technical Aerospace Reports* (1963-), and *Nuclear Science Abstracts* (1948-76). Produced by a computer, entries contained the title of the report with the accession number, hardcopy and microfiche prices, and one or more of the above abstract indexes with the citation to volume and issue. The index is continued in *Government Reports Announcement and Index* (see entry 354).

356. **Introduction to United States Public Documents.** 3rd ed. Morehead, Joe. Littleton, CO: Libraries Unlimited, 1983. 309p.

Designed for students and librarians, Morehead's text is concerned with federal publications—the relationship between their production and distribution, and their control, access, and management in libraries and information centers. The first four chapters discuss the Government Printing Office, the Superintendent of Documents, the depository library system, and administration of documents collections. The remaining seven chapters cover publications of the federal hierarchy, beginning with general guides. A Name/Subject Index and Title/Series Index provide quick access to information, and the thorough, well-structured table of contents approaches the functions of an index.

357. **Monthly Catalog of United States Publications.** U.S. Superintendent of Documents. Washington, DC: Government Printing Office, 1895- . monthly.

Printed by the U.S. Government Printing Office and distributed by the Superintendent of Documents, this bibliography of government publications does not include classified documents, documents that are published directly by the issuing agency, or are contracted for by the U.S. government agencies. Monthly indexes are cumulated annually.

Important scientific documents are included from agencies such as the National Bureau of Standards, the National Oceanic and Atmospheric Administration, Geological Survey, the Bureau of Mines, and the National Research Council. A more recent source of subject retrieval is *Cumulative Subject Index to the Monthly Catalog of U.S. Government Publications, 1900-1971* (compiled by William W. Buchanan and Edna M. Kanely. Washington, DC: Carrollton Press, 1973-1975).

358. **Monthly Checklist of State Publications.** Washington, DC: Library of Congress, Processing Department, Exchange and Gifts Division, 1910- . monthly.
Lists only documents submitted by state issuing agencies to the Library of Congress.

359. **Report Series Codes Dictionary.** 3rd ed. Aronson, E. J., ed. Detroit, MI: Gale Research, 1986. 647p.
This guide to the alphanumeric codes used to identify technical reports includes 25,500 codes designating the various agencies of the Department of Defense, the Atomic Energy Commission, their contractors (including industrial, educational, and professional organization), agencies of the U.S. government, and similar agencies of foreign governments. The second edition has doubled the number of entries cited in the first and reflects the phenomenal increase in the report literature, which is now estimated to encompass as much as half a million publications a year. Useful data include a glossary, a bibliography of articles on technical codes, and sources of the codes included here. The text proper is divided into three color-coded sections: (1) "Reference Notes — 48 explanations of series designations or of the practice of assigners in expanding on a series designation"; (2) a list of report series codes, arranged by the first letter found in the code, with identification of the related agency; (3) corporate entries with related report series codes.

360. **State Government Reference Publications: An Annotated Bibliography.** 2nd ed. Parish, David W. Littleton, CO: Libraries Unlimited, 1981. 355p.
The author has selected and annotated 1,756 of the most important state reference publications from the 50 states and the U.S. territories.

361. **UNESCO List of Documents and Publications.** New York: UNESCO; distr., New York: UNIPUB, 1979- .
A compiled list of all publications, documents, and articles in periodicals issued by UNESCO during 1972-1976, 1977-1980, and 1981-1983. Broken down into five sections including a list of acronyms used, an annotated list, personal name index, conference index, and subject index.

362. **U.S. Government Manual.** Washington, DC: Office of the Federal Register, National Archives and Record Service; distr., Washington, DC: U.S. Government Printing Office, 1935- . annual.
Previously appearing as *U.S. Government Organization Manual*, this annual provides recent information on the functions and administrative structure of U.S. government agencies. The names of the principal officers in charge of each department are given along with an explanation of the authority and activities of the department. For the researcher this manual aids in identifying federal agencies responsible for the production of scientific reports. Organizational charts are included.

363. **U.S. Government Research and Development Reports.** Washington, DC: Clearinghouse for Federal Scientific and Technical Information, 1946-1971. frequency varies.

Appeared previously under the titles: *Bibliography of Scientific and Industrial Reports* (1946-49); *Bibliography of Technical Reports* (1946-49); and *U.S. Government Research Reports* (1954-64). It has since been superseded by *Government Reports Announcement and Index* (see entry 354). This source informs the public as to the availability of new reports of U.S. government sponsored research and development not appearing in *Nuclear Science Abstracts* (1948-76) and *STAR* (see entry 1808).

364. **U.S. Government Scientific and Technical Periodicals.** Yannerella, Philip A., and Rao Aluri, comps. Metuchen, NJ: Scarecrow Press, 1976. 263p.

Each entry in this directory of U.S. government scientific and technical periodicals includes SuDocs classification number, date of first issue, starting date of latest title and/or SuDocs classification number, latest frequency, issuing agency and its address, depository item number, subscription price, history, and several other informational items.

3   Astronomy

Astronomy has felt a tendency to move into several subfields, most marked by an "astro" prefix. In this, astronomy is clearly like other traditional areas of science. In the broad sense, astronomy is the science of matter in outer space. It deals with the composition, energy, relative position, mass, size, and chemical makeup of celestial bodies. Included in celestial bodies are asteroids, clusters, comets, galaxies, meteoroids, natural and sometimes artificial satellites, nebulae, planets, stars, space between bodies, and all other forms of cosmic matter.

Astronomy is one of the oldest sciences, evidenced by the interest and attention given the sky and celestial bodies by early man. Although serious scientific interest waxed and waned prior to the Copernican Revolution, the underlying fascination remained high.

The invention of the telescope was a watershed event in astronomy. Previously, all investigation relied on visual observation of bodies. Only certain bodies were visible or at a high enough order of magnitude to be seen. The telescope enhanced the ability to see beyond what was visible only to the naked eye. The introduction of such an instrument also allowed for an even finer measurement by refining the measurement of parallax and motions. Teamed with instruments such as spectrographs, even more detailed information was available.

The propensity of astronomy, like other sciences, to utilize methodologies and techniques from other areas was born early. An example is the use of photographic plates to study the physical makeup as well as the relative motion of stellar bodies. Much work was done at the beginning of this century with applications of physics to astronomy. This branch of astronomy is astrophysics.

A short jump, scientifically, from light radiation to radio waves opened up the field of radio astronomy. Basically, the radio telescope is a large radio receiver which can be tuned to specific frequencies. Primarily this branch of astronomy examines all or a portion of the electromagnetic radiation from a celestial body in the nonvisible wavelengths. Work utilizing radio telescopes led directly to underlying evidence for the Big Bang theory of the birth of the universe.

Much astronomical work today is even more mathematical and theoretical than previously. The ability of the astronomer to build apparatus to push back the boundaries of knowledge has not kept pace with the ability of the theoretician to conceptualize. Astronomy literature has begun to be more theoretical and less experimental. As long as funding for larger and more complicated apparatus continues to be in short supply, the literature will reflect the astronomer's attempt to model what cannot yet be observed.

Some care must be taken in use of this section. Astronomy has undergone a set of discipline-shaking events and discoveries. Of particular note is the vast amount of data gathered as a result of probes and new observations. These new sets of data are being incorporated into the literature as rapidly as possible. Some sources are listed here which contain information that is not totally current. The new information will take some time to work its way into the literature, and specifically the secondary literature. Those who use this section are cautioned to go beyond the sources listed here to the primary literature for specific, factual information.

GUIDES TO THE LITERATURE

365. **Astronomy and Astronautics: An Enthusiast's Guide to Books and Periodicals.** Lusis, Andy. London: Mansell, 1986. 360p.

QB43.2
.L87
1986
Sci
Ref

A handy collection development tool that is extremely current and covers everything from the history of astronomy to the future. Contains nearly 1,000 entries including radical hypotheses and lesser-known periodicals. An extensive index is provided.

366. **Astronomy and Astrophysics: A Bibliographical Guide.** Kemp, D. London: MacDonald Technical & Scientific, 1970. 584p.

Z5151
.K45
Sci
Ref

This guide lists and evaluates the general reference media in astronomy. A specialized subject list follows the general section. The arrangement of the subject list is mainly chronological and includes the number of references and the time period covered by the bibliography. The list is evaluative, which is the main reason the work is included here. The work does cite in excess of 3,500 items but should not be considered comprehensive in any one area.

367. **History of Modern Astronomy and Astrophysics.** DeVorkin, David H. New York: Garland, 1982. 434p.

Z5154
.H57
D48
Sci
Ref

A selected annotated bibliography beginning with the invention and application of the telescope to astronomy. Emphasis on mid-nineteenth to mid-twentieth centuries. Includes both popular and scholarly works but with a preference for works in English.

ABSTRACTS, INDEXES, AND BIBLIOGRAPHIES

368. **Aeronautics, Aerospace and Astronomy.** Washington, DC: NTIS, 1980- . quarterly.

A database covering aeronautics, aerospace, and astronomy with a focus on the military aspects. This is available on CD-ROM.

369. **Astronomy and Astrophysics Abstracts.** Berlin: Springer, 1969- . semiannual.

QB1
.A796
Sci

This superseded *Astronomischer Jahresbericht* (Berlin: G. Reimer, 1899-1968). Coverage is international with the emphasis in English. Author's abstracts are used whenever possible. Various subdivisions and categories group like items together. Some entries, usually those with limited relevance to astronomy, have no abstracts. Author and subject indexes are included.

370. **Bibliographie generale de l'astronomie.** rev. ed. Houzeau, J., and A. Lancaster. West Orange, NJ: Saifer, 1964. 3v.

Z5151
.H84
1964

Items are arranged according to an internal system, featuring a scholarly introduction and manuscript locations. An author index is included.

Z5151
.S38
1982
Sci
Ref

371. **Bibliography of Astronomy 1970-1979.** Seal, Robert A., and Sarah S. Martin. Littleton, CO: Libraries Unlimited, 1982. 407p.

Intended primarily to fill the gap between Kemp's work and the present, this is an introduction of the field and a selection aid. The present work is more comprehensive, with extensive author, title and subject indexes. A superb work.

Ø16
.523016
B582
Sci

372. **Bibliography of Natural Radio Emissions from Astronomical Sources.** Ithaca, NY: Cornell University Press, 1961- . annual.

An annual bibliography of radio astronomy containing approximately 800 items in each volume. Important for its compilation of emissions. Used by researchers to differentiate between new and previously cataloged emissions.

Z6033
.M5
B73
Sci
Ref

373. **Bibliography on Meteorites.** Brown, Harrison Scott. Chicago, IL: University of Chicago, 1953. 686p.

Although an older imprint, this work arranges the world's literature on meteorites and related subjects from 1491 to 1950 in chronological order. Almost 9,000 items are listed making this the most complete historical source for information on meteorites. Of particular note is the care taken with bibliographic accuracy—most of the citations were checked with the original sources. An author index is included.

QB843
.B55
D36
.1985
Sci

374. **Black Holes: An Annotated Bibliography, 1975-1983.** Danko, Steven. Metuchen, NJ: Scarecrow, 1985. 282p.

Arranged by source document making it difficult to search by subject. Author and title index are provided. This is an important contribution to a current area which, unfortunately, is made difficult to use by its format.

ENCYCLOPEDIAS

375. **All about Telescopes.** 6th ed. Brown, Sam. Barrington, NJ: Edmund Scientific, 1985. 192p.

This is a nontechnical book intended for those wishing to build telescopes or desiring further information on their construction in general. Both theory and practice of telescopes and their use are covered. Additional information is given on sky observation, photography, and optics.

QB45
.M728
1990
Sci

376. **Amateur Astronomy.** Moore, Patrick. New York: Norton, 1968. 328p.

Formerly *Amateur Astronomer* (London: Butterworths, 1971), this work combines a readable text with charts and tables. It is intended for the amateur, as the title indicates. The tables and charts included are presented clearly and can be used with a minimum of prior knowledge.

QB43.2
C35
1977
Sci
Ref

377. **Cambridge Encyclopedia of Astronomy.** Mitton, Simon, ed. New York: Crown, 1977. 481p.

A standard tool containing excellent illustrations. Covers a historical treatment of the study of the universe to 1977. The editor made a conscious decision to place the work at the upper edge of utility for amateurs but still not technical enough to be a professional source. The articles are anonymous and varied in both approach and style. Overall, they present a clear discussion, focused on synthesis of particular problems. Still recommended because it is not a "fact-oriented" work. Its focus on synthesis helps it retain a place here.

378. **Concise Encyclopedia of Astronomy.** 2nd ed. Weigart, Alfred, and Helmut Zimmerman. London: Hilser, 1976. 532p.

Translated from the German. This is a valuable one-volume reference for astronomers. The second edition is considerably revised and well illustrated.

QB14
.W413
1968
Sci

379. **Encyclopedia of Astronomy: A Comprehensive Survey of Our Solar System, Galaxy and Beyond.** Ronan, Colin, ed. New York: Hamlyn, 1979. 240p.

This is a useful text that covers the field of astronomy and space science. Describes in detail various instruments, launch vehicles, and satellites. Contains biographical sketches of astronomers from the Greeks to the present. Includes diagrams and photographs. Indexed and cross-referenced.

380. **Extraterrestrial Encyclopedia.** Angelo, Joseph A. New York: Facts on File, 1986. 256p.

Deals with earthlings moving to areas beyond Earth, *not* aliens. Good cross-referencing with a considerable number of photographs. A short bibliography is provided at the end of the work.

QB54
.A523
1985
Sci
Ref

381. **Illustrated Encyclopedia of Astronomy and Space.** rev. ed. Ridpath, Ian. New York: Thomas Y. Crowell, 1979. 240p.

This is a good, general purpose encyclopedia suitable for the total novice to the serious amateur. The slant of the work is clearly in the direction of the United States and the U.S.S.R. There is an index, but the work suffers from the lack of a bibliography. The overall intent of the work is to be a popular treatment of the field as opposed to a professional source.

QB14
.I44
1976
Sci

382. **Illustrated Encyclopedia of Space Technology: A Comprehensive History of Space Exploration.** 4th ed. Gatland, Kenneth, et al. New York: Harmony, 1985. 301p.

A one-volume encyclopedia covering the past, present, and future of the space age. Included are photographs, drawings, diagrams, and maps, along with a glossary, index, and chronology from 360 B.C. through 1980.

TL788
.I44
1981
Sci Ref

383. **Illustrated Encyclopedia of the Universe.** Lewis, Richard S. New York: Harmony, 1983. 320p.

An outstanding tool with specific emphasis on recent space exploration with the goal of explaining and assisting readers to understand the cosmos. Extensive color pictures (some in double spreads), drawings, brief bibliographies for each of the 20 chapters, and a specific subject index is included. This is a reference work with universal appeal.

384. **Larousse Guide to Astronomy.** Baker, David. New York: Larousse, 1978. 288p.

The Larousse attention to detail and excellence is evident. The work tends to have a somewhat British slant but is excellent overall.

385. **McGraw-Hill Encyclopedia of Astronomy.** Parker, Sybil P., ed. New York: McGraw-Hill, 1983. 450p.

A good tool with over 200 articles on theoretical, observational, and experimental aspects of astronomy. The work has a considerable number of photographs and figures, and contains entries covering the general fields of astronomy. Some biographical sketches and illustrations are found. The definitions are clear and concise.

QB501
K75
Sci

386. **Solar System.** Kuiper, G. P., and B. M. Middlehurst. Chicago, IL: University of Chicago, 1953-1963. 4v.

This is a standard reference work in the field. It contains bibliographic references for chapters and an analytic index of subjects and definitions in each volume. It is a required item for any research collection.

TL789
.S16
Sci Ref

387. **The UFO Encyclopedia.** Sachs, Margaret. New York: Putnam, 1980. 408p.

Consists of entries alphabetically arranged relating to UFO phenomena. Provides information on people, locations of sightings, interest groups, technical terms, and publications. Extensively cross-referenced.

QB1
.Y4
Sci
Ref

388. **Yearbook of Astronomy.** Moore, Patrick, ed. New York: Wiley, 1962- . annual.

Up-to-date regarding constellations; planets; phases of the moon; longitudes of the sun, moon, and planets; and some events to come. An article section deals with current topics. No index is provided.

DICTIONARIES

QB14
.K55
1961a
Sci
Ref

389. **Astronomical Dictionary in Six Languages.** Kleczek, Josip. New York: Academic, 1961. 972p.

This is a multilingual dictionary included here because of the one-stop translation ability offered by the work. Its chief benefit is the inclusion of six languages. The key term is always English with equivalent terms given in Russian, German, French, Italian, and Czech. The non-English terms are related back to the English by means of an accession number.

390. **Dictionary of Astronomy: Terms and Concepts of Space and the Universe.** Nicholson, Iain. New York: Barnes & Noble, 1980. 249p.

A comprehensive, reliable source of information on all aspects of astronomy including satellites, meteors, asteroids, and "intelligent life in the universe."

QB14
.T43
Sci

391. **Dictionary of Astronomy, Space, and Atmospheric Phenomena.** Tver, David F., Lloyd Motz, and William K. Hartmann. New York: Van Nostrand Reinhold, 1979. 281p.

Contains broad coverage of current advances in meteorology, space exploration, and astronomy as well as physics and mathematics. Many entries are accompanied by tables of data and line drawings.

QB500
.P52
1986
Sci Ref

392. **Dictionary of Space.** Plant, Malcolm. Harlow, England: Longman, 1986. 270p.

This is a concise dictionary of space and space technology that includes persons, organizations, and abbreviations. Good cross-referencing.

QB14
.H66
1980
Sci
Ref

393. **Glossary of Astronomy and Astrophysics.** 2nd ed. Hopkins, Jeanne. Chicago, IL: University of Chicago, 1980. 196p.

A revised and enlarged edition of the 1976 work of the same name, this is a comprehensive dictionary of astronomical and astrophysical terms. The major drawback to the work is its lack of illustrations, tables, or photographs. Definitions range from the simplistic to those intelligible only to experts. Recommended due to the breadth of its definitions.

QB14
.M57
Sci

394. **Key Definitions in Astronomy.** Mitton, Jacqueline. Totowa, NJ: Littlefield Adams, 1982. 168p.

Provides the most useful and important terms in the field of astronomy and covers those likely to be found in most popular journals, newspapers, and in news reports. It is limited in scope, but is a good source for the educated layperson.

395. **Longman Illustrated Dictionary of Astronomy & Astronautics: The Terminology of Space.** Ridpath, Ian. Chicago, IL: Longman Trade, 1987. 224p.

QB14
.R54
1987
Sci
Ref

This general dictionary will find greatest use in the hands of novices. The definitions are grouped according to topic, making the index a critical piece of the work. The groupings can be confusing and an impediment to the use of the dictionary at times. The resourceful or persistent user will find the illustrations good and the definitions up-to-date. Recommended for all general collections.

HANDBOOKS AND FIELD GUIDES

396. **Air Almanac.** Washington, DC: U.S. Government Printing Office, 1933- . 3 times/yr.

Gov Doc
D 213.7
: 992

Issued jointly by Her Majesty's Nautical Almanac Office, this compendium contains data necessary for air navigation. It contains a wealth of data, a good proportion of which relates to celestial nighttime navigation. This particular focus makes the work valuable for astronomy.

397. **Amateur Astronomer's Handbook.** 3rd ed. Muirden, James. New York: Harper & Row, 1983. 472p.

QB64
.m85
1983
Sci

Useful for the amateur in setting up a systematic study of the sky. Tables are given listing recurring phenomenon, and reading lists and a glossary are helpful. Arranged by title and scope, this work is intended for amateurs.

398. **Amateur Astronomer's Handbook.** 4th ed. Sidgwick, John Benson. Hillside, NJ: Enslow, 1982. 568p.

QB44
.S558
1971
Sci

Contains advanced technical information on astronomy both theoretical and practical. An extensive bibliography is a very useful component of the book. A companion work, *Observational Astronomy for Amateurs* (London: Faber & Faber, 1971), is geared to more practical astronomy. An advanced tool for amateurs.

399. **Apparent Places of Fundamental Stars.** Heidelberg, West Germany: Astronomisches Rechen-Institut, 1940- . annual.

QB9
.J5
Sci

Lists the mean and apparent location for over 1,500 stars, giving right ascension and declination, mean place, magnitude, and spectral class. Useful for both the amateur and the professional astronomer. This is a prime tool for a research collection.

400. **Astronomical Almanac.** Washington, DC: U.S. Government Printing Office, 1981- . annual.

QB8
U6
A77
Sci
Ref

Supersedes *American Ephemeris and Nautical Almanac* (Washington, DC: U.S. Government Printing Office, 1852-1980). Data for astronomy, space sciences, geodesy, surveying, navigation, and other applications are provided, along with tables containing information on virtually any astronomy question. Also included is a list of the computed positions celestial bodies will occupy on certain dates. The almanac covers phenomenon such as eclipses. This is a professional tool for professional and advanced amateur astronomers.

QB64
.T7
1983
Sci

401.   Astronomy and Telescopes: A Beginner's Handbook. Traister, Robert J., and Susan E. Harris. Blue Ridge Summit, PA: TAB Books, 1983. 200p.

The emphasis is on theory, construction, and use of telescopes and auxiliary equipment for the new amateur astronomer. A good introduction is presented as well as some valuable information of the buyer, users, or builder of telescopes.

QB64
.R58
1979
Sci Ref

402.   Astronomy Data Book. 2nd ed. Robinson, J. Hedley, and James Muirden. New York: Halsted, 1979. 272p.

A compilation of tables and data brought together in one convenient place. This second edition updates tables and observed data from the 1972 edition. The glossary is expanded, but few other changes were made in this edition. It remains a good handbook of greatest utility to an amateur observer.

403.   Astronomy Handbook. Muirden, James. New York: Prentice-Hall, 1987. 189p.

Most topics in astronomy are covered in this well-illustrated handbook. Presuming no prior knowledge of astronomy, this is a beginning astronomer's handbook.

QB64
.B85
1978
Sci
Ref

404.   Burnham's Celestial Handbook: An Observer's Guide to the Universe beyond the Solar System. rev. and enl. ed. Burnham, Robert, Jr. New York: Dover, 1978. 3v.

Originally a looseleaf format, this source has now become the most comprehensive guide to celestial objects in English. It is arranged alphabetically by constellation and contains both illustrative and descriptive information. Mythology and origin of cosmological names are covered. This work is indispensable for a variety of reasons.

QB44
.O6
1954
Sci

405.   Field Book of the Skies. rev. ed. Olcott, William Tyler. Hebron, CT: Susan P. Howell Enterprises, 1982. 176p.

This is one of the best sources for the experienced amateur. It is arranged in an outline format with information on constellations and individual stars. Mythological origins for names of constellations are given. Overall, it is an excellent source for all but the professional.

QB64
.m4
Sci

406.   Field Guide to the Stars and Planets, Including the Moon, Satellites, Comets, and Other Features of the Universe. 2nd ed. Menzel, Donald Howard, and Jay Pasachoff. Boston: Houghton Mifflin, 1983. 473p.

This is a completely revised and enlarged edition of the 1964 work. It is a popular guide compared favorably with Olcott (see entry 405). Monthly sky maps and atlas charts have replaced the maps and charts of the earlier edition. Extensive tables and a good index make this an excellent tool.

QB477
.P3
Sci

407.   Handbook of Radio Sources. Pacholczyk, A. G., ed. Tucson, AZ: Pachart Publishing, 1978- . v. 1- .

Contains a considerable amount of data on quasars and galaxies. A professional handbook for practicing astronomers.

QB526
.F6
C48
Sci

408.   Handbook of Solar Flare Monitoring and Propagation Forecasting. Cherman, Carl M. Blue Ridge Summit, PA: TAB Books, 1978. 194p.

This handbook for the beginning astronomer contains information on flare monitoring and flare effects. Discusses theories as to causes of flares and means to predict future ones.

409. **Handbook of Space Astronomy and Astrophysics.** Zombeck, M. V. New York: Cambridge University Press, 1982. 326p.

QB 136
Z65
1990
Sci
Ref

A compilation of often inaccessible information in tables, graphs, and formulas for use across a broad range of the physical sciences. Information is included on all aspects of astronomy and astrophysics, the Earth's atmosphere and environment, relativity and atomic physics.

410. **Handbook of the Constellations.** Vehrenberg, Hans, and Dieter Blank. Dusseldorf, West Germany: Treugesell-Verlag, 1984. 197p.

QB64
.V4
1977
Sci

This work provides indexing to well-known constellations. For each constellation a list of bright stars, double stars, variable stars, clusters, and nebulae are given. An easy to read map of each constellation is provided, making this an excellent choice for amateurs.

411. **Master List of Nonstellar Optical Astronomical Objects.** Dixon, Robert S., and George Sonneborn, comps. Columbus, OH: Ohio State University Press, 1980. 835p.

QB65
.D56
Sci
Ref

A listing of nonstellar objects based on 270 catalogs. Refers astronomers to the original catalogs and decreases chances of pseudodiscovery. A standard reference for professional astronomers.

412. **Mysterious Universe: A Handbook of Astronomical Anomalies.** Corliss, William R. Glen Arm, MD: Sourcebook Project, 1979. 710p.

QB52
.M97
Sci

A handbook of astronomical illustrations intended primarily for the layperson without prior knowledge of astronomy.

413. **Observer's Handbook.** 74th ed. Bishop, Roy L., ed. Cambridge, MA: Sky Publishing, 1981.

QB9
.R7
Sci Ref

An in-depth handbook for use as an aid for amateur astronomers. A one-stop source for astronomy, including predictions for Canada and the United States.

414. **Pictorial Guide to the Planets.** 3rd ed. Jackson, Joseph H., and John H. Baumert. New York: Harper & Row, 1981. 246p.

523
J13
Sci

A good overall treatment of the solar system. All planets are analyzed in detail with special emphasis on the earth and moon. The absence of a bibliography is a flaw; however, the work still gives the reader a clear compilation of information on the planets. This edition concentrates on space hardware to some extent. A good discussion of the U.S. space program to 1980 is included.

415. **Planet Jupiter: The Observer's Handbook.** 2nd ed. rev. Moore, Patrick. London: Faber & Faber, 1981. 240p.

QB661
.P4
1981b
Sci

Gives a complete description of Jupiter as observed from Earth with visual observations of color, position, rotation, and surface detail. Contains diagrams, tables, photographs, a glossary, and an index. The user should be aware that the newest information gleaned from both observation and satellite probe is not included.

416. **Standard Handbook for Telescope Making.** rev. ed. Howard, N. E. New York: Harper & Row, 1984. 356p.

QB88
H76
1984
Sci

This is a description of how to build a telescope, written in a clear and concise format. It is a revised edition of the 1959 edition which used an 8-inch f/7 Newtonian reflector as an example. Intended for the amateur experimentalist or the curious amateur wishing to know both the theory and the practice of telescopes.

QB63
H68
Sci
Ref

417. **Telescope Handbook and Star Atlas.** rev. ed. Howard, N. E. New York: Thomas Y. Crowell, 1975. 226p.

This is a companion to *Standard Handbook for Telescope Making* (see entry 416). There are 14 charts specifically compiled for use at the telescope. There are some flaws in the work but they tend to be in the nature of proofreading errors. Overall, this is an excellent introduction for use by novice astronomers. Included here because of its ease of use for the beginning astronomer, as opposed to its currency.

QB63
.R53
1985
Sci Ref

418. **Universe Guide to Stars and Planets.** Ridpath, Ian. New York: Universe, 1985. 384p.

An amateur star watcher's guide. Includes star maps for 88 major constellations. Northern and Southern latitude and star maps for each month of the year are provided.

QB64
.W36
1986
Sci

419. **Webb Society Deep-Sky Observer's Handbook.** Jones, Kenneth Glyn, ed. Short Hills, NJ: Enslow, 1975- . irregular.

Each volume covers a class of objects. It includes a review article, background information, positions, magnitudes, charts, and various other information. This is an excellent reference work. Volume titles are: volume 1: *Double Stars*, volume 2: *Planetary and Gaseous Nebulae*, volume 3: *Open and Globular Clusters*, volume 4: *Galaxies*, and volume 5: *Clusters of Galaxies*. Volume 1 was revised in 1985.

QB65
.W48
1985
Sci

420. **Whitney's Star Finder: A Field Guide to the Heavens.** 4th ed. Whitney, Charles. New York: Knopf, 1985. 111p.

This work does not pretend to be an astronomical primer. It is what its title says—a star finder. It is a good, practical guide which introduces theory by means of explanation of practical constructs.

ATLASES AND STAR CATALOGS

QB68
H43
Sci

421. **Astronomical Photographic Atlas.** Heck, A., and J. Manfroid. Liége, Belgium: Desoer, 1977. 222p.

An album of astronomical photographs, including the moon, sun, planets, comets, star fields, galaxies, and clusters of galaxies.

QB65
.V413
1983
Sci
Ref

422. **Atlas of Deep-Sky Splendors.** 4th ed. Vehrenberg, Hans. Dusseldorf, West Germany: Trueldorf-Verlag, 1983. 240p.

Contains photographic charts and a description of all Messier objects and more than 300 celestial wonders. Sections on the Messier catalog, Lacaille's catalog, and Schmidt's contributions to astronomical photography are included. An index of objects is given.

QB641
.C75
Sci
Oversize

423. **Atlas of Mercury.** Cross, Charles A., and Patrick Moore. New York: Crown, 1977. 48p.

Comprehensive treatment of the planet Mercury. Based on the Mariner 10 pioneer voyage. The atlas portrays surface features in map form.

QB883
.Y35
Sci

424. **Atlas of Representative Stellar Spectra.** Yamashita, Yasumasa, K. Nariai, and Yuji Norimoto. New York: Wiley, 1978. 129p.

This work consists of 45 plates containing spectra of 197 MK standard stars. The work uses citations from published literature to identify spectral features. Energy level diagrams are included and make this source particularly useful.

425. **Atlas of the Planets.** Doherty, Paul. New York: McGraw-Hill, 1980. 143p.

This guide to the planets and solar system for amateur astronomers provides detailed descriptions of planetary features, observing hints, nomenclature, and other useful information.

Map
QB605
.D62
1980

426. **Atlas of the Solar System.** Moore, Patrick, and Gary Hunt. New York: Rand McNally, 1983. 464p.

This compilation pulls together much new data on the planets, their satellites, and the sun, and displays them with considerable diversity. The combination of historical perspective with current thought and knowledge makes this an excellent work. A glossary, voluminous tables, bibliographies, and an extensive index complete the work.

QB501
.A84
1983
Sci
Ref

427. **Atlas of the Universe.** rev. ed. Moore, Patrick, ed. Chicago, IL: Rand McNally, 1981. 271p.

An excellent and beautifully laid out atlas containing stunning photographs and other illustrations. A catalog of stellar objects, glossary, and a "Beginner's Guide to the Heavens" are also included.

QB44
.M5425
Sci Ref
Oversize

428. **Bright Star Catalogue.** 4th ed. rev. Hoffleit, Dorrit, and Carlos Jaschek. New Haven, CT: Yale University Observatory, 1982. 472p.

This is a scholarly catalog of over 9,000 stars suitable for professional or advanced amateur astronomers. It includes name, number, infrared source, equatorial coordinates for 1900 and 2000, spectral class, and rotational velocity.

QB843
.B75
B74
1982
Sci Ref

429. **Cambridge Photographic Atlas of the Planets.** Briggs, Geoffrey, and Fredric Taylor. Cambridge, England: Cambridge University Press, 1986. 256p.

This text examines each planet from Mercury out to Saturn with many photographs from spacecraft, maps, processes, and nomenclature for surface features.

430. **Catalog of the Universe.** Murdin, Paul, David Allen, and D. Malin. London: Book Club Association, 1980. 256p.

This is a volume of photographs of galaxies, stars, and planets which places emphasis on southern celestial objects. The text provides background and history for each photograph. A glossary and notes on special photographs and techniques are included.

431. **Isophotometric Atlas of Comets.** Hogner, W., and N. Richter. New York: Springer, 1980- . 2 parts.

A selective collection of photographs needed for physical research of comets. Photographs are from the period 1902-1967.

QB722
.H613
1980
Sp.Coll.

432. **National Geographic Picture Atlas of Our Universe.** rev. ed. Gallant, Roy. Washington, DC: National Geographic Society, 1986. 284p.

An atlas emphasizing the solar system but with an informative introduction to the history of astronomy. Sections on individual members of the solar system, stars, and galaxies are provided.

QB68
.G34
Main
Juve.
Coll.

433. **Nearby Galaxies Atlas.** Tully, R. Bent, and J. Richard Fisher. New York: Cambridge University Press, 1987. 1v. (various paging).

The atlas is in three sections. The first is a collection of two-dimensional sky maps showing nearby galaxies. The second section is a graphic demonstration of the distribution of the nearby galaxies. The final section deals with the structure of galaxies. Overall, this

QB857
.T85
1987
Sci
Over size

is an important work because it maps the sky using a focus larger than the Milky Way Galaxy. Highly recommended for specialized collections.

QB65
M8
1978
Map Ref

434. **New Concise Atlas of the Universe.** rev. ed. Moore, Patrick. New York: Rand McNally, 1978. 190p.

An atlas in four parts. Topics covered include: part 1, the Earth from space; part 2, the moon; part 3, the solar system; and part 4, the stars. Little change from the previous (1974) edition. Index is incomplete.

435. **Palomar Observatory Sky Survey.** Pasadena, CA: California Institute of Technology, 1949-1955.

Consists of red and blue sensitive photographs covering the entire sky − 33 degrees to + 90 degrees declination. This is the best quality with the most complete coverage of any atlas in existence.

QB851
.94
Sci
Oversize

436. **Revised New General Catalog of Nonstellar Astronomical Objects.** Sulentic, Jack W., and William G. Tifft. Tucson, AZ: University of Arizona Press, 1973. 384p.

This work is a correction of the *New General Catalog of Nebula and Clusters of Stars* (London: Royal Astronomical Society, 1888-1895). One object of the work is to ease the problem of finding objects in the *Palomar Observatory Sky Survey* (see entry 435). This is a collection of basic data for a large percentage of all bright objects other than stars.

QB857
.V38
1976
Sci

437. **Second Reference Catalogue of Bright Galaxies: Containing Information on 4,364 Galaxies with References to Papers Published between 1964 and 1975.** Vaucouleurs, Gerard de, Antoinette de Vaucouleurs, and Harold G. Corwin, Jr. Austin, TX: University of Texas Press, 1976. 396p.

This supplement to the *Reference Catalogue of Bright Galaxies* (Austin, TX: University of Texas, 1964) lists 4,364 of the brightest galaxies. Some effort has been expended to include all galaxies that have attracted special attention in recent years. It is composed of two parts—the first is the catalog proper; the second contains references to literature published between January 1964 and July 1965. This is a clear professional tool with little utility for the public or even the amateur.

QB65
.T54
1981b
Sci
Oversize

438. **Sky Atlas 2000.0.** Tirion, Wil. New York: Cambridge University Press, 1981. 26 leaves.

An atlas for the epoch 2000.0 including 45,300 stars to visual magnitude 8.0 and 2,500 sky objects. Contains charts with stars, clusters, and nebulae.

439. **Star Atlas.** rev. ed. Heweliusz, Jan. Tashkent, USSR: FAN Press, 1978. 54 leaves.

An important work because it was first published in 1690 as a result of observing stars with the naked eye. This is the last and most accurate star atlas of pretelescopic observations.

440. **Star Atlas.** Mitton, Jacqueline, and Simon Mitton. New York: Crown, 1979. 31p.

A star guide for the novice astronomer. Data are applicable for all time zones. Latitudes and longitudes are given on a worldwide basis.

Q66
.S57
Sci

441. **Star Catalog.** Washington, DC: Smithsonian Institution, 1971. 4v.

A comprehensive catalog for the epoch and equinox of 1950.0 giving positions and motions of 258,997 stars. It combines information found in a number of other star catalogs. This is, in effect, a master catalog. A massive tool, it is available in machine readable form.

442. **Stars and Stellar Systems: Compendium of Astronomy and Astrophysics.** Kuiper, G. P., and B. M. Middlehurst, eds. Chicago, IL: University of Chicago Press, 1982. 9v.

Volumes titles are: volume 1, telescopes; volume 2, astronomical techniques; volume 3, basic astronomical data; volume 4, clusters and binaries; volume 5, galactic structures; volume 6, stellar atmospheres; volume 7, nebular and interstellar matter; volume 8, stellar structure; and volume 9, galaxies and the universe. Speculative topics have been de-emphasized to ensure the continuing value of this comprehensive reference.

QB88 .K8 Sci

443. **True Visual Magnitude Photographic Star Atlas.** Papadopoulos, C. Oxford, England: Pergamon, 1979-80. 3v.

A very useful tool that presents stars in their "apparent magnitude" or as the eye sees them through a telescope. As such, it can be used by both professional and amateur astronomers alike.

QB815 .P28 Sci

DIRECTORIES

444. **Biographical Dictionary of Scientists: Astronomers.** Abbott, David, ed. New York: Bedrick Books, 1984. 204p.

This volume in the series covers different scientific fields. One-half to two-page biographies are provided on astronomers from past to present. Contains no bibliographies.

QB35 .B56 1984 Sci Ref

445. **Directory of Physics and Astronomy Staff Members.** New York: American Institute of Physics, 1959/60- . annual.

Lists physics and astronomy personnel with address and telephone number. Also included is a list of faculty and staff at a particular institution. No biographical data are given.

QC47 .N75 D57 Sci Ref

446. **Graduate Programs in Physics, Astronomy, and Related Fields.** New York: American Institute of Physics, 1986. 967p.

A guide listing information on doctoral and master's degree programs in the United States and Canada. It is arranged geographically with information on the faculty, research specialties, course requirements, financial aid, and other pertinent information.

QC30 .A552a Sci Ref

447. **Observatories of the World.** Marx, Siegfried. New York: Van Nostrand, 1982. 200p.

This is a directory of optical and radio astronomical observatories. Meteorological and seismic observatories are excluded. The arrangement is by country then subdivided by optical or radio. Information consists of founding date, location, list of equipment, and programs.

QB81 .M3913 Sci

4 General Biology

Biology is the science of living systems. Such a broad definition suggests that biology is inherently interdisciplinary. An examination of both the sources listed below and the actual literature of biology will also suggest the multifaceted nature of biology.

In some senses, biology is an extremely old science. Records dating from at least 3000 B.C. indicate that people had a reasonable knowledge of living systems and biological principles. It was not until the age of Greece that what we know as ancient biology became a science. The Arabic world continued the study of biology and was a major force in the transmission of biological information into the Renaissance. Beginning with the Renaissance, advances in biology and allied fields came much more quickly. As the telescope was a milestone in the development of astronomy, so was the microscope an event of much importance in biology.

Use of tools such as the microscope opened up a previously unseen world to the biologist and strained the concepts held to that point. Work by Louis Pasteur and Robert Koch laid the groundwork for microbiology. Robert Hooke's discovery of the cell and his examination of the cell's characteristics began the area of cellular biology. It was to a great extent the discovery of the cell that led to a fascination with uncovering the secret of life via biology investigation. Rediscovery of Gregor Mendel's work with genetics (flawed though it is by data manipulation) and an increase in the use of chemical and physical models for biological phenomena were precursors to such events as the DNA structure discovery.

The field of biology has grown to the point that the term *biology* has become inadequate to those in the discipline. Few practice biology, but rather are investigators in particular branches of biology. Most scientific disciplines can say the same, but it is especially prevalent in biology and physics. This has considerable impact on the provision of information service in the biological sciences. Knowledge of general biology is likely to be of limited use to the information provider. As biology becomes more specialized, so will the questions put to the information center. A concomitant consequence is the diffusion of reference sources for the biological sciences. The wide variety presented here is only a sampling of the specialized materials in this broad field.

The future of biology appears to be one of continued expansion and greater use of chemical and physical techniques. The already complicated methodologies of biology will only become more complicated in the future.

GUIDES TO THE LITERATURE

448.   **Guide to Sources for Agricultural and Biological Research.** Blanchard, J. Richard, and Lois Farrell. Berkeley, CA: University of California Press, 1981. 735p.

Each chapter contains an annotated bibliography plus a brief discussion of the various areas in food production, wildlife management, and environmental sciences.

449.   **Library Research Guide to Biology: Illustrated Search Strategy and Sources.** Kirk, Thomas G. Ann Arbor, MI: Pierian Press, 1978. 84p.

A guide to the basic tools for gathering information in the biological sciences. The appendices are particularly important, containing lists of reviews, guides to the literature, and basic reference sources. A section on use of *Chemical Abstracts* (see entry 675) and *Zoological Record* (see entry 1013) is very useful.

450.   **Literature of the Life Sciences.** Kronick, David A. Philadelphia: ISI Press, 1985. 219p.

This is not meant to be a definitive guide to the literature. It deals with basic issues concerning the information systems in each discipline, including history and terminology/vocabulary problems. Descriptions of primary information systems are given. This is a good basic guide.

451.   **Recent Publications in Natural History.** New York: American Museum of Natural History, 1983- . quarterly.

A bibliography of scholarly and general works published by commercial publishers, universities, and scientific institutions. Books are included. This is an excellent checklist for new materials.

452.   **Smith's Guide to the Literature of the Life Sciences.** 9th ed. Smith, Roger C. Minneapolis, MN: Burgess, 1980. 223p.

This is a guide to library research and not a handbook on the literature of the life sciences. The book deals more with the items such as the preparation of scientific papers than with any discussion of the structure of the life sciences literature.

453.   **Use of Biological Literature.** 2nd ed. Bottle, R. T., and H. V. Wyatt, eds. London: Butterworths, 1972. 379p.

A good, first-stop guide for graduate students in biology. Specific chapters are devoted to literature reviews, the use of the library, and the conduct of biological research. Dated, but still a reasonable source.

454.   **Using the Biological Literature.** Davis, Elisabeth B. New York: Dekker, 1981.

This annotated guide to the literature is aimed at graduate students and undergraduates. A good guide in terms of generalities and much better than Bottle and Wyatt's work (see entry 453), though the two set out to do different things. Davis's book is more of a literature guide than Bottle and Wyatt's book. This point and its more recent publication date make it the choice between the two.

ABSTRACTS, INDEXES, AND BIBLIOGRAPHIES

455. Biological Abstracts. Philadelphia: Biosciences Information Service, 1926- . semimonthly.

This is the best and most comprehensive biological abstracting service available. Written in English, the abstracts are arranged into some 85 categories. The author, biosystematic, generic, and subject indexes are a particularly strong part of this service. A concept index can be found in earlier volumes and cumulative indexes are issued semiannually. This publication constitutes the major portion of the BIOSIS database.

456. Biological Abstracts/RRM. Philadelphia: Biosciences Information Service, 1980- . semimonthly.

This is the successor to *BioResearch Index* (see entry 458), which covers reviews, reports, selected patents, books, and meetings. The concept index is no longer provided. A cumulative index is published semiannually.

457. Biological and Agricultural Index. New York: Wilson, 1916/1918- . monthly.

This elementary level index covers the fields mentioned for the beginning student and layperson. It now covers approximately 200 journals, an increase of approximately 50 journals. There are quarterly and annual cumulations. This service is now available both online and in CD-ROM format.

458. BioResearch Index. Philadelphia: Biosciences Information Service, 1967-1979. 16v.

This service is now of historical significance. It includes material taken from annual institutional reports, bibliographies, letters, notes, preliminary reports, reviews, selected government reports, popular journals, symposia, and trade journals. Its most important aspect is the diversity of material used to compile the work. It is continued by *Biological Abstracts/RRM* (see entry 456).

459. Catalog of the Library of the Marine Biological Laboratory and the Woods Hole Oceanographic Institution. Boston: G. K. Hall, 1971. 12v. **Journal Catalog.** 1971.

Covers the collection of the institutions spanning the last 300 years of marine biology and oceanography. These are two of the premier libraries in their areas and their catalogs are an excellent checklist for research collections desiring improvement.

460. Catalogs of the Scripps Institution of Oceanography Library. Boston: G. K. Hall, 1971. 12v.

What Woods Hole is to the East Coast, Scripps is to the West Coast. This is an excellent library, with an excellent collection. Use of the catalog and supplements are a valuable tool for building collections.

461. Catalogues of the Library of the Freshwater Biological Association. Boston: G. K. Hall, 1979. 6v.

These catalogs represent one of the best collections in the world on limnology. The range is from the mid-nineteenth century to the present. The coverage includes all areas of limnology with emphasis on freshwater algae, planktonic and benthic invertebrates, fishes, and lake sediment.

462. CSA Neurosciences Abstracts. Bethesda, MD: Cambridge Scientific Abstracts, 1983- . monthly.

Coverage of approximately 5,000 journals, books, and conferences. Both vertebrates and invertebrates are included. The emphasis is on basic research rather than clinical aspects or neurosurgery. Author and subject indexes together with monthly and annual cumulative indexes provide easy access.

463. **Current Advances in Microbiology.** New York: Pergamon, 1984- . monthly.

This is a selective index to the field of microbiology, excellent in certain fields and weak in others. The quality varies with each volume.

464. **Current Awareness in Biological Sciences.** Oxford, England: Pergamon, 1983- . 144/yr.

This continues *International Abstracts of Biological Sciences* (Oxford, England: Pergamon, 1954-1983). The strengths of the service are in physiological and biochemical aspects of anatomy, animal behavior, biochemistry, endocrinology, experimental medicine, microbiology, pathology, and pharmacology. Abstracts are signed and are, for the most part, excellent.

465. **Ecology Abstracts.** Bethesda, MD: Cambridge Scientific Abstracts, 1980- . monthly.

This continues *Applied Ecology Abstracts* (1975-1979). It covers approximately 5,000 primary journals, conferences, bibliographies, books. Author and subject indexes are found in each issue. Cumulated annually.

466. **Index to Illustrations of the Natural World: Where to Find Pictures of the Living Things of North America.** Thompson, John, comp. Hamden, CT: Archon, 1983. 265p.

An alphabetical listing of the species of plants and animals found in North America for which illustrations can be found. There are indexes to scientific names, book titles, and book code letters.

467. **Index to Illustrations of Living Things outside North America.** Munz, Lucile, and Nedra G. Slauson. Hamden, CT: Archon Books, 1981. 441p.

This is a companion to the *Index to Illustrations of the Natural World* (see entry 466). It contains the same type of information for species of plants and animals found outside North America.

468. **Life Sciences Collection.** Bethesda, MD: Cambridge Scientific Abstracts, 1981- . monthly.

A database containing abstracts of information in the fields of animal behavior, biochemistry, ecology, entomology, genetics, immunology, microbiology, toxicology, and virology. Available from DIALOG.

469. **Natural History Index-Guide.** 2nd ed. Altsheler, Brent, comp. New York: H. W. Wilson, 1940. 583p.

This is a particularly important piece for historical and retrospective collections. It contains entries on material published from 1800 to 1940. The arrangement is classified. This is an expert list, drawn up by prominent scientists and explorers. For this reason alone, it is an important work.

470. **Oceanic Abstracts.** Louisville, KY: Data Courier, 1980- . v. 17- . 6/yr.

Former titles were *Oceanic Index* (1972-1979) and *Oceanic Citation Journal* (1964-1971). Coverage includes biology, fisheries, geology, remote sensing, meteorology, oceanography, acoustics, optics, positioning, and a multitude of additional areas bounded only by their commonality with regard to dealing with the ocean. Books, journals, pamphlets, government publications, and symposia are all covered. This is a very comprehensive service, available from DIALOG as an online database.

471.   **Oceanographic Index.** Sears, Mary, comp. Boston: G. K. Hall, 1976.
Author Cumulation 1971-1974. 1v.
Regional Cumulation 1971-1974. 1v.
Subject Cumulation 1971-1974. 2v.
Marine Organisms, Chiefly Planktonic Cumulation 1946-1973. 3v.
The titles above are listings and cumulations of the literature held by the Marine Biological Laboratory and the library of the Woods Hole Oceanographic Institution. Due to their age they are primarily of historical interest, but should serve well in that regard.

472.   **VETDOC UDB/VETDOC.** 1968- .
Database which covers the worldwide journal literature on veterinary applications of drugs, hormones, vaccines, and growth inducements. Available from SDC.

ENCYCLOPEDIAS

473.   **Cambridge Encyclopedia of Life Sciences.** Friday, Adrian, and David S. Ingram, eds. Cambridge, England: Cambridge University Press, 1985. 432p.
An undergraduate-oriented encyclopedia with good basic information. Entries are too basic for students at the graduate level and higher.

474.   **Concise Encyclopedia of Biochemistry.** Scott, Thomas, and Mary Brewer. Berlin: Walter de Gruyter, 1983. 516p.
This is a translation of Brockhouses' *ABC Biochemie* (Berlin: Walter de Gruyter, 1983) with unsigned entries of varying length. A good first source but not recommended for in-depth usage.

475.   **Encyclopedia of the Biological Sciences.** 2nd ed. Gray, Peter, ed. Huntington, NY: Krieger, 1981. 1027p.
This is a good, basic encyclopedia. It contains some biographical information but concentrates on biology, ecology, physiology, genetics, anatomy, and taxonomy. The entries range in length and scope. Some entries are signed. This is a good, but not superior work. It provides information in a clear and accurate manner.

476.   **Evolution of Life.** Gamlin, Linda, and Gail Vines. New York: Oxford University Press, 1987. 248p.
The work is divided into four parts. The first part deals with evolution, genetics, and classification. The second part examines the development of fungi, algae, angiosperms, lower invertebrates, arthropods, echinoderms, lower chordates, fish, amphibians, reptiles, birds, and mammals. The third section explores the chemistry of life by discussing the role of amino acids, enzymes, collagen, nucleic acid, and DNA. The final section discusses developmental processes such as fertilization, embryo growth, and regeneration. Accompanied by a wealth of illustrations and an excellent glossary and index, this is a welcome addition to any library.

477. **Grzimek's Encyclopedia of Ethology.** Grzimek, Bernard, ed. New York: Van Nostrand Reinhold, 1977. 705p.

QL751
.G77
1977
Sci
Ref

  A highly useful work, but with a decided European slant. For this reason, it should not be considered the authoritative volume on animal behavior. The coverage of the work varies from excellent to superficial. For a single volume, this source does an admirable job of pulling together diverse material on a still emerging field.

478. **Grzimek's Encyclopedia of Evolution.** Grzimek, Bernard, ed. New York: Van Nostrand Reinhold, 1976. 560p.

QH366.2
G7
Sci Ref

  This is an authoritative and thorough overview of the subject. As an encyclopedia, it suffers from some major flaws such as the mention of experiments or bibliographic material without references. The suggested bibliography contained in the work does not correct this deficiency. This is more of a treatise than an encyclopedia, and is placed here because of its title and the admittedly good overview it supplies the reader. The chapters on geologic evolution are particularly good.

479. **Wildlife in Danger.** Fisher, James, et al. New York: Viking, 1969. 368p.

QL88
.F48
Sci

  This is a listing together with a history and description of plants and animals in danger of extinction. The arrangement is by class of endangered animal or plant: mammals, birds, reptiles, amphibians, fishes, and plants. It is an excellent work, but because it needs an update it should be used with some caution.

DICTIONARIES

480. **Cambridge Illustrated Dictionary of Natural History.** Lincoln, R. J., and G. A. Boxshall. New York: Cambridge University Press, 1987. 413p.

QH13
.L56
1987
Sci
Ref

  Natural history is defined by this work as the study of plants, animals, and microorganisms which make up the living world. It excludes such potential areas as meteorology, geology, and biochemistry. The language is clear and concise but the definitions tend to be very brief. The limited scope and simplified definitions exclude this for most academic and specialized collections. It is recommended for public and general purpose collections.

481. **Dictionary of Biology.** 6th ed. Abercrombie, Michael, C. J. Hickman, and M. L. Johnson. New York: Penguin Books, 1977. 309p.

QH13
.A25
1973
Sci

  Intended for the layperson or the beginning student, the coverage of this dictionary is general biology. About 2,000 definitions are given, most of which are short. This is a good generalized source, but not for professional use.

482. **Dictionary of Biology: English/German/French/Spanish.** 2nd ed. rev. and enl. Haensch, Gunther, and Gisela Haberkamp de Anton. New York: Elsevier, 1981. 680p.

QH302.5
H3
1981
Sci

  Covering all of biology, this source is arranged by the English term followed by German, French, and Spanish equivalents. A good one stop polyglot dictionary.

483. **Dictionary of Biotechnology.** Coombs, J. New York: Elsevier, 1986. 330p.

TP248.
16
C66
1992
Sci
Ref

  This is a listing of more than 4,000 terms, most of which are defined in less than 50 words. The result is that this dictionary, written by an expert and prolific author, is uneven and sometimes useless. Illustrations and cross-references are exceedingly spare. The major recommendation for this work is that it focuses on the biology portion of the biotechnology field. It is useful as a quick reference source only.

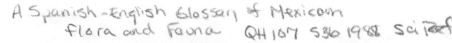

A Spanish-English Glossary of Mexican flora and Fauna   QH107 S36 1988 Sci Ref

RB114
.L4
Sci

484. Dictionary of Comparative Pathology and Experimental Biology. Leader, Robert W., and Isabel Leader. Philadelphia: W. B. Saunders, 1971. 238p.

This work supplies expanded definitions in terms of comparative animal data. Much of the information is presented in tabular form. It is included here as one of the first books to systematize biology in terms of man being no different from other animals. The viewpoint permeates the work, resulting in an alternative view. It is intended for specialists in the field. A glossary, unusually wide in scope, is also included. Emphasis is given to terminology relating genetics to disease.

QH540.4
.L56
Sci Ref

485. Dictionary of Ecology, Evolution, and Systematics. Lincoln, R. J., G. A. Boxshall, and P. F. Clark. Cambridge, England: Cambridge University Press, 1982. 298p.

Contains short entries with no illustrations. A series of appendices consisting of maps, diagrams, tables, and lists complete the work. Good general information is provided.

RT-
(QL750.3
I4513
1989
Sci
Ref)

486. Dictionary of Ethology and Animal Learning. Harre, Rom, and Roger Lamb, eds. Cambridge, MA: MIT Press, 1986. 171p.

Information here was selected, updated, and supplemented from material originally published in the *Encyclopedic Dictionary of Psychology* (Guilford, CT: Dushkin, 1986). This is a good reference tool in a specific area.

QH442
.O43
1985
Sci Ref

487. Dictionary of Genetic Engineering. Oliver, Stephen G., and John M. Ward. Cambridge, England: Cambridge University Press, 1985. 153p.

Contains short, unsigned entries. This is a valuable reference tool because of the currency of the subject covered.

QH13
.G68
Sci Ref

488. Dictionary of the Biological Sciences. Gray, Peter. Malabar, FL: Krieger, 1986. 602p.

Though dated (a reprint of the 1967 edition), this dictionary is still very useful for the college student because of its comprehensive coverage and format. Words derived from the same root are grouped together with cross-references.

QH302.5
R63
Sci Ref

489. Dictionary of Theoretical Concepts in Biology. Roe, Keith E., and Richard G. Frederick. Metuchen, NJ: Scarecrow Press, 1981. 267p.

This work provides access to the literature on named theoretical concepts by citing original sources and reviews in which these concepts are elucidated. Contains 1,166 concepts, but definitions are not given. Material referenced is primarily in English. Coverage is complete through 1979.

490. Lexicon de Biologie. New York: Herder, 1983- . 8v.

Volumes 1-6 are completed. A comprehensive lexicon of biology using international sources. This is an excellent source for information both in general terms and for specific information.

491. Macmillan Dictionary of Life Sciences. 2nd ed. Martin, E. A., ed. London: Macmillan, 1983. 396p.

This edition expands the first edition (1976) by 300 entries. The focus remains on students and laypersons. The definitions are more complete than the majority of dictionaries in the area.

492. McGraw-Hill Dictionary of Biology. Parker, Sybil P. New York: McGraw-Hill, 1984. 384p.

Material here was previously published in the *McGraw-Hill Dictionary of Scientific and Technical Terms* (see entry 229), and there is no reason to have both. However, if the larger work is not available, this is an excellent dictionary.

493. **McGraw-Hill Dictionary of the Life Sciences.** Lapedes, Daniel N., ed. New York: McGraw-Hill, 1976. 907p.

QH302.5
M3
Sci Ref

Contains short, and in some cases very short, definitions on over 20,000 terms. The appendices are most interesting and include the U.S. customary system, the metric system, a description and explanation of the SI system, plus basic plant and animal taxonomy.

494. **Oxford Dictionary of Natural History.** Allaby, Michael. Oxford, England: Oxford University Press, 1985. 688p.

QH13
.O9
1985
Sci
Ref

In this dictionary plants and animals are described under their scientific names with their common name listed in parentheses and in cross-references to the main entry. Entries are short with no illustrations, and a bibliography is provided at the beginning of the book. This work covers a very broad subject area and is therefore best suited to amateurs and undergraduates.

495. **Source Book of Biological Names and Terms.** 3rd ed. Jaeger, Edmund Carroll. Springfield, IL: Thomas, 1966. 323p.

QH83
J3
1955

The date of this publication is not an important issue. The intent is to list the derivation of biological names. Greek, Latin, and other origins are given, usually with short definitions of the original term. A short biography of persons of special interest is included. The index allows the work to be used as a dictionary to Greek and Latin roots.

496. **Synopsis and Classification of Living Organisms.** Parker, Sybil P. New York: McGraw-Hill, 1982. 2v.

QH83
.S9P
Sci
Ref

A systematic position of all living organisms presented in synoptic articles for all taxa down to the family level. Articles are signed and include references. An excellent starting point for detailed reference questions.

HANDBOOKS AND FIELD GUIDES

497. **Biological Research Method.** 2nd ed. Holman, H. H. New York: Hafner, 1969. 272p.

574.
O72
H747
Sci

Despite its age, this practical guide is very useful. It focuses on animal experimentation and animal product research. The greatest utility of the book is its discussion of the components of the research process in biology. These processes are still viable today and make the book valuable for beginning researchers and those interested in the research component of biology.

498. **Biology Data Book.** 2nd ed. Altman, Philip L., and Dorothy S. Dittmer. Bethesda, MD: Federation of American Societies for Experimental Biology, 1972-1974. 3v.

QH310
A392
Sci
Ref

This work is a compendium of basic data for the biological sciences. Tables list the various properties of biological substances and information on both materials and methods. An inclusive taxonomic table and a geologic distribution key are provided. This is a necessary source of information for researchers.

499. **CRC Handbook of Biological Effects of Electromagnetic Fields.** Polk, Charles, ed. Boca Raton, FL: CRC Press, 1986. 576p.

QP82.2
E43
C73
1986
Sci

A three-part presentation of the state of the art knowledge as it relates to the effects of electromagnetic fields on living matter. The first part covers dielectric premittivity and electrical conductivity of biological materials. The second part covers the effects of direct current and low frequency fields. The final section covers the effects of radio frequency fields which include microwaves. This is a valuable resource for both the professional biologist and the interested layperson. The nonprofessional will have some difficulty, however.

500. CRC Handbook of Cell Biology of Aging. Cristofalo, Vincent J., ed. Boca Raton, FL: CRC Press, 1985. 608p.

QH608
.C73
1985
Sci

This handbook summarizes the literature on aging and cell biology. It is especially useful because its objective is to gather a wide range of sources as opposed to a narrower strategy. The volume is essentially broken into three sections. The first deals with the effect of aging on cells and their behavior during the aging process. The second section discusses the problem from a tissue specific stance with a concentration on existing data, where available. The final section deals with mammalian cell cultures. This is an excellent starting point for beginners and a solid reference point for professionals in the field.

QK99.A1
D83
1985
Sci Ref

501. CRC Handbook of Medicinal Herbs. Duke, James A. Boca Raton, FL: CRC Press, 1985. 677p.

Arranged alphabetically by Latin name, this handbook is generally nontechnical and highly readable. This is an unusual handbook for CRC but is done with their usual expertise and excellent results.

502. Cytology in Evolution of Parthenogenesis. Suomalainen, Esko, et al., ed. Boca Raton, FL: CRC Press, 1987. 208p.

This is a condensation of the existing knowledge of parthenogenesis in the animal kingdom. The book is beneficial not only to those working in the field, but to those in allied fields as well. It is a careful analysis of the existing knowledge with a sense of clear direction for the field. It covers the most recent advances in the field and relates them to existing theory. A necessary addition to any research collection in the area.

QP520
.D37
1986
Sci Ref

503. Data for Biochemical Research. 3rd ed. Dawson, Rex, et al. Oxford, England: Clarendon Press, 1986. 580p.

A well-indexed handbook with data useful for applied biochemistry. Illustrations and a bibliography are included along with a useful compilation of physical properties within tables.

QH453
D484
1988
Sci

504. Developmental Genetics of Higher Organisms. Malacinski, G. M., ed. New York: Macmillan, 1987. 550p.

This volume presents a survey of contemporary research in developmental genetics. It emphasizes the developmental genetics of the whole embryo rather than selected parts. In this respect, this is a welcome departure from the treatment this subject has received in the past. This volume should have considerable influence on developmental biology.

QP601
B2435
Sci
Ref

505. Enzyme Handbook. Barman, Thomas E. New York: Springer, 1969- . irregular.

This is a listing of enzymes (over 800) arranged by the Enzyme Commission classification. To be included, an enzyme must have been fully described in the literature. A full description consists of molecular weight, specific gravity, specificity, and kinetic properties. Systematic names are included in the index. This is an excellent and necessary source for researchers.

506. **Large Scale Cell Culture Technology.** Lyderson, B. K., ed. New York: Macmillan, 1987. 275p.

This work focuses on approaches to the large scale culture of animal and plant cells. Continuous culture, process control, selective membranes, and cell immobilization are all considered and discussed. Of particular interest are the experimental results which show the practical utility of the approaches. An excellent discussion of techniques, backed by empirical data.

507. **Manual of Clinical Microbiology.** 4th ed. Lennette, Edwin H. Washington, DC: American Society for Microbiology, 1985. 1149p.

A reference tool covering laboratory data primarily in medical aspects of microbiology. Areas focus on fungi, bacteria, and viruses. Included are classification and nomenclature. Bibliographic references, extensive subject indexes, and author indexes are very helpful.

508. **New Generation Guide to the Wild Flowers of Britain and Northern Europe.** Fitter, Alistair. Austin, TX: University of Texas Press, 1987. 320p.

This is a good catalog of plant species in its defined area. Unfortunately, the illustrations are too small to be of much use in identification, and the only arrangement of the work is systematic. The textual portion of the book is very well done. This is a difficult book to recommend because it has both strengths and weaknesses. As a text it is good; as anything else it is second-rate.

509. **Peterson Field Guide Series.** Boston: Houghton Mifflin, 1947- .

These are the benchmark series for both amateurs and professionals. The following titles in the series are of interest to the biological sciences.

Animal Tracks. Murie, Olaus J. Norwalk, CT: Easton Press, 1985. 375p.

Bird Nests. Harrison, Hal H. Norwalk, CT: Easton Press, 1986. 279p.

Birds of Texas and Adjacent States. Peterson, Roger T. Norwalk, CT: Easton Press, 1985. 304p.

Field Guide to Mexican Birds. Peterson, Roger T., and Edward L. Chalif. Norwalk, CT: Easton Press, 1973. 298p.

Field Guide to Mushrooms: North America. McKnight, Kent H., and Vera B. McKnight. 1987. 429p.

Field Guide to Pacific States Wildflowers. Niehaus, Theodore F., and Charles L. Ripper. 1976. 432p.

Field Guide to the Birds. 4th ed. Peterson, Roger T. 1980. 384p.

Field Guide to the Birds of Britain and Europe. 4th ed. Peterson, Roger T., and P. A. D. Mountford. 1983. 241p.

Field Guide to Reptiles and Amphibians of Eastern and Central North America. 2nd ed. Conant, Roger. 1975. 429p.

Field Guide to Western Birds. 2nd ed. Peterson, Roger T. 1969. 366p.

Field Guide to Western Reptiles and Amphibians. 2nd ed. rev. Stebbins, Robert C. 1985. 336p.

Mammals. Burt, W. H. Norwalk, CT: Easton Press, 1986. 289p.

510. **Phospholipids and Cellular Regulation.** Kuo, J. F., ed. Boca Raton, FL: CRC Press, 1985. 2v.

An excellent source for information in this particular area. The material presented is highly technical, intended only for the specialist in the area. As the regulation and control of individual cells becomes a highly investigated area, works such as this will increase in terms of utility. This is a clear choice for the professional researcher and the research collection.

511. **Picture-Key Nature Series.** Dubuque, IA: William C. Brown, 1946- . irregular.

This is a good series of introductory texts in biology for the beginner. Each volume is fully illustrated and focuses on a particular topic. Titles of interrest here include:

How to Know the Aquatic Plants. Prescott, George W. 1980. 158p.

How to Know the Butterflies. Ehrlich, Paul R. 1961. 262p.

How to Know the Cacti. Dawson, E. Yale. 1963. 158p.

How to Know the Eastern Land Snails. Burch, John B. 1962. 214p.

How to Know the Economic Plants. Jaques, Harry E. 1958. 174p.

How to Know the Fall Flowers. Cuthbert, Mabel J. 1948. 199p.

How to Know the Freshwater Algae. 3rd ed. Prescott, George W. 1978. 293p.

How to Know the Freshwater Fishes. 3rd ed. Eddy, Samuel. 1978. 215p.

How to Know the Grasses. 3rd ed. Pohl, Richard W., ed. 1978. 200p.

How to Know the Insects. 3rd ed. Jaques, Harry E. 1978. 409p.

How to Know the Lichens. Hale, Mason E. 1979. 246p.

How to Know the Mammals. 4th ed. Booth, Ernest S. 1982. 198p.

How to Know the Mosses and Liverworts. 2nd ed. Conrad, Henry S. 1979. 302p.

How to Know the Protozoa. 2nd ed. Jahn, L. 1979. 279p.

How to Know the Seaweeds. 2nd ed. Dawson, E. Yale. 1978. 141p.

How to Know the Spiders. 2nd ed. Kaston, B. J. 1978. 272p.

How to Know the Spring Flowers. 2nd ed. Verhoek, Susan. 1982. 244p.

How to Know the Tapeworms. Schmidt, Gerald D. 1970. 266p.

How to Know the Trees. 3rd ed. Miller, Howard A., and H. E. Jaques. 1978. 263p.

How to Know the Trematodes. Schell, Stewart C. 1970. 355p.

How to Know the True Bugs: (Hemiptura: Hetroptera). Slater, James A., and Richard M. Baranowski. 1978. 256p.

How to Know the Water Birds. Jaques, Harry E. 1970. 159p.

How to Know the Weeds. 3rd ed. Wilkinson, R. E., and Harry E. Jaques. 1979. 235p.

How to Know the Western Trees. 2nd ed. Baerg, Harry J. 1973. 179p.

Plant Families, How to Know Them. 2nd ed. Jaques, Harry E. 1948. 177p.

512. **Putnam's Nature Field Books.** New York: Putnam, 1915- . irregular.
These are handy books suitable for the beginner. Each volume covers a particular area. Those related to the biological sciences include:

Birds of the Ocean. 2nd ed. Alexander, Wilfrid B. 1963. 306p.

Field Book of American Trees and Shrubs. Mathews, F. Schulyer. 1915. 465p.

Field Book of Common Mushrooms. 3rd ed. Thomas, William S. 1948. 369p.

Field Book of Eastern Birds. Hausman, Leon A. 1946. 659p.

Field Book of Insects of the U.S. and Canada. 3rd ed. Lutz, Frank E. 1948. 510p.

Field Book of Ponds and Streams. Morgan, Ann. 1930. 448p.

Field Book of Seashore Life. Miner, Roy W. 1950. 888p.

Field Book of Snakes of the U.S. and Canada. Schmidt, Karl P., and D. Dwight Davis. 1941. 365p.

New Field Book of American Wild Flowers. Rickett, Harold W. 1963. 414p.

New Field Book of Freshwater Life. Klots, Elise B. 1966. 398p.

New Field Book of Nature Activities and Hobbies. Hillcourt, William. 1970. 400p.

New Field Book of Reptiles and Amphibians. Cochran, Doris M., and Colman J. Gain. 1970. 359p.

513. **Role of the Cell Surface in Development.** Rao, K. V. Boca Raton, FL: CRC Press, 1987. 2v.
This is a multidisciplinary approach to the cellular and molecular basis of animal development. The role of the plasma membrane in controlling cell adhesion and locomotion is the primary focus of the work. There is a range of developmental systems considered, and the problems in experimental embryology are discussed. This is a particularly valuable set for researchers involved in this field.

514. **Statistical Tables.** 2nd ed. James, Rohlf F., and Robert R. Sokal. San Francisco: Freeman, 1981. 219p.
A compendium of statistical tables and interpretations of statistical tables in the biological sciences, social, and earth sciences. Mathematical tables are not given in most cases. Each table contains an explanation, instructions for finding data, and the source of the data.

QH323.5
.R63
1981
Sci Ref

515. **Statistical Tables for Biological, Agricultural, and Medical Research.** 6th ed. Fisher, Ronald Aylmer, and Frank Yates. New York: Hafner, 1974. 146p.
This is a compilation of statistical tables useful in the biological disciplines. A brief discussion accompanies each of the tables, and a bibliography of material related to statistical methods is included. This is an excellent source compiled by two of the giants in statistics.

QH324
.F52
1963
Sci
Ref

516. **UFAW Handbook on the Care and Management of Laboratory Animals.** 6th ed. London: Longman Scientific & Technical, 1987. 933p.
This handbook was written by experts in the field at the request of the University Federation for Animal Welfare. It is the basic compendium of rules by which laboratory

SF406
.U54
1972
Sci

animals are treated. Now in its sixth edition, the size of the volume indicates the complexity and the seriousness of the issue. This is a timely source which will be of interest to those engaged in research involving animals and for those concerned about humane treatment of laboratory animals.

DIRECTORIES

Q145
.S4
Sci

517.   **Naturalists Directory International.** South Orange, NJ: PCL Publications, 1975- . annual.

Arranged geographically, this directory consists of a listing of professional and amateur naturalists. The information on each entry includes name, address, and subject of interest. Provided also is a list of museums and societies and a list of pertinent periodicals. A bias toward North American naturalists in the work should be watched.

(cultures of ?)

QR64.5
.W67
Sci Ref

518.   **World Directory of Collections of Microorganisms.** Martin, S. M., comp. New York: Wiley, 1972. 560p.

International in scope, this work lists the major collections of microorganisms. There is an index to provide access by geographic area and name of microorganism, and cross-references from common names of organisms are given. The information on collections is reported in English, French, German, Japanese, Russian, and Spanish. A one of a kind reference tool.

CELL BIOLOGY

Abstracts, Indexes, and Bibliographies

QR65
.S5
Sci Ref

519.   **Abstracts of Microbiological Methods.** Skerman, V. B. D., ed. New York: Wiley, 1969. 883p.

Although this source of information is showing some age, it is still a useful tool for methodological research into microbiology. In essence, this is a listing of methodologies used successfully by microbiologists. The list is in the form of abstracts of the methods, and is arranged alphabetically by the name of the method. These are subdivided into author, identification of the organism under study, a citation to the original literature, and, in some cases, a short bibliography.

QH442
.M46
1993
sci Ref

520.   **Genetic Engineering, DNA and Cloning: A Bibliography in the Future of Genetics.** Menditto, Joseph, and Debbie Kirsch. New York: Whitston, 1983. 783p.

This is a good bibliography consisting of books, periodicals, newspaper articles, and government documents. It is an excellent starting point for the beginner.

521.   **Microbiology Abstracts.** London: Information Retrieval, 1965- . monthly.

This excellent source is issued in three sections: A, *Industrial and Applied Microbiology*; B, *Bacteriology*; and C, *Algology, Mycology, and Protozoology*. Book notices and notification of proceedings are featured in each section. An author index is found in the monthly issues.

522.   **Virology Abstracts.** London: Information Retrieval, 1967- . monthly.

An abstracting tool which does a very good job covering isolation and identification, phage studies, culture, immunology, viral infection of man and animals, and methodology and techniques of virology. Abstracts are short but indicative, though as a majority are not evaluative. Annual author and subject indexes.

523.   **Zentralblatt fuer Mikrobiologie.** Jeng, West Germany: Fisher, 1986- .
Continues *Zentralblatt fuer Bakteriologie, Parasitenkunde, Infectionskrankheiten und Hygiene* 1976-1986. This tool provides international coverage of information on microbiology and hygiene. The subject analysis is overly broad for most researchers. Of particular interest is a section on book reviews.

Encyclopedias

524.   **Encyclopedia of Biochemistry.** Williams, Roger John, and Edwin M. Lansford. QP512
Huntington, NY: Krieger, 1977. 876p.   .W5
Although 10 years old, this is still an important work because over half of its articles Sci
are signed by leaders in the field, with approximately 270 short unsigned articles filling out   Ref
the remainder of the book. Bibliographic references are provided.

525.   **Encyclopedia of Microscopy and Microtechniques.** Gray, Peter. New York: Krieger, QH203
1982. 638p.   G8
Microscopy can be employed in a variety of fields. The emphasis of this encyclopedia   Sci
is on biological science; hence, it has been included here. The majority of the articles in the
work deal with techniques and methodologies. Most have bibliographies attached. The
articles are liberally illustrated with tables and formulas. This is an excellent tool in a narrow, but important area.

Dictionaries

526.   **Dictionary of Genetics.** 3rd ed. King, Robert C. New York: Oxford University QH427
Press, 1985. 480p.   .K55
The intent of this dictionary is to list terms not commonly found in general biological   1990
dictionaries that are specific to genetics. This means that a great number of the terms listed   Sci
and defined are new to the field or to genetics in particular and biology in general. There is   Ref
a list of important persons in genetics arranged in chronological order. This is an excellent
source for genetics.

˅ Molecular Biology

527.   **Dictionary of Microbiology.** Singleton, Paul, and Diana Sainbury. New York: QR9
Wiley, 1978. 481p.   .S56
This work concentrates on the environment of microorganisms as well as on the actual   1987
microorganism. It is extremely comprehensive, not only giving definitions, but techniques,   Sci
tests, and microbial taxa.   Ref

528.   **Enzyme Nomenclature.** Commission on Biological Nomenclature. Amsterdam, QP601
Netherlands: Elsevier, 1973. 443p.   I54
This is the standard reference work for determining the names of enzymes, and is an   1979
important tool for controlling pseudo-discovery and reinvention. The work contains   Sci
recommendations of symbols for enzyme kinetics, and is indexed by subject and enzyme.

QR9
.525
Sci

529. Glossary of Bacteriological Terms. Samson, P. London: Butterworths, 1975. 155p.

Bacteriology has advanced considerably since 1975; however, this glossary remains an excellent source of medical laboratory terms in bacteriology. It is useful for students and professionals because of its short and concise definitions. A good desk dictionary even given its age.

QH431
.B53
Sci Ref

530. Glossary of Genetics in English, French, Spanish, Italian, German, Russian. Bias-Ducroux, Francoise. New York: Elsevier, 1970. 436p.

An indispensable tool for professionals in the field. It is listed here because of its multilingual nature. Some care needs to be taken in the use of definitions, but it remains an excellent, comprehensive multilingual glossary of genetic terms. Entries are listed in alphabetical order based on the English term. Every term is given an identifying number and is followed by the equivalents in French, Spanish, Italian, German, and Russian. Alphabetical indexes in the non-English languages allow access to the English term. Russian entries are listed in a separate section but are also coded to the English equivalent.

Handbooks and Laboratory Guides

QR6
.C2
Sci Ref

531. CRC Handbook of Microbiology. 2nd ed. Laskin, Allen I., and Hubert Lechevalier, eds. Boca Raton, FL: CRC Press, 1987. 448p. v.VIII.

A comprehensive and current source of information in the field of microbiology. For all intents, this should be used as the first stop and, in a great number of cases, as the last stop for detailed information in the field. The focus is on composition, activities, and adverse effects of microorganisms. This is an excellent source for any collection with a research focus.

QH231
.M4
1972
Sci

532. Electron Microscopy: A Handbook for Biologists. 3rd ed. Mercer, E. H., and M. S. C. Birbeck. London: Blackwell, 1972. 145p.

A good introduction to the preparation of material for examination using an electron microscope. There is a wealth of information on buffers, fixatives, embedding media, and the like. Due to the age of the book, this material should be used primarily for background as opposed to actual methodological practice. Because this book provides an excellent, brief, and practical set of instructions, it is included here.

533. Guide to Microscopical Methods. Grimstone, A. V., and R. J. Skaer. Cambridge, England: Cambridge University Press, 1972. 134p.

This work is noteworthy for its attempt to systematize the methodologies reported in the literature. A partial list of the items covered includes bacteria, protozoa, insects, blood, plants, and mammalian tissues. Common techniques are described in sufficient detail to enable them to be carried out without further information. Additional references are given for less common techniques.

QP514.2
Y83
1971
Sci

534. Guidebook to Biochemistry. 4th ed. rev. Yudkin, Michael, and Robin Offord. New York: Cambridge University Press, 1980. 261p.

This is an introduction to concepts in biochemistry and macromolecular chemistry. It is divided into three sections: Section 1 outlines the relation between structure and function in macromolecules. Section 2 covers cellular metabolic reactions. Section 3 introduces molecular genetics and the control of protein synthesis. This is a wealth of information on a fairly wide area in terms of methodology and is an important work for most research collections.

535. **Handbook of Biochemistry and Molecular Biology.** 3rd ed. Fasman, Gerald D. QP514.2
Cleveland, OH: CRC Press, 1976. Sections A-C.   .F73
    An excellent handbook providing the researcher with information in the areas of
biochemistry and molecular biology. It is divided into sections, each amounting to a   1989
separate handbook. Depending on the needs of the researcher one or more of the sections   Sci
will suffice as a bench manual. Research collections will want to have all sections.   Ref

536. **Handbook of Intermediate Metabolism of Aromatic Compounds.** Goodwin, Brian QP801
L. London: Chapman & Hall, 1976. 799p.
    A narrow source, but one with a wealth of data on a subject for which there are few   .A75
other choices in terms of handbooks. The intent is to list the metabolic reactions of   G66
aromatic compounds by both description and a reference to the primary literature. It is   1976b
divided into two sections. The first deals with a review of metabolic enzymes and reactions.   Sci
The second section, the major portion of the book, deals with metabolic reactions com-   Ref
pound by compound.

537. **International Code of Nomenclature of Bacteria.** International Association of QR11
Microbiological Societies. Washington, DC: American Society of Microbiology, 1976.   .I5
180p.   Sci
    This is a revised edition of the *International Code of Nomenclature of Bacteria and
Viruses* (Ames, IA: Iowa State College Press, 1958). A new edition is sorely needed, but the
current edition is still important because of its listing of approved and rejected names.

538. **Staining Procedures Used by the Biological Stain Commission.** 4th ed. Clark, QH237
George, ed. Baltimore, MD: Williams & Wilkins, 1981. 512p.   .C66
    This is a list of the different staining procedures used in laboratories of the commis-   1981
sion members. It is not a complete listing of all staining procedures, and the procedures
listed are not meant to be normative. Because of the prestige of the Biological Stain Com-   Sci
mission, these procedures tend to be the standard methods used. A bibliography and index   Ref
are included.

Treatises

539. **Comprehensive Biochemistry.** Florkin, M., and E. H. Stotz, eds. New York: QD415
Elsevier, 1962- . irregular.   .F54
    This is a renowned treatise in biochemistry. Currently there are 36 volumes in print,   Sci
and each volume has a special title and editor. There are extensive bibliographic references
in each volume, making it an excellent source not only for information in the treatise itself,
but for current, important literature as well.

540. **Enzymes.** 3rd ed. Boyer, P. D., ed. New York: Academic Press, 1970- . irregular. QP601
    This is probably the most authoritative treatise dealing with enzymes. It is especially   .E523
well known for its treatment of enzymes and enzyme catalysts at the molecular level. Ex-   Sci
cellent documentation and a clear presentation. There are replete bibliographic references
with author and subject indexes.

541. **Methods in Enzymology.** Colowick, Sidney P., and Nathan O. Kaplan, eds. New QP601
York: Academic Press, 1955- .   .M56
    This is a collection of the methods used in the study of enzymes. It is comprehensive   Sci
and scholarly in its treatment, and easily serves as an adjunct to *Enzymes* (see entry 540).
Each volume covers a specific topic and is edited by an authority in the field.   Ref

QH581.2
M64
1983
Sci

542. **Molecular Biology of the Cell.** Alberts, Bruce. New York: Garland, 1983. 1146p.

Five authors, including James D. Watson, compiled an integrated and detailed picture of the molecular basis of life. This is an excellent work for the scientist and nonscientist alike.

QH581.2
D37
1986
Sci

543. **Molecular Cell Biology.** Darnell, J. E. New York: Scientific American Books, 1986. 1187p.

Complete coverage of cytology and molecular biology is provided in this well-illustrated book with comprehensive indexes and topical bibliographies. Serves as an up-to-date introductory text with glossary and bibliographies.

Directories

QH442
.G4565
Sci
Ref

544. **Genetic Engineering and Biotechnology Related Firms Worldwide Directory.** 5th ed. Sittig, Marshall, and Robert Noyes. Kingston, NJ: Sittig & Noyes, 1987/88. 919p.

Includes research laboratories, production plants, investors, potential investors, construction companies, and information organizations. A good source for information in this fast-moving area.

5 Botany and Agriculture

Botany, the study of plants, may be approached from several different perspectives. As examples, the study may take the form of classification, form and structure, diseases, or heredity, to mention only a few.

The study of plants and their categories began early in history. It clearly was the early man's advantage to be able to pass down to successive generations the uses for various plants. Scientific botany, as we know it, probably began with the ancient Greeks and Romans. Theophrastus, the father of botany, wrote extensively about form, classification, and natural history.

The invention of the microscope and the wealth of information it unlocked for the botanist was immense. Combined with a normative scheme for classification suggested by Linnaeus, botany had the major tools with which to develop the botanical sciences we know today. Darwin's explorations, best known for their biological consequences, were instrumental in allowing botanists to build evolutionary structures.

Today botany is a fast moving science with branches in several areas such as chemistry, physics, and zoology.

Agriculture began evolving when people first cultivated wild plants and domesticated animals. The ability to produce a dependable food supply on a consistent basis was a major impetus for the beginning of agriculture.

As a science, agriculture has grown from a trade school subject to that of a full fledged academic discipline. Modern agriculture incorporates statistics, genetics, botany, and several other hard sciences. The result is a restructuring of the agricultural sciences curriculum and units on university and college campuses. Considerably more time and effort, in terms of research methodologies and techniques, are now being seen in agriculture. The informational support for such services is multidisciplinary while it also retains a base in the traditional agriculture literature.

ABSTRACTS, INDEXES, AND BIBLIOGRAPHIES

545. **Abstracts of Mycology.** Philadelphia: Biosciences Information Service, 1976- . monthly. *QK600 .A22 Sci*

    This abstracting journal is a major source for references and abstracts pertaining to fungi and lichen. The majority of the papers are already reported in *Biological Abstracts* (see entry 455), *BioResearch Index* (Philadelphia: Biosciences Information Service, 1967-69), and *Biological Abstracts/RRM* (see entry 456). This source pulls together specific literature from these general sources. Each issue includes author, biosystematic, CROSS, and subject indexes.

546.   Agrindex. Rome: AGRIS Coordinating Centre, 1975- . monthly.

Contains materials related to agriculture which have been contributed by participating centers around the world. One such center is the National Agricultural Library. Coverage is extensive, including books, journals, atlases, and technical reports. Material listed in the source can usually be obtained from Agrinet, the world network of agriculture libraries, and is also available as a loadable database. This is an excellent source for materials from developing countries and about developing countries. It often identifies materials which would not otherwise be used.

547.   Asher's Guide to Botanical Periodicals. Amsterdam, Netherlands: A. Asher, 1973- . 15/yr.

This is a table of contents journal awareness service notable because of the speed with which it is produced. Included once a year are conference proceedings and symposia. Author and subject indexes are provided. This could be considered an alternative to *Current Contents* (see entry 179), though it is not as extensive in its coverage. Some European bias can be detected.

548.   Bibliography of Plant Viruses and Index to Research. Beale, Helen Purdy, comp. and ed. New York: Columbia University Press, 1976. 1495p.

A means to access the literature dealing with viruses that attack plants. A range of periodicals are scanned, increasing the breadth. Given the age, it should be used with some caution in a research environment. It is included here because of its excellent coverage of the literature to 1975.

549.   Botanical Abstracts. Baltimore, MD: Williams & Wilkins, 1918-1926. 15v. monthly.

A set now important for its retrospective coverage of the literature of the period. In classified arrangement, each entry gives a complete citation. It was superseded by *Biological Abstracts* (see entry 455).

550.   Botanical Bibliographies: A Guide to Bibliographic Materials Applicable to Botany. Swift, Lloyd H. Minneapolis, MN: Burgess, 1970. 804p.

This is a bibliography of bibliographies in the botanical sciences which is excellent for historical materials. Composed of four parts, it is a useful guide to background material. Part 1, "General Bibliography," contains sections on library classification, periodicals, book reviews, and abstracts. Part 2 focuses on background literature and references to mathematical, physiochemical and general life sciences sources. Part 3 on botanical literature, limits itself to the pure science, reference works, and specialized sources. Part 4 on literature of applied areas of plant study lists citations on applied botany. Though it was designed specifically for the beginning graduate student, it should be used with caution at that level.

551.   CAB Abstracts. Commonwealth Agricultural Bureaux, 1972- .

An online file of agricultural and biological information, containing all records in the main abstract journals published by the Commonwealth Agricultural Bureaux (CAB).

552.   Catalog of the Royal Botanic Gardens, Kew, England. Boston: G. K. Hall, 1973. 9v.

The Royal Botanic Gardens are one of the best in the world. Further adding to their prestige is the amount of scholarly work that continues to emanate from them. This makes the catalog an important collection development tool for other libraries. The published catalog is classified by the Dewey Decimal Classification system for some subjects, while the Bentham and Hooker Botanical Classification is employed for systematic works on specific plant groups and species. The collection is especially rich in plant taxonomy, economic botany, early works, as well as plant cytology, physiology, and biochemistry.

553. **CRIS/USDA.** U.S. Department of Agriculture, 1983- .
A database for agriculturally related research projects. It covers current research in agriculture and related sciences, and is available from DIALOG.

554. **Entomology: A Guide to Information Sources.** Gilbert, Pamela, and Chris J. Hamilton. London: Mansell, 1983. 237p.
This is both an introduction and a source book for entomology. Arranged by subject instead of systematic group, it is valuable as an alternate method of entry to the subject.

QL468.2 G54 1983 Sci Ref

555. **Excerpta Botanica.** Stuttgart, Germany: Fischer, 1959- . 4/yr.
This is one of the foremost sources for information in botany and allied areas. Arranged in several sections, each issue deals with selected countries and is then subdivided by botanical classes. Section A, "Taxonomica et Chrologica," is a series of references to systematic botany. The annotations in this section are either in English, French, or German. The choice of language is mainly dependent on the original language of the material being annotated. This section also abstracts periodical literature of herbaria, gardens, museums, congresses, biographies, and bibliographies. Section B, "Sociologica," is an international bibliographic listing of mainly monographic material on plant geography and ecology. There are no annotations in this section. Each new issue focuses on selected countries and then is further subdivided by botanical categories. The entire work is a major source to the literature of botany.

QK1 E9 Sci

556. **Farm and Garden Index.** Wooster, OH: Bell & Howell, 1978- . quarterly.
The index purports to cover about 120 agricultural and horticultural periodicals. It has excellent coverage of materials ranging from the highly technical to the mundane. The focus is on practice and considerably less on theory. Good cross-indexing is available for the novice or first-time user.

Z5071 .A3 F3 Sci

557. **Flowering Plant Index of Illustration and Information.** Isaacson, Richard T., comp. Boston: G. K. Hall, 1979. 2v. **Supplement**, 1982. 2v.
An index which indicates where illustrations in over 100 different titles may be found. Arranged both by common name and by botanical name, this is an invaluable reference tool for anyone from the school child locating a picture for an assignment to a world class researcher needing an illustration. It is indispensable.

558. **Gardening: A Guide to the Literature.** Isaacson, Richard J. New York: Garland, 1985. 198p.
An annotated bibliography arranged by broad subject area. Within each subject area titles are arranged by the compiler with the most important or useful titles first. It is written with the general gardener in mind.

SB450 .97 .I82 1985 Sci Ref

559. **Geographical Guide to Floras of the World.** Blake, Sidney Fay. Washington, DC: U.S. Government Printing Office, 1942-1961. 2v.
This is an excellent work that is still quite useful despite its age. It catalogs the literature on floras by continent, country, and region. Annotations to the various entries

Z5358 .A12 B5 Sci Ref

are short but to-the-point. Popular works and local areas are not included, so the geographical range can be quite large. In two parts, part 1 contains entries on Africa, Australia, North America, South America, and the Oceanic islands. Part 2 is a listing of entries for Western Europe. The second part is somewhat different from the first in its treatment. First, works on pteridophytes, weeds, and poisonous plants are included. The second part also indicates a library location, if known, for libraries other than the National Agriculture Library.

560. **Gray Herbarium Index, Harvard University.** Boston: G. K. Hall, 1968. 10v. **Supplement**, 1978.

    The Gray Herbarium is an internationally recognized collection of materials. This is a catalog of its impressive collection of material on vascular plants of the Western Hemisphere. Mainly an index with multiple entries to name and literature citations, it is an excellent starting point for producing a bibliography in this specialized area. The material here will certainly need to be updated with more recent material from other sources, however.

561. **Guide to Information Sources in the Botanical Sciences.** Davis, Elisabeth B. Littleton, CO: Libraries Unlimited, 1987. 175p.

    Well organized for efficient use, this work is divided into three sections: bibliographic control, ready-reference sources, and additional sources. Each section begins with a practical introduction that indicates coverage. The annotations are sometimes not evaluative and subjects are not included in the index. Although selective, it is a good addition to guidebooks on botany literature.

562. **Index Bergeyana.** Buchanan, Robert E., ed. Baltimore, MD: Williams & Wilkins, 1966. 1472p.

    An impressive work which examines material that was not covered, or covered only marginally, in Bergey's *Manual of Determinative Bacteria* (Baltimore, MD: Williams & Wilkins, 1974). An annotated bibliography dealing with bacteria taxa, the majority of its annotations are critical and evaluative in nature, making this work a selection for inclusion here even given its age. There is a long bibliography, even for botany, which is arranged by author of the cited material. Overall, this is an evaluative tool for the literature prior to 1966 which is not covered in Bergey.

563. **Index Kewensis. Planetarum Phanerogamarum Nomina et Synonyma Omnium Generum et Specierum a Linnaeo Usque ad Annum MCCCCLXXXV Complectens.** Oxford, England: Clarendon, 1893-1895. 4v. 1299p. **Supplement**, 1886-95- . irregular.

    This amounts to the bible for the purposes of naming flowering plants, and its only rival is the *International Plant Index* (New Haven, CT: New York Botanical Garden, 1962-). This is the forerunner of the comprehensive indexes in names of plants. The supplements have deviated markedly from the five-year frequency, but continue to add names to the master listing.

564. **Index of Fungi.** Kew, England: Commonwealth Mycological Institute, 1940- . semiannual.

    This is a standard registry containing the names of new varieties, species, and genera of fungi. The entries are gleaned from the world literature dealing with fungi. Well indexed, it is a valuable tool in this particular area.

+ 67-76

565. **Index to American Botanical Literature, 1886-1966.** Torrey Botanical Club. Boston: Z5358
G. K. Hall, 1969. 4v. **Supplement, 1977.**

.A4

This is essentially a catalog of material concerning botany which has been published
since 1886. The entries cover a range consisting in part of taxonomy, phylogeny, and
floristics of the fungi, pteridophytes, bryophytes, and spermatophytes; morphology,
anatomy, cytology, genetics, physiology, and pathology of the same groups; plant ecology;
and general botany. The work is valuable for its checklist features for older material and is
particularly useful for turn of the century material.

T6

Sci

Ref

566. **Index to Plant Distribution Maps in North American Periodicals through 1972.** Z5354
Phillips, W. Louis, and Ronald L. Stuckey. Boston: G. K. Hall, 1976. 686p.

.E1

A specific source for specific information, this work compiles and indexes plant
distribution maps in North American periodicals. The internal order is by the taxon mapped. In the instances where there are more than one set of illustrations for a particular taxa,
the entries are chronological. Each entry includes the name of the taxon mapped, type of
map, geographical distribution, periodical reference, and author of the article. The source
includes a list of books containing plant distribution maps, geographically arranged.

P55

Sci

Ref

567. **Information Sources in Agriculture and Food Science.** Lilley, G. P., ed. Boston: S494.5
Butterworths, 1981. 603p.

D6

This basic guide to the literature gives a short introduction to the various fields of
agricultural research followed by the sources themselves. Recommended for beginning
graduate students in the field.

J5

Sci

Ref

568. **International Bibliography of Vegetation Maps.** Kuchler, A. W., comp. Lawrence, Z664
KS: University of Kansas Libraries, 1965-1970. 4v.

.K2

In the same manner that *Index to Plant Distribution Maps in North American
Periodicals through 1972* (see entry 566) deals with vegetation maps for North America,
this source deals with vegetation maps for botanical, agricultural, and biological geographic studies. The items are noted by geographical area and then by date. The entries for each
map include title, color, scale, author, legend transcript, and location and date published.

no.21
etc.
Map
Coll.

569. **Range Science: A Guide to Information Sources.** Vallentine, John F., and Phillip L. Z5074
Sims. Detroit, MI: Gale, 1980. 231p.

.R27

An annotated guide to range science sources, including periodicals, books, organizations, and government reports, that also discusses manual and online search techniques.
The structure of the literature manual does not sacrifice practical considerations.

v33

Sci

Ref

570. **Trees and Shrubs of the United States: A Bibliography for Identification.** Little, Z5356
Elbert L., and Barbara H. Honkala. Washington, DC: U.S. Government Printing Office,
1976. 56p.

.T8

This listing is subdivided by the classifications of popular tree and shrub guides
published in the United States. In some cases highly technical monographs are included,
but not with enough frequency to recommend this as a comprehensive bibliography. In addition to the federal materials expected, some state government documents are included.
This is a good source of material with a long literature life.

L56

Sci

A 1.38:
1336
Gov
Doc

ENCYCLOPEDIAS

571. **Atlas of Plant Life.** Edlin, Herbert. New York: John Day, 1973. 128p.

This is a geographical representation of plant life on a continent by continent basis. In addition to the vegetation distribution maps, there are also sections on climate. An interesting section on the spread of plants by man completes the work. The index is arranged using the common name, and the Latin equivalent is given in a table. Excellent graphics are used to convey a complex concept in this well prepared atlas.

572. **Chilton's Encyclopedia of Gardening.** Stangl, Martin. Radnor, PA: Chilton, 1975. 206p.

This is a basic gardening book covering the initial planning of the garden to harvesting. It contains sections on tools, insecticides and pest control, and fertilizers. This is a good first source as well as a continuing source for basic gardening information. Not well indexed, it is still serviceable.

573. **Colour Atlas of Poisonous Plants.** Frohne, Dietrich. London: Wolfe, 1984. 291p.

Covers those plants which are indigenous or naturalized in central and western Europe, as well as important decorative and house plants. Contains many color photographs. The distinctive European slant makes this less useful for U.S. readers, but researchers will find it helpful.

574. **Diseases and Pests of Ornamental Plants.** 5th ed. Pirone, Pascal P. New York: Wiley, 1978. 566p.

The book begins with a summary of various plant diseases, pests and damaging insects, and the control of both diseases and pest problems. The second part of the book contains information on specific diseases grouped by the name of the host. Each disease or pest is described with an accompanying recommendation for control or eradication. The book has numerous illustrations and footnotes that lead to primary literature. The comprehensive nature of this book makes it a natural choice for both amateur gardeners as well as professionals.

575. **Encyclopedia of American Forest and Conservation History.** Davis, Richard C., ed. New York: Macmillan, 1983. 2v.

The goal in compiling this major work was to produce the standard authoritative guide and reference to the history of forestry, conservation, forest industries, and other forest related subjects in the United States. Articles are both factual and interpretive. Major articles are signed and most include a bibliography. Photographs are selected from the Forest History Society Media Archives.

576. **Encyclopedia of Ferns: An Introduction to Ferns, Their Structure, Biology, Economic Importance, Cultivation, and Propagation.** Portland, OR: Timber Press, 1987. 433p.

This is not a complete encyclopedia of all living ferns, an identification manual, or a classification of ferns. It is an encyclopedia of ferns which are cultivated. In this more restricted area, this is an excellent contribution. The coverage is international, including many uncommon ferns. Once the actual scope of the work is understood, this is an excellent reference source for public and academic libraries.

577. **Encyclopedia of Mushrooms.** Dickinson, Colin, and John Lucas, eds. New York: Crescent, 1983. 280p.

This book is somewhat mistitled. It is an encyclopedia in that the first part concerns the basics of mushrooms. These include a section on biology, the basic mushroom, and the use of mushrooms by man. The second part of the book is clearly not an encyclopedia but a field guide to the identification of specific mushrooms. Both sections are well done, but some indication of the true nature of the work should be included in the title.

578. **Illustrated Encyclopedia of Indoor Plants.** Beckett, Kenneth, and Gillian Beckett. Garden City, NJ: Doubleday, 1977. 192p.

This is a guide to house plants with a large number of illustrations that help convey the information on ideal growing conditions and methods of taking cuttings and transplanting of plants. This is a good, general guide which will be of interest to public libraries.

579. **International Code of Botanical Nomenclature.** Stafleu, F. A., ed. Boston: Junk, 1983. 472p.

This book spells out the rules and norms for establishing botanical names. The present code is the result of continued meeting of the International Botanical Congress. The text is in English, French, and German. This is a major item for inclusion in a research or university collection.

QK96
.S7
Sci
or
QK11
.I4
Sci

580. **Living Plants of the World.** Milne, Lorus, and Margery Milne. New York: Random House, 1975. 336p.

A layperson's descriptive guide to most common plants, this work provides excellent descriptions and uses for many species of plants. The illustrations in both color and black and white are excellent and are well integrated into the book. This would be an excellent choice for public libraries.

QK45
.M54
Sci

581. **McGraw-Hill Encyclopedia of Food, Agriculture and Nutrition.** Lapedes, Daniel N., ed. New York: McGraw-Hill, 1977. 732p.

A good, solid work which discusses the relations between food, agriculture, and nutrition. Of particular note are the entries dealing with the world food problem and the various areas of agricultural productivity. The longer articles have bibliographies. In general, this sets out to cover the production and provision of food. It manages to meet its goal but with broad brush strokes. Recommended for its breadth of coverage.

TX349
.M2
Sci
Ref

582. **Morphologic Encyclopedia of Palynology.** Kremp, Gerhard Otto Wilhelm. Tucson, AZ: University of Arizona Press, 1968. 263p.

An encyclopedic dictionary which uses the original literature to define the terminology relating to spores and pollen. There are numerous plates which complement the descriptions. The majority of the descriptions are lengthy and involve considerable detail. This is an excellent source book for this particular area.

583. **New York Botanical Garden Illustrated Encyclopedia of Horticulture.** Evertee, Thomas H. New York: Garland, 1980-82. 10v.

The primary objective was a comprehensive description and evaluation of horticulture in the United States and Canada by amateurs and professionals. Most plant names are entered under the genus with cross references from the common name. Tips for home or garden cultivation are included. There is no bibliography.

SB317.58
E94
Sci
Ref

584. **Oxford Encyclopedia of Trees of the World.** Hora, Bagard, ed. New York: Crescent, 1986. 288p.

QK475
.O93
sci Ref

Aimed at the undergraduate level, this encyclopedia presents many color photographs and diagrams. It provides good basic information but does not serve as an in-depth source of information.

585. **Pocket Encyclopedia of Plant Galls in Colour.** rev. ed. Darlington, Arnold. New York: Philosophical Library, 1975.

In addition to considerable discussion of plant galls, this work doubles as a field guide to galls and the parasites responsible for their growth. Color illustrations are provided for each gall identified. The arrangement of the work is by host plant, subdivided by type of gall. A final section of the book discusses the life cycle of plant galls. This is a well done source that contains information difficult to uncover elsewhere.

586. **Rodale's Illustrated Encyclopedia of Herbs.** Kowalchik, Claire, and William H. Hylton, eds. Emmaus, PA: Rodale Press, 1987. 545p.

The strong point of this volume is its format. The major portion of the page is used for text with an outer column used for description, illustrations, and growing conditions. The text is clearly written and the illustrations are well done. This is recommended for public and nonacademic collections.

587. **Tanaka's Cyclopedia of Edible Plants of the World.** Tanaka, Tyozaburo. Tokyo, Japan: Yugaku-sha Publishing Co., 1976. 924p.

This book lists edible plants by Latin name. The entry for each plant listed consists of common name, distributions, edible parts, recipes, and literature citations. Two types of plants are not included: fodder and drugs. Almost a handbook, the work is fairly complete and without any discernible major geographic bias.

588. **Tobacco Encyclopedia.** Voges, Ernst, ed. Mainz, Germany: Tobacco Journal International, 1984. 468p.

Divided into two parts, part 1 consists of a short entry dictionary of tobacco related terms. Part 2 consists of short, unsigned articles arranged by subject area, such as history, leaf types, cultivation, and curing.

DICTIONARIES

589. **Agricultural Terms.** 2nd ed. Phoenix, AZ: Oryx Press, 1978. 122p.

Contains a list of terms used as subject headings in the *Bibliography of Agriculture* (Phoenix, AZ: Oryx, 1980-). This is a good locator for specific terms, but is not a major dictionary source.

590. **Ainsworth and Bisby's Dictionary of the Fungi.** 7th ed. Hawksworth, D. L., B. C. Sutton, and G. C. Ainsworth. Kew, England: Commonwealth Mycological Institute, 1983. 445p.

Contains short definitions with references. This is a good, basic dictionary without frills.

591. **Black's Agricultural Dictionary.** 2nd ed. Dalal-Clayton, D. B. London: A&C Black, 1985. 432p.

Primarily covering British agriculture, this reference source is for students, farmers, and others in agriculture.

592. Botanical Latin: History, Grammar, Syntax, Terminology, and Vocabulary. 3rd ed. rev. Stearn, William T. North Pomfret, VT: David & Charles, 1983. 566p.

A dictionary of Latin terms together with the botanical rules for forming the names of plants. There are discussions of plant habitats, geographical names, color terms, and symbols and abbreviations. Provided are a general bibliography to like works, along with a vocabulary listing that reduces the need for a Latin dictionary. Recommended for both the novice and the professional alike.

QK 10
.S7
1973
Sci
Ref

593. Collegiate Dictionary of Botany. Swartz, Delbert. New York: Ronald Press, 1971. 520p.

This is a specialized dictionary in that common botanical terms which can be found in other dictionaries are not included here. The entries are gathered from a variety of sources, most coming from the primary literature. A distinct U.S. bias in the terms and their usage can be detected. Latin names are normally not included here, since they can be located in other dictionaries. This is recommended because of its distinct contribution to the area and because it does not overlap to a great extent with *Dictionary of Botany* (see entry 594).

QK9
.S88
Sci
Ref

594. Dictionary of Botany. Little, R. John, and C. Eugene Jones. New York: Van Nostrand Reinhold, 1980. 400p.

This dictionary does not include archaic or seldom used words. It contains very short entries and some illustrations are provided. This is a useful beginning dictionary and is more up to date than *Collegiate Dictionary of Botany* (see entry 593) but with surprisingly little overlap.

QK9
.L735
Sci
Ref

595. Dictionary of Cultivated Plants and Their Regions of Diversity. 2nd ed. Zeven, A. C., and J. M. J. de Wet. Wageningen, West Germany: Centre for Agricultural Publishing and Documentation, 1982. 263p.

The aim of this dictionary is to give the reader quick reference to the regions of diversity of cultivated plants. Arranged by geographic region of the world, it contains many maps showing distributions. Known somatic chromosome numbers and genome formulae are also provided. A botanical name index is included, making this an excellent source for some elusive information.

SB71
.Z46
1982
Sci
Ref

596. Dictionary of Economic Plants. 2nd ed. Uphof, Johannes Cornelius Theodorus. New York: Stechert-Hafner, 1968. 591p.

This is a dictionary of plants important to the agricultural economy. The entries are arranged by Latin name with a cross-reference to the common name. There is a brief description of the plant which includes geographic dispersion, the product or use of the plant, and some illustrations. Over 9,500 plant species are detailed. This is included here because it contains concise information on a wide variety of plants.

QK9
.U6
1968
Sci
Ref

597. Dictionary of Gardening. 2nd ed. Chittenden, Fred J., and Patrick M. Synge, eds. Oxford, England: Oxford University Press, 1974. 4v.

This is a scholarly production which includes terms used in gardening and horticulture. This is not a reference for novice gardeners, but is more a professional's tool. The work was sponsored by the Royal Horticultural Society. Some entries are quite lengthy and almost encyclopedic in depth.

SB450
.95
.D53
1992
Sci
Ref

598. Dictionary of Nutrition and Food Technology. 5th ed. Bender, Arnold E. London: Butterworths, 1982. 309p.

TX349
.B4
1982
Sci Ref

A multipurpose dictionary which deals with chemistry, biochemistry, microbiology, and mechanical engineering as they might relate to nutrition and food sciences. The distinctive slant of the definitions gives this work a recommendation for any research or teaching collection in nutrition and food science.

599.   Dictionary of Plants Used by Man. Usher, George. New York: Hafner, 1974. 619p.
Plants which are edible as well as inedible are covered here. If there is food value or economic value, this work will normally list the plant. The arrangement of the book is alphabetical by plant genus, and the entry for each plant consists of the vernacular name, country of origin, brief description of the genus, and the total number of species.

600.   Dictionary of the Flowering Plants and Ferns. 8th ed. Willis, John Christopher. Cambridge, England: Cambridge University Press, 1985. 1245p.
This dictionary was first published in 1897, which is the primary reason for its inclusion here. It is a scholarly work that excludes common plant names, plant products, and general terms. A listing of accepted plant names with references to Bentham and Hooker's *Genera Plantarum* (London: A. Black, 1862) and Engler's *Syllabus* (Berlin: Borntracger, 1954) is an important feature of the book. For a number of entries, brief characteristics of subfamilies are given. This is an excellent source for original descriptions of flowering plants and ferns.

601.   Dictionary of Useful and Everyday Plants and Their Common Names. Howes, F. N. Cambridge, England: Cambridge University Press, 1975. 290p.
This work, together with Willis's *Dictionary* (see entry 600) gives an excellent overview of the plant world. Howes includes the majority of the very elements that Willis excludes. The entries here consist of general botanical terminology, trade names and common names of plants and commercial plant products. The arrangement is by Latin names, countries of origin, and practical uses. Most short essays included have to do with the more general topics. This is an excellent companion work to Willis.

602.   Elsevier's Dictionary of Botany. Amsterdam, Netherlands: Elsevier, 1979. 2v.
In addition to supplying definitions, this dictionary lists French, German, Latin, and Russian equivalents of the English terms. The first volume covers plant names. The second is a dictionary of basic terms. A good dictionary with the added value of being multilingual.

603.   Elsevier's Lexicon of Plant Pests and Diseases. Merino-Rodriques, Manuel, comp. Amsterdam, Netherlands: Elsevier, 1966. 351p.
This work is divided into two sections: (1) zooparasites and (2) phytoparasites. Terms are entered in Latin, English, French, Italian, Spanish, and German. This makes the dictionary useful for multilingual needs. Although dated, it contains terms in common usage with a worldwide linguistic focus.

604.   Glossary of Botanic Terms with Their Derivation and Accent. 4th ed. Jackson, Benjamin Dayden. London: Duckworth, 1960. 481p.
This is the English language botanical dictionary of choice. Terms, with their Latin equivalents, derivation, and pronunciation, are listed together with short, but to the point, definitions. Generic terms are listed, allowing the nonspecialist an entry point to terms. Even given its age, it commands the respect and faithful following of botanists. It is highly recommended for public or academic libraries of virtually any size.

605. **Glossary of Mycology.** rev. ed. Snell, Walter H., and Ester A. Dick. Cambridge, MA: Harvard University Press, 1971. 181p.

    A special feature of this dictionary is the color terms from *Repertoire de Couleurs* (Paris: Societe François des Chrysanthemistes, 1905). Other than this feature, the work is a very adequate glossary covering terms dealing with fungi research and its applications.

606. **Hortus Third: A Concise Dictionary of Plants Cultivated in the United States and Canada.** New York: Macmillan, 1976. 1290p.

    A very important work that identifies all species and varieties of plants cultivated in North America. There is a description of the geographic spread, the use, and the methods of cultivation of each plant listed. Common plant names are contained in the index with references to the Latin name in the text. A necessary tool for research and technical libraries.

607. **Index Nominum Genericorum (Plantarum).** Utrecht, Netherlands: Bohn, Scheltema and Holkema, 1979. 3v. **Supplement,** 1986. 126p.

    Together with the supplement, this is a listing of valid generic names of plants that have been named in the botanical literature. There is a citation to the first publication of the name. This is a very important work for research collections and to anyone interested in the history of a particular plant name.

608. **Russian-English Botanical Dictionary.** Macura, Paul. Columbus, OH: Slavica, 1982. 678p.

    An extensive listing of Russian, English, and Latin names of plants, trees, shrubs, fungi, and lichens. A large number of biological and botanical terms can also be found.

609. **Vocabularium Botanicum.** Steinmetz, E. F. Amsterdam, Netherlands: Steinmetz, 1953. 362p.

    A dictionary of terms used in the trade literature and catalogs. It is multilingual with terms arranged by Latin or Greek followed by an equivalent term or terms in Dutch, German, English, and French. At this point, its use is predominantly historical; however, it is a good source for trade terms that are difficult to trace.

HANDBOOKS AND FIELD GUIDES

610. **Atlas of United States Trees.** Washington, DC: U.S. Government Printing Office, 1971-81. 6v.

    Each volume in this magnificent series contains an introduction with an explanation of the maps that follow. A discussion of the scientific and common names of the trees for each region is provided, along with notations on rare and endangered species. Volume 1 of this first-rate atlas covers conifers and temperate hardwoods. Volume 2 covers the trees and common shrubs of Alaska, and volume 3 covers minor western hardwoods. Minor eastern hardwoods are covered in volume 4, and the trees of Florida are covered in volume 5.

611. **Audubon Society Field Guide to North American Wildflowers, Eastern Region.** Niering, William A., and Nancy C. Olmstead. New York: Knopf, 1983. 887p.

612. **Audubon Society Field Guide to North American Wildflowers, Western Region.** Spellenberg, Richard. New York: Knopf, 1979. 862p.

Together these guides cover all wildflowers on the North American continent. Pictures of individual wildflowers are arranged by color with a full description of the flower. Scientific names and common names are listed, together with the vernacular and regional names. This is a well conceived and well done field guide series. Recommended for any library.

613. **Basic Plant Pathology Methods.** Dhangra, Onkar D., and James B. Sinclair. Boca Raton, FL: CRC Press, 1985. 376p.

This is an excellent entry point for determining a particular plant disease. The procedures described in this thorough source range from the sterilization of the test apparatus to chemical control. A large section also deals with biological control.

614. **Bergey's Manual of Systematic Bacteriology.** Holt, John G., and Noel R. Krieg. Baltimore, MD: Williams & Wilkins, 1984- . v. 1- .

This is a classified listing of bacteria cited in the world literature. Included in the listings are descriptions taken from the primary literature, such as the identification of elements. A specific tool for in-depth research centers.

615. **Chemistry of Plant Hormones.** Takahashi, Nobutaka, ed. Boca Raton, FL: CRC Press, 1986. 282p.

A discussion of the chemistry of the five principal hormone groups is the main thrust of the work. There is a review of the history of each group, its isolation and detection, metabolism, and structural determination. The result is an excellent work delineating the role of growth regulators in higher plants. It is highly recommended for research collections.

616. **Common Weeds of the United States.** U.S. Department of Agriculture. Washington, DC: U.S. Government Printing Office, 1971. 463p.

A selective compilation of common weeds found mainly in crop lands, grasslands, aquatic areas, and some noncrop land weeds. There is a great deal of detail given in each entry, to the point of being a scientific analysis. Maps of geographic distribution are included. For those interested in weeds on a level beyond that of the layperson, this is an excellent source.

617. **Complete Book of Mushrooms.** Rinaldi, Augusto, and Vassili Tyndalo. New York: Crescent, 1985. 310p.

Though this is an excellent handbook for amateur mushroom hunters, it is flawed by the lack of geographic location notations for some mushroom varieties. Divided into two parts, the first part is a description of the mushroom, including its flavor, odor, and whether or not it is poisonous. A majority of the entries have color illustrations. The second part is a more general description of mushrooms. A listing of information on cooking, nutrients, and preserving mushrooms is provided.

618. **Conifers.** Rushford, Keith D. New York: Facts on File, 1987. 232p.

This is a handbook aimed at the informed but nonresearch focused reader. The definitions, descriptions, and bibliography are intended for the layperson. This is a good choice for public and nonresearch collections.

619. **CRC Handbook of Plant Science in Agriculture.** Christie, B. R., ed. Boca Raton, FL: CRC Press, 1987. 2v.

A new handbook composed of expert papers on all aspects of plant science in agriculture. The scope of the work runs from a discussion of chromosome numbers through a discussion of drug crops. Volume 1 has 304 pages, volume 2 contains 288 pages. This is a well done source.

620.   **CRC Handbook of Processing and Utilization in Agriculture.** Wolff, Ivan A., ed. Boca Raton, FL: CRC Press, 1982- . 2v.
   Dealing primarily with agricultural processes which occur after harvest, volume 1 covers animal products, while volume 2 deals with horticultural products. This is a handbook of processes based on the literature of agriculture and botany. Specific to an agriculture collection or to field botany.

S698
.C7
1982
Sci
Ref

621.   **Economics of Agricultural Policies.** Gardner, B. New York: Macmillan, 1987. 385p.
   Concentrates on the development and application of tools for analysis of governmental policy in agriculture. The slant is toward econometric models and their effective use in the area of agriculture. Topics include price support programs, price stabilization, international trade, and cooperatives. This is an excellent tool for those who study agriculture in statistical and economic modes.

HD1761
.6245
1987
Main

622.   **Edible Plants of the Prairie: An Ethnobotanical Guide.** Kindscher, Kelly. Lawrence, KS: University Press of Kansas, 1987. 276p.
   This work is the result of the author's 80-day trek across the prairies. It will find an audience among those who are interested in native fruits and vegetables of the prairie used by prehistoric peoples, Native Americans, early explorers, and others. Though it will be of limited interest, it is the only material of its kind.

623.   **Families of Flowering Plants Arranged According to a New System Based on Their Probable Phylogeny.** 3rd ed. Hutchinson, John. Oxford, England: Clarendon Press, 1973. 2v.
   The author is one of the outstanding botanists of his day. This work is included here not because of its acceptance, but because it is a different system from the standard of Linnaeus. Bentham and Hooker are an example of yet another system. This is a necessary book for botanical research collections.

QK97
.H82
1973
Sci
Ref

624.   **Flowers of Europe: A Field Guide.** Polunin, Oleg. London: Oxford University Press, 1969. 662p.
   This basic guide to wildflowers in Europe provides bare to adequate information on flowers and their habitat and uses. A glossary of French, German, and Italian names of flowers is listed. Color photographs of some flowers are provided in the appendix.

QK281
.P65
Sci

625.   **Forestry Handbook.** 2nd ed. Wenger, Karl F. New York: Wiley, 1984. 1335p.
   Written for the practicing field forester, this handbook contains methods, formulas, tables, conversion factors, and other data commonly used in the United States and Canada. It includes many tables, charts, and diagrams.

SD373
F58
1984
Sci Ref

626.   **Guide to Standard Floras of the World.** Frodin, D. G. Cambridge, England: Cambridge University Press, 1984. 619p.
   In bibliography form, this is a one-volume guide to the most useful nominally complete floras and checklists dealing with the vascular plants of the world and their component parts. It is arranged by geographic region.

QK45.2
.F76
1984
Sci
Ref

627.   **Guide to the Study of Lichens.** Duncan, Ursula K. Arbroath, Angus, Scotland: Buncle, 1959. 164p. **Supplement,** 1965. 144p.

589.1
D912
Sci

A comprehensive guide to the families and genera of lichen. The arrangement of the works is systematic with good cross-referencing. A glossary and bibliography round out the work. This is a very specific book of greatest utility to the specialist.

628. Handbook of Soils and Climate in Agriculture. Kilmer, Victor J., ed. Boca Raton, FL: CRC Press, 1982. 445p.

An excellent handbook containing much information of utility to soil conservationists as well as to those in agriculture. Contains up-to-date data and interpretations.

629. Living Trees of the World. Everett, T. H. London: Thames & Hudson, 1969. 315p.

In order to be included in this book the plant must be 20 feet tall when mature. In effect, this is the working definition of a tree in this source. Included are pteridiphytes, gymnosperms, angiosperms, monosotyledons, and dicotyledons. A comprehensive identification handbook.

630. Manual of Grasses of the United States. Hitchcock, A. S. New York: Dover, 1971. 2v.

Covers virtually every aspect of grasses in the United States. A large portion of the book is devoted to synonyms of grasses that have appeared at one time or another in the botanical literature. The two volumes include identification keys, narrative descriptions, ranges, and drawings of common grasses of the United States. This is an extremely comprehensive work.

631. Models in Plant Physiology and Biochemistry. Newman, David W., and Kenneth G. Wilson, eds. Boca Raton, FL: CRC Press, 1987. 3v.

Comprised of contributions by leading scientists, this work features models consisting of one or more illustrations followed by a brief description of the model. The first volume features models of photosynthesis, proteins, and lipids. Volume 2 is concerned with nitrogen, sulfur, and secondary compounds. The final volume deals with transport phenomena, molecular biology, and biotechnology. This is an excellent source for theoretical discussions of plants and processes related to plants.

632. Mosses with Hand Lenses and Microscope. Grout, Abel Joel. Ann Arbor, MI: University Microfilms, 1979. 416p. 5 parts.

This is a standard field handbook for the identification of mosses. Some illustrations aid in the identification, but the majority of the book is descriptive. A good choice for the amateur through the seasoned specialist.

633. Mushrooms of North America. Miller, Orson K. New York: Dutton, 1985. 368p.

This is a guide to mushrooms and other fungi including puffballs, earthstars, and tongue fungi. Each of the entries is described in very close detail. With the addition of excellent photographs and an illustrated glossary, this is a first-rate source. The completeness of the entry extends to the mushroom's edibility, habitat, and range. Highly recommended for any collection whose users have an interest in mushrooms.

634. Mycology Guidebook. rev. ed. Stevens, Russell B. Seattle, WA: University of Washington Press, 1981. 712p.

This is an expert manual written by experts. The intent is to supply material for those teaching introductory mycology courses. As such, it includes teaching aids. Because of the care taken by eminent researchers in the area, this is a definitive work and is not intended for the novice.

635. **North American Range Plants.** Stubbendieck, J., Stephan L. Hatch, and Katie J. Hirsch. Lincoln, NE: University of Nebraska Press, 1986. 465p.

The 200 species in this book were selected because of their abundance, desirability, or noxious properties. Nomenclature, life span, origin, inflorescence, physical characteristics, a line drawing, distribution map, and forage value are included in each entry.

636. **North American Trees (Exclusive of Mexico and Tropical United States): A Handbook Designed for Field Use, with Plates and Distribution Maps.** 3rd ed. Preston, Richard J. Cambridge, MA: MIT Press, 1976. 399p.

This is a good, basic field handbook for tree identification. The descriptions are usually accompanied by line drawings of the tree. Individual entries include leaf form, habitat, and twig and bark characteristics at the minimum. Additional information such as fruit, floral design, and value are given as necessary. A manual for the novice through the specialist level.

637. **Organic Gardener's Complete Guide to Vegetables and Fruits.** Emmaus, PA: Rodale Press, 1982. 510p.

A practical guide for the home gardener, using completely natural organic methods. Part 1 deals with vegetables; part 2 with fruits. Early chapters cover garden planning, basic planting methods, and basic cultural techniques. The majority of the book covers 57 vegetable and 45 fruit crops.

638. **Plant Disease Handbook.** 4th ed. Westcott, Cynthia. New York: Van Nostrand Reinhold, 1979. 803p.

A guide book to specific diseases, the host plant, and the control of the disease. There is some discussion of the history of the disease, but the majority of the work is descriptive. Cross-references are drawn between the host, the disease, and the control. A glossary, bibliography, and list of agricultural experiment stations is also included. This is an excellent work, although the sections dealing with control could be updated.

639. **Plant Protoplasts.** Fowke, Larry C., and Fred Constabel, eds. Boca Raton, FL: CRC Press, 1985. 256p.

An excellent source for information on plant protoplasts. It deals with isolation and culture, regeneration, fusion, the cell cycle and protoplasts, and biotechnology issues. The range of material covered in this volume is very large, yet it is done well. Recommended for research collections.

640. **Plants of the World.** de Wit, H. C. D. London: Thames & Hudson, 1967-1968. 3v.

This is a translation from the Dutch of a three-part handbook. Part 1 treats the higher plants, monocotyledons and some dicotyledons. Part 2 lists the remainder of the dicotyledons. Part 3 treats the lower plants, including ferns, fungi, mosses, and lichens. Entries include a description, distribution, habitat, uses, and a history of the name of the plant.

641. **Poisonous Plants: A Colour Field Guide.** Woodward, Lucia. Newton Abbot, England: David & Charles, 1985. 192p.

A quick guide to toxicity and treatment which provides a color photograph with each entry. It is recommended for most general libraries.

642. **Seed Identification Manual.** Martin, Alexander Campbell, and William D. Barkley. Los Angeles, CA: University of California Press, 1973. 221p.

A catalog of photographs arranged by general location. Following the photographs is a systematic arrangement of identification points. This is an excellent source because of the photographs and the deductive methodology used by the book to aid in the process of identification. It is recommended for agriculture and botanical libraries.

643. Trees of North America and Europe. Phillips, Roger. New York: Random House, 1978. 224p.

A two-part identification guide. The first part consists of a leaf index which, in turn, supplies an index number to the second and main part. Part 2 includes a basic entry on each tree, including a photograph or drawing. This is a competitor to *Living Trees of the World* (see entry 629). Between the two, identification of most trees in North America and Europe is possible. Recommended for most libraries.

644. Westcott's Plant Disease Handbook. 4th ed. Horst, R. Kenneth. New York: Van Nostrand Reinhold, 1979. 803p.

An impressive work divided into two sections. The first deals with plant diseases and their pathogens. A description of the disease is provided along with a recommended control. The common name or names of the disease are also included. The second section lists common plants and the diseases to which they are susceptible. In terms of identification and short description, this is a necessary part of most reference collections.

645. Wild Flowers of the United States. Rickett, Harold William. New York: McGraw-Hill, 1966-1975. 6v. **Index**, 1975. 152p.

An authoritative and comprehensive guide to the wildflowers of the United States. The descriptions, however, are not necessarily written for the specialist. The layperson will find this a very intelligible work. Color photographs or line drawings are provided with each entry. This is a catalog of extant wildflowers in the United States. Given its comprehensive nature, it is highly recommended for most libraries.

TREATISES

646. Fungi: An Advanced Treatise. Ainsworth, G. C., and A. S. Sussman. New York: Academic Press, 1965-1973. 4v.

This is a very authoritative work dealing with the cell, the basic organism, and clusters of fungi. A taxonomic review section and author and subject indexes are provided. While somewhat dated at this point, this is still highly cited and used by botanists.

647. Illustrated Reference on Cacti & Other Succulents. 2nd ed. rev. Lamb, Edgar. London: Blandford Press, 1978. 4v.

The focus of the work is horticultural. As a survey of the succulents of the world it makes a chief contribution to horticultural research. Also of note are the growing instructions for each of the succulents discussed. A specialized source for research collections.

648. Plant Pathology: An Advanced Treatise. Horsfall, James Gordon. New York: Academic Press, 1959-1960. 3v.

This is an important work because it takes a different track in examining plant disease. The direction is toward disease concepts rather than specific diseases. It is an excellent, well-documented work. Volume 1 covers scope, importance and history of plant pathology; pathological processes; defense devices; predispositions of the diseased plant; and therapy. Volume 2 covers pathogenicity and its inhibition, and volume 3 discusses diseased population of plants and epidemics and their control.

DIRECTORIES

649. **Agricultural and Veterinary Sciences International Who's Who.** 3rd ed. Harlow, England: Longman, 1987. 2v.

Part 1 covers biographical profiles alphabetically arranged by surname. Part 2 is a country and subject index. A current source of information on notables in the two fields.

650. **Animal Health Yearbook 1986. Annuaire de la Sante Animale. Anuario de Sanidad Animal.** Lanham, MD: UNIPUB, 1987. 222p.

SF600
.F6
Sci

Targeted toward those in need of information on international trade in livestock and livestock products. The scope is truly international with glossaries in Arabic, Chinese, German, and Russian. The volume is current through 1986 and will be of interest to specialized collections only.

651. **Biographical Dictionary of Botanists Represented in the Hunt Institute Portrait Collection of the Hunt Botanical Library at the Carnegie-Mellon University.** Boston: G. K. Hall, 1972. 451p.

QK26
.H83
Sci

Mainly of interest for historical purposes, as one must have a portrait hanging in the Hunt Library to be included. Good biographical information is provided for each individual. Includes botanists, horticulturists, and others who work with plants.

652. **Dictionary of British and Irish Botanists and Horticulturists Including Plant Collectors and Botanical Artists.** Desmond, Ray. London: Taylor & Francis, 1977. 747p.

QK26
.D47
1977
Sci
Ref

A directory of British and Irish botanists and horticulturists. Entries provide name; dates and places of birth and death; education, awards, honors, and selected publications; biographical references in books and periodicals; locations of plant collections, herbaria, manuscripts, drawings, and portraits; and any plant commemorating the individual. Predominantly useful for retrospective information.

653. **FAO Fertilizer Yearbook.** Rome: FAO, 1985. 35v.

S633
.F64
Sci

Compiled as a result of responses from questionnaires sent to 200 countries, the bulk of the work concerns nitrogen, phosphate, and potash fertilizers. Separate sections in Spanish, French, and English repeat the information. The consumption, use, and export of fertilizers is included, making this one of the most comprehensive compilations of information on fertilizers. A technical source for researchers and academic libraries.

654. **Great Botanical Gardens of the World.** Hyams, Edward. London: Bloomsbury, 1985. 288p.

QK71
.H9
Sci
Oversize

This is less a directory than a guidebook to some of the most renowned botanical gardens in the world. Grouped by continent, each entry gives a history and nature of the collection, any specialties, and the current research activities of the garden. Excellent photography makes this an exceptional directory as well as guidebook.

655. **Index Herbariorum: A Guide to the Location and Contents of the World's Public Herbaria.** 6th ed. Lanjouw, Joseph, and F. A. Stafleu. Utrecht, Netherlands: International Bureau for Plant Taxonomy and Nomenclature of the International Association for Plant Taxonomy, 1974. 2 parts.

QK95
.L3
Sci

Issued in two parts, this is a guide to herbaria around the world. Part 1, *Herbaria*, gives directory information for herbaria, arranged alphabetically by cities. Included are a list of publications and loan and exchange regulations. Part 2, *Collectors*, lists collectors, alphabetically arranged, with dates, locations, and the range of their collections. A unique reference source.

6 Chemistry

Chemistry is the science of transformation. Early man can be said to have practiced chemistry by cooking plant and animal matter over a fire. Modern chemistry, however, has stronger roots in the medieval attempts to convert base materials into gold. The alchemy of the Middle Ages produced the groundwork on which a considerable portion of modern chemistry rests.

The publication of Libavius's textbook, *Alchemia*, signaled the start of chemistry as a science. During the seventeenth through the beginning of the nineteenth centuries several important discoveries were made. These included the discovery of oxygen, the study of gases in general, and the formulation of the concept of chemical elements. With Dalton's atomic theory, the science of chemistry now had a conceptual model to frame several discoveries.

Discoveries in chemistry and the addition of new elements necessitated the normalization of both nomenclature and definition. Mendeleyev formulated what is now known as the table of periodic elements. He not only formulated the table, but based on perceived gaps in the table, suggested the future discovery of particular elements.

Beginning with the twentieth century, chemistry became more conscious of physics (and vice versa). The application of spectroscopy and the laws of thermodynamics suggested new avenues and discoveries in chemistry. The advent of quantum mechanics and its use in chemistry, quantum chemistry, led to additional advances.

Chemistry is now generally divided into organic chemistry and inorganic chemistry. There are other areas, but not as large, such as physical chemistry, analytical chemistry, and chemical physics.

The chemical literature is exceedingly broad. Some argue too broad. The future of chemistry is to continue to broaden as the techniques of physics, particularly, allow chemists to probe ever deeper into the structure of elements and the bonds they use. This can only mean the information required by the chemist will become increasingly more diverse and outside the realm of chemistry as defined by traditional libraries.

Despite these potential problems, chemistry is one of the best indexed and abstracted disciplines in science and technology. The premier abstracting and indexing tool in all of science, *Chemical Abstracts* (see entry 675), continues to control the literature of chemistry very well. Ancillary services, such as structure searching increase the potential of supplying the chemist with needed information. Even considering the expansion of chemistry, the tools are in place and expanding to allow good coverage of this discipline.

GUIDES TO THE LITERATURE

656. **Chemical Publications: Their Nature and Use.** 5th ed. Mellon, Melvin Guy. New York: McGraw-Hill, 1982. 419p.

QD8 .5
M44
1982
Sci Ref

Concentrates on the description of the standard reference tools in the field of chemistry. The descriptions are excellent for the most part, though sometimes tend to be too brief. A discussion of the uses to which the tools might be put is included.

657. **Communication, Storage and Retrieval of Chemical Information.** Ash, Janet E. Chichester, England: Ellis Horwood Ltd., 1985. 297p.

QD8.3
C66
1985
Sci

Primarily intended for those who both generate and use the chemical literature. An emphasis is placed on online databases, making this a very valuable source for those interested in entry level information about online services in chemistry.

658. **Guide to Basic Information Sources in Chemistry.** Anthony, Arthur. New York: Wiley, 1979. 219p.

QD8.5
A57
1979
Sci

This is a first stop source for nonprofessionals with a focus on pure chemistry as opposed to multidiscipline areas. The prime reason for its inclusion here is the fact that it examines literature from the user's standpoint.

659. **How to Find Chemical Information: A Guide for Practicing Chemists, Educators and Students.** 2nd ed. Maizell, Robert E. New York: Wiley, 1987. 402p.

QD8.5
M34
1987
Sci
Ref

This is a completely new edition of the 1979 work of similar title. It has been considerably expanded to include a greater range of information as well as updated information, and has increased 54 percent in page count over the first edition. Remaining a systematic guide to the literature of chemistry for students and librarians, it finds excellent utility not only in pure chemistry but in chemical engineering as well.

660. **Literature of Matrix Chemistry.** Skolnik, Herman. New York: Wiley, 1982. 297p.

As a result of its focus toward the serious practitioner or student of chemistry, this is a more difficult source than most guides to the literature. Chemical engineers will find this useful as well, though it is not a good source for general or beginning students.

661. **Use of Chemical Literature.** 3rd ed. Bottle, R. T., ed. London: Butterworths, 1979. 306p.

QD8.5
B6
1979
Sci
Ref

This is the classic guide to the literature. It is included here for that reason and because it contains excellent discussions of periodical literature and indexing and abstracting services. The individual sources mentioned may be dated, but this is still important for its view of the structure of the chemical literature.

ABSTRACTS, INDEXES, AND BIBLIOGRAPHIES

662. **American Chemical Society Primary Journal Database (CFTX).** Columbus, OH: American Chemical Society, 1980- . semimonthly.

An online database which provides quick access to the most current information in the chemical literature. Available from BRS.

663. **Analytical Abstracts.** London: Royal Society of Chemistry, 1954- . monthly.

Covers the field of analytical chemistry, continuing the lapsed section C of *British Abstracts* (see entry 666). Although monthly, the timeliness of this source is its major weakness. Material found here is often far behind the publication schedule of current journals.

664. **Bibliographic Atlas of Protein Spectra in the Ultraviolet and Visible Regions.** Kirschenbaum, Donald M., ed. New York: Plenum, 1984. 523p.

Covers the field of spectroscopic analysis of proteins. Even within this small area, the focus is only on a select area of the spectrum. Its indexing, however, betrays nothing of a special nature and is useful to researchers in any number of areas.

665. **Bibliography of Paper and Thin-Layer Chromatography 1970-73 and Survey of Applications.** Macek, Karel, et al. New York: Elsevier, 1976. 744p.

Because chromatography is such an important tool in chemistry, this bibliography, published as supplements to *Journal of Chromatography* (Amsterdam, Netherlands: Elsevier, 1958-), is an important addition to a research collection. The bibliography contains literature references not only to methodology related papers, but to advances in the underlying theory as well.

666. **British Abstracts.** London: Bureau of Abstracts, 1926-1953.

This was an important abstracting tool, included here for its retrospective coverage. It contained notoriously poor indexing and is primarily of historical importance at present.

667. **CA Search.** Columbus, OH: Chemical Abstracts Service, 1967- . semimonthly.

Provides a variety of information and references to chemistry related documents. Composed primarily of journal article references, all areas of chemistry are covered. This is an excellent database from a world-class provider. Available from DIALOG.

668. **CAOLD.** Columbus, OH: Chemical Abstracts Service.

This online file contains references to substances cited in *Chemical Abstracts* (see entry 675) prior to 1967. The database is being expanded backwards and uses the *CA* accession number, document type (for patents only), and registry numbers as index terms.

669. **CApreviews.** Columbus, OH: Chemical Abstracts Service, 1988- .

A literature alert online database which provides bibliographic information for documents not yet added into *Chemical Abstracts* File (see entry 675). The availability of material six to eight weeks prior to finding it online in *CA* is a major service improvement.

670. **CAS Online.** Columbus, OH: Chemical Abstracts Service, 1967- .

A series of online databases beginning with 1967 to the present which covers chemical science literature from over 12,000 journals, patents from 26 countries, books, conference proceedings, and government research reports.

671. **CASREACT.** Columbus, OH: Chemical Abstracts Service, 1988- .

This online database contains reaction information indexed by registry number. It may be searched using a substance in the reaction (reactant, product, reagent, solvent, or catalyst). The file is restricted to material published since 1985.

672. **CASSI Cumulative 1907-1984.** Columbus, OH: Chemical Abstracts Service, 1985. *QD1*
    A cumulative work containing information on serials and nonserials monitored by *C53* CAS and held by libraries throughout the world. It is an invaluable tool to locate libraries *Sci Ref* holding materials on chemistry. Complete bibliographic information for nearly 60,000 *Main* publications is included. Quarterly supplements beginning in 1985 add to its utility. *Ref*

673. **Chembooks: New Books and Journals.** Basel, Switzerland: Karger Libri, 1969- . annual.
    An annual bibliography covering pure and applied chemistry. Brief annotations are provided for items arranged under 22 subject areas. This is a good reference tool for keeping up with new materials in chemistry.

674. **Chemdex/Chemdex2/Chemdex3/.** 1972- .
    A series of dictionary files online, citing literature from 1972 to the present.

675. **Chemical Abstracts.** Columbus, OH: American Chemical Society, 1907- . weekly. *QD1*
    This is the most comprehensive scientific abstracting service in English of any field in *A51* science. Descriptive indexes are arranged in a range of sections under broad headings. *Sci Ref* Monographs are included. A multitude of spinoff products are available in both hard copy and online form. This is an excellent abstracting service with excellent products, and should serve as a model for other services. Available online as CHEMCON.

676. **Chemical Exposure.** Chemical Effects Information Center, 1974- .
    An online database of chemicals identified in human tissue, body fluids, and food animals. A wide range of information related to exposure to chemicals and pharmaceutical is contained within. Available from DIALOG.

677. **CHEMNAME.** Columbus, OH: Chemical Abstracts Service, 1967- . quarterly.
    An online substance searching and identification database. Provides nomenclature, trade names, synonyms, and substructure searching. Available from DIALOG.

678. **CHEMSEARCH.** Columbus, OH: Chemical Abstracts Service. semimonthly.
    An online dictionary listing of the most recently cited substances in *CA SEARCH* (see entry 667). This is a companion file to *CHEMNAME* (see entry 677). Available from DIALOG.

679. **CHEMSIS.** Columbus, OH: Chemical Abstracts Service, 1982- .
    An online dictionary, nonbibliographic file containing chemical substances cited once during a Collective Index Period of *Chemical Abstracts* (see entry 675). Available from DIALOG.

680. **ChemSmart.** Philadelphia: ISI, 1987.
    This is a software package allowing the user to build, search, and display chemical structure and reactions with a personal computer. It comes with a basic library of 250 organic compounds drawn from *Index Chemicus* (see entry 690). Additional specialized databases are available. This is an interesting and generally well written piece of software. It is a partial alternative to structure searching in the CAS files.

681. **CHEMZERO.** Columbus, OH: Chemical Abstracts Service, 1965- .
    An online dictionary, nonbibliographic file containing those chemical substances for which there are no citations in *Chemical Abstracts* (see entry 675). Available from DIALOG.

QD117
.C5
G34
Sci

682. Chromatography Abstracts. Barking, England: Elsevier, 1986- . 7/yr.

Formerly *Gas and Liquid Chromatography Abstracts* (1970-85) and *Gas Chromatography Abstracts* (1958-69). Annual cumulative author and subject indexes are arranged in two parts: (1) gas, and (2) liquid. Because of the importance of chromatography in chemistry, this is a significant source for abstracts. The frequency of publication aids in maintaining currency of the material.

683. CIN. Columbus, OH: Chemical Abstracts Service, 1974- .

An online citation database to the business literature in the chemical industry. Available from DIALOG and SDC.

TP910
Sb22
Sci
Ref

684. Colour Index. 2nd ed. Yorkshire, England: Society of Dyers and Colourists, 1956-1958. 4v.

Supplemented in 1963, this is an exhaustive index to the commercially produced dyes of the world. Its three parts contain coverage of commercial name and hue, C.I. (Colour Index) number, and an index which includes dye and pigment makers. This is a major source for both chemists and chemical engineers involved in the dye industry.

685. Current Abstracts of Chemistry. Philadelphia: ISI Press, 1960- . weekly with quarterly and annual cumulations.

This is an excellent source with an excellent track record in terms of timeliness. As with most ISI publications, its major drawback is the use of its own abbreviation system. It is highly recommended, however, even given this nonstandard system.

686. Current Chemical Reactions. Philadelphia: ISI Press, 1979- . monthly with annual cumulations.

This is a major source for current information on chemical reactions. Like other materials from ISI, a nonstandard abbreviation system is used; however, this is still an excellent source overall.

QD551
.J62
Sci

687. Electroanalytical Abstracts. Basel, Switzerland: Birkhauser Verlag, 1963- . bimonthly.

Specializing in fundamental, physiochemical, and analytical electrochemistry, the abstracts contained in this work are descriptive but short. This is a good source, though it has considerable problems covering the world literature in a timely fashion given the wide scope of the work.

Z5524
.P5
H58
Sci Ref

688. Equilibrium Properties of Fluid Mixtures-2: A Bibliography of Experimental Data on Selected Fluids. Hiza, M. J., A. J. Kidnay, and R. C. Miller. New York: Plenum, 1982. 246p.

Covers material related to available experimental phase equilibria and thermophysical properties data on mixtures of selected low molecular weight fluids. Designed primarily for the design engineer, data analyst, and the experimental chemist, this is a professional source without handholds for the novice.

Z5524
.C55
S5
Sci

689. Guide to Gas Chromatography Literature. Signeur, Austin V. New York: Plenum, 1964- .

A guide to literature cited in the field of the theory, methodology, and application of gas chromatography. It is arranged by author and includes subject indexes. This is a good source, though it is not evaluative.

690. **Index Chemicus: Annual Cumulative Index—1986.** Philadelphia: ISI, 1987. 576p.

An annual cumulation of material from 112 source journals, providing an excellent blend of chemistry, clinical chemistry, and pharmaceutical titles. The data gleaned from the source journals by means of citation analysis are analyzed and tabulated in several different ways. This is an excellent tool but prone to the same problems as most ISI publications in that there is little or no editorial work done, allowing misspellings, plurals, and inconsistencies to hinder an effective search. The majority of this can be overlooked because of the unique nature of the publication. It is recommended for those involved in organic chemistry, but should be used with care as a direct literature tool.

691. **Literature Guide to the GLC of Body Fluids.** Signeur, Austin V. New York: Plenum, 1982. 385p.

Contains references from the scientific literature on the determination of substances found in the analysis of human fluids using gas chromatographic methods for the mid-1950s through 1981. This is a virtual storehouse of information on the application of a particular methodology to a specific area. Even though the material is now somewhat dated, the specificity of the source makes it important.

692. **Physical and Chemical Properties of Water: A Bibliography: 1957-1974.** Hawkins, Donald T. New York: Plenum, 1976. 556p.

The focus of this work is fundamental properties of water. Divided into two bibliographies, part 1 covers the literature from 1957 through 1968, and part 2 covers 1969 to 1974. It cites nearly 3,600 references to monographs, government documents, patents, dissertations, and journal articles. Sections are arranged by subject, and a separate author and permuted title (KWIC) index is provided for each. The majority of the references are drawn from *Chemical Abstracts* (see entry 675). The age of this work is a major drawback, but it is included here because of its basic nature and because there is no other comparable source available.

Z5524 . W35 H38 1976 Sci Ref

ENCYCLOPEDIAS

693. **Encyclopedia of Chemical Reactions.** Jacobson, Carl Alfred, and C. A. Hampel. New York: Van Nostrand Reinhold, 1946-1959. 8v.

An alphabetical arrangement of chemical reactants, first by the formula of the reactant, then by the reagent. Equations are accompanied by a description of the reaction conditions. This is a good basic course for standard reactions that is well organized and relatively easy to use.

QD155 .J3 Sci Ref

694. **Encyclopedia of Chemistry.** 4th ed. Considine, Douglas M., ed. New York: Van Nostrand Reinhold, 1984. 1082p.

This update of a well-respected reference book on chemistry covers over 1,300 topics and contains an alphabetical index with cross-references. A standard work which has stood the test of time, it is used by both professionals and novices alike.

QD5 V37 1984 Sci Ref

695. **Encyclopedia of Electrochemistry of the Elements.** Bard, Allen J., ed. New York: Dekker, 1973- .

Provides a critical, systematic, and comprehensive review of the electrochemical behavior of the elements and their compounds. As an ongoing series, it strives for currency and is generally successful. A very good source.

QD552 .5 .E5 Sci Ref

Encyclopedia of Chemical Technology   TP9 Sci Ref
E685

696. **Encyclopedia of Terpenoids.** Glasby, John S. New York: Wiley, 1982. 2v.

Items are arranged alphabetically by name, and a short list of references accompanies each entry. The coverage of the literature extends to the end of 1979. Volume 2 contains the formula index. Although almost 10 years old, this is still a good source for basic and particular information. It pulls together literature otherwise difficult to synthesize, but should be used with care because of its age.

QD421
654
Sci
Ref

697. **Encyclopedia of the Alkaloids.** Glasby, John S. New York: Plenum, 1975- . irregular. [current to 1983].

Designed for professional chemists and biochemists, this tool contains compounds arranged in alphabetical order by substance. Considerable information on each compound is given together with commentaries. The material at the beginning of this series must be used with caution, but the later material is very good and justifies its inclusion here.

QD5
M36
1993
Sci

698. **McGraw-Hill Encyclopedia of Chemistry.** Parker, Sybil P., ed. New York: McGraw-Hill, 1983. 1195p.

Contains articles by experts in fields of inorganic, organic, physical, and analytical chemistry. There is a set of page references, cross-references to topics, illustrations, photographs, and line drawings in addition to equations. The material here comes directly from the *McGraw-Hill Encyclopedia of Science and Technology*, 5th ed. (see entry 207). There is no need to have both.

QD262
F5
Sci
Ref

699. **Reagents for Organic Synthesis.** Fieser, Louis Frederick, and Mary Fieser. New York: Wiley, 1967- . irregular.

An encyclopedia of chemical reagents including information on each reagent and references to the literature. Significant uses of the particular reagent are also indicated. Of interest is a flow sheet showing reaction conditions and the yield. This is a good work with much technical and professional information which is recommended for its technical focus.

QD5
V37
1984
Sci
Ref

700. **Van Nostrand Reinhold Encyclopedia of Chemistry.** 4th ed. Considine, Douglas M., ed. New York: Van Nostrand Reinhold, 1984. 1082p.

A one-volume tool with alphabetically arranged entries and a detailed subject index. The editor assumes a minimal background in chemistry. This is an excellent source and very well done. It is recommended to all libraries with patrons interested in chemistry as well as to specialized information centers.

DICTIONARIES

TP9
.G28
Sci

701. **Chemical Synonyms and Trade Names: A Dictionary and Commercial Handbook Covering over 35,500 Definitions.** 8th ed. rev. Cooke, Edward I., and Richard W. I. Cooke. Oxford, England: Technical Press, 1978. 769p.

The age of this work should be overlooked, for this is still a major sourcebook for the laboratory or the field. The revised edition adds many new terms. It does need an update, but the information contained here is invaluable because it is so elusive.

QD5
.B57
Sci
Ref

702. **Concise Etymological Dictionary of Chemistry.** Bevan, Stanley C., et al. London: Applied Science Publishers, 1976. 140p.

An excellent dictionary that continues to find utility in libraries and information centers despite its age. Because the focus of the work is not on new knowledge, it remains reasonably current.

703. **Dictionary of Chemical Terminology in Five Languages.** Amsterdam, Netherlands: Elsevier, 1980. 600p.

    Contains chemical terminology in English, German, French, Polish, and Russian with an emphasis on English entries. This is a good general polyglot dictionary and a clear necessity for libraries and information centers accessing foreign language material.

704. **Dictionary of Chemistry and Chemical Technology.** Gross, Helmut. Amsterdam, Netherlands: Elsevier, 1984. 633p.

    Translating from German to English only, this is generally more up-to-date than the *Dictionary of Chemical Terminology in Five Languages* (see entry 703), though it translates fewer languages.

705. **Dictionary of Chromatography.** 2nd ed. Denney, Ronald C. London: Macmillan, 1982. 229p.

    Written as a quick reference tool for students, laboratory technicians, or general scientists, this source provides good coverage of an important area in chemistry. References to literature sources containing more in-depth information are included along with major equations covering theoretical chromatography.

706. **Dictionary of Electrochemistry.** 2nd ed. Hibbert, D. B., and A. M. James. London: Macmillan, 1984. 300p.

    This is a companion to James's *Dictionary of Thermodynamics* (see entry 710). The definitions are long and there are numerous references to literature. Overall, this is an excellent source both for definitions and supporting literature. Primarily for use by chemists, but could be of use to others.

707. **Dictionary of Named Effects and Laws in Chemistry, Physics, and Mathematics.** 4th ed. Ballentyne, Denis William George, and D. R. Lovett. New York: Barnes & Noble, 1980. 346p.

    An invaluable source for named effects, this is a list of organic compounds arranged in alphabetical order with references to the literature. The references are to the publication announcing the original preparation of the compound. For particular questions, this is an excellent source.

708. **Dictionary of Organic Compounds.** 5th ed. New York: Chapman & Hall, 1982. 4 supplements to 1986.

    This is a very comprehensive dictionary containing molecular formula index, heteroatom index, and chemical abstracts service registry number index. Together with the supplements, this is a prime source for information on compounds and is highly recommended for major collections or very specialized collections.

709. **Dictionary of Organometallic Compounds.** London: Chapman & Hall, 1984- . 3rd supplement, 1987.

    Like the *Dictionary of Organic Compounds* (see entry 708), this is a comprehensive work covering the international field of organometallic compounds. Together with the supplements, this is a major source for information in this area. It is highly recommended for major collections or very specialized collections.

710. **Dictionary of Thermodynamics.** James, A. M. New York: Wiley, 1976. 262p.

    This companion work to *Dictionary of Electrochemistry* (see entry 706) contains lengthy definitions with references to pertinent literature including other reference books and textbooks. It is a good source despite its age, written by an expert in the field.

QD5
.D67
1983
Sci Ref

711.   **Elsevier's Dictionary of Chemistry Including Terms from Biochemistry.** Dorian, A. F. Amsterdam, Netherlands: Elsevier, 1983. 685p.

Contains terms in English, French, Spanish, Italian, and German. A general dictionary for general reference, it is included here because of its polyglot nature.

712.   **Facts on File Dictionary of Chemistry.** 2nd ed. Daintith, John, ed. New York: Facts on File, 1981. 233p.

This is a good, all-purpose dictionary directed toward the layperson with no knowledge of chemistry. It has been included here for that reason and is recommended for public and other nontechnical libraries.

TP9
.6286
1987
Sci Ref

713.   **Gardner's Chemical Synonyms and Trade Names.** 9th ed. Pearce, Jill, ed. Brookfield, VT: Gower Publishing, 1987. 1081p.

This is a quick-reference dictionary of chemical synonyms and trade names in commercial usage. Entries consist of brief definitions, chemical formulas, and manufacturers (when available). An appendix lists company names worldwide, although the bias is clearly toward U.S. and British corporations. This is a good quick reference tool suitable for virtually any collection with some interest in chemistry.

QD5
H34
1982

714.   **Glossary of Chemical Terms.** 2nd ed. Hampel, Clifford A., and Gessner Hawley. New York: Van Nostrand Reinhold, 1982. 306p.

The emphasis of this work is on major chemical classifications, important terms, chemical processes, elements and compounds, and biographies of prominent chemists. It is a good, well-rounded dictionary, recommended for all collections.

715.   **Grant and Hackh's Chemical Dictionary Containing the Words Generally Used in Chemistry, and Many of the Terms Used in Related Sciences.** 5th ed. Grant, Roger, and Claire Grant, eds. New York: McGraw-Hill, 1987. 641p.

An authoritative dictionary covering words and phrases in chemistry and other related fields. It is designed for those who deal with chemical formulas either directly or indirectly. Entries are accompanied by high quality figures and numerous tables. A distinction is made between U.S. and British usage. Trademarks are identified in some cases.

QD5
.C5
1987
Sci
Ref

716.   **Hawley's Condensed Chemical Dictionary.** 11th ed. Sax, N. Irving, and Richard J. Lewis. New York: Van Nostrand Reinhold, 1987. 1288p.

This is a quick reference tool with highly technical descriptions of chemicals and processes. In some cases encyclopedic definitions are given for chemical phenomena and terminology. Of particular note is its concentration on identification of a wide range of trademarked products. Trademarked materials are keyed to a list of manufacturers. This is an excellent source because of the definitions and because of the identification of trademarks. This edition reflects an increased emphasis on current environmental and health aspects of chemicals and energy sources. Another excellent addition is the inclusion of CAS registry numbers for over 3,000 substances.

QD5
.M356
1985
Sci
Ref

717.   **McGraw-Hill Dictionary of Chemical Terms.** Parker, Sybil P. New York: McGraw-Hill, 1985. 470p.

Contains short definitions. No photographs, drawings, or charts are provided, but variant spelling for entries, acronyms, abbreviations, and symbols is given. This is a good, but not outstanding, dictionary.

718. **Miall's Dictionary of Chemistry.** Sharp, D. W. A. Harlow, England: Longman, 1981. 501p.

This is a selective dictionary covering various branches of chemistry. Particular attention is paid to industrial processes. It is useful only as a secondary dictionary and should not be the primary dictionary in any collection.

QD5
M618
1981
Sci Ref

719. **Vocabulary of Organic Chemistry.** Orchin, Milton, et al. New York: Wiley, 1980. 609p.

This work contains definitions of the most common and important terms in organic chemistry. Entries are arranged in order of their importance and hierarchy in organic chemistry. Both beginning students of chemistry at the undergraduate level and libraries and information centers dealing with chemical questions would be interested in this source.

QD291
.C55
1980
Sci
Ref

HANDBOOKS AND TABLES

720. **Beilstein Guide: A Manual for the Use of Beilstein's Handbuch der Organischen Chemie.** Weissbach, Oskar. Berlin: Springer, 1976. 95p.

This is an excellent introduction to the use and purpose of one of the major tools in chemical literature. Any library or information center which has the *Handbuch der Organischen Chemie* (see entry 756) should have a copy of this guide.

QD251
B439
1976
Sci Ref

721. **Chemical Formulary: Collection of Commercial Formulas for Making Thousands of Products in Many Fields.** Vol. 27. New York: Chemical Publishing, 1987. 358p.

This latest volume in the *Chemical Formulary* offers almost 600 formulas. It is classified into nine categories covering adhesives, foods and beverages, cosmetics, coatings, detergents, drugs, metal treatments, polishes, and elastomers, polymers, and resins. Together with the previous 26 volumes, more than 115,000 formulas have been published. Recommended for chemistry collections in academia and industry.

TP151
.C53
Sci

722. **Chemical Technicians' Ready Reference Handbook.** 2nd ed. New York: McGraw-Hill, 1981. 867p.

Contains detailed instructions on how to perform each step of normal laboratory procedures. This will find good use in college and technical school libraries, and serves as a good companion to a course in chemistry or as a refresher in techniques.

QD61.S58
1990
Sci
Ref

723. **Chemicals in Conservation: A Guide to Possible Hazards and Safe Use.** Clydesdale, Amanda. Edinburgh, Scotland: Scottish Society for Conservation and Restoration, 1982. looseleaf.

Covers carcinogens, toxic and hazardous materials, incompatible chemicals, flammability, and first aid. Also included are banned chemicals that may still be found in the environment. Terms used in the text are explained in the glossary. This is a professional handbook.

TP149
C58
1982
Sci
Ref

724. **CRC Handbook for Solubility Parameters and Other Cohesion Parameters.** Barton, Allan F. M. Boca Raton, FL: CRC Press, 1983. 594p.

This is an excellent handbook containing not only tables and charts, but essays on the field. There are references to the original literature from which both the essays and the tables and charts were drawn. This is a professional source for professionals.

725.   **CRC Handbook of Chemistry and Physics 1987-1988: A Ready-Reference Book of Chemical and Physical Data**. 68th ed. Weast, Robert C., et al., eds. Boca Raton, FL: CRC Press, 1987. 1v. (various paging).

This is the premier reference handbook for chemistry and physics. It is often used in other areas because of its excellent mathematical tables. In some ways, the handbook is difficult to use for the uninitiated, but the information derived is well worth the effort. This is an absolute must for any library with reference questions in the physical and chemical sciences.

726.   **CRC Handbook of Chromatography: Inorganics**. Qureshi, Mohsin, ed. Boca Raton, FL: CRC Press, 1986. 384p.

A comprehensive handbook valuable when doing routine analysis or developing new methods of chromatography of organic materials. It is divided into three sections. Section 1 covers background material, section 2 summarizes existing data in graphic and tabular form, and section 3 is a listing of important literature in the area. Serves as an excellent handbook for a professional chemist.

727.   **CRC Handbook of Chromatography: Polymers**. Smith, Charles G., et al. Boca Raton, FL: CRC Press, 1982. 200p.

A workbench reference tool for scientists and researchers using chromatographic systems for the analysis of polymers. A wide range of material is covered, mostly in tabular form. This is an excellent tool for the research scientist or institution.

728.   **CRC Handbook of Clinical Chemistry**. Werner, Mario, ed. Boca Raton, FL: CRC Press, 1982- .

Volume 1 was published in 1982, and volumes 2 and 3 in 1985. A compendium of information, data and methods is provided for those whose work involves clinical chemistry. Extensive details and bibliographies for specific applications of various techniques are also included, along with many tables and figures. This is a highly recommended handbook for specialized collections and research libraries.

729.   **CRC Handbook of Data on Organic Compounds**. Weast, Robert C., and Melvin J. Astle, eds. Boca Raton, FL: CRC Press, 1985. 2v.

An indispensable source for data on organic compounds, this work includes CAS registry number for nearly all compounds and Beilstein References for all compounds for which references could be located.

730.   **CRC Handbook of Organic Analytical Reagents**. Cheng, K. L., Keihei Ueno, and Toshiaki Imamura. Boca Raton, FL: CRC Press, 1982. 534p.

Limited to reagents for metals and some anions, this handbook contains almost nothing for organic analysis. It is a very specific source for specific uses.

731.   **CRC Handbook of Tables for Organic Compound Identification**. Rappaport, Z. Boca Raton, FL: CRC Press, 1983. 563p.

Covers compounds, dissociation constants of phenols, organic acids, and organic bases. An invaluable tool for identification purposes, it can be used both as a reference book in a library and as a bench handbook by a chemist.

732.   **CRC Handbook Series in Inorganic Electrochemistry**. Meites, Louis, P. Zuman, Elinor B. Rupp, and Ananthakrishnan Narayanan, eds. Boca Raton, FL: CRC Press, 1980- .

A comprehensive reference set that contains information on the electrochemical behavior of inorganic substances, including the complexes of metal ions with organic ligands. A key to literature citations and an author index is provided in each volume. This is an excellent source.

733. **Crystal Data Determinative Tables.** 3rd ed. National Bureau of Standards Crystal Data Center. Swathmore, PA: JCDDS, 1986.

QD908 D663 Sci

This includes entries for organic crystalline materials, along with cell parameters, space group, structure, density, and chemical name and formula. It is particularly useful in a laboratory or research setting.

734. **Eight Peak Index of Mass Spectra.** 3rd ed. Nottingham, England: Royal Society of Chemistry, 1983. 3v. in 7v.

QC454 M3 E33 1983 Sci Ref

Serves as an aid to compound identification and molecular weight index while providing point of entry to mass spectral collections. This work covers a large number of spectra which increases its utility. This is a professional source for the use of professionals in either a laboratory or research library setting.

735. **Gmelin's Handbuch der Anorganischen Chemie.** Leipzig, Germany: Verlag Chemie, 1924- . irregular.

QD151 G52 Sci Ref

This is the most comprehensive work on inorganic chemistry in the world. The entire work is coded for machine searching in the Gmelin Institute. It is arranged according to the Institute's classification system. A highly technical tool recommended only for those individuals and institutions who are engaged in research in inorganic chemistry.

736. **Guide to Beilstein's Handbuch.** Vestling, Martha M., and Janice T. Liebe. Boca Raton, FL: Huley Associates, 1977. 32 slides with cassette.

QD251 B438 1975 Media

Contains a discussion and guide to the *Handbuch der Organischen Chemie* (see entry 756). A valuable tool for beginning students in chemistry and for those who must deal with the chemical literature, it is included because it is a slide and cassette approach to the use of the *Handbuch*, as opposed to a straight textual guide.

737. **Handbook of Analytical Derivatization Reactions.** Knapp, D. R. New York: Wiley, 1979. 741p.

QD78 K63 Sci Ref

Even given its age, this is an outstanding reference on the preparation of derivatives of organic compounds. It contains indexes that allow easy access to information and is helpful to scientists working with gas chromatography, mass spectrometry, or liquid chromatography. This work needs an update, but is still useful.

738. **Handbook of Anion Determination.** Williams, W. John. London: Butterworths, 1979. 630p.

QD561 W628 Sci

Another useful handbook despite its age. In this case, the specificity of the handbook is the grounds for its inclusion. The work deals with organic and inorganic anion determination and separation. Anions are treated separately with discussion of the accuracy of various methods. Theory, equations, and procedures are given and ample reference lists are included. This work needs an update but is useful as it is.

739. **Handbook of Applied Chemistry.** Hopp, Vollrath, and Ingo Henning. Washington, DC: Hemisphere, 1983. 1v. (various paging).

TP151 H5813 1983 Sci

This is a useful source of basic information that includes industrial processes and use of substances. It will be of use to chemists, chemical engineers, and graduate students. A good, basic source for college, university, and professional collections.

740. **Handbook of Bimolecular and Termolecular Gas Reactions.** Kerr, Alistair, and Stephen J. Moss, eds. Boca Raton, FL: CRC Press, 1981-1987. 3v.

This is an excellent compendium of both data and discussion of bimolecular and ter-molecular gas reactions. The data presented are up-to-date as are the discussions. References are given back to the original literature supporting the data or discussion. This is an excellent source for research and professional collections.

741. **Handbook of Chemical Equilibria in Analytical Chemistry.** Kotrlby, Stanislav, and Ladislav Sjucha. Chichester, England: Horwood, 1985. 414p.

This is an excellent source, well conceived and executed. Contains considerable infor-mation of great utility to analytical chemists. The processes described cover the predomi-nant areas of interest in the field. Together with the description is a discussion with references to the original literature. Highly recommended for research collections.

742. **Handbook of Chemical Microscopy.** 4th ed. Mason, C. W. New York: Wiley, 1983. 505p.

Includes material on scanning microscopy as well as microscopical qualitative tests. All aspects of physical methods and chemical analysis are covered. This is a very practical yet highly specialized work and is recommended for research collections.

743. **Handbook of Chemical Property Estimation Methods: Environmental Behavior of Organic Compounds.** Lyman, Warren J., William F. Reehl, and David H. Rosenblatt, eds. New York: McGraw-Hill, 1982. 977p.

A comprehensive handbook on existing techniques for estimating physio-chemical properties of organic chemicals of environmental concern. It discusses transport, proper-ties, and importance of chemicals, and includes references and lists of symbols and sources of data. This is an excellent choice for research collections.

744. **Handbook of Computational Chemistry: A Practical Guide to Chemical Structure and Energy Calculations.** Clark, T., ed. New York: Wiley, 1985. 332p.

A practical guide to performing chemical structure and energy calculations which deals specifically with the three most commonly used programs: MM2, MOPAC, and GAUSSIAN 82. A clear choice for any laboratory or research collection.

745. **Handbook of Enzyme Inhibitors (1965-1977).** Jain, M. K. New York: Wiley, 1982. 447p.

As the title indicates, this work covers material only through 1977. It is an excellent source for retrospective material and discussions of ten-year-old procedures. Contained within are almost 5,000 compounds that function as enzyme inhibitors in over 3,000 pro-cesses, listing the name, process it inhibits, type of inhibition constant, and the reference. This handbook should be used with care and is included here because of its excellent coverage of the time period indicated.

746. **Handbook of Heats of Mixing.** Christensen, James J., Richard W. Hanks, and Reed M. Izatt. New York: Wiley, 1982. 1586p.

This compilation of enthalpy changes for mixing of liquids consists of a table that summarizes the published literature value through 1980 under the headings of the various substances. The information includes temperature, pressure, error, literature references, method and condition of measurement of change, and purity of material used. Provided are three indexes: empirical formula, synonym, and reference. This is an excellent profes-sional tool.

747. Handbook of Intermediary Metabolism of Aromatic Compounds. Goodwin, Brian L. London: Chapman & Hall, 1976. 799p.

This is included because it is virtually a one-of-a-kind reference tool. Very specialized in its focus and in its use, it is an accurate informative reference on aromatic metabolism and enzymatic reactions. An alphabetical listing of compounds is provided. This source should be used with caution due to its age.

QP801
.A75
G66
1976
b
Sci Ref

748. Handbook of Laboratory Distillation. 2nd ed. [rev. 3rd ed.] Krell, Erich. New York: Elsevier, 1982. 524p.

A standard reference manual in the field of distillation in the laboratory. An introduction to practical work with apparatus and a description of fundamentals and calculations of the separation process is included. This is also beneficial for distillation on the industrial scale and is recommended for college through research libraries.

QD63
.D6
K713
1963
Sci

749. Handbook of Metal Ligand Heats and Related Thermodynamic Quantities. 3rd ed. rev. Christensen, James J., and Reed M. Izatt. New York: Dekker, 1983. 783p.

This new edition contains data through 1980 for 1,547 separate ligands. It should be used as a companion to various published tables and is highly recommended for technical and research collections.

QD504
.C528
1983
Sci Ref

750. Handbook of Modern Analytical Instruments. Khandpur, Righbir Singh. Blue Ridge Summit, PA: TAB Books, 1981. 588p.

This handbook is intended for the actual users of analytical instruments. Its primary use will be at the undergraduate level because of its level of treatment. It includes the principles of construction and operation of electromechanical, spectrometric, and chromatographic instruments.

QD53
K63
Sci

751. Handbook of Naturally Occurring Compounds. Devon, T. K., and A. I. Scott. New York: Academic, 1972- .

If a structure has been assigned a naturally occurring compound, the compound will normally be found here. Polymeric compounds, synthetic derivatives, and degradation products are excluded. Access is by alphabet, molecular weight, and molecular formula indexes. This is an excellent source with considerable data on compounds. It is recommended for research and technical collections.

QD415.7
D48
Sci

752. Handbook of Practical Organic Micro-Analysis: Recommended Methods for Determining Elements and Groups. Bance, S. New York: Halsted, 1980. 206p.

This is a clear and concise presentation of organic microanalysis techniques. It provides detailed laboratory procedures with emphasis on quantitative elemental analysis, and is a clear choice for laboratory technicians as well as researchers.

QD272
M5
B36
Sci

753. Handbook of Reactive Chemical Hazards. 3rd ed. Boston: Butterworths, 1985. 1852p.

A useful tool if seeking stability data on single specific compounds, data on possible violent interaction between two or more compounds, general data on a class of compounds, or structures associated with a known hazardous group or fire related data. Highly recommended for laboratory and research collections.

TS5.3
H3
B73
1990
Sci Ref

754. Handbook of Spectroscopy. Robinson, J. W., ed. Boca Raton, FL: CRC Press, 1974- . 3v.

QD95
.H27
Sci Ref

Currently contains three volumes providing information on the major fields of spectroscopy. The last volume was published in 1981. This is now both a retrospective and a survey of the field. Well done and very thorough, it is recommended for research libraries and information centers.

RA1193
.S58
1991
Sci Ref

755.   **Handbook of Toxic and Hazardous Chemicals and Carcinogens.** 2nd ed. Sittig, Marshall. Park Ridge, NJ: Noyes, 1981. 950p.
Gives a concise form of chemical, health, and safety information on toxic and hazardous chemicals and is a valuable addition to research libraries.

QD251
.B423
1979
Sci Ref

756.   **Handbuch der Organischen Chemie.** Beilstein, Friedrich Konrad. Berlin: Springer, 1918-1940.
This is the classic work in organic chemistry. All concern about the age of the material is irrelevant, for this is an essential source for any serious research library or information center with an emphasis on chemistry. The contents of the various volumes are listed below. This is the largest compilation of physical data related to organic chemistry. The publication of the English-language 5th supplementary series has been in progress since 1984. The 5th supplementary series will cover 1960-1979.

I.   *Die Literatur von 1910-1919 umfassend.* 1938-1948.

II.   *Die Literatur von 1920-1929 umfassend.* 1941-1955.

III/IV.   *Die Literatur von 1930-1959 umfassend.* 1956-1974.

IV.   *Die Literatur von 1950-59 umfassend.* 1972- .

QD51
.H35
1986
Sci Ref

757.   **Hazards in the Chemical Laboratory.** Bretherick, L., ed. London: Royal Society of Chemistry, 1986. 604p.
Contains introductory sections on health, safety, fire protection, first aid, and toxicology followed by an alphabetical directory of approximately 500 flammable, explosive, corrosive and/or toxic substances with information on toxic effects, proper first aid and how to deal with spills and fires. A timely and important addition to a research library or information center.

QC457
.S983
Sci
Ref

758.   **Infrared Band Handbook.** 2nd ed. Szymanski, Herman A., and Ronald E. Erickson. New York: Plenum, 1970. 1491p. 2v.
Though dated, this is an important tool. It is a comprehensive treatment of most structural groups and their environments. Arrangement is by wave length, physical state, special formation, structural group, and reference number. It is included here because it contains a wealth of data on a subject with a present low growth rate.

QD65
.H25
Sci
Ref

759.   **Lange's Handbook of Chemistry.** 13th ed. Dean, John A., ed. New York: McGraw-Hill, 1985. 1v. (various paging).
This is a good general purpose reference tool that provides access to chemical and physical data used both in the laboratory and in manufacturing. Extensive entries on pure and applied chemistry make this a valuable source for chemical engineers as well. It is highly recommended for all levels.

760.   **Methoden der Organischen Chemie.** Houben, Josef, and Thedor Weyl, eds. Stuttgart, Germany: G. Thieme, 1952- .
Written in German, this is the world authority on laboratory methods in organic chemistry. Detailed descriptions of methodology with discussions of underlying theories are provided. This is an essential source for any serious collection in chemistry.

761. **Official Methods of Analysis.** 14th ed. Washington, DC: Association of Official Analytical Chemists, 1984. 1141p.

This work contains quantitative and qualitative analytic methods for foods, fertilizers, pesticides, drugs, and cosmetics. A treasure house of material on methodology in chemistry, it also includes a section on preparation of standard solutions. A clear and necessary choice for any serious research organization.

SS87
A73
Sci

762. **Oxide Handbook.** Samsonov, G. V., ed. New York: Plenum, 1982. 463p.

This work is not precisely titled. It is in reality an entry point to the Russian literature on oxides. Very little literature other than Russian is included. Once the focus is understood, this is a very good source and is recommended for research collections only.

QD181.O1
F5813
1982
Sci Ref

763. **Parent Compound Handbook.** Columbus, OH: American Chemical Society, 1976. 2v.

This is a major component of *Chemical Abstracts* (see entry 675) listing parent compounds and related information. The majority of this information is now online, and this is the remaining hard copy version. It supersedes the *Ring Index* (Washington, DC: American Chemical Society, 1960-1965). Each parent compound contains structural data, identifier, CAS registry number, and Wiswesser Line Notation. There is no need to have this if the CAS files are available online.

QD291
.P29
Sci

764. **Purification of Laboratory Chemicals.** 2nd ed. Perrin, D. D., W. L. F. Armarego, and D. R. Perrin. Oxford, England: Pergamon, 1980. 568p.

This reference work tabulates applications and methods for purifying chemical reagents and classes of compounds. It is not a general source, but is very specific both in its focus and the material it presents. For the serious collection in a working laboratory or research institution, this is a necessary source.

TP156
.P83
P47
1988
Sci Ref

765. **Reagents for Organic Synthesis.** Fieser, Louis Frederick, and Mary Fieser. New York: Wiley, 1967-1986. 12v.

This is a comprehensive listing of reagents. Each reagent has listed its structural formula, molecular weight, physical constants, method of preparation or purification, suppliers, and significant uses. This is a bench handbook as well as a library reference book and is recommended for research institutions only.

QD262
FS
Sci
Ref

766. **Ring Systems Handbook.** Columbus, OH: Chemical Abstracts Service.

Contains information formerly found in the *Patterson Ring Index* and the *CAS Parent Compound Handbook* (see entry 763). Issued every four years, the handbook is a basic tool for chemical research.

QD291
.R55
Sci Ref

767. **Standard Methods for the Examination of Water and Wastewater.** 16th ed. Washington, DC: American Public Health Association, 1985. 1268p.

Details methods of examination and analysis. This is an excellent handbook covering basic through expert material in one volume and is a clear choice for chemists and engineers alike. Its greatest utility is found in professional collections or in research collections.

QD142
A5
Sci
Ref

768. **Tabliktlsy Spektral'nykh Linifi Atomov i Ionov.** Stringanov, A. R., and G. A. Odinktlsova. Moskva, USSR: Energoizdat, 1982. 311p.

In Russian, this is a classification into tabular form of the emission spectra of 22 elements. Each element is listed with wavelength, intensity and classification for each spectral line. In addition to spectrum of neutral atoms, spectra of several of their ions are

QC453
.Z313
1970
Sci

given. This is a highly specialized source requiring some familiarity with Russian. It is an excellent source, but only for the most technical of organizations.

769. **Toxic and Hazardous Industrial Chemicals Safety Manual.** Tokyo: International Technical Information Institute, 1986. 700p.

Provides the world chemical and other industries with up-to-date and accurate information as to treatment and disposal of chemicals. More than 200 industrial chemicals are listed in alphabetical order, giving properties, hazardous potentials, and handling and storage. This is a timely and useful source for almost any library.

TREATISES

770. **Advanced Treatise on Physical Chemistry.** Partington, James Riddick. New York: Wiley, 1949- .

A mathematical treatment of physical chemistry with each volume covering a separate topic. To date five volumes of this classic treatise have been published, the last in 1954. An excellent piece of work, it is very important for its comprehensive retrospective and introspective coverage of mathematical chemistry. It is recommended only for major research libraries.

771. **Comprehensive Chemical Kinetics.** Bamford, C. H., and C. F. H. Tipper, eds. Amsterdam, Netherlands: Elsevier, 1969- .

Covers the theory and practice of kinetics of organic, inorganic, and polymerization reactions. In the field of kinetics in chemistry, this is a comprehensive source covering not only the normative theories, but competing theories as well. It is recommended for major research libraries only.

772. **Comprehensive Heterocyclic Chemistry.** Katritzky, Alan R., and Charles W. Rees, eds. Oxford, England: Pergamon, 1984. 8v.

Presents a comprehensive account of fundamental heterocyclic chemistry, with the emphasis on basic principles and unifying correlations. Volume 8 contains a physical data index, author index, subject index, and ring index. This is an excellent source for research libraries.

773. **Comprehensive Inorganic Chemistry.** Bailar, J. C., et al., ed. Oxford, England: Pergamon, 1975. 5v.

A curious treatise because of its ease of use. Not only is it concise, but it is thorough. It has been expertly edited to include only that which is important. Elements and groupings of elements are discussed from their discovery to the present. The index is particularly well done. It is highly recommended, even considering its age, to research libraries.

774. **Comprehensive Organic Chemistry.** Barton, D., and W. D. Ollis, eds. Oxford, England: Pergamon, 1979. 6v.

This is a classic treatise for organic chemistry. It describes the major classes of organic compounds including some synthetic compounds. The original literature underlying the work is referenced throughout the text. It contains excellent indexes and is highly recommended for research and academic libraries.

775. **Comprehensive Organometallic Chemistry.** Wilkinson, Geoffrey. Oxford, England: Pergamon, 1982. 9v.

Covering contemporary organometallic and carbon monoxide chemistry, this is a well done treatise on a specialized topic. The original literature is liberally referenced and the indexing is reasonable. A good choice for specialized research and academic collections.

776.   **Comprehensive Treatise on Inorganic and Theoretical Chemistry.** Mellor, Joseph William. London: Longman, 1922-1937. 16v. with supplements.

QD 31 M52 Sci Ref

Arranged by periodic table, this source covers inorganic chemistry thoroughly. The focus here is somewhat broader than *Comprehensive Inorganic Chemistry* (see entry 773), lessening its utility as a comprehensive source. What it lacks in comprehensiveness, it makes up for in synthesis. It brings together inorganic and theoretical chemistry very well and is recommended for academic and research collections.

777.   **Rodd's Chemistry of Carbon Compounds: A Modern Comprehensive Treatise.** 2nd ed. Rodd, E. H. New York: Elsevier, 1964- . irregular.

QD 251 R62 Sci

This is the most comprehensive treatise available on carbon compounds. References to original literature are provided and each volume has its own index. A clear classic and a necessary choice for any major chemistry collection with research interests.

778.   **Treatise on Analytical Chemistry.** 2nd ed. Kolthoff, Izaak Maurits, and P. J. Elving. New York: Wiley, 1978- . irregular.

QD 75.2 K64 Sci

This is a treatise for the advanced and experienced chemist. It covers the field of analytical chemistry, including inorganic and organic compounds. There is a large portion of the work devoted to analytical chemistry in industry, making this an important work for chemical engineers as well as practicing chemists. It is highly recommended for academic and research collections.

DIRECTORIES

779.   **American Chemists and Chemical Engineers.** Miles, Wyndham D., ed. Washington, DC: American Chemical Society, 1976. 544p.

QD 21 .A43 Sci Ref

The imprint of this work does it an injustice. This reference tool provides information on prominent men and women in science over a span of 300 years. It is not a current directory but more of a biographical directory of some of the greats in the field.

780.   **Biographical Dictionary of Scientists, Chemists.** Abbott, David. New York: Bedrick, 1984. 203p.

Coverage includes the ancients to the comtemporary. Short biographic sketches are the rule. This is a good source, especially when teamed with *American Chemists and Chemical Engineers* (see entry 779).

781.   **Chem Sources.** (U.S.A) Remington, NJ: Directories Publishing, 1958- . annual.

TP 12 C44 Sci Ref

This is a current sourcebook for chemicals and suppliers, and an excellent source for some very ephemeral information. A tradename section is included. It is highly recommended for libraries and information centers serving experimental research or production units.

782.   **ChemBUYDirect: International Chemical Buyers Directory.** Derz, Friedrich W., ed. Berlin: Walter de Gruyter, 1974- .

A comprehensive international guide to providers of chemicals, this is an excellent source for information that is sometimes very difficult to come by. It contains indexes which provide full name and address. Recommended for libraries and information centers having ongoing experimental research or production components.

783.   **Directory of Graduate Research.** Washington, DC: American Chemical Society, 1985. 1260p.

Universities and colleges offering doctoral and master's degrees in six fields are covered. This is an excellent tool for information on graduate schools, location of teaching personnel, and information on graduate research. It is recommended for any academic library.

784.   **Directory of World Chemical Producers.** 2nd ed. Oceanside, NY: Chemical Information Services, 1984/85. 575p.

Covers nearly 50,000 product listings (including cross-references) manufactured by over 5,000 chemical producers in 59 countries. It is divided into two parts which list products and producer addresses. This is a good tool for finding chemical information and information on the producers of the chemicals. It is recommended for any library or information center serving a production or experimental research unit.

7 Geosciences

Because the geosciences deal with the investigation of the earth and those forces acting upon it, it follows that a large amount of the sources listed here will fall under the categories of geology and meteorology. The science of geology is of particular interest because of a fairly recent upheaval involving the emergence of plate tectonics. Plate tectonics became the dominant explanatory theory in geology during the 1960s and acted to rejuvenate the literature of geology.

The science of meteorology has fascinated individuals since the time of early man. Because they required consistent cycles for agriculture, the ancients put considerable effort into studying the cycles of meteorological events. To a large extent, the reasons behind the study of meteorology today remain much the same.

The advent of satellite observation and increased use of sophisticated computer modeling has increased the accuracy of measurement and prediction of the meteorologist. Such new techniques are evident in the literature and will require some reshaping of libraries and library services.

The geosciences can be compared to astronomy in some senses. The inclusion of techniques and methodologies from other disciplines has created a series of "geo" areas. Excellent examples of these areas are geophysics and geochemistry. Each combines the most rigorous elements of chemistry or physics and applies the results to the study of the earth. The result for the information provider is a crossing of traditional boundaries. The current trends, if they continue, will increase the interdisciplinary study in the geosciences.

GUIDES TO THE LITERATURE

785. **Geologic Reference Sources: A Subject and Regional Bibliography to Publications and Maps in the Geological Sources.** 2nd ed. Ward, Dederick C., et al. Metuchen, NJ: Scarecrow Press, 1981. 560p.

An excellent guide to geological literature with the majority of items listed published since 1950. It is intended as an introduction to the literature, but has few annotations.

786. **Geologists and the History of Geology: An International Bibliography for the Origins to 1978.** Sarjeant, William A. S. New York: Arno Press, 1980. 5v. **Supplement 1979-1984.** Malabar, FL: Krieger, 1987. 2v.

Volume 1 is entitled *Important Events in the History of Geology*; volumes 2 and 3, *Biographies of Geologists and References to Their Works*; volume 4, *Country and Specialty Indexes*; and volume 5, *Index of Authors, Editors, and Translators.* This is an impressive and excellent reference work for any major research collection made even more useful with the supplement.

QC804
B78
1985
Sci

787. **History of Geophysics and Meteorology: An Annotated Bibliography.** Brush, Stephen G., Helmut E. Landsberg, and Martin Collins. New York: Garland, 1985. 450p.

This is a selected bibliography of approximately 2,000 items. A broad range of the geophysical sciences are covered, including general histories and some biographies. The literature coverage includes the USSR, Europe, and North America. This is an excellent source of material published up to 1982 and is recommended for serious geoscience collections with a research focus.

Z692
M3
P68
Maint
Maps

788. **Map Librarianship.** 2nd ed. Larsgaard, Mary. Littleton, CO: Libraries Unlimited, 1987. 382p.

A practical text offering guidance in selection, classification, and computer applications. Sample policies, map sources, and a glossary round out the volume. This is a well done work, and should be the first choice of any book on the subject.

Z692
.M3
M52
maps

789. **Map Librarianship.** 2nd ed. Nichols, Harold. London: Clive Bingley, 1982. 272p.

A good, solid book on map librarianship with occasional bibliographic notes. Sections touch on some mapping services and map cataloging. There is little improvement over the first edition in terms of writing style, which makes this work a secondary source.

QC981
B8
1988
SciRef

790. **Selective Guide to Climatic Data Sources.** Hatch, Warren L. Washington, DC: U.S. Department of Commerce, NOAA, 1986. 1v. (various paging).

Acquaints potential users with the forms in which climatological data are available, both published and unpublished. Most items covered are available from the National Climatic Data Center. Arrangement is by format of material.

Z7935
.645
Sci
Ref

791. **Sources of Information in Water Resources.** Giefer, Gerald F. Port Washington, NY: Water Information Center, 1976. 290p.

Covers secondary sources pertinent to water and water management issues. It is not comprehensive, but serves as a starting place for further literature searching. Its major drawback is the age of the material, though coverage of sources included is excellent.

Z6031
.W67
1973
Sci
Ref

792. **Use of Earth Sciences Literature.** Wood, D. N., ed. Hamden, CT: Archon Books, 1973. 459p.

A good systematic coverage of the earth sciences suitable for the beginning student or novice. Chapters discuss libraries and use of libraries, the differences between primary and secondary literatures, the place of maps, and the performance of literature searches. Individual titles mentioned in the book should be used with care, but the overall structure of the book and its approach to the literature is excellent.

ABSTRACTS, INDEXES, AND BIBLIOGRAPHIES

QE71
A27
Sci

793. **Abstracts of North American Geology.** Washington, DC: U.S. Geological Survey, 1966-1971. 6v.

This has been superseded by *Bibliography and Index of Geology* (see entry 798). It contains abstracts of technical papers and of books together with citations to cartographic material on the geology of North America. The internal arrangement is by author. It is included here because it is still utilized by geological researchers.

794. **Annotated Bibliographies of Mineral Deposits in Europe: Northern Europe In-** TN55 **cluding Examples from the U.S.S.R. in Both Europe and Asia.** Ridge, J. D. New York: R49 Pergamon, 1984- . irregular.

1984
Sci

795. **Annotated Bibliographies of Mineral Deposits in the Western Hemisphere.** Ridge, J. D. Boulder, CO: Geological Society of America, 1972. 681p.

These bibliographies list mineral deposits first by continent and country. For the United States and Canada, listing is by state or province. It is indexed by author, deposit, age of mineralization, minerals produced, and deposits ranked by Lindgren classification. Considered to be the definitive series on mineral deposits.

796. **Annotated Bibliography of Economic Geology.** Urbana, IL: Economic Geology TN260 Publishing Co., 1928-1966. 38v.

A56
Sci

Though dated, this is a classic work covering all aspects of mining and petroleum geology. The arrangement is by subject with author indexes in the annual volumes. This is an excellent source for historical papers and classics in the field.

797. **Antarctic Bibliography.** Washington, DC: U.S. Government Printing Office, Z6005 1965- . irregular.

A7

An international bibliography covering all aspects of Antarctic exploration. Biology, A55 expeditions, geology, logistics, equipment, atmospheric physics, and political geography Sci Ref are all covered. Indexing is by author, title, and geographic area.

798. **Bibliography and Index of Geology.** Alexandria, VA: American Geological In- QE1 stitute, 1969- . monthly.

G21

This is the hard copy version of the GeoRef database (see entry 811). Thirty-one Sci volumes were published as *Bibliography and Index of Geology Exclusive of North America* Ref (1933-1968). Each issue of this index to books, papers, and maps dealing with geology contains author and subject indexes. International in scope, this is the prime index for North American geology.

799. **Bibliography of Fossil Vertebrates.** New York: Geological Society of America, Z6033 1928- . irregular.

P2

Compiled on a five-year basis, some were published as an issue of the society's B48 *Memoirs* or *Special Papers*. They are arranged alphabetically by author with a systematic Sci and detailed subject index. A comprehensive work.

800. **Bibliography of North American Geology.** Washington, DC: U.S. Government QE75 Printing Office, 1923-1971. 49v.

B59
Sci

A subseries of the *U.S. Geological Survey Bulletin* (Washington, DC: U.S. Govern- ment Printing Office, 1949-), each volume covers the geological literature for that year. It OR is arranged by author with a subject index, and is continued by *Bibliography and Index of* CD-ROM *Geology* (see entry 798).

Sci Ref

801. **Bibliography of Theses in Geology, 1965-1966.** Ward, Dederick C., and T. C. QE77 O'Callaghan. Washington, DC: American Geological Institute, 1969. 255p.

W37
1969

802. **Bibliography of Theses in Geology, 1967-1970.** Ward, Dederick C. Boulder, CO: Sci Ref Geological Society of America, 1973. 274p.

These two works are a continuation of yet earlier works by John and Halka Chronic. QE1 Although all material covered here is also contained in *Dissertation Abstracts International* G216 (Ann Arbor, MI: University Microfilms, 1969-), the coverage here is in depth. It is includ- No. 143 ed here because of that reason.

Sci Ref

QE 1
B865
Sci
Journ.

803. British Geological Literature (New Series). London: Brown's Geologic Information Service, 1972- . quarterly.

What *Bibliography and Index of Geology* (see entry 798) is to North American geology this index is to British geology. Arranged by broad subject areas with an author index, it provides short annotations. The annotations are poorer in quality than those of *Bibliography and Index of Geology.*

QC983
A5
Sci

804. Climatological Data. New York: U.S. Weather Bureau, 1948- . monthly.

Arranged by state, this is a summary of reports of U.S. Weather stations. A plethora of information is contained in these reports and in their compilation. Of interest primarily to the amateur through professional meteorologist, this summary provides more than enough data and variants of data sets to satisfy all reasonable needs.

Z6028
N58
Main Ref

805. Dictionary Catalog of the Map Division, New York Public Library. Boston: G. K. Hall, 1971. 10v.

Contains listings for a depository collection of U.S. Army Map Service maps, foreign maps, manuscript and early printed maps, and treatises and works on all aspects of cartography.

QE26.2
P67
1983
Sci

806. Earth Sciences: An Annotated Bibliography. Porter, Roy. New York: Garland, 1983. 192p.

This work does not include standard histories of sciences, unpublished works (dissertations), or general bibliographical guides to the history of science. Arranged thematically, it is indexed by author, geologist mentioned, and major departments in the history of geology. The title is somewhat misleading.

807. Geoarchive. Geosystems, 1969- .

Available from DIALOG, this is a geoscience database indexing more than 100,000 references each year.

Z6001
.V28
Main Ref + Sci Ref

808. Geography and Earth Science Publications, 1968-1972: An Author, Title, and Subject Guide to Books Reviewed, and an Index to the Reviews. Van Balen, John, comp. Ann Arbor, MI: Pierian Press, 1978.

809. Geography and Earth Science Publications, 1973-1975: An Author, Title, and Subject Guide to Books Reviewed, and an Index to the Reviews. Ann Arbor, MI: Pierian Press, 1978. 2v.

These provide comprehensive coverage of the books published in geography, geology, and related earth sciences. The scope is international. Citations are listed alphabetically by author, followed by subject and title indexes. It is dated, but given that modern geology uses much more older material than other sciences, this is an important work.

QE500
U53
Sci
Ref

810. Geological Abstracts. Norwich, England: GeoAbstracts, 1986- . bimonthly.

This is a continuation of *Geophysical Abstracts* (Norwich, England: GeoAbstracts, 1977-), which in turn continued the U.S. Geological Survey's *Geophysical Abstracts.* It is published in four parts, each issued six times a year: *Geophysics and Tectonics, Economic Geology, Paleontology and Stratigraphy,* and *Sedimentary Geology.* Abstracts are arranged under broad subject categories. No annual subject and author indexes are provided, making the service more of a current awareness resource.

811. **GeoRef.** American Geological Institute, 1967- .

A geological reference file online that covers geosciences literature from journals, conferences, symposia, and monographs. Available from DIALOG and SDC.

812. **GeoRef Serials List and KWOC Index.** Alexandria, VA: American Geological Institute, 1985. 4v.

A comprehensive list of serials cited in the GeoRef database between 1967-1985. The serial titles are listed alphabetically with publisher information, CODEN and ISSN numbers, notes regarding previous titles and other information. The second volume consists of a KWOC index of titles. This would be a useful supplement to *Bibliography and Index of Geology* (see entry 798).

813. **Geotitles Weekly.** London: GeoServices, 1969- . weekly.

This current awareness service for the geosciences focuses on news, subject classification, and source and author. The major plus here is the weekly nature of the publication. Although not evaluative, it does serve its purpose as a current awareness service.

814. **Guide to USGS Geologic and Hydrologic Maps.** McLean, VA: Documents Index, Inc., 1986. 612p.

USGS maps are listed according to categories such as oil and gas investigator's maps, state hydrologic unit maps, and hydrological investigations atlases. Information included under each listing consists of scale, magnetic-contour intervals, and size of map. Area-subject, subject-area, and coordinate indexes are included. This is especially useful in a depository library or research unit.

815. **Index of State Geological Survey Publications Issued in Series.** Corbin, John Boyd. Metuchen, NJ: Scarecrow Press, 1982. 449p.

Covers all numbered monographic publications in series issued by the state geological surveys or equivalents from 1963 to 1980. Any unnumbered material was omitted. Arranged by state, title of series, and numerically, author and subject indexes are included. This is a good source, but is less comprehensive than the title suggests.

816. **Meteorological and Geoastrophysical Abstracts.** Washington, DC: American Meteorological Society, 1950- . monthly.

This work is devoted to current abstracts on meteorological and geoastrophysical papers. Boundary layer problems and general atmospheric science are emphasized. An annual cumulative author and subject index is provided. This is an excellent source with good abstracts. Available from BRS and DIALOG as an online database.

817. **Mineralogical Abstracts.** London: Mineralogical Society of Great Britain, 1920- . quarterly.

Covers books, reports, and periodical literature in mineralogy with an international scope. Arranged by subject with annual topographical index, this is a good, solid abstracting tool. It has less of a European slant than might be expected.

818. **Monthly Weather Review.** Washington, DC: U.S. Government Printing Office, 1872- .

Contains articles on meteorology and summaries of weather phenomenon. It is a good source for technical articles on weather forecasting and weather phenomenon. This is a secondary source and should be considered only for serious collections wishing to round out their holdings.

819. **Publications of the Geological Survey, 1879-1961.** Washington, DC: U.S. Government Printing Office, 1964. 457p.

820. **Publications of the Geological Survey, 1962-1970.** Washington, DC: U.S. Government Printing Office, 1971. 586p.

821. **New Publications of the Geological Survey.** Washington, DC: U.S. Government Printing Office, 1984- . monthly.
These titles are a checklist to the myriad publications of the U.S. Geological Survey. All series are listed, including map series. Serves as an excellent current awareness tool as well as a checklist. The material for 1971-1984 consists of individual titles and is not a distinct part of a series.

822. **Zentralblatt fuer Geologie und Palaeontologie. Teil 1: Allgemeine Angewandte, Regionale und Historische Geologie.** Stuttgart, Germany: E. Schweizerbart'sche Verlagbuchhandlung, 1955- . 7/year.

823. **Zentralblatt fuer Geologie und Palaeontologie. Teil 2: Historische Geologie und Palaeonotologie.** Stuttgart, Germany: E. Schweizerbart'sche Verlagbuchhandlung, 1950-64. 17v.

824. **Zentralblatt fuer Mineralogie. Teil 1: Kristallographie und Mineralogie.** Stuttgart, Germany: E. Schweizerbart'sche Verlagbuchhandlung, 1807- . 7/year.

825. **Zentralblatt fuer Mineralogie. Teil 2: Gesteinkunde, Technische Mineralogie, Geochimie und Lagerstattenkunde.** Stuttgart, Germany: E. Schweizerbart'sche Verlagbuchhandlung, 1807- . 7/year.
These make up a comprehensive list to the world's literature in geology, paleontology, and mineralogy. An excellent work, it is well indexed and thoroughly international in scope. An essential set of titles for any serious research collection in the geosciences.

ENCYCLOPEDIAS

826. **Cambridge Encyclopedia of Earth Sciences.** Smith, David G., ed. Cambridge, England: Cambridge University Press, 1982. 496p.
This glossy encyclopedia reads like a textbook and has many color illustrations. It covers all aspects of geology from physics and chemistry of the earth to extraterrestrial geology. There are a glossary, a list of further readings, and an index. Because of the wealth of illustrations and its scope, this is a worthwhile addition to any undergraduate collection.

827. **Climates of the States.** 3rd ed. Ruffner, James A. Detroit, MI: Gale Research, 1985. 1200p.
This is in major part a reprint of two U.S. government documents, *Climates of the States* (Port Washington, NY: Water Information Center, 1974) and *Local Climatological Data* (Ashville, NC: National Climatic Center, 1952). New material is predominantly in the form of introductory and explanatory material. Even though the imprint date is new, the material is dated for the most part. Recommended for research collections.

828. **Color Encyclopedia of Gemstones.** 2nd ed. Arem, Joel E. New York: Van Nostrand Reinhold, 1987. 248p.

Lists basic mineralogical and gemological data on known species and a variety of gemstones. An alphabetic arrangement by mineral species is the basic entry point. An excellent guidebook to gemstones, it is a bench reference tool for in-depth work rather than a field guide.

829. **Deserts of the World: An Appraisal of Research into Their Physical and Biological Environments.** MacGinnies, William G., ed. Tucson, AZ: University of Arizona Press, 1968. 788p.

In cooperation with the Office of Arid Land Studies of the University of Arizona, the book contains a wealth of information from the most general to the most specific on 13 major desert areas. Flora, fauna, surface and groundwater hydrology, and climate are fully discussed. The literature referenced should be used with caution; however, this is a one-of-a-kind reference tool and is highly recommended for research collections.

830. **Encyclopedia of Applied Geology.** Finkel, Charles W. New York: Van Nostrand Reinhold, 1984. 644p.

Volume 13 in the *Encyclopedia of Earth Sciences* series, this is a scholarly work with long chapters on alphabetically arranged topics. Graphs and illustrations are well designed for each term or discipline, and lists of references are provided at the end of each major article. A listing of geological abstracts and indexes, computer databases, periodicals, and other texts and reference works begins the volume. An excellent tool for any university library.

831. **Encyclopedia of Climatology.** Oliver, John E., and Rhodes W. Fairbridge, eds. New York: Van Nostrand Reinhold, 1987. 986p.

This is basically an update and revision of the 1967 *Encyclopedia of Atmospheric Sciences and Astrogeology* (New York: Van Nostrand Reinhold, 1967). The articles are written by experts and are intended for scholars in the field. Of particular note are articles covering unexpected topics such as art and climate, and crime and climate. Highly recommended for academic and some public libraries.

832. **Encyclopedia of Geomorphology.** New York: Van Nostrand Reinhold, 1986. 1295p.

833. **Encyclopedia of Geochemistry and Environmental Sciences.** New York: Van Nostrand Reinhold, 1972. 1321p.

834. **Encyclopedia of Sedimentology.** New York: Academic Press, 1978. 901p.

These three encyclopedias were all edited by Rhodes Whitmore Fairbridge. Intended for the college to graduate level student, the subject of each volume is covered in very good detail, although the level of the fourth is not consistent throughout the series. These are excellent sources, edited with care, but are becoming dated.

835. **Encyclopedic Dictionary of Physical Geography.** Oxford, England: Blackwell, 1985. 528p.

Contains relatively short, signed entries, some with references. This is a good general purpose reference source recommended for general reference collections and for undergraduate collections.

836. **McGraw-Hill Encyclopedia of Ocean and Atmospheric Sciences.** Parker, Sybil P., ed. New York: McGraw-Hill, 1980. 580p.

Covers all aspects, especially basic, of ocean and atmospheric sciences. Articles are signed and are alphabetically arranged. Some articles come directly from *McGraw-Hill Encyclopedia of Science and Technology* (see entry 207), and as a result, *Ocean and Atmospheric Sciences* is not recommended if the collection already contains *Science and Technology*.

837. **Oilfields of the World.** 3rd ed. Titratsoo, E. N. Houston, TX: Gulf Publications, 1986. 392p.

A very well done volume describing all geologic and geographic aspects of the world's oilfields. Tables and statistics are well presented, making this an excellent source for world petroleum information.

QE770
J6
1970
Sci

838. **Treatise on Invertebrate Paleontology.** Moore, Raymond C., ed. New York: Geological Society of America, 1953- . irregular. [presently in 31 parts].

This is the most comprehensive and authoritative treatise on invertebrate paleontology published. Each entry consists of a full description, illustrations, drawings, and bibliographic citations. It is a necessity for any research institution in which paleontology is studied.

839. **Weather Almanac: A Reference Guide to Weather, Climate, and Air Quality in the United States and Its Key Cities, Comprising Statistics, Principles, and Terminology....** 5th ed. Ruffner, James A., and Frank E. Bair. Detroit, MI: Gale Research, 1987. 811p.

Both the title and the work are comprehensive. The work consists of a compilation of weather and climatic data throughout the United States. Tables, charts, maps, and diagrams help provide focus to information dealing with severe weather conditions, yearly weather records, air quality data, marine weather, and world weather summaries.

DICTIONARIES

840. **Challinor's Dictionary of Geology.** 6th ed. Wyatt, Anthony. Cardiff, England: University of Wales Press, 1986. 374p.

A good basic dictionary with up-to-date definitions of terms new in the field. This is a solid standard work recommended for any library.

841. **Dictionary of Earth Sciences.** Stiegler, Stella E., ed. Totowa, NJ: Rowman & Allanheld, 1983. 301p.

Consists of definitions of words and phrases dealing with either contemporary or historical usage in geology, paleontology, geophysics, meteorology, and other related sciences. A good first stop for basic information.

QE392
R42
1982
SciRef

842. **Dictionary of Gemology.** Read, P. G. London: Butterworths, 1982. 240p.

Provides short descriptions of the principal gem materials as well as definitions of associated scientific terms and gemological instruments. Serves as a dictionary good for all libraries.

843. **Dictionary of Geological Terms.** 3rd ed. rev. New York: Anchor Press, 1984. 571p.

A small and concise dictionary which both defines terms and places them in relation to other terms and concepts. The book explores geology by "examining the meaning and usage of names and terms that stand for the more significant things, facts and concepts of science." An excellent approach, it is carried off in like fashion.

844. **Dictionary of Petrology.** Tomkeieff, S. I. New York: Wiley, 1985. 680p.   QE423
Encompassing the terminology of sedimentary, metamorphic, and igneous petrology, T65
this dictionary includes synoptic tables which group together associated terms and make 1983
this useful as a thesaurus as well. This is an excellent source and is recommended for Sci Ref
serious collections.

845. **Dictionary of Rocks.** Mitchell, Richard Scott. New York: Van Nostrand Reinhold, 1985. 228p.
This is the first dictionary in the English language devoted exclusively to the names of rocks. As such, it is a highly recommended text with good definitions and illustrations.

846. **Dinosaur Dictionary.** Glut, Donald F. New York: Bonanza Books, 1984. 218p.
A listing in alphabetical order of almost all dinosaurs known to paleontologists with cross-references to other or similar genera. A complete description is given for each entry, often including the date and place of discovery of fossils. Drawings help illustrate bone fragments and other material. Recommended for any library.

847. **Geological Nomenclature.** Visser, W. A., ed. Utrecht, Netherlands: Bonn, Scheltema & Holkema, 1980. 540p.
This is a multilingual (English, Dutch, French, German, and Spanish) compilation of nomenclature compiled by the Royal Geological and Mining Society of the Netherlands. The entries are in English first and are arranged in subject categories. Terms are indexed linguistically. This is a very useful tool for those dealing with geology in Dutch, French, German, or Spanish.

848. **Glossary of Mineral Species.** Fleischer, Michael. Tucson, AZ: Mineralogical Record, 1987. 227p.
An alphabetical list of the names, symmetry, and chemical composition of mineral species, this is an excellent source for the identification and study of minerals. It is recommended for undergraduate through professional collections.

849. **McGraw-Hill Dictionary of Earth Sciences.** Parker, Sybil P., ed. New York: McGraw-Hill, 1984. 837p.
Contains very short definitions of over 15,000 terms, but no pictures, maps, or diagrams are provided. Many definitions are drawn from the *McGraw-Hill Dictionary of Scientific and Technical Terms* (see entry 229), 3rd edition, so there is no reason to have both.

850. **Nomenclature of Petrology: With References to Selected Literature.** Holmes, Arthur. New York: Hafner, 1971. 284p.
A very dated work but still useful for its definition of British and American geological terms—terms which are often not compatible. This work can be used as a translation bridge.

851. **Penguin Dictionary of Physical Geography.** Whittow, John B. London: Allen Lane, 1984. 591p.
Consists of short entries with no references and provides an explanation of the differences between British and American usage. It is recommended as a general dictionary in the field for all collections.

852. **Petroleum Dictionary.** Tver, David F., and Richard W. Berry. New York: Van Nostrand Reinhold, 1980. 374p.

The intent of this dictionary is to be a combination dictionary-handbook covering all aspects of the petroleum industry. Overall it succeeds if for no other reason than because it is the only work of its type at present. It is recommended for research collections.

HANDBOOKS, MANUALS, AND FIELD GUIDES

853. **AGI Data Sheets for Geology in the Field, Laboratory, and Office.** 2nd ed. Dietrich, R. V., J. T. Dutro, Jr., and R. M. Foose, comps. Falls Church, VA: American Geological Institute, 1982- . irregular.

A compendium of quick facts both general and specific such as symbols for fluvial sequences as well as trigonometric tables and lists of bibliographies, abstracts, and indexes. There is no index, but the table of contents is very descriptive. A useful ready reference guide with references at the end of some data sheets, this is recommended for research collections.

854. **Alkaline Rocks and Carbonatites of the World.** Woolley, Alan R. Austin, TX: University of Texas Press, 1987. 4 parts.

The first of four parts, covering North and South America, provides access to the literature and descriptions of alkaline and carbonatites known in North and South America. Expected in the series are three additional parts to cover Africa; USSR; and Asia, Europe (exclusive of the USSR), Australia, Antarctica, and the Oceanic islands. Recommended for research institutions.

855. **The Atmosphere.** Schaeffer, Vincent J., and John A. Day. Norwalk, CT: Easton, 1985. 359p.

A good basic guide to the complexities of the atmosphere. The intended audience is the novice, and the work does an excellent job in reaching this audience. It is recommended for general and other nontechnical collections.

856. **Audubon Society Field Guide to North American Rocks and Minerals.** New York: Knopf, 1978. 850p.

This is an older work, included here because it is an excellent field guide for the amateur. Complete identification information is given for all rocks and minerals normally encountered in North America. A glossary, bibliography, rock-forming minerals, chemical elements, and localities are also included. Recommended for general collections but not for research or specialized collections.

857. **CRC Handbook of Atmospherics.** Volland, Hans, ed. Boca Raton, FL: CRC Press, 1982. 2v.

Each chapter is written by an expert in the field and many references are given. This is not a novice's handbook, but is intended for, and will be used by, professionals in the field.

858. **Field Guide to Rocks and Minerals.** 4th ed. Pough, Frederick H. Boston: Houghton Mifflin, 1976. 317p.

Like the *Audubon Society Field Guide* (see entry 856), this is an amateur's guide to rocks and minerals. Provided are excellent color photographs and coverage of over 270 minerals grouped by chemical composition. Chapters describing the tenets of mineralogy and home laboratory techniques are included. Recommended for general, nonresearch collections.

859. **Handbook of Applied Meteorology.** Houghton, David D., ed. New York: Wiley, 1985. 1461p.

An authoritative, concise, and comprehensive reference for meteorological knowledge and the technology designed for professionals outside the meteorological profession. Consists of five parts covering fundamentals, measurement, applications, impact of meteorology on society, resources for meteorological data and knowledge. An excellent professional source for professionals.

860. **Handbook of Physical Properties of Rocks.** Carmichael, Robert S. CRC Press, 1982- . [currently 3v.].

Primarily tabular, this is an excellent source for esoteric information on the properties of rocks. Much general information can be found here as well. A highly recommended source for technical and research collections.

QE431.6 P5 C18 Sci Ref

861. **Larousse Guide to Minerals, Rocks, and Fossils.** Hamilton, W. R., A. R. Woolley, and A. C. Bishop. New York: Larousse, 1978. 320p.

An illustrated guide to minerals, rocks, and fossils, this is done in the expected style of Larousse with beautiful illustrations complementing an excellent text. The excellence of the text and the illustrations are the prime reasons for its inclusion here.

862. **Reference Handbook on the Deserts of North America.** Bender, Gordon L., ed. Westport, CT: Greenwood Press, 1982. 594p.

This is a very technical encyclopedia of the deserts of North America. Each desert region is given a chapter with an extensive discussion of geology, hydrology, zoology, botany, climatology, ecology, and anthropology of the desert region. There is an extensive bibliography at the end of each chapter, and author, subject, and common name indexes at the end of the book. This is a good, very technical and comprehensive reference source.

863. **Simon and Schuster's Guide to Rocks and Minerals.** Prinz, Martin, George Harlow, and Joseph Peters, eds. New York: Simon & Schuster, 1978. 607p.

A combination field guide, handbook, and reference work on mineralogy, this is a good general guide containing more information than most field guides. The nature of mineralogy allows works with older imprints to remain valuable, which is the case with this particular work.

864. **Smithsonian Meteorological Tables.** 5th imprint. Washington, DC: Smithsonian Institution, 1984. 527p.

Designed for the meteorologist, this is a bench handbook which contains all the pertinent tables and data necessary to interpret and compile meteorological reports. A professional source of little utility to the amateur, it is recommended for technical and research collections only.

865. **Systems of Mineralogy.** 7th ed. Dana, J. D., et al., eds. New York: Wiley, 1944-1962. 3v.

This is the most comprehensive classification system of minerals published. Chemical and physical characteristics are described for each entry making this a classic work with current utility in any research or technical collection.

866. **Times Books World Weather Guide.** Pearce, E. A., and C. G. Smith. New York: New York Times Books, 1984. 480p.

Temperature, humidity, and precipitation data for selected world cities are provided in this guide along with a short description of climatic conditions in selected countries. A traveler's guide to world weather, it contains a short glossary, temperature conversion, description of wind chill, and relative humidity. Recommended for general collections.

867.   **World Climates: With Tables of Climatic Data and Practical Suggestions.** Rudloff, Willy. Stuttgart, Germany: Wissenschaftliche Verlagsgesellschaft, 1981. 632p.

This is a scholarly work similar to the *Times Books World Weather Guide* (see entry 866). Nearly 1,500 weather stations are covered. The introduction discusses man's interaction with climate and major world climatic regions. It is recommended for research collections.

868.   **World Survey of Climatology.** New York: Elsevier, 1969-85. 15v.

Each volume covers the climate of a different geographical region. Many diagrams, maps, and tables are included making this an excellent world source of information.

ATLASES

869.   **Atlas of Economic Mineral Deposits.** Dixon, Colin J. Ithaca, NY: Cornell University Press, 1979. 143p.

Covers mineral deposits for 48 major economic minerals. A listing of each location, the geological setting, and locator maps of the deposit are included. Photographs, maps, and text are all included in the same volume. The value of this work lies in the integration of the maps with the textual and photographic information. Recommended for technical collections.

870.   **Climatic Atlas of Europe. Maps of Mean Temperature and Precipitation.** Geneva, Switzerland: World Meteorological Organization, 1970- .

871.   **Climatic Atlas of North and Central America. Maps of Mean Temperature and Precipitation.** Geneva, Switzerland: World Meteorological Organization, 1979- .

Sponsored by the World Meteorological Organization and based on WMO specifications, this atlas displays the following information: monthly and annual mean temperatures, annual range of temperature, and monthly precipitation. The maps are color coded to allow easy visual inspection of changes in measurements. This is the most authoritative source on the subject and is highly recommended for research collections.

872.   **National Atlas of the United States.** Washington, DC: U.S. Government Printing Office, 1970. 417p.

An outstanding work containing expertly drawn and printed maps which illustrate all aspects of geoscience as they pertain to the United States. This is a classic work.

DIRECTORIES

873.   **Directory of Geoscience Departments, United States and Canada.** 25th ed. Alexandria, VA: American Geological Institute, 1986. 232p.

University and college programs in the geosciences are arranged by state and then institution. Addresses, telephone numbers, and names of faculty are listed for each institution, and specialty codes are given to each faculty member listed according to their field of interest. A section lists those departments offering field courses and camps. This is a useful annual directory for university students.

874. **Directory of Information Resources in the United States: Geosciences and Oceanography.** Washington, DC: Library of Congress, 1981. 375p.

Based on the DOE/RECON database this directory is arranged alphabetically by title of the organization. A subject list is also provided. It is recommended for technical and research collections.

875. **Earth and Astronomical Sciences Research Centres.** Fitch, Jennifer M., ed. Essex, England: Longman, 1984. 742p.

Arranged by country, this is a world directory of approximately 3,500 organizations involved in research. A name and subject index are included. This is a very well organized and substantive directory of interest to research scientists in geology and astronomy.

876. **Geoscience Software Directory for the IBM PC and Compatibles.** Boston: International Human Resources Development Corp., 1985- . irregular.

Application software available in the geosciences are listed alphabetically by keyword in title. Each listing has information concerning the program, price, publisher and address, hardware requirements, and a brief description of the program. There is a helpful subject index to return to the program listing. Although this is not an exhaustive directory, it is a useful compilation.

877. **Map Collections in the United States and Canada.** 4th ed. Carrington, David K. New York: Geography and Map Division of Special Libraries Association, 1985. 178p.

This is a directory to American cartographic collections, excluding private collections. The arrangement is alphabetical by state and by city within state or province. Given the nature of cartographic collections it is a very well done source recommended for research collections.

878. **World Directory of Map Collections.** 2nd ed. Ristor, Walter W., ed. Munich: K. G. Saur, 1986. 405p.

A listing of collections in over 45 countries, it is arranged by country, then by city with information on each facility. Serves as a good directory for world information, though the individual country information is not as replete as it could be. Given the scope of the work, it could be included in any research collection.

8   Mathematics

Mathematics is the study of numbers, sets of points, various abstract elements, and, most importantly, the relations between them and the operations performed on them. Some consider mathematics a language, some a tool, some an art. Most consider mathematics a science. It is this aspect which is the basis for the selection of materials below.

Mathematics can be divided into pure mathematics and applied mathematics. Applied mathematics deals with solutions to practical problems. Such problems might consist of anomalies in physics, economics, navigation, and the like. Pure mathematics is more concerned with the study of abstract properties or numbers and systems without regard to practical applications.

The field of mathematics is one of the best disciplines in the sciences in terms of bibliographic control. Axioms which were discovered 2,000 years ago are still valid and utilized. Monographs and journal collections rarely are unused because of changes in theory.

Most of the sociological work done in the area of mathematics suggests that the mathematician attacks a particular, well defined problem and sees it through to conclusion. This indicates the mathematician needs fewer resources than other areas of science. It also suggests the mathematician needs more intense use of particular materials than other branches of science.

Overall, mathematics is one of the most stable scientific and technical areas in terms of its literature. Particularly in the area of pure mathematics, relatively little literature use is required. Because of this stability, the sources listed below will have an overall earlier imprint date than those in other areas. This is a reflection of the usage of literature by the mathematician as well as the extremely long half-life of the mathematics literature.

GUIDES TO THE LITERATURE

879.   **Current Information Sources in Mathematics: An Annotated Guide to Books and Periodicals, 1960-72.** Dick, Elie M. Littleton, CO: Libraries Unlimited, 1973. 281p.

This supplement to Parke's *Guide to the Literature of Mathematics and Physics* (New York: Dover, 1958) covers the most important monographic English language publications from 1960 through 1972. The listing includes bibliographic citation and an annotation. Reference books, periodicals, and publishers are also included.

880. **Guide to Tables in Mathematical Statistics.** Greenwood, J. A., and H. O. Hartley. Princeton, NJ: Princeton University Press, 1962. 1014p.

QA276. 25 G7. Sci Ref

Sponsored by the Committee of the Division of Mathematics of the National Academy of Sciences-National Research Council, this is a classified arrangement complemented by a contents listing of books of tables. It is updated by *Statistical Theory and Methods Abstracts* (see entry 905). Because mathematical tables change infrequently, this is still a valuable tool.

881. **How to Find Out in Mathematics: Guide to Sources of Information.** 2nd ed. Pemberton, John E. Oxford, England: Pergamon, 1969. 193p.

A guide that is now a classic. Covering the waterfront for mathematics on a surface level, it includes such topics as careers for mathematicians in addition to discussions of source materials for the study of mathematics. It is dated, but still useful to librarians as well as students.

882. **Use of Mathematical Literature.** Dorling, A. R., ed. London: Butterworths, 1977. 260p.

Unlike Pemberton's guide (see entry 881), this is a graduate level guide that covers the general character of mathematical literature including the structure of the discipline, major organizations and journals, and reference materials. Topics covered include the history of mathematics; combinatorics; rings and algebras; group theory; measure and probability; topology; and mathematical programming. It is recommended for research collections.

ABSTRACTS, INDEXES, AND BIBLIOGRAPHIES

883. **Author Index of Mathematical Reviews.** Providence, RI: American Mathematical Society, 1961- . annual.

Continues *The Twenty Year Author Index, 1940-1959* and the *Author Index, 1960-1964*, published in 1961 and 1964 respectively. Included are complete citations and references to volumes of *Mathematical Reviews* (see entry 902) that contain corresponding abstracts. This is a first-rate source.

884. **Bibliography of Basic Texts and Monographs on Statistical Methods. 1945-60.** 2nd ed. Buckland, William R., and Ronald A. Fox. New York: Hafner, 1963. 297p.

This selection of English-language entries on statistical methods and their applications is arranged by broad subject category with an author index. It is an excellent jumping off point for statistical material of the period, though it should be used with some care, as statistical theory has evolved some since its publication.

885. **Bibliography of Early Modern Algebra, 1500-1800.** Rider, Robin E. Berkeley: University of California, Office for History of Science and Technology, 1982. 171p.

Outlines the development of algebra from 1500 through 1799 with information on the history of the development of algebraic theory and an examination of the publication practices and patterns of the period. Arranged chronologically with a full author index, this is an important piece for the history of mathematics. It chronicles, in bibliographical format, the rebirth of algebra.

886. **Bibliography of Multivariate Statistical Analysis.** Anderson, T. W., et al. Huntington, NY: Krieger, 1977. 642p.

A compilation of the literature on multivariate analysis up to 1966 for articles, and up to 1970 for monographs. The editors have taken great care in assembling the materials, and this is as complete a bibliography on the subject as exists within this time period. It provides excellent background information on multivariate analysis and should be considered for any research collection.

887. **Bibliography of Statistical Literature.** Kendall, Maurice G., and Alison G. Doig. New York: Arno, 1981. 3v.

This is a comprehensive listing of the significant contributions to statistics since the sixteenth century. For current information one should consult *Statistical Theory and Methods Abstracts* (see entry 905). Special note should be taken that this work was put together by Maurice Kendall, one of the giants in the field of statistics.

888. **Bibliography on Time Series and Stochastic Processes.** Wold, Herman. Edinburgh, Scotland: Oliver & Boyd, 1966. 516p.

Covers research on time series and stochastic processes up to 1965. For current information on this topic consult *Statistical Theory and Methods Abstracts* (see entry 905). This is an excellent bibliography in an especially interesting area of mathematics, and is recommended as a research tool for academic collections.

889. **Computer and Control Abstracts.** London: Institution of Electrical Engineers, 1966- . monthly. (*Science Abstracts* Section C).

This abstract journal covers systems and control theory; control and computer technology; and systems and equipment. The abstracts tend to be short and informative, but in most cases are not evaluative. Because the abstracts are in English, the language of the original material is given. This is a necessity for any research and development or scholarly collection.

890. **Computer and Information Systems Abstract Journal.** Bethesda, MD: Cambridge Scientific Abstracts, 1962- . monthly.

An abstract journal concentrating on computer software, applications, mathematics, and electronics. The original title was *Information Processing Journal*, which changed to *Computer and Information Systems* and was then published under the current title in 1978. Abstracts are descriptive and well done. A major tool for research collections.

891. **Computer Literature Bibliography, 1946-1967.** Youden, W. W., ed. New York: Arno Press, 1970. 381p.

This is now an excellent tool for beginning literature in the computer area. It contains citations from journals, books, workshop reports, and conference proceedings. The work was originally published by the U.S. National Bureau of Standards in two volumes, covering the years 1946-1963 and 1964-1967. This is not a source for current information, but is of great historical value.

892. **Computing Reviews.** New York: Association for Computing Machinery, 1961- . monthly.

The reviews are short and signed. The arrangement of the journal is classified and emphasizes machine aspects over software. Features, multiple reviews, and some authors' rebuttals appear occasionally. This is an excellent source for forthright and to-the-point hardware reviews in the computing industry.

893. **Cumulative Index to Mathematics of Computation 1970-1984, Volumes 24-43.** Providence, RI: American Mathematical Society, 1987. 503p.

This is a cumulative index to one of the primary journals in mathematical literature. It is divided into author, subject, and key areas, and is a necessary tool for any collection that has *Mathematics of Computation* (see entry 903).

894. **Current Mathematical Publications.** Providence, RI: American Mathematical Society, 1969- . 17/yr.

Formed by the merger of *Contents of Contemporary Mathematical Journals* and *American Mathematical Society: New Publications*, this amounts to a prepublication announcement of items to be reviewed in *Mathematical Reviews* (see entry 902). Items are listed by subject and then alphabetically by author, with complete bibliographic citation. An excellent source for current awareness.

895. **Guide to Mathematical Tables.** Lebedev, Aleksandr Vasil'evich, and R. M. A. Fedorova. Oxford, England: Pergamon, 1960. 586p.

This is a translation of the Russian *Spravochnik Po Matematicheskikh Tablits*. It is similar to Fletcher's *Index to Mathematical Tables* (see entry 897) but omits many of the more obscure tables with which Fletcher's work is afflicted. Because of the translation and the age of the imprint, some of the tables are in material that is currently out of print. It should be used with care, but is an excellent source for tabular information.

896. **Index of Mathematical Papers.** Providence, RI: American Mathematical Society, 1973- . annual.

This is an author and subject index to *Mathematical Reviews* (see entry 902). In the same way that *Mathematical Reviews* is an indispensable tool for a research collection, the index to the reviews is just as important to the same audience.

897. **Index to Mathematical Tables.** 2nd ed. Fletcher, Alan. Reading, MA: Addison-Wesley, 1962. 2v.

This is a classic index to tables for the mathematical sciences. Its scope is international and the time period covered is the sixteenth century to 1961. Tables must be considered "working" tables to be included, and only tables of historical interest are excluded. The two volumes are arranged in four parts as follows: volume 1 contains part 1, "Historical Introduction" and "Index According to Functions"; volume 2 contains part 2, "Bibliography" (of sources of tables); part 3, "Errors" (in published tables); and part 4, "Index to Part I." Information given for each table in part 1 includes number of decimals or figures, interval and range of argument, facilities for interpolation, authorship, and date. The only weakness of the work is that it includes a number of esoteric tables. Depending on the application, this may not be a weakness.

898. **Information Science Abstracts.** New York: Plenum, 1966- . quarterly.

First published as *Documentation Abstracts*, this publication concentrates on approximately 350 journals in the fields of documentation and information science. It is an excellent tool for theoretical material which bridges the mathematical and information science areas.

899. **Integer Programming and Related Areas: A Classified Bibliography, 1978-1981.** von Randow, R., ed. New York: Springer-Verlag, 1982. 338p.

Reproduced in all capital letters from a computer output, this bibliography provides useful information on the applications of integer programming, complexity, dynamic programming, graph theoretic results, packing, and shortest paths. It is most useful to researchers and graduate students in mathematical economics and related fields.

900. Jahrbuch uber die Fortschritte der Mathematik. Berlin: Walter de Gruyter, 1868-1942. 60v.

Although it has now ceased publication, this is included here because it was the major abstracting tool for mathematics prior to the publication of *Mathematical Reviews* (see entry 902). Written in German, it provided international coverage using a classified subject arrangement. It is an essential tool for any research library with mathematical interests prior to 1940.

901. Japanese Mathematics: A Bibliography. Honda, Shojo, comp. Washington, DC: Library of Congress, 1982.

This bibliography of printed books and manuscripts from the Asian Division of the Library of Congress covers pre-Meiji Japanese mathematics from the seventeenth century to 1867. Entries are arranged alphabetically with Romanized title using the Hepburn system.

902. Mathematical Reviews. Providence, RI: American Mathematical Society, 1940- . monthly.

This is the major abstracting tool in mathematics, providing comprehensive, international coverage of mathematical works in many different areas of mathematics. Most abstracts are in English, but French and German abstracts are also included. Numbered consecutively, each abstract gives the author, title, periodical citation and/or publisher. Monographs are also included with a price following the citation. Individual journal issues on a given topic may be reviewed as a whole, if appropriate. Titles of articles in French, German, and English are given in their original language, while those in other languages are translated into English with a notation of the original language. The abstracts themselves are arranged by subject and are signed. Reprints from other abstracting services are identified, if they are used. An author index and a brief subject index to the categories are provided and include symposia, proceedings, biographical collections, and bibliographies. It is important to note that this abstracting service uses its own method of transliterating Russian, which varies considerably from the method of the Library of Congress. Recommended as an absolute necessity for any research oriented collection in the mathematical sciences or allied fields.

903. Mathematics of Computation. Washington, DC: National Research Council, 1943- . quarterly.

A publication devoted to reporting advances in numerical analysis, application of computer methods, mathematical tables, and aids to computation in general. A particular feature of the work is a section titled "Reviews and Descriptions of Tables and Books," which lists unpublished tables that are available from the editorial office by request. Volumes 1 through 13 were called *Mathematical Tables and Other Aids to Computation.* This is an excellent tool for researchers, and should be considered by any research collection.

904. MATHFILE. American Mathematical Society, 1973- .

A database providing coverage of the mathematical research literature of the world. Available from BRS and DIALOG.

905. **Statistical Theory and Method Abstracts.** Edinburgh, Scotland: Oliver & Boyd, 1959-1970; London: Longman, 1971- . quarterly.

An excellent tool for keeping abreast of the statistical literature. The journal was formed by the merger in 1964 with *International Journal of Abstracts: Statistical Theory and Methods* (1954-1963). The arrangement of the journal is by classification, using headings such as probability, distributions, variance analysis, experiment design, sampling, new tables, and stochastic theory and time series analysis. It is recommended for research and academic collections.

ENCYCLOPEDIAS

906. **Encyclopedia of Computer Science and Engineering.** 2nd ed. Ralston, Anthony, ed. New York: Van Nostrand Reinhold, 1983. 1664p.

This is a good, general encyclopedia, intended for the layperson or nonspecialist in the field. It has signed articles which cover the entire range of computer science. For this reason, it is not recommended for research collections, but is a candidate for academic and public library collections.

907. **Encyclopedia of Computer Science and Technology.** Belzer, Jack, et al. New York: Dekker, 1975- .

This general encyclopedia covering the computer field and the broad spectrum of components is not an in-depth piece of work, but is an excellent overview for anyone interested in the field. Its prime audience will be academic and public libraries.

908. **Encyclopedia of Mathematics and Its Applications.** Reading, MA: Addison-Wesley, 1976- .

Volume 1 is entitled *Integral Geometry and Geometric Probability, Section-Probability*, 1976; volume 2, *The Theory of Partitions, Section-Number Theory*, 1976; volume 3, *The Theory of Information and Coding, Section-Probability*, 1977; and volume 4, *Symmetry and Separation of Variables, Section-Special Functions*, 1977. Volume 7 was published in 1979. Volumes 12 and 14, part 2, *Extension and Applications*, came out in 1981, and volume 15, *The Logic of Quantum Mechanics*, was published in 1981. This is a massive work with much to recommend it. The individual volumes are extremely well done and are recommended for any research collection.

909. **Encyclopedia of Statistical Sciences.** Katz, Samuel, and Norman L. Johnson, eds. New York: Wiley, 1982- .

Containing a wide range of statistical theory, methodology, and applications in the fields of natural sciences, engineering, and social sciences, this encyclopedia is helpful to nonstatisticians as well as practicing statisticians. It is recommended for academic and research collections.

910. **Encyclopedic Dictionary of Mathematics.** 2nd ed. Ito, Kiyosi, ed. Cambridge, MA: MIT Press, 1987. 4v.

The majority of the entries in this translation of a Japanese encyclopedia are specific as opposed to general. The biographical information included through the work is an added benefit. This source should be well used because of the coverage and the fine indexing that accompanies it. Recommended for academic libraries.

911. **Fundamentals of Mathematics.** Behnke, H., ed. Cambridge, MA: MIT Press, 1974. 3v.

This is a translation of the German work, *Grundzuge der Mathematik*. The original is a classic in the field of mathematics, making the translation just as important. Because the coverage is extensive, this is highly recommended for research collections.

912. **Mathematics Encyclopedia.** Shapiro, Max S., ed. Garden City, NY: Doubleday, 1977. 289p.

A good general work which covers all branches of mathematics. It includes tables, formulas, and symbols, and is an appropriate reference for high school students and teachers.

913. **VNR Concise Encyclopedia of Mathematics.** Gellert, W., ed. New York: Van Nostrand Reinhold, 1977. 760p.

This is the English version of *Kleine Enzyklopädie Mathematik* which covers all fields and includes both photographs and biographies. It is concise, as the title suggests, and is not intended for the expert in the field or the practicing mathematician. Recommended for public and nonresearch collections.

DICTIONARIES

914. **American National Dictionary for Information Processing Systems.** ANSI Committee X3. Homewood, IL: Dow Jones-Irwin, 1984. 430p.

This is not a general dictionary of the computing fields, but rather is intended as an adjunct to a standards collection. Any collection involved in the computer sciences and the standards surrounding the field should have this source.

915. **Barnes & Noble Thesaurus of Computer Science.** Godman, Arthur. New York: Barnes & Noble, 1984. 262p.

This is a very interesting work. The emphasis is on interconnections of both the terms and the components of a computer. A unique color coding scheme is employed to assist the reader in connecting parts of the computer. The major drawback is its orientation toward British usage. Other than this caveat, it is an excellent choice for most public and academic libraries.

916. **Computer Dictionary and Handbook.** 3rd ed. Sippl, Charles J., and Roger J. Sippl. Indianapolis, IN: Howard W. Sams, 1980. 928p.

Contains well written and clear definitions, usually with extensive explanations. Cross-references are given. The handbook portion contains textbook type information on computer systems principles, systems design, and languages.

917. **Dictionary of Computing and New Information Technology.** 2nd ed. Meadows, A. J., M. Gordon, and A. Singleton. New York: Nichols, 1984. 229p.

Emphasized are words most likely to be found in library and online systems. This source will find greatest use among librarians uncomfortable with computing. It also contains a collection of words and phrases used in England and Western Europe and not usually found in U.S.-oriented dictionaries. It is a good basic source.

918. **Dictionary of Data Processing: Including Applications in Industry, Administration, and Business.** 4th ed. Wittmann, Alfred, and Joel Klos. New York: Elsevier, 1984. 281p.

This is a polyglot dictionary containing terms in English, French, and German. The main entry in English is referred to in the French and German entries. This will be a useful volume in organizations with a multinational focus.

919. **Dictionary of Gaming, Modelling and Simulation.** Gibbs, G. Ian. London: Sage Publications, 1978. 159p.

Including numerous statistical tests, mathematical formulas, and helpful illustrations that explain some terms, this source is recommended for public libraries as well as academic libraries with collections in electrical engineering, statistics, and computer science.

920. **Dictionary of Logical Terms and Symbols.** Greenstein, Carol Horn. New York: Van Nostrand Reinhold, 1978. 188p.

An excellent source to the notation used in higher level mathematics such as logic, engineering, and computer science. Columnar tables for translation from one system to another are provided. This is an excellent source for any library dealing with high level mathematics.

921. **Dictionary of Mathematics.** Glenn, J. A., and G. H. Littler. Totowa, NJ: Barnes & Noble, 1984. 230p.

Specifically targeted to a British audience, this dictionary is useful because of the universality of mathematics. The definitions are concise, but accurate. The type is very small, allowing a great deal of information to be packed into a relatively few number of pages. Recommended for academic and most public libraries.

922. **Dictionary of Statistical Terms.** 4th ed. rev. Kendall, M. G., and W. R. Buckland. New York: Longmans, 1982. 213p.

Statistical terms, definitions, and many new concepts are presented in a clear and easy-to-read format. A helpful reference aid for those in the statistical consultation field, it is recommended for academic libraries.

923. **Dictionary of Symbols of Mathematical Logic.** Feys, R., and F. B. Fitch, eds. Amsterdam: North Holland, 1973. 171p.

An explanatory text outlining the concepts and notations of the formal deductive systems of symbolic logic used in standard mathematical and philosophical works. A more detailed explanation of symbols is provided in this work than in the *Dictionary of Logical Terms and Symbols* (see entry 920).

924. **Encyclopedic Dictionary of Mathematics.** Iyanaga, Shokichi, and Yukiyosi Kawada, eds. Cambridge, MA: MIT Press, 1977. 2v.

This is an excellent dictionary compiled by international experts in mathematics. Entries from all fields of mathematics contain cross-references. Recommended for specialists and advanced students.

925. **Illustrated Computer Dictionary.** rev. ed. Spencer, Donald D. Columbus, OH: Merrill, 1983. 209p.

This is a nontechnical guide to the history and present state of computers. It includes entries for both hardware and software, and is recommended for general and nontechnical collections.

926. International Dictionary of Applied Mathematics. Frieberger, W. F., ed. Princeton, NJ: Van Nostrand Reinhold, 1960. 1173p.

Geared for the advanced scientist in engineering and the physical sciences, this is an excellent encyclopedic dictionary, even given its age. Most definitions are moderate to extensive in length.

927. MAST. Minimum Abbreviations of Serial Titles—Mathematics. Tompkins, Mary L. North Hollywood, CA: Western Periodicals, 1969. 427p.

A unique tool, this work attempts to standardize abbreviations of serial titles and to provide an entree into deciphering cryptic abbreviated titles sometimes found in citations. Its listing of serials in the area of mathematics is also helpful.

928. Mathematics Dictionary. 4th ed. James, Glenn, ed. New York: Van Nostrand Reinhold, 1976. 509p.

A good, general dictionary covering calculus through probability and statistics, this includes bibliographic sketches of individuals who have made contributions to mathematics. It is the mainstay of any good mathematics reference collection and is highly recommended to the point of necessity.

929. McGraw-Hill Dictionary of Computers. Parker, Sybil P., ed. New York: McGraw-Hill, 1984. 452p.

This is a paperback spinoff of *McGraw-Hill Dictionary of Scientific and Technical Terms* (see entry 229) that concentrates on computer-related terms and electronics. There is no reason to have this title if the full dictionary is available. The hardback version is more descriptively titled, *McGraw-Hill Dictionary of Electronics and Computer Technology.*

930. Penguin Dictionary of Data Processing. 3rd ed. Chandler, Anthony. Harmondsworth, England: Penguin, 1985. 488p.

This is a small dictionary of data processing terms intended for the user of computers. It is not a particularly good first stop reference, though it is an excellent tool for those who have some familiarity with computers. It successfully fills a gap in the computer dictionary area and is recommended for public and academic libraries.

931. Prentice-Hall Standard Glossary of Computer Terminology. Edmunds, Robert A. Englewood Cliffs, NJ: Prentice-Hall, 1985. 489p.

The coverage here is extensive with a considerable amount of space devoted to acronyms and abbreviations. The structure is hierarchical, with a set of terms defined as "key." This is a drawback, forcing the user to flip between entries before building a complete definition. An assumption of some knowledge beyond the amateur status is made. This is recommended despite some imperfections.

932. Quantities and Units of Measurement: A Dictionary and Handbook. Drazil, J. V. London: Mansell, 1983. 313p.

This is a revised and expanded version of the 1971 work, *Dictionary of Quantities and Units.* Divided into two parts, the first is a dictionary of units of measurement and their symbols and abbreviations. The second is a dictionary of quantities and selected constants. There is no real discussion of origins nor is there any real description of the units or symbols. However, this is a recommended work for academic and research collections.

HANDBOOKS AND TABLES

933. ASM Handbook of Engineering Mathematics. Belding, William G., ed. Metals Park, OH: American Society for Metals, 1983. 697p.

Contains key equations of the basic mathematic equations and theorems used in the design and manufacturing environment of typical metalworking companies. It is directed toward the engineer or engineering student with a basic knowledge of college-level mathematics.

934. Barlow's Tables of Squares, Cubes, Square Roots, Cube Roots and Reciprocals of All Integers Up to 12,500. 4th ed. Barlow, Peter, and L. J. Comrie, eds. New York: Chemical Publications, 1960. 258p.

This handbook is comparable to the *CRC Handbook of Mathematical Sciences* (see entry 937) and is the British equivalent to the CRC tables.

935. Biometrika Tables for Statisticians. 3rd ed. Pearson, Egon Sharpe, and H. O. Hartley, eds. London: Biometrika Trust, 1976. 2v.

QA 276 .P33 Sci Ref

A magnificent piece of work by two giants in the field of statistics, this is the handbook of choice for many statisticians and is referred to by almost every statistics textbook written. It is a required title in any mathematical or statistics oriented collection.

936. Collected Algorithms from ACM. New York: Association for Computing Machinery, 1978- . looseleaf.

This is a compilation of algorithms published in *Communications of the ACM* (New York: Association for Computing Machinery, 1958-) and *Transactions on Mathematical Software* (New York: Association for Computing Machinery, 1975-). Each entry lists the identifying title of the algorithm, source, author, institutional address, certification status of the algorithm, and remarks. It is a highly recommended title for mathematical research collections.

937. CRC Handbook of Mathematical Sciences. 6th ed. Beyer, William H., ed. Boca Raton, FL: CRC Press, 1987. 872p.

QA 47 H324 1978 Sci Ref

Formerly the *CRC Handbook of Tables for Mathematics*, this is a standard desk reference for most mathematicians and others involved in mathematical fields. It is a world class handbook highly recommended for any library or collection.

938. CRC Handbook of Tables for Probability and Statistics. 2nd ed. Beyer, William H. Boca Raton, FL: CRC Press, 1968. 642p.

QA 276 .25 B48 1968 Sci

This is a collection of standard statistical tables and a short description of the underlying distributions which produce them. The tables and sections include probability and statistics; normal distribution; binomial, Poisson, hypergeometric, and negative binomial distribution; student's t-distribution; chi-square distribution; F-distribution; order statistics; range and studentized range; correlation coefficient; nonparametric statistics; quality control; miscellaneous statistical tables; and miscellaneous mathematical tables. It is a required handbook in most statistically oriented collections.

939. CRC Standard Mathematical Tables. 28th ed. Beyer, William H., ed. Boca Raton, FL: CRC Press, 1987. 688p.

Consisting of math tables selected to aid scientific, engineering, industrial, and educational personnel, this work includes numerical tables, logarithmic tables, trigonometry tables, binomial functions, and differential equations. It is required for almost any collection.

940. Eight-Place Tables of Trigonometric Functions for Every Second of Arc, with an Appendix on the Computation to Twenty Places. Peters, Jean. Bronx, NY: Chelsea, 1968. 954p.

This work does precisely what its title indicates. Because the computations going into the table were done with such care, this is accepted as one of the most authoritative sets of tables for the field. It is highly recommended for both theoretical and applied mathematics collections.

941. Engineering Mathematics Handbook: Definitions, Theorems, Formulas, Tables. 3rd ed. Tuma, Jan H. New York: McGraw-Hill, 1987. 498p.

This is a major work for both mathematics and engineering. Broken into sections detailing the type of mathematics covered, it is intended as a desktop reference and fulfills its ambition well. The definitions are well constructed, beginning with basic concepts and quickly moving to more involved areas. Highly regarded by mathematicians and engineers, this is recommended for any mathematics or applied mathematics collection.

942. Guide to the Applications of the Laplace and Z-transforms. 2nd ed. Doetsch, Gustav. New York: Van Nostrand Reinhold, 1971. 240p.

Specifically designed to aid in the practical applications of the Laplace transformation, this is a professional handbook for the practicing mathematician. It is recommended for research collections.

943. Handbook for Linear Regression. Younger, Mary Sue. North Scituate, MA: Duxbury Press, 1979. 569p.

This reference handbook examines simple and multiple linear regression methods. It contains a subject index and four appendices that add to its usefulness. Some background knowledge of statistics and matrix analysis is helpful but not required. Recommended to undergraduate libraries.

944. Handbook of Applicable Mathematics. Ledermann, Walter, ed. Chichester, England: Wiley, 1980-1985. 6v.

A reference set concerning the practical aspects and applications of mathematics. Articles do not require extensive knowledge of particular mathematical topics. Volumes cover algebra, geometry, probability, and statistical analysis. An extensive bibliography is included at the end of each article.

945. Handbook of Applied Mathematics: Selected Results and Methods. 2nd ed. Pearsen, Carl E., ed. New York: Van Nostrand Reinhold, 1983. 1307p.

This book of mathematical procedures and applications for solving scientific and engineering problems includes formulas for vector analysis, tensors, and complex variables.

946. Handbook of Hypergeometric Integrals: Theory, Applications, Tables, Computer Programs. Exton, Harold. New York: Halsted Press, 1978. 316p.

An ordered list of analytical formulas, this is a useful reference for mathematicians, statisticians, physicists, and computer analysts.

947. Handbook of Mathematical Functions with Formulas, Graphs and Tables. U.S. National Bureau of Standards. New York: Wiley-Interscience, 1972. 1046p.

Incorporates numerical tables of mathematical functions. For those without easy access to computers, the tables serve as preliminary surveys of problems before the actual programming is attempted on the computer.

948. **Handbook of Mathematics.** Kuipers, L., and R. Tinman, eds. Oxford, England: Pergamon, 1969. 782p. (International Series of Monographs in Pure and Applied Mathematics, Vol. 99).

This is a well known and respected handbook on general mathematics. Translated by I. N. Sneddon from the Dutch *Handboek der Wiskunde* it includes history of mathematics, number systems, linear algebra, analytical geometry, analysis, sequences and series, theory of functions, ordinary differential equations, special functions, vector analysis, partial differential equations, numerical analysis, the Laplace transform, probability, and statistics. It is highly recommended for research collections.

949. **Handbook of Numerical and Statistical Techniques.** Pollard, J. H. Cambridge, England: Cambridge University Press, 1977. 349p.

This well-arranged handbook of statistics and statistical techniques is easy to use and highly recommended. The majority of the examples are in the life sciences.

950. **Handbook of Numerical Matrix Inversions and Solution of Linear Equations.** Westlake, Jean. Huntington, NY: Krieger, 1975. 171p.

This work is included because of its emphasis on computer solutions to the linear equations presented. The coverage includes direct methods, interactive methods, error measures, and scaling. It is recommended for research collections.

951. **Handbook of Operations Research.** Moder, Joseph J., and Salah E. Elmaghraby. New York: Van Nostrand Reinhold, 1978. 2v.

Volume 1 is titled *Foundations and Fundamentals*; volume 2, *Models and Applications*. Theory and concepts of operational research are covered, as well as areas of application. This is highly recommended for any research collection.

952. **Handbook of Probability and Statistics with Tables.** 2nd ed. Burington, Richard Stevens, and Donald Curtis May. New York: McGraw-Hill, 1970. 462p.

This handbook includes a chapter on nonparametric methods and some material in the areas of regression theory, variance analysis, and sampling techniques. Many formulas, definitions, specialized tables, and other material for ready reference use are provided. The coverage is basic, but substantial.

953. **Mathematics Manual: Methods and Principles of the Various Branches of Mathematics for Reference, Problem Solving, and Review.** Merritt, Frederick S. New York: McGraw-Hill, 1962. 378p.

This is a basic manual included here because it contains excellent coverage of methods of mathematics for various branches of the field. The coverage ranges from arithmetic through higher mathematics including matrices, tensors, probabilities, and statistics. Definitions, theorems and corollaries are provided throughout. Examples and references to additional literature are also included. This is recommended for academic libraries.

954. **Operations Research Handbook: Standard Algorithms and Methods with Examples.** Eiselt, H. A., and H. von Frajar. New York: Walter de Gruyter, 1977. 398p.

Contains algorithms in the field of computer programming. All algorithms are presented in form of principles, description, and examples. Recommended for applied mathematics collections in academic and research settings.

955. **Outliers in Statistical Data.** 2nd ed. Barnett, V., and T. Lewis. Chichester, England: Wiley, 1984. 463p.

An updated edition of a standard reference work on outliers, this work provides relevant illustration and tabulation as well as suggestions for further research. It is a definite must for any researcher involved in correlation or regression.

956. **Selected Tables in Mathematical Statistics.** Providence, RI: American Mathematical Society, 1970- . irregular.
This series of tables pulls together not only the selected tables, but some discussion of the underlying distributions. This multivolume work appears to be well on its way to becoming the definitive, scholarly set of tables and descriptions in the area of mathematical statistics. It is highly recommended for any research collection.

957. **SI Metric Handbook.** Feirer, John L. New York: Scribner, 1977. 1v. (various paging).
This work is included here as a standard reference to the SI system of measurement. Because a great deal of science and technology is now conducted in SI measurement, this is a useful translation tool for those unfamiliar with the system. Recommended for all libraries with science and technology interests.

958. **Statistical Tables for Biological, Agricultural and Medical Research.** 6th ed. Fisher, Ronald Aylmer, and Frank Yates. New York: Hafner, 1963. 146p.
A comprehensive collection of tables and bibliography on sources on statistical method. It should be noted that these tables are compiled by two giants in the field of statistics. This is a required title for any research collection.

QA276.25
N43
Sci

959. **Statistics Tables: For Mathematicians, Engineers, Economists and the Behavioral and Management Sciences.** Neave, H. R. London: Allen & Unwin, 1978. 87p.
A collection of statistical tables helpful to a broad range of students. It is recommended for general academic and college collections.

960. **Table of Series and Products.** Hansen, Eldon R. Englewood Cliffs, NJ: Prentice-Hall, 1975. 523p.
This is a listing of series that can be used to express a mathematical function as a sum of more elementary functions. The closed form for a given series is also provided. A necessary source for mathematicians and research collections.

961. **Tables of Physical and Chemical Constants and Some Mathematical Functions.** 15th ed. Kaye, G. W. C., and T. H. Laby, ed. London: Longman, 1986. 477p.
Contains updated information in the fields of general physics, chemistry, and mathematical functions. Footnote references are provided throughout, and all tabulated values are in SI units. This is an excellent source for tabular information and is highly recommended for research collections.

DIRECTORIES

962. **Computer Directory and Buyer's Guide.** Newtonville, MA: Berkley Enterprises, 1955- . annual.
Contains a wealth of information on all areas of the computer industry. The depth of coverage in the areas varies with each year but sections containing overviews of the technical advances of the year are provided. It is an excellent source for up-to-date information on firms, products, and services, and is especially useful because of the fast moving nature of the computing industry.

963. **Computer Yearbook and Directory.** Detroit, MI: American Data Processing, 1966- . annual.

There are two sections to this yearbook. One is a state-of-the-art review section and the second is a directory section. Like the *Computer Directory and Buyer's Guide* (see entry 962) this is an invaluable source for information on a fast moving area. The state-of-the-art sections are somewhat useful for historical purposes.

964. **International Directory of Computer and Information System Services.** London: Europa Publications, 1969- . irregular.

This is a true directory, listing names, addresses, telephone numbers, and principle officers of both institutions and companies in the computing industry. The focus is clearly on Western institutions and companies, but some entries for other countries are included.

965. **Mathematical Sciences Professional Directory.** Providence, RI: American Mathematical Society, 1987. 196p.

Covers the administrative structure, boards and committees of the American Mathematical Society and other related professional associations. Addresses for individuals listed under the professional organizations are provided, as well as those for publishers and editors of mathematical journals. Indexed by colleges and universities, this is a comprehensive directory of clear worth.

966. **Men of Mathematics.** Bell, Eric Temple. New York: Simon & Schuster, 1965. 590p.

This is an account of 34 persons who were instrumental in the development of mathematics. The two criteria for inclusion were (1) the known appeal of the man's life and character, and (2) the importance of the man's works to modern mathematics. This is recommended for general collections.

967. **Women of Mathematics: A Bibliographic Sourcebook.** Grinstein, Louise S., and Paul J. Campbell, eds. Westport, CT: Greenwood Press, 1987. 292p.

This is a compilation of material dealing with women mathematicians born prior to 1925 and recognized by the mathematical community in some manner. Forty-three mathematicians are included. Unlike other sources, this offers reasonably in-depth explanations of the work of these women. It is recommended for academic and professional collections because of its level of treatment.

[handwritten margin notes: QA 28 .W66 1987 Sci Ref]

968. **World Directory of Mathematicians.** 8th ed. Mostow, G. D., ed. Helsinki, Finland: International Mathematical Union, 1986. 950p.

Mathematicians of the world are listed with their address and occasionally with their title and affiliation. A geographical listing by country provides name only. This is an important tool for world information in mathematics.

9 Physics

Physics is the science which deals with nature in its most abstract form. Consisting of both physical experiment and mathematical description, its basic goal is the study and description of natural phenomena in inanimate nature.

Physics has two basic divisions: experimental physics and theoretical physics. Somewhat analogous to a mathematician, the theoretical physicist is in need of a great deal of literature. The experimental physicist is less literature-based and is closer to the technologist in terms of literature use.

Theoretical physics makes great use of mathematics and applied mathematics in an effort to model the universe. The experimental physicist is interested in verifying the theories of the theoretical branch. While this is a gross generalization, it does point out two very distinct camps in the physics community.

Physics has attracted a great deal of attention since World War II, particularly for its advances in the area of nuclear physics. More recently, investigations into the nature of matter on the subatomic level have been the object of attention. These investigations engendered the subatomic, elementary particle "zoo" of quarks, antiquarks, and gluons among others.

Physics as a discipline is very wide and encompasses a great number of subfields and specialties. As a topic, it is rarely discussed at the research front area. Smaller, more compact areas are the focus of modern physics. Libraries and information centers should recognize that physics is more of an administrative division within a university structure rather than an intellectual division.

GUIDES TO THE LITERATURE

969. **Information Sources in Physics.** Shaw, Dennis F., ed. London: Butterworths, 1985. 456p.

This is a descriptive source book for using the physics literature. The 20 chapters discuss the various indexing and abstracting services and what sources are available in various fields of physics. Each area is broken down into various source materials. An extensive name index and subject/title index is provided. Several sources in quantum physics are dated and should be used with care.

970. **Use of Physics Literature.** Coblans, Herbert, ed. London: Butterworths, 1975. 290p.

A book intended for scientists, engineers, students, and librarians. The first five chapters are related to libraries, the structure and control of physics literature, and the basic general reference tools in physics. The remaining chapter covers specific subject literature related to subfields of physics, such as history of physics, theoretical physics, nuclear and atomic physics, and instrumentation. A more up-to-date literature source book is Shaw's *Information Sources in Physics* (see entry 969). This is included because of its good treatment of the literature structure in physics.

ABSTRACTS, INDEXES, AND BIBLIOGRAPHIES

971. **Acoustics Abstracts.** Brentwood, England: Multi-Science Publishing Co., 1967- . monthly.

This service covers the primary areas of vibration, shock, audio frequencies, ultrasonics, noise, and the physiological and psychological aspects of sound and bioacoustics. Indexes by author and subject are produced annually.

972. **CINDA 84 (1982-1984): The Index to Literature and Computer Files on Microscopic Neutron Data.** Vienna: International Atomic Energy Agency, 1984. 279p.

Covers the literature on measurements, calculations, reviews, and evaluations of neutron cross-sections and other microscopic data. The data are gathered from books, journals, conference proceedings, and other laboratory findings. In tabular form, the arrangement is by element and mass number. Abbreviations are utilized extensively, making the volume somewhat difficult to use. It is recommended for research collections.

973. **Current Papers in Physics.** London: Institution of Electrical Engineers, 1966- . bimonthly.

This current awareness service consists of titles of research articles from the world's physics journals. Assuming the titles are illustrative of the material, this is an excellent means of keeping abreast in allied areas of physics.

974. **Current Physics Index.** New York: American Institute of Physics, 1975- . quarterly.

The intent is to provide information about physics research published in a core set of journals. The arrangement is by subject, and the entries include title, author, affiliation, and bibliographic description. No attempt is made to be evaluative.

975. **General Physics Advance Abstracts.** New York: American Institute of Physics, 1985- . semimonthly.

Geared to quickening the pace of getting physics literature to the field, this contains brief abstracts of material in a select list of physics journals. Its intent is to act as a current awareness service. Recommended for research collections.

976. **INIS Atomindex: An International Abstracting Service.** Vienna: International Atomic Energy Agency; distr., New York: UNIPUB, 1970- . monthly. 1976- . semimonthly.

This is the premier abstracting tool for nuclear physics. In addition to strictly scientific areas, economic, legal, and social aspects are covered, as well as patents, technical reports, and standards. *Nuclear Science Abstracts* (Washington, DC: Atomic Energy Commission, 1948-1976) was discontinued in favor of this publication.

977. **INSPEC.** Hitchin Herts, England: Institution of Electrical Engineers, 1969- .

One of the portions of the INSPEC database corresponds to *Physics Abstracts* (see entry 979). The file is updated monthly and is available from DIALOG, SDC, and BRS.

978. **Physical Review Abstracts.** New York: American Institute of Physics, 1976- . semimonthly.

An abstract of papers already accepted for publication in the *Physical Review* (New York: American Institute of Physics, 1970-) and *Physical Review Letters* (New York: American Institute of Physics, 1970-). Both of these publications are major series in physics. The abstracts are descriptive and generally brief. It has been included here because of the timeliness with which the abstracts are prepared. Recommended for any collection where *Physical Review* or *Physical Review Letters* is used.

979. **Physics Abstracts.** London: Institution of Electrical Engineers, 1898- . semimonthly.

In 1941, *Physics Abstracts* became Section A of *Science Abstracts*. Section B is titled *Electrical and Electronics Abstracts* and section C, *Computer and Control Abstracts*. This is the only abstracting service which purports to cover all of physics. Its coverage is distinctly international, including journals, technical reports, books, dissertations, patents, and conference papers. The abstracts are short and descriptive as opposed to evaluative. There is an indication, taken from the original document, of the author's affiliation. The internal arrangement is classified on the following order: (0) general; (1) physics of elementary particles and fields; (2) nuclear physics; (3) atomic and molecular physics; (4) classical areas of phenomenology; (5) fluids, plasmas, and electrical discharges; (6) condensed matter, including its structure, thermal, and mechanical properties; (7) condensed matter, including electronic structures, electrical, magnetic, and optical properties; (8) cross-disciplinary physics and related areas of science and technology; and (9) geophysics, astronomy, and astrophysics.

980. **Physics Briefs.** New York: American Institute of Physics, 1979- . semimonthly.

Issued in cooperation with Deutsche Physikalische Gesellschaft and the Fachinformationszentrum Energie, Physik, Mathematik, this journal covers the majority of physics and some allied areas. The coverage is international and includes books, journals, technical reports, patents, theses, and conference papers. Journals considered to be especially important are abstracted completely. Not as complete overall as *Physics Abstracts* (see entry 979), it is still more timely.

981. **Referativnyi Zhurnal. Fizyka.** Moscow: Institut Nauchno-Tekhnicheskoi Informatsii, 1954- . monthly.

This is one of the world's best abstract journals with well-written abstracts usually done by experts. The abstracts are mostly descriptive, and at times can be evaluative. The amount of time it takes the abstract to reach the journal is the major drawback of this work. Other than this one problem, which is not unusual for abstract journals, this is an excellent source.

982. **Rheology Abstracts: A Survey of World Literature.** New York: Pergamon, 1958- . quarterly.

Covering the world literature in rheology, the abstracts are descriptive and generally short. Annual author and subject indexes are provided.

983. **Solid State Abstracts Journal.** Cambridge, MA: Cambridge Communications Corporation, 1957- . 7/yr.

Contains material on physics, metallurgy, crystallography, chemistry, and device technology of solids. The coverage includes primary documents as well as books. The work appears to be designed for those with some knowledge in the use of physics literature. *Science Research Abstracts Journal*, Part A (Riverdale, MD: Cambridge Scientific Abstracts), is now incorporated into this title.

984. **SPIN.** New York: American Institute of Physics, 1975- . monthly.

SPIN (Searchable Physics Information Notices) provides indexing and abstracting of major U.S. and Russian physics and some astronomy journals. The majority of the material cited is from the publications of the AIP. Available from DIALOG.

ENCYCLOPEDIAS

985. **Concise Encyclopedia of Solid State Physics.** Lerner, Rita G., and George L. Trigg. New York: Addison-Wesley, 1983. 311p.

Contains signed articles with references from the larger *Encyclopedia of Physics* (see entry 987). This is basically a spinoff work and is important only if the larger work is not available.

986. **Encyclopaedic Dictionary of Physics: General, Nuclear, Solid State, Molecular** QC5
Chemical, Metal and Vacuum Physics, Astronomy, Geophysics, Biophysics, and Related E52
Subjects. Thewlis, James, ed. New York: Pergamon, 1961-1964. 9v. **Supplement,** 1966- . Sci Ref
irregular.

Also known as *Thewlis's Encyclopaedic Dictionary of Physics*, this work covers all aspects of physics and related areas such as mathematics, astronomy, chemistry, and hydraulics. Each entry is signed and is written for a professional audience. This is not a dictionary for the undergraduate or casual inquiry. It is updated with regular supplements.

987. **Encyclopedia of Physics.** 3rd ed. Besancon, Robert M., ed. New York: Van QC5
Nostrand Reinhold, 1985. 1378p. E546
This is a concise, one-volume edition covering the entire field of physics. Each subject 1985
article was written by an expert and is signed. Articles on new developments since the Sci
publication of the second edition have been added. Designed to give uniform coverage, the Ref
encyclopedia presents articles written on three different levels: those on the main divisions
of physics are intended for readers with little background in the subject; those on the subdivisions are aimed at readers with more knowledge; and those on the more finely divided areas are geared toward readers with fairly sound backgrounds in both physics and mathematics.

988. **Handbuch der Physik (Encyclopedia of Physics).** Flugge, S., ed. Berlin: Springer, QC176
1955- . 54v. .A3
First published from 1926-1929 in 24 volumes and an index. The second edition covers C66
the following topics: 1-2, mathematical methods; 3, principles of classical mechanics and 1983
field theory; 4, principles of thermodynamics and relativity; 5, principles of quantum Sci
theory; 6, elasticity and plasticity; 7, crystal physics; 8, fluid dynamics; 9, fluid mechanics; Ref
11, acoustics; 12, thermodynamics of gases; 13, thermodynamics of liquids and solids;
14-15, low-temperature physics; 16, electric fields and waves; 17-18, dielectrics; 19-20, electrical conductivity; 21-22, electron emission, gas discharges; 23, electrical instruments;

24, fundamentals of optics; 25, crystal optics, diffraction; 26, light and matter; 27-28, spectroscopy; 29, optical instruments; 30, X-rays; 32, structural research; 33, corpuscular optics; 34, corpuscles and radiation in matter; 35-36, atoms; 37(1), atoms (pt. 3), molecules (pt. 1); 37(2), molecules (pt. 2); 38(1), external properties of atomic nuclei; 38(2), neutron and related gamma ray problems; 39, structure of atomic nuclei; 40-42, nuclear reactions; 44-45, nuclear instrumentation; 46, cosmic rays; 47-49, geophysics; 50-54, astrophysics.

This is the absolute authority in the physics world for published information. It is the only systematic encyclopedic treatise covering the entire domain of physics. The work is trilingual — German, English, and French. Many volumes are entirely in English; others have English contributions; and all have added title pages in English. The subject indexes in each volume are often pressed into service as informal lexicons.

TA418
.52
P8
Sci
Ref

989. **Thermophysical Properties of Matter.** Touloukian, Y. S. New York: Plenum, 1970-1979. 13v. in 15v.

This is a massive undertaking which resulted in the generation of a series of tables for science and technology. Each volume normally contains three sections of varying length: text, numerical data with source references, and an index. Most of the material is in tabular or graphic format, with explanatory text accompanying each bit of data.

990. **Zahlenwerte und Funktionen aus Naturwissenschaften und Technik — Neue Serie. 1961-1985. (Numerical Data and Functional Relationships in Science and Technology — New Series. 1961-1985).** Berlin: Springer-Verlag, 1987.

This is a direct competitor to *Thermophysical Properties of Matter* (see entry 989) in certain areas. The scope of this work is broader, however. It has an excellent collection of tabular information on the fundamental properties of physics, chemistry, astronomy, and geophysics. The first edition was published in 1883 under the title *Physikalisch-Chemische Tabellen*. The volumes and their contents are:

Vol. 1, *Atom-und Molekularphysik*
Vol. 2, *Eigenschaften der Materie in Ihren Aggregatzustanden*
Vol. 3, *Astronomie und Geophysik*
Vol. 4, *Technik*

New Series:

Group I, *Kernphysik und Kerntechnik (Nuclear Physics and Technology)*
Group II, *Atom-und Molekularphysik (Atomic and Molecular Physics)*
Group III, *Kristall-und Festkorperphysik (Crystal and Solid State Physics)*
Group IV, *Makroskopische und technische Eigenschaften der Materie (Macroscopic and Technical Properties of Matter)*
Group V, *Geophysik und Weltraumforschung (Geophysics and Space Research)*
Group VI, *Astronomie, Astrophysik und Weltraumforschung (Astronomy, Astrophysics and Space Research)*

DICTIONARIES

991. **Cambridge Illustrated Thesaurus of Physics.** Richards, Teresa. Cambridge, England: Cambridge University Press, 1984. 256p.

This thesaurus is broken down into the various subjects of physics with terms of the subject defined. The definitions are very brief and include cross-references. The index is good and is necessary to access specific terms. Though it deals little with quantum physics, this work would be useful for quick, short definitions of general physics.

992. **Concise Dictionary of Physics and Related Subjects.** 2nd ed. rev. Thewlis, J. Oxford, England: Pergamon, 1979. 370p.

This is based in part on the *Encyclopaedic Dictionary of Physics* (see entry 986). The result is a minor updating of the older work. The intent of the dictionary is to give students and nonspecialists an entree to physics terminology. It differs therefore from the earlier work in terms of scope. The terms defined are not all strictly in physics, some come from astronomy, photography, and allied areas. Recommended for academic and some public libraries.

993. **Dictionary of Spectroscopy.** 2nd ed. Denney, R. C. London: Macmillan, 1982. 205p.

A standard dictionary format covering the modern and traditional types of spectroscopy. Most entries have a reference to literature in the field, providing a means of additional information sources. The audience is undergraduates and those with some training in the area.

994. **Dictionary of the Physical Sciences.** Emiliani, Casare. New York: Oxford University Press, 1987. 365p.

The definitions here range from a single sentence to several paragraphs. For the majority of cases, the definitions are more complex than those found in the *McGraw Hill Dictionary of Scientific and Technical Terms* (see entry 229). Aimed at the professional in science, this is more than a dictionary and contains tables of data in the physical sciences more in the fashion of a handbook. It is a clear choice for more technically and professionally oriented collections.

995. **Elsevier's Dictionary of Nuclear Science and Technology in Six Languages: English/American-French-Spanish-Italian-Dutch and German.** 2nd rev. ed. Clason, W. E., comp. Amsterdam: Elsevier, 1970. 787p.

This is, as the title suggests, a polyglot dictionary. The entries are arranged by the English word followed by the equivalents in French, Spanish, Italian, Dutch, and German. The layout of the entry is tabular. Each language has a separate index referring the English word. Although dated, it is still valuable for its multilingual nature.

996. **English-Russian Physics Dictionary.** Tolstoi, D. M., ed. Oxford, England: Pergamon, 1978. 848p.

Included here because of the large amount of Russian material comprising physics literature, this Russian-English dictionary is a requirement for complete coverage of the literature. All basic areas of physics are covered. Recommended for any research oriented collection.

997. **Macmillan Dictionary of Physics.** Lord, M. P. London: Macmillan, 1986. 330p.

Written for the undergraduate level, this work contains short, unsigned articles on over 4,000 terms. Recommended for any academic and most public libraries.

998. **McGraw-Hill Dictionary of Physics.** Parker, Sybil P., ed. New York: McGraw-Hill, 1984. 646p.

With a few additions, this is basically composed of all the physics terms found in the *McGraw-Hill Dictionary of Physics and Mathematics* (1978). This dictionary contains definitions of terms in physics, mathematics, and other related fields, such as fluid mechanics and mineralogy.

HANDBOOKS

QC 161.5
A43
1985
Sci
Ref

999. AGA Gas Handbook. Ahlberg, Kersti, ed. Lindingho, Sweden: AGA AB, 1985. 582p.

This work contains "general information about the physical and chemical properties, application, handling and transportation of 67 gases." Primarily for engineers and technicians, it is arranged alphabetically by name of gas. A subject index is provided. Recommended for research and highly technical collections only.

QC61
.A5
1963
Sci

1000. American Institute of Physics Handbook. 3rd ed. Gray, Dwight E., ed. New York: McGraw-Hill, 1972. 1v. (various paging).

This is one of the most respected handbooks in all science. It supplies tables, reference materials, and descriptions of areas by leaders in individual fields. Descriptions are brief, but very well done. Each section covers a field of physics, from definitions and concepts through the many subtopics of that particular field. An excellent index helps the user locate specific data. It is recommended for technical and research collections, although some public libraries will find it useful as well.

1001. CRC Handbook of Fast Neutron Generators. Gyula, J. Csikai, ed. Boca Raton, FL: CRC Press, 1987. 2v.

Contains review problems and methods in science where neutrons produced in the $^3H/d$, $n/^4He$ and $^2H/d$, $n/^3He$ reactions play a major role. Included are discussions of experiments as well as possible uses for the generators. This is a professional source for use in a research collection.

1002. Eight Peak Index of Mass Spectra. 3rd ed. Nottingham, England: Mass Spectrometry Data Centre, 1983. 3v. in 7v.

An invaluable reference source, this contains the eight most abundant ions in 66,720 mass spectra. It is indexed by molecular weight, elemental composition, and most abundant ions.

QC161.5
K43
1983
Sci Ref

1003. Gas Tables. 2nd ed. Keenan, Joseph. New York: Wiley, 1980.

Consisting of 62 tables of thermodynamic properties, this source contains excellent material drawn from other handbooks and from original literature. There are two versions of this handbook, one in English units and another in SI unit notation.

QC369
.H35
Sci Ref

1004. Handbook of Optics. Driscoll, Walter G., ed. New York: McGraw-Hill, 1978. 1v. (various paging).

Intended for the optical systems designer and engineer, a considerable amount of the book is taken up with tabular and graphic information. A minimum of description is present; however, extensive lists of references to the literature are provided.

1005. Infrared Spectra Handbook of Common Organic Solvents. Philadelphia: Sadtler, 1983. 400p.

This handbook lists the infrared reference spectra of 400 common solvents grouped by chemical class and contains information extremely difficult to obtain otherwise.

QC61
.K3
1986
Sci
Ref

1006. Tables of Physical and Chemical Constants and Some Mathematical Functions. 15th ed. Kaye, George William Clarkson, and T. H. Laby. London: Longman, 1986. 320p.

Each of the sections begins with a well-written and effective introduction. The tables frequently contain notes to the literature, not only detailing the source of the tables, but the background for the underlying tenets as well. All tables are in SI units.

1007. **Thermometry.** Schooley, James F. Boca Raton, FL: CRC Press, 1986. 256p.

An excellent single source for discussions of the development of temperature scales and the use, construction, and theory of thermometers. Tables and figures as well as references to the literature round out the work. This is an excellent source book for the particular area. Recommended for research collections.

1008. **Vapour Pressures of Pure Substances.** 2nd ed. Boublik, Tombais, Vojtiech Fried, and Eduard Hbala. New York: Elsevier, 1984. 972p.

A compendium of the vapor pressures of pure substances, compiled from other handbooks and original literature. This material will be of most use to experimental and theoretical physicists engaged in research.

DIRECTORIES

1009. **Biographical Dictionary of Scientists: Physicists.** Abbott, David, ed. New York: Bedrick, 1984. 212p.

This is a new biographical series covering the ancients to contemporary physicists. A one-half-to-two-page biography is provided for each entry. Bibliographies are not included.

1010. **World Nuclear Directory.** Wilson, C. W. J., ed. Harlow, England: Longman, 1985. 387p.

Provides profiles of organizations and laboratories which are carrying out or funding research and development projects within nuclear science. Arrangement is alphabetical by entry.

10   Zoology

As the study of animals, traditional zoology made a simple distinction between the plant and animal kingdoms. Zoology dealt with animals; botany dealt with plants. Modern zoology has refined this distinction so that the zoologist today investigates organisms which are not animals, monera, protista, or fungi.

The ancient Egyptians had a rudimentary concept of blood circulation, functions of organs, and disease. It was not until Aristotle, however, that the cornerstones of what we know as modern zoology were laid. Aristotle's contributions in taxonomy, anatomy, physiology, and genetics are the basis for modern zoology.

The focus of zoology has remained primarily in these four areas. The benefit to the library is the constancy of the areas. However, zoology has benefited from techniques in other disciplines. The electron microscope, for example, allows more finely delineated study of living organisms and their structures. The stability of the literature does make bibliographic control much easier than in other disciplines such as physics, as an example.

ABSTRACTS, INDEXES,
AND BIBLIOGRAPHIES—GENERAL

1011. Bibliography of Reproduction: A Classified Monthly Title List Compiled from the World's Research Literature. Vertebrates, Including Man. Cambridge, England: Reproduction Research Information Service, 1963- . monthly.

This work attempts to cover the literature of biology, medicine, agriculture, and veterinary science with respect to reproductive topics. An author and animal index is provided in each issue. The indexes are cumulated semiannually. Overall the coverage is good, though an English language bias exists.

1012. Nomenclator Zoologicus: A List of the Names of Genera and Subgenera in Zoology from the Tenth Edition of Linnaeus 1758 to the End of 1955. Neave, Sheffield Airey, ed. London: Zoological Society of London, 1939-1965. 7v.

This is a listing of zoological names accepted by the scientific community during the period 1758 to 1955. The arrangement is alphabetical with each entry giving a citation to the name and original literature reference. This is a major tool for tracing nomenclature in zoology.

1013. **Zoological Record.** London: Zoological Society of London, 1865- . annual.
This is the most comprehensive bibliography of the world's zoological literature in terms of scope and coverage, and is also an excellent source for taxonomic references. Composed of several sections, it is somewhat difficult to use because of a lack of an overall index. Nonetheless, it is still the premier indexing tool for zoological literature. Available as an online database from DIALOG 1978- .

ABSTRACTS, INDEXES, AND BIBLIOGRAPHIES—INVERTEBRATES

1014. **Abstracts of Entomology.** Philadelphia, PA: Biosciences Information Service, 1970- . monthly.
Coverage includes pure and applied literature on insects and spiders. Other arachnids are covered with varying degrees of completeness. Abstracts are descriptive and generally short. Recommended for research collections only.

1015. **Entomological Nomenclature and Literature.** 3rd ed. rev. and enl. Chamberlain, Willard Joseph. Westport, CT: Greenwood Press, 1970. 141p.
This is a bibliography of insect nomenclature arranged in chronological order. There are separate annotated bibliographies of serials and general works. Although dated, this is still a good source of information for nomenclature and is recommended for academic and research organizations.

ABSTRACTS, INDEXES, AND BIBLIOGRAPHIES—VERTEBRATES

1016. **Aquatic Sciences and Fisheries Abstracts.** London: Information Retrieval, Ltd., 1971- . monthly.
This is an excellent source of material related in any way to physical and chemical oceanography, limnology, aquatic biology, ecology, and pollution effects on fishes. The broad subject categories impede retrieval somewhat in the hard copy version. Includes author, taxonomic, and geographic indexes in each issue. Cumulative author indexes are issued semiannually. Originally published as *Aquatic Biology Abstracts* (1969-1971), the change of title occurred when the *Abstracts* merged with *Current Bibliography for Aquatic Sciences and Fisheries* (1958-1971). Available online from 1978 to present from DIALOG.

1017. **Bibliography of Birds.** Strong, Reuben Myron. Chicago: Natural History Museum, 1939-1959. 4v.
This is a major reference work for information related to anatomy, behavior, biochemistry, embryology, poultry, culture, and related subjects. The material is dated in some places; however, it is included here because it pulls together a massive amount of material. The coverage is comprehensive to 1926 and then selective to 1938. Of particular note is the fact that all the references were checked against the original literature to verify accuracy. This is a special tool for research and academic collections.

1018. **Bibliography of Fishes.** Dean, Bashford. New York: American Museum of Natural History, 1972. 3v.
Coverage focuses on the habitat, structure, development, pathology, physiology, and distribution of fishes. The bibliography is arranged by author making it less useful for the

casual user. This is a professional tool to be used by one already somewhat familiar with the literature. Of particular note is the pre-Linnaean material referenced. Although showing some age, this is still an excellent bibliography used widely by zoologists.

1019. **Dictionary Catalog of the Blacker-Wood Library of Zoology and Ornithology, McGill University, Montreal.** Boston: G. K. Hall, 1966. 9v.
This entry is included because of the first-rate nature of the Blacker-Wood collection. As a checklist of predominantly historical material, it is an excellent entry point for a serious researcher. The reputation of the Blacker-Wood collection as a research center is a major impetus for inclusion.

1020. **Dolphins and Porpoises: A Comprehensive Annotated Bibliography of the Smaller Cetacea.** Truitt, Deborah. Detroit, MI: Gale Research, 1974. 582p.
Although dated, this source is included because of its depth of coverage. The entries range from 560 B.C. through 1972 and include journal articles, books, and report literature. The work is not entirely scientific, because titles from fiction, mythology, and children's stories are provided as well. Foreign language materials are well represented, with non-Roman titles converted. Descriptive annotations are usually found for each entry. This is an excellent, if somewhat eclectic, research tool.

1021. **Introduction to the Literature of Vertebrate Zoology.** Wood, Casey Albert, ed. New York: Arno, 1974. 643p.
This work was prepared by one of the giants in the field. It is based on materials chiefly found in the McGill University Library system: the Blacker Library, the Wood Library, and the Osler Library. Given the scope and collection of these libraries, this is not a drawback but a positive point. Contains a good introduction, is showing some age, but overall is important for its historical and systematic introduction to vertebrate zoology.

1022. **Laboratory Animal Science.** Joliet, IL: American Association for Laboratory Animal Science, 1950- . bimonthly.
Contains material related to care and usage of laboratory animals. The material is brief, but informative. A particularly timely publication.

1023. **Laboratory Animals: An Annotated Bibliography of Informational Resources Covering Medicine—Science (Including Husbandry)—Technology.** Cass, Jules, ed. New York: Hafner, 1971. 1v. (various paging).
In some ways, this complements the periodical title, *Laboratory Animal Science* (see entry 1022). Sections delineate such topics as normal anatomy, physiology and psychology, disease, abnormalities and injuries, nutrition and diet, breeding programs, colony design and maintenance, procurement and use of animals, and periodical and other publication sources. The material is presented in a descriptive format with some critical annotations. The clear emphasis is on vertebrates. A good retrospective resource in an area receiving much attention.

ENCYCLOPEDIAS

1024. **Atlas of Animal Migration.** Jarman, Cathy. New York: Thomas Y. Crowell, 1974. 124p.
Contains a good description of the migratory patterns and emigration of several major migratory groups. The emphasis of the work is more on migration, and it is included here

because of its straightforward discussion of the phenomenon. Recommended for college and public library collections.

1025. Atlas of Wildlife. Nayman, Jacqueline. New York: John Day, 1972. 124p.

An interesting book included for its completeness. It begins with a section on fauna differences and similarities, focusing on the continental drift theory as an explanation. Another section deals solely with island fauna. The clarity of the book is the major reason for its inclusion. It is recommended for public and college collections.

1026. Encyclopedia of Animal Care. 12th ed. West, Geoffrey P., ed. Baltimore, MD: Williams & Wilkins, 1977. 867p.

This is an American version of *Black's Veterinary Dictionary* (London: A & C Black, 1976). The emphasis is on first-aid and preventive medicine, veterinary techniques of interest to the farmer, and public health matters. This is not intended as a state-of-the-art publication. It is a practical encyclopedia, which extends its currency considerably beyond the publication date. Recommended for general collections.

1027. Encyclopedia of Aquatic Life. Banister, Keith, and Andrew Campbell, eds. New York: Facts on File, 1985. 349p.

Not as comprehensive as the title indicates, this work still manages to be a good introduction to aquatic life for the layperson. The articles are all signed by experts in the field, and a good glossary is provided for the instances where technical terms are unavoidable. Recommended for general collections.

1028. Encyclopedia of Birds. Perrins, Christopher M., and Alex L. A. Middleton, eds. New York: Facts on File, 1985. 445p.

Well illustrated, this is a compilation of articles by authorities in ornithological research. Not as detailed as *Dictionary of Birds* (see entry 1042), this is still an excellent beginning encyclopedia. It is recommended for general collections, school, and public libraries.

1029. Encyclopedia of Mammals. Macdonald, David, ed. New York: Facts on File, 1984. 895p.

This is an amateur or layperson's encyclopedia. The work is authoritative and relatively complete, given its scope. All illustrations are in color. For a more scholarly treatment of mammals, consider Walker's *Mammals of the World* (see entry 1103). Recommended for public and college collections.

1030. Grzimek's Animal Life Encyclopedia. Grzimek, Bernhard, ed. New York: Van Nostrand Reinhold, 1984. 13v.

This encyclopedia was originally published in Germany. The arrangement of the work is by animal groupings: mammals, birds, fish and amphibians, reptiles, insects, mollusks and echinoderms, and lower animals. The material related to each grouping is further subdivided into animal orders and families. The overall tone of the work is descriptive without introduction of controversial issues. Recommended for public, college, and some university collections.

1031. Hyman Series in Invertebrate Biology: Zoological Sciences. Hyman, Libbie Henrietta. New York: McGraw-Hill, 1940-1967. 6v.

This is a well known and respected treatise covering morphology, physiology, and embryology of the invertebrates. It is included here because it is still used by zoologists as a source of references. Recommended for research collections only.

QL674
.H229
Sci
Ref

1032. **Illustrated Encyclopedia of Birds: All the Birds of Britain and Europe in Color.** New York: Marshall Cavendish, 1979. 5v.

There are excellent photographs and drawings in this translation from a 1971 Italian work. Names of birds are given in English, French, Italian, Spanish, and German, along with the Latin name. The descriptive material on each entry includes habitat, identification, call, reproduction, food, distribution and movements, and subspecies. Although somewhat dated, the work is still worthwhile for the good description and excellent illustrations.

X

1033. **International Wildlife Encyclopedia.** Burton, Maurice, and Robert Burton, eds. New York: Marshall Cavendish, 1969-1970. 20v.

This is a first-rate encyclopedia. Each article has descriptive information including geographic distribution and a map. The text is very descriptive and tends to cover each entry thoroughly. The breadth of the work is impressive and is matched by the depth of the articles. Highly recommended for any library or information center.

1034. **Living Sea: An Illustrated Encyclopedia of Marine Life.** Burton, Robert, Carole Devaney, and Tony Long. New York: Putnam, 1976. 240p.

The text in this encyclopedia is rather skimpy and not overly informative. The illustrations, however, are excellent and qualify the work for inclusion here. Divided into five main sections, it covers invertebrates, fish, reptiles, seabirds, and mammals. Recommended for both general and research collections because of the illustrations only.

1035. **Macmillan Illustrated Animal Encyclopedia.** Whitfield, Philip, ed. New York: Macmillan, 1984. 600p.

This is a mistitled encyclopedia. Rather than covering the entire animal kingdom, it covers very well the vertebrates. The intended audience is the general reader and the work generally hits its target. Few errors mar the work and, as a whole, it can be recommended for most general collections.

1036. **New Larousse Encyclopedia of Animal Life.** New York: Larousse, 1980. 640p.

A very good general reference work fully living up to the high Larousse standards. It begins with simple unicellular life and completes its systematic coverage with complex animals. Each chapter generally covers one phylum. This is a clear choice for virtually any library or information center.

QL45
T7
Sci

1037. **Traite de zoologie: Anatomie, systematique, biologie.** Grasse, Pierre Paul. Paris: Masson, 1948- . 17v.- .

Malcles discusses this title in *Les Sources du travail bibliographique* (Geneva, Switzerland: E. Droz, 1950). His overall comment is that this work is the only true treatise on zoology. It is compared favorably with *Handbuch der Zoologie: eine Naturgeschichte der Stamme des Tierreiches* (Berlin: Walter de Gruyter, 1968). An older work to which Grasse's work can be compared is *The Cambridge Natural History* (London: Macmillan, 1895-1909). It should be clear this is a necessary title for any serious research collection. The other titles listed above are either much older or not as complete.

1038. **World Encyclopedia of Fishes.** Wheeler, Alwyne. London: Macdonald, 1985. 368p.

Arranged into two sections, the first is a series of color photographs of selected species. The second section is a "dictionary" arranged by scientific name. A good general purpose encyclopedia in the field recommended for university and research collections.

DICTIONARIES

1039. **Amphibian Species of the World: A Taxonomic and Geographical Reference.** Frost, Darrel R., ed. Lawrence, KS: Allen Press, 1985. 732p.

This is the first book of its kind to serve as a "dictionary" to species names while complying with the requirements of the third edition of the *International Code of Zoological Nomenclature* (see entry 1053). This is an easy-to-use reference tool that is an important contribution to the taxonomic structure and literature and is highly recommended for any serious zoological collection.

1040. **Birdwatcher's Dictionary.** Weaver, Peter. Calton, England: Poyser, 1981. 155p.

Intended for beginners and experienced birdwatchers, this dictionary covers scientific terms, slang, and common names used in Britain. Recommended for public and general collections.

QL676
W35
Sci
Ref

1041. **Dictionary of American Bird Names.** rev. ed. Choate, Ernest A., and Raymond A. Paynter. Boston: Harvard Common Press, 1985. 226p.

This was updated as a result of the appearance of the sixth edition of the American Ornithologist's Union's *Check-list of North American Birds* (see entry 1078). The first part is a listing of common names, which includes brief etymology and derivation of common phrases derived from the bird name. The second part is a listing by scientific name. Finally, a biographical appendix and an English/Latin glossary are included. This is an upper level dictionary but still of excellent utility to general as well as research collections.

1042. **Dictionary of Birds.** Campbell, Bruce, and Elizabeth Lack, eds. Vermillion, SD: Buteo Books, 1985. 670p.

QL673
D54
1985b
Sci
Ref

Published for the British Ornithologists' Union, this work contains signed articles on different types of birds and general bird subjects. References (generally in English) are included with the larger entries. This is more of an encyclopedic dictionary and is highly recommended for any serious collection in ornithology.

1043. **Dictionary of Entomology.** Leftwich, A. W. New York: Crane-Russak, 1976. 360p.

This is intended for the amateur entomologist or naturalist with an interest in insects and students of zoology. The work deliberately excludes definitions of general biological terms except where absolutely necessary. Considered to be a good choice for a general dictionary in the area for college and public libraries.

1044. **Dictionary of Herpetology.** Peters, James Arthur. New York: Hafner, 1964. 391p.

Brief definitions are given for terms relating to snakes, including notation of conflicting meanings. There are cross-references for some material. Although dated, this is a good source for basic information and is recommended for college and public libraries.

1045. **Dictionary of Zoology.** Leftwich, A. W. London: Constable & Co., Ltd., 1973. 478p.

QL9
.L4
1973
Sci
Ref

This is a student dictionary on general zoology. Included with the general dictionary are appendices on classification and nomenclature, translation of Greek terms, and a short bibliography. The bibliography is very much out of date; however, the rest of the dictionary is still useful as a student dictionary, which was its original intent. Recommended for general, but not research, collections.

1046. **Entomologisches Wörterbuch mit besonderer Berucksichtigung der Morphologischen Terminologie.** von Keler, S. Berlin: Akademie-Verlag, 1963. 774p.

A very complete and thorough dictionary intended for the scholar in the field. There are good discussions of conflicts in meaning and interpretations for various terms. The definitions are very well done, making this a highly recommended source for any research collection.

1047. **Glossary of Entomology: Smith's "An Explanation of Terms Used in Entomology."** De La Torre-Bueno, Jose Rollin. New York: New York Entomological Society, 1978. 336p.

This is a difficult dictionary to annotate. It is not solely intended for the novice, but is still relatively basic in its coverage. It is recommended for college and some university collections, though specialized public library collections may also be interested.

1048. **Glossary of Some Foreign-Language Terms in Entomology.** Ericson, R. O. Washington, DC: U.S. Government Printing Office, 1961. 59p.

This is a brief glossary showing some age. It is included here because of its compactness and for its good, short definitions. This is a good choice for a desk reference to use with Czech, Danish, Dutch, French, German, Polish, Russian, and Swedish literature. The terms are interfiled alphabetically with language designations and the English equivalent.

1049. **New Dictionary of Birds.** Thomson, A. L. London: Nelson, 1964. 928p.

The title is not an indication of the reason the work is included here. The care with which the work has been put together is the prime reason. Sponsored by the British Ornithologists' Union, this text gives good definitions of ornithological terms together with explanations of American, British, and other native bird names. An index of generic names is provided. Recommended for research collections only.

1050. **University Dictionary of Mammals of the World.** 2nd ed. Burton, Maurice. New York: Thomas Y. Crowell, 1968. 307p.

This is a good general purpose dictionary which covers a wide variety of mammals. The entries are descriptive, concentrating on characteristics, habits, habitat, distribution, breeding, longevity, and food. Recommended for general collections.

HANDBOOKS – GENERAL

1051. **Animal Life of Europe: The Naturalist's Reference Book.** Graf, Jakob. London: Warne, 1968. 595p.

A cross between a field manual and a desk reference, this is an aid to identification of insects, birds, fish, mammals, and reptiles of Europe. Assisting in the goal are good illustrations. This is a solid choice for most collections.

1052. **Biological Research Method.** 2nd ed. Holman, H. H. New York: Hafner, 1969. 272p.

This is not specifically a biological research methods handbook. It focuses on animal research. Chapters are oriented towards data collection, records and their interpretation, mathematical and statistical methods, and the organization and preparation of scientific papers. A useful handbook for those involved in animal research.

1053. **Code Internationale de Nomenclature Zoologique.** 3rd ed. International Commission on Zoological Nomenclature, adopte par le XXe Congres Internationale de Zoologie. [**International Code of Zoological Nomenclature**, 3rd ed. adopted by the XXth International Congress of Zoology]. Berkeley, CA: University of California Press, 1985.

The text is in French and English. "The object of the code is to promote stability and universality in the scientific names of animals and to ensure that the name of each taxon is unique and distinct" (preface). The draft of the code was discussed and modified in London in 1958 by the Colloquium on Zoological Nomenclature. In its final form, the code sets forth the rules and regulations for assigning scientific names to animals and groups of animals with proper form of citation. Glossaries in both English and French are provided.

1054. **Controlled Wildlife.** Estes, Carol, and Keith W. Sessions. Lawrence, KS: Association of Systematics Collections, 1983. 3v.

These volumes provide information on wildlife (plant and animal) regulated by federal and state law. Its work will be of little interest to the general reader, but of high utility to the research and zoo community. This is an important work and should be considered by all major public and research collections.

KF5640
C66
1983
Sci
Ref

1055. **List of Common and Scientific Names of Fishes from the United States and Canada.** 4th ed. Robins, Richard, et al. Bethesda, MD: American Fisheries Society, 1980. 174p.

Covers all species of known freshwater fish of the United States and Canada as well as species along the continental shelf to a depth of 200 meters. Should be used as an aid to avoid confusion in nomenclature. This is a valuable tool for research and academic collections.

QL618
A49
1980
Sci
R4

1056. **Natural History Notebook of North American Animals.** National Museum of Natural Sciences. Englewood Cliffs, NJ: Prentice-Hall, 1985. 160p.

This work is divided into two sections. The first is an album of prehistoric animals and extinct wildlife. The second is a description of animals today. Each animal is covered in approximately one page and is illustrated with a drawing. This will be of chief interest to school and public libraries.

1057. **New York Aquarium Book of the Water World: A Guide to Representative Fishes, Aquatic Invertebrates, Reptiles, Birds, and Mammals.** Bridges, William. New York: American Heritage Press, 1970. 287p.

The title is accurate in that this is not a complete listing of water creatures. Those which are included are examined in detail and accompanied by full-color illustrations. The emphasis is on animals of the seas, such as jellyfish, clams, shrimp, corals, octopuses, penguins, sea turtles, sea snakes, and crocodilians. This is an excellent choice for public and college libraries.

1058. **Poisonous and Venomous Marine Animals of the World.** 2nd ed. rev. Halstead, Bruce W. New York: Darwin Press, 1987. 1500p.

Deals with toxic marine animals of the world over a broad expanse of time—from antiquity to the present. Contains an unusually large number of illustrations, some in color. Those references which are cited are well documented. This is an excellent work for any general to research collection.

1059. **Principles of Receptor Physiology.** Loewenstein, Werner R., ed. Berlin: Springer, 1971. 600p.

This is a very complete reference tool on the physiology of nervous tissue in higher and lower life forms. The areas covered are general receptors, enteroreceptors, muscle type receptors, electroreceptors and other unusual lower animal senses, auditory system, vestibular system, photoreceptors, visual photochemistry and photophysics, and central processing of visual information. This is an impressive tool that, even given its age, is still highly regarded.

1060. **World of Venomous Animals.** Freiberg, Marcos, and Jerry G. Walls. Neptune, NJ: T.F.H. Publications, 1984. 191p.

A good source for information and illustrations on the world's poisonous animals. Restricted to animals that can bite or sting, the book contains information on the animals, the poison, and a section on treatment. It can be a welcome addition to the scholarly and to the general interest collection.

HANDBOOKS—INVERTEBRATES

1061. **Audubon Society Book of Insects.** Line, Les, Lorus Milne, and Margery Milne. New York: Abrams, 1983. 260p.

The large format and distinctive printing added to the excellent photographs make this a masterpiece. The audience is intended to be the general public. The text and care with which this book was produced make it an excellent choice for almost any collection. Although it appears at first glance to be a "coffee-table" publication, it is destined to be a classic.

1062. **Butterflies: A Colour Field Guide.** Devarenne, M. London: David & Charles, 1983. 180p.

This handbook illustrates and describes common butterflies of Europe and North America. The color photographs are of consistent high quality but do not always show both wing surfaces. This makes identification from the photographs difficult. The selective nature of the work makes it a supplemental title for most collections. Recommended for general and some research collections.

1063. **Collector's Guide to Seashells of the World.** Eisenberg, Jerome M. New York: McGraw-Hill, 1981. 237p.

Covering over 2,600 species, the emphasis of this work is on the most popular families. Serves as a good first start reference. It is not as complete as *Compendium of Seashells* (see entry 1064), but is more of a field guide and is recommended for all types of collections.

1064. **Compendium of Seashells.** Abbott, R. Tucker, and S. Peter Dance. Melbourne, FL: American Malacologists, 1986. 411p.

Intended for the amateur shell collector, this bibliography is arranged by taxon and is indexed by popular and scientific name. This is a good general handbook and identification guide, and is recommended for all types of collections.

1065. **Comprehensive Insect Physiology, Biochemistry, and Pharmacology.** Oxford, England: Pergamon, 1985. 13v.

The intent is to "provide an up-to-date summary and orientation on the physiology, biochemistry, pharmacology, behavior and control of insects that would be of value to research workers, teachers, and students" (preface). Special attention is paid to the literature from 1950 to the present. Highly recommended for university and research collections.

1066. **Destructive and Useful Insects: Their Habits and Control.** 4th ed. rev. Metcalf, Clell L., and W. P. Flint. New York: McGraw-Hill, 1967. 1087p.

An excellent collection of information and description on North American insect pests. Line drawings and halftones complete the descriptive component. The major contribution of this work is the control methodology suggested for the various pests covered. Recommended for all research collections.

1067. **Insects of the World.** Linesenmaier, Walter. New York: McGraw-Hill, 1972. 392p.

A good guide arranged systematically with the exception of the social and aquatic insects. This quirk will irritate some researchers and confuse some readers. The focus of the handbook is to define the insect as a living organism within the zoological world. The work is replete with illustrations, which are a major reason for its inclusion. A good piece for most libraries.

1068. **Oxford Book of Insects.** Burton, John, et al. New York: Oxford University Press, 1984. 201p.

This is an excellent text as long as one understands the focus is on Great Britain. Very few insects from other parts of the world are covered. What it does, however, it does well. Intended for the layperson, it should be considered for specialized collections and some research collections.

1069. **Oxford Book of Invertebrates: Protozoa, Sponges, Coelenterates, Worms, Mollusks, Echinoderms and Arthropods (Other Than Insects).** Nichols, David, and John A. L. Cooke. London: Oxford University Press, 1979. 218p.

This is an excellent work with an excellent format. Pages alternate between color illustrations and facing pages of text. The illustrations tend to be drawn to a single scale to aid in relative comparison with other entries. Designed for popular use, the work will still find good use in a research collection.

1070. **Primitive Oribatids of the Palaeartic Region.** Balogh, J., and S. Mahunka. New York: Elsevier, 1983. 372p.

This is a highly technical volume of a projected three-volume set. This volume includes all species described through 1980. There is no other work of comparable scope, making this a necessity for research collections.

1071. **Shell Book.** Rogers, Julia Ellen. Boston: Bransford, 1951. 503p.

A very popular field handbook for the identification of shells, it was first published in 1908 and includes illustrations and listings of popular names. Designed for on-site use, it is a welcome addition to any public or college collection.

1072. **Shrimps, Lobsters, and Crabs of the Atlantic Coast of the Eastern United States, Maine to Florida.** Washington, DC: Smithsonian Institution Press, 1984. 505p.

This is the first coverage of the decapod crustaceans of the entire Atlantic coast of the United States. It is a technical handbook which will serve as a field guide only to the trained zoologist. Highly recommended for any professional research collection in zoology.

1073. **Spiders of the World.** Preston-Mafham, Rod, and Ken Preston-Mafham. New York: Facts on File, 1984. 191p.

The preface to this work is consumed with disclaimers. It does hit its target audience well and should be considered for purchase by general collections but not research collections.

1074. **World of Butterflies.** Sbordoni, Valerio, and Saverio Forestiero. Poole, England: Blandford, 1985. 312p.

An excellent source, it contains a survey of the butterfly and moth families along with discussions of coloration, evolution, distribution, and migration. The illustrations and descriptions are not overly technical, making this a good choice for general as well as research collections.

HANDBOOKS – BIRDS

1075. **Birds of the Wetlands.** Hancock, James. New York: Facts on File, 1984. 152p.

This is a carefully edited handbook covering birds in wetland areas of the world. The major contribution of the work is the number of color photographs of birds, some very rare. The importance of wetlands as an ecosystem, and the birds which depend on them, are vividly displayed here. Recommended for any collection.

1076. **Birds – Their Latin Names Explained.** Gotch, A. F. Poole, England: Blandford, 1981. 348p.

Outlines the derivation of the scientific names of 1,850 species of birds. Most are well known, while some are rare or near extinction. Birds from all parts of the world are covered. This is a good source for translation of scientific names of birds and recommended for all types of collections.

1077. **Check-list of Birds of the World.** Mayr, Ernst, and G. E. W. Cottrell, eds. Cambridge, MA: Museum of Comparative Zoology, 1979- . irregular.

This is an ongoing scholarly work, listing ornithological genus, species, and subspecies with bibliographic sources. Highly recommended for all research collections.

1078. **Check-list of North American Birds.** 6th ed. New York: American Ornithologist's Union, 1983. 877p.

Prepared by the committee on classification and nomenclature of the Union. An authoritative source and highly recommended for all research collections.

1079. **Checklist of the World's Birds: A Complete List of the Species, with Names, Authorities, and Areas of Distribution.** Gruson, Edward S. New York: Quadrangle/New York Times Book Co., 1976. 212p.

Intended more for the layperson than *Check-list of Birds of the World* (see entry 1077) and *Check-list of North American Birds* (see entry 1078), this is still an excellent source. The material was obtained from authoritative sources and is well presented, making it a good choice for general collections.

1080. **Complete Birds of the World.** Walters, Michael. Newton Abbot, England: David & Charles, 1980. 340p.

An attempt to list all bird species which have lived in post-Pleistocene times, the entries of this work follow the sequence of *Check-list of Birds of the World* (see entry 1077). Entries include scientific name, authority who first used the name, English name, distribution, habitat, food, and incubation period. An excellent tool for a variety of questions.

1081. **Cranes of the World.** Johnsgard, Paul A. Bloomington, IN: Indiana University Press, 1983. 257p.

This is essentially an update of Lawrence Walkinshaw's 1973 book of the same title and is an excellent addition to Johnsgard's already impressive list of titles. This work continues his tradition of synthesizing a massive amount of published and unpublished material. The book is overly technical for the amateur, but will be of considerable interest to the researcher.

1082. **Field Guide to the Birds of North America.** Scott, Shirley L., ed. Washington, DC: National Geographic Society, 1983. 464p.

In addition to this title, *Audubon Society Master Guide to Birding* (Knopf, 1983), and *Birds of North America* (Golden, 1983) were published in 1983. Of this excellent group, this title is the best due to the painstaking attention to detail which includes illustrations of juvenile, immature, and seasonal plumage of females and birds in flight. The illustrations are second to none. The text is presented facing the illustrations and is written by experts in the field. A highly recommended source.

1083. **Field Guide to the Nests, Eggs, and Nestlings of North American Birds.** Harrison, Colin. Toronto: Collins, 1984. 416p.

A good identification guide to eggs, nests, and nestlings utilizing color illustrations. This is a very comprehensive guide and worthy of consideration by all types of libraries.

1084. **Handbook of North American Birds.** Palmer, Ralph S. New Haven, CT: Yale University Press, 1962- . irregular.

This is an excellent handbook series approaching the encyclopedic. The published as well as some unpublished literature is synthesized to describe both sexes of each species, to cover plumage at all ages and in all seasons, and to give measurements, weight, hybrids, and geographical variations. Additional points covered include voice, habitat, distribution, migration, banding status, reproduction, survival, habits, and food. This is a quality series and should be considered by any research collection.

1085. **North American Birds.** Milne, Lorus, and Margery Milne. Englewood Cliffs, NJ: Prentice-Hall, 1969. 340p.

This is oriented to the amateur ornithologist. The textual material is easier for the layperson. For a more scholarly handbook, consult *Handbook of North American Birds* (see entry 1084). This handbook does its job very well and should be considered by public and college libraries.

HANDBOOKS—FISH

1086. **FAO Species Catalogue. Vol. 2: Scombrids of the World: An Annotated and Illustrated Catalogue of Tunas, Mackerels, Bonitos, and Related Species Known to Date.** New York: UNIPUB, 1983. 137p.

This is the second volume in a series of species catalogs produced by FAO and is intended primarily for those involved in scombrid fisheries. The catalog is completed by line drawings. Highly recommended for anyone involved with the Scombridae.

1087. **FAO Species Catalogue. Vol. 3: Cephalopods of the World: An Annotated and Illustrated Catalogue of Species of Interest to Fisheries.** New York: UNIPUB, 1984. 277p.

Like volume two in this series, this is an impressive catalog of 173 cephalopod species of interest to fisheries. It supplies a key to the cephalopod families that cannot presently be found elsewhere. An excellent resource for research and fishery use.

1088. **Fishes of North America.** Herald, Earl Stannard. New York: Doubleday, 1972. 254p.

An identification and field manual primarily for the amateur. Very impressive underwater photographs of various fishes are included. Recommended for public and general collections.

1089. **Fishes of the World.** 2nd ed. Nelson, Joseph S. New York: Wiley, 1984. 523p.

Originally published by Nauka (Leningrad) in 1971, this is a professional's tool, designed for the researcher. The concise presentation presumes familiarity with the subject. An excellent source for research collections.

1090. **Freshwater Fishes of the World.** Sterba, Gunther. London: Studio, 1974. 2v.

This is a major reference tool systematically arranged with the focus on basic identification and maintenance of the fish in aquaria. Many line drawings and some color illustrations accompany the text. Since its original publication in Germany in 1959, this work has been considered a major tool and is highly recommended for research collections.

1091. **Handbook of Freshwater Fishery Biology.** Carlander, Kenneth D. Ames, IA: Iowa State University Press, 1969- . irregular.

Predominantly a collection of highly specialized data on individual fish, the majority of the information is in tabular form, arranged by species. The conservationist and the biologist will find a great deal of data with which to work. The scope of the work covers North America (United States and Canada). Though somewhat dated, this is an excellent source for research collections.

1092. **Living Fishes of the World.** Herald, Earl Stannard. Garden City, NY: Doubleday, 1972. 304p.

The age of this work is overcome by the quality of its underwater photographs. Written for the amateur and student, this book is recommended for general collections because of the excellent photography.

1093. **Tropical Fish Identifier.** Walker, Braz. New York: Sterling, 1980. 256p.

This is a concise identification tool for the amateur. A color photograph, coupled with a fairly short description, completes each entry. This is an excellent tool for general collections.

HANDBOOKS – AMPHIBIANS AND REPTILES

1094. **Living Amphibians of the World.** Cochran, Doris M. Garden City, NY: Doubleday, 1967. 199p.

Predominantly for the amateur and pet fancier, the text includes brief descriptions usually accompanied by color photographs. A general section on amphibians and a section on the care of amphibians as pets completes the work. This is useful in a general collection.

1095. **Living Snakes of the World in Color.** Mehrtens, John M. New York: Sterling Publishing, 1987. 480p.

The major contribution of this work is its color photography for use in identification of snakes. Five hundred and forty color photographs add to the considerable worth of this volume. In some cases, more than one photograph is included for a particular species. This is an excellent identification guide but it is not for the weak of heart.

1096. **Reptiles of the World: The Crocodiles, Lizards, Snakes, Turtles and Tortoises of the Eastern and Western Hemisphere.** Ditmars, Raymond Lee. London: Lane, 1933. 321p. QL644 .635 Sci

This is a very popular handbook focused on identification. The age of this tool should not be considered a large problem because the reptiles of North America are still recognizable. The descriptive information is supplemented by plates of illustrations. Recommended for general collections.

1097. **Turtles of the United States.** Ernst, Carl H., and Roger W. Barbour. Lexington, KY: University Press of Kentucky, 1972. 347p. QL666 .C5 E76 Sci (out)

This is probably the most comprehensive handbook on U.S. turtles in existence. Detailed accounts of species in the U.S. emphasize behavior, ecology, and conservation. A good bibliography for the period 1950 through 1970 is provided. Recommended for research collections.

HANDBOOKS—MAMMALS

1098. **Complete Guide to Monkeys, Apes, and Other Primates.** Kavanagh, Michael. New York: Viking Press, 1983. 224p.

This is a simply written but very accurate survey of the primates. It will find greatest usage from general readers. Kavanagh acknowledges that some classifications may be a problem and recognizes more species in this work than most writers. A good addition to general collections.

1099. **Handbook of Living Primates: Morphology, Ecology and Behavior of Nonhuman Primates.** Napier, John Russell, and P. H. Napier. London: Academic Press, 1976. 456p.

This handbook deals with the functional morphology of primates, profiles of primate genera, and supplementary and comparative data including taxonomic features, habitats, appendages, and their uses. This is a scholarly text for use by scholars and is recommended for research collections only.

1100. **Hoofed Mammals of the World.** Mochi, Ugo, and T. Donald Carter. New York: Scribner, 1971. 268p.

Included primarily for the excellent illustrations, this handbook does contain a compendium of all living species, many subspecies, and a few recently extinct forms. It is recommended for research collections.

1101. **Mammals of North America.** 2nd ed. Hall, Eugene Raymond. New York: Wiley, 1981. 2v.

A major source book in mammalogy, this work is arranged by order, family, genus, and subgenus. The exhaustive description for each entry is enhanced by distribution maps, literature citations, and illustrations. An extensive bibliography is included. This is a highly recommended source for major research collections.

1102. **Primates of the World: Distribution, Abundance, and Conservation.** Wolfheim, Jaclyn H. Seattle, WA: University of Washington Press, 1983. 831p.

"The purpose of this volume is to synthesize the information now available describing the distribution, abundance, habitats, and factors affecting natural populations of each primate species." This is a major work of importance in terms of primate geography.

1103.   **Walker's Mammals of the World.** 4th ed. Nowak, Ronald, and John L. Paradiso. Baltimore, MD: Johns Hopkins Press, 1983. 2v.

Each volume contains its own subject index. Volume 1 also contains a chart showing world distribution of genera of recent mammals. Volume 2 contains the complete citation for literature cited in both volumes. This is a comprehensive account of recent genera of mammals arranged by taxonomic classification. The illustrations are excellent.

QL737
.C4
Mbb
1984
Sci

1104.   **World's Whales: The Complete Illustrated Guide.** Minasian, Stanley M., Kenneth C. Balcomb, and Larry Foster. Washington, DC: Smithsonian Books, 1984. 224p.

The information here is accurate and up-to-date. The text is standard, but the illustrations are superb. Not all species are illustrated, but those which are are very well done. This is the most complete collection of cetacean photographs available and is highly recommended for research collections.

DIRECTORIES

1105.   **Animals Next Door: A Guide to Zoos and Aquariums of the Americas.** Gersh, Harry. New York: Fleet Academic, 1971. 170p.

This is a good directory to zoos and aquariums, public and private, in the Western Hemisphere. The information given contains name, address, hours, fees, collection statistics, publications, educational programs, and directors. A good general purpose tool badly in need of updating, it is included here because of its uniqueness.

1106.   **International Zoo Yearbook.** London: Zoological Society, 1960- . annual.

This is an international source listing animal populations in zoological gardens and aquaria. Included with the work is a subject index. This source should be recommended for specialized collections.

1107.   **Lions and Tigers and Bears: A Guide to Zoological Parks, Visitor Farms, Nature Centers, and Marine Life Displays in the United States and Canada.** Ulmer, Jefferson G., and Susan Gower. New York: Garland, 1985. 230p.

The subtitle very accurately describes this work. It is extremely useful for its coverage of lesser known facilities and is a good choice for any collection.

1108.   **World Wildlife Guide.** Ross-Macdonald, Malcolm, ed. New York: Viking Press, 1972. 416p.

A directory of areas where wildlife might be seen, the title of this work is somewhat misleading. The focus of the work is on national parks, reserves and sanctuaries, state parks, and other accessible wildlife areas in various countries. For each entry, information is usually given on fauna, flora, landscapes, facilities for accommodation and transportation, and location directions. A good tool for general collections.

11 General Engineering

Engineering deals with the design and operation of tangible artifacts. As a discipline, it was not normally distinguished from science until early in the nineteenth century. In fact, most of the scientific discoveries of the ancient world were made by persons we would now call engineers.

Engineering as a discipline emanates from the need to create and manufacture efficient tools for day-to-day life as well as to increase comfort and extend scientific knowledge. The ancient engineers were mostly master builders and inventors. The pyramids of Egypt and the inventions of Greek engineers are testaments to the vitality of engineering at the time.

Engineering, and particularly the study of mechanics, during the Renaissance led to several major scientific discoveries. Studies of gravitation as a force are but one example.

Beginning with the industrial revolution, engineering became somewhat separated from science. Although engineering was still based on and still developed scientific principles, the concept of the engineer as distinct from the scientist became more widespread and accepted.

Modern engineering is a diverse field. In some respects, the term *engineering* is an analogue to the term *science*. True to form, modern engineering is using and sometimes suggesting scientific principles and techniques. Heavily dependent on mathematics, engineering helps to drive science in areas such as chemistry and materials science; promoting advances in computer chip technology as one example.

The information requests of the engineer are as diverse as the engineers themselves. The literature of engineering also runs the gamut from the house organ to the highly specialized theoretical journal. Engineers are noted for their reliance on and need for handbooks. Their questions to an information center are usually of the short answer type and findable in one or more handbooks. As can be noted within this chapter, the plethora of handbooks on almost any subject make this easier than it might be otherwise.

The literature of engineering, and there is a great deal of it, belies Derek Price's claim of a papyrophobic group. On the whole the engineering community produces a considerable number of information requests on an astoundingly wide range of topics. The state of the engineering literature in the future will continue to move toward emulation of the sciences in terms of literature cited and, therefore, needed from the information center.

GUIDES TO THE LITERATURE

1109. Finding and Using Product Information: From Trade Catalogues to Computer Systems. Wall, Raymond A., ed. Aldershot, England: Gower, 1986. 336p.

The emphasis is on components and materials. Section 1 discusses information sources, and section 2 represents views of designers and designer-related services — special subject areas and industrial sectors where product information needs are particularly great. A particularly useful tool for locating otherwise fugitive material.

1110. Guide to Basic Information Sources in Engineering. Mount, Ellis. New York: Wiley, 1976. 196p.

Now a classic in the field, this book is included because it covers the literature on the basis of its structure and type as opposed to serving strictly as a source book. It covers four broad categories entitled "Technical Literature — What It Is, Where to Find It," "Books," "Periodicals and Technical Reports," and "Other Sources of Information." Under each category there are entries for bibliographies, dictionaries, encyclopedias, handbooks, guides to literature, and histories. This is recommended for large collections only.

1111. How to Find Out about Engineering. Parsons, S. A. J. New York: Pergamon, 1972. 271p.

This is a dated book, but one which can still find some utility in its discussion of the use of libraries. It includes several sections documenting the sources of mechanical, mining, electrical, nuclear, civil, and aeronautical engineering.

1112. Information Resources for Engineers and Scientists: Workshop Notes. 4th ed. Maiorana, Charlie. Washington, DC: INFO/tek, 1985. 1v. (various paging).

A guide to technical information written for engineers and the librarians who work with them. About 50 categories of reference sources are covered, including technical reports, conference proceedings, and abstracts and indexes. This is a well done source in the style and format engineers will find attractive.

1113. Information Sources in Engineering. 2nd ed. Anthony, L. J., ed. Boston: Butterworths, 1985. 579p.

The "aim is to bring together sources of information into a single convenient form. Arranged by I — primary information sources (reports, journals, trade catalogs), II — secondary information sources (indices and abstracts, online information, reference sources), and III — specialized subject fields (machines, computers, electronic engineering). Each article is written by a different person, describing subject sources and types of material out there" (preface). This is a good, solid source book.

1114. Lesko's New Tech Sourcebook: A Directory to Finding Answers in Today's Technology-Oriented World. Lesko, Matthew. New York: Harper & Row, 1986. 726p.

This book "leads you to a wide range of information sources in major areas of high technology," listing professional societies, trade associations, government offices, businesses, and research centers. Also lists magazines, journals and information source directories; recommended online databases; and companies and educational institutions that can be consulted for information. A highly recommended source.

1115. Patenting Manual. 2nd ed. Hale, Alan M. Buffalo, NY: SPI, 1983. 381p.

Explains the processes associated with the activities of inventing and patenting in nonlegal language and contains a comprehensive glossary of related terms. This proves to be a necessity for anyone working in the patent field.

1116. **Scientific, Engineering, and Medical Societies Publications in Print, 1980-1981.** Kyed, James M., and James M. Matarazzo. New York: Bowker, 1981. 626p.

This is a standard reference to publications of 365 professional societies of the United States, Canada, Great Britain, and international societies. The societies are arranged alphabetically and include name, address, telephone number, and payment policy. The publications are divided into three broad categories of books, periodicals, and nonprint materials. The section on books provides information on author, edition, publication date and price; serials include title, frequency, and price. Nonprint materials cover information such as films, slides, cassettes, filmstrips, etc. Author, subject, and periodical indexes are given. This work proves to be an essential addition to all research and special library collections.

1117. **Use of Engineering Literature.** Mildren, K. W., ed. Boston: Butterworths, 1976. 621p.

This is a survey of the various fields of engineering. The chapters include information on classification and materials. Dated now, this is mainly useful for the discussion on library arrangement of materials and for retrospective information.

1118. **What Every Engineer Should Know about Engineering Information Resources.** Schenk, Margaret T., and James K. Webster. New York: Dekker, 1984. 216p.

The index is a quick means of locating an item in a variety of formats including technical reports, periodicals, and tables. Each chapter provides a brief description of format, and includes a list of representative reference tools. This is a good, readable book of information on sources and the primary literature in engineering, though some of the literature references are dated.

ABSTRACTS, INDEXES, AND BIBLIOGRAPHIES

1119. **AGARD Index of Publications, 1980-1982 North Atlantic Treaty Organization.** Langley Field, VA: AGARD, 1984. 139p.

A NASA database was used to compile this tool containing abstracts and indexes for AGARD publications. Combined with something similar to the *Criss-Cross Directory* (see entry 1132), it would be very handy. There are five different indexes, and the information is easily accessible. This work would be an asset to specialized collections.

1120. **Applied Science and Technology Index.** New York: H. W. Wilson, 1913- . monthly (except August) with quarterly and annual cumulations.

This is an index in the Wilson format to the theoretical sciences and their engineering applications. It includes pure physics, chemistry and geology, mathematics, metallurgy, and computer science. Substantial coverage of science applications is included. Though not a research tool, it is recommended for college and public, and some school, collections. Available online and on CD-ROM from Wilson.

1121. **Arthur D. Little/Online.** Cambridge, MA: Arthur D. Little, 1977- . monthly.

An index to the non-proprietary information sources of the Arthur D. Little Company, covering industries, technologies, and management. Available from DIALOG.

1122. **ATINDEX.** Sydney, Australia: J. Noyce, 1980- . quarterly.

A quarterly indexing service to the literature of appropriate technology (agriculture, education, energy, food, health, housing, transportation, rural and urban environment, among others) which scans major periodicals for articles that discuss techniques appropriate to the concept of "small is beautiful."

1123. **Bibliographic Guide to Technology.** Boston: G. K. Hall, 1976- . annual.

This is a thorough subject bibliography that deals with engineering and technology. It is designed for use in conjunction with other bibliographic guides, and the listing consists of current publications cataloged by the Library of Congress and the Research Libraries of the New York Public Library. All entries are arranged alphabetically and include title, subject heading, and main and added entries. Of interest to acquisition, reference, and cataloging departments of science libraries.

1124. **CLAIMS Compound Registry.** IFI/Plenum.

An online file consisting of a dictionary of specific chemical compounds. Each record includes a specific registry number, main compound name, synonyms, molecular formula, and fragment codes and terms. Available from DIALOG.

1125. **CLAIMS/CHEM.** IFI/Plenum, 1947- .

An online listing of U.S. chemical and chemically related patents available from DIALOG. Some foreign equivalents are included.

1126. **CLAIMS/CITATION.** IFI/Plenum, 1947- .

Available from DIALOG, this is an online file referencing patent numbers cited in the U.S. Each record includes a U.S. patent number plus patent numbers cited to that patent by other U.S. patents.

1127. **CLAIMS/CLASS.** IFI/Plenum.

An online file containing the classification code and title dictionary for all classes and all subclasses of the U.S. Patent Classification System. This file corresponds to the *Manual of Classification* (see entry 349) and is available from DIALOG.

1128. **CLAIMS/GEM.** IFI/Plenum, 1975- .

United States general, electrical, and mechanical patents in an online database available from DIALOG.

1129. **CLAIMS/UNITERM.** IFI/Plenum, 1950- .

An online file which gives access to chemical and chemically related patents. Contains subject indexing for each chemical patent from a controlled vocabulary designed to facilitate retrieval of chemical structures and polymers. Available from DIALOG.

1130. **CLAIMS/US Patents Abstracts.** IFI/Plenum, 1982- .

Online files containing patents listed in the general, chemical, electrical, and mechanical sections of the *Official Gazette* (see entry 345) of the U.S. Patent Office. Available from DIALOG.

1131. **CLAIMS/US Patents Abstracts Weekly.** IFI/Plenum.

An online companion to *CLAIMS/US Patents Abstracts* (see entry 1130) which includes the most current weekly update and records from the current month. Available from DIALOG.

1132. **Criss-Cross Directory of NASA "N"-Numbers and DOD "AD"-Numbers, 1962-1978.** Chicago, IL: SLA-Aerospace Division, 1984. 449p.

This does exactly what its title states. It is possible to trace from AD to N; from NASA TT or TN to N. Hopefully, there will be directories covering the period prior to 1962 and following 1978. This is an invaluable tool in a technical report collection of any size.

1133. **EI Engineering Conference and Index.** New York: Engineering Information, 1985- . annual.

A comprehensive record of international engineering conference literature from published and available literature, this first volume of ECI covers 91,000 papers representing over 1,600 conferences. It is available online from EI Engineering Meetings database.

1134. **EIMET.** 1982- .

An online database covering significant papers from published proceedings of engineering and technical conferences. Available from SDC.

1135. **Engineering Index Monthly.** New York: Engineering Index, Inc., 1884- . monthly with annual cumulation.

This is the premier, general purpose engineering and technology abstracting service in English. It abstracts in excess of 3,500 journals. Books, reports, and anything the editors consider pertinent in 20 or more languages are included. Each entry provides a complete citation followed by an abstract. The abstracts are, for the most part, descriptive only. The publication is also available online from several vendors including BRS, CISTI, DIALOG, European Space Agency, INKA, NERAC Inc., Pergamon InfoLine, SDC Orbit Search Service, and STN International. In addition to printed and online versions, the CD-ROM products *Compendex Aerospace Engineering, Compendex Chemical Engineering,* and *Compendex Electrical and Computer Engineering* are available.

1136. **New Technical Books.** New York: New York Public Library, 1951- . 10 issues/yr.

This list covers published monographic material in the pure and applied physical sciences, mathematics, engineering, industrial technology, and related fields published in the United States, plus some noteworthy foreign books. Arranged by DDC, it is a serviceable classified list which might find utility as a checklist in college and public libraries.

1137. **NTIS.** Springfield, VA: National Technical Information Service (NTIS), 1964- .

Published as a result of governmental contracts, this database covers technical information, journals, monographs, and reports. It is available from BRS, DIALOG, and SDC.

1138. **PIE: Publications Indexed for Engineering.** New York: Engineering Societies Library, 1974.

Lists almost 3,000 serial and nonserial publications abstracted and indexed by the Engineering Societies Library. Includes a list of abbreviations for scientific and engineering terms.

1139. **Standards.** 1963- .

An online database covering a diverse range of standards and specifications developed under the auspices of the SAE and ASTM. Available from SDC.

1140. **Standards & Specifications.** 1950- .

This database provides access to governmental and industry standards. Available from DIALOG.

1141. SUPERINDEX.
A database consisting of indexes from professional level reference books in science, engineering, and medicine. Available from BRS.

1142. Technology Book Guide. Swanson, Gerald, ed. Boston: G. K. Hall, 1974- . annual with monthly cumulation.
English- and French-language books and serial titles are classified by the Library of Congress in all subfields of engineering technology. This is a good listing of new material in technological fields and is recommended for college and university collections.

1143. World Patents Index. 1963- .
This database consists of files containing data from over three million inventions represented by over six million patent documents from patent issuing authorities around the world. Available from DIALOG.

1144. WPI/WPIL. 1977- .
This authoritative database consists of patent specifications issued by the patent offices of 24 major industrial countries. Available from SDC.

ENCYCLOPEDIAS

TA330
S59
1976
Sci
Ref

1145. Encyclopaedic Dictionary of Mathematics for Engineers and Applied Scientists. Sneddon, I. N., ed. New York: Pergamon, 1976. 800p.
This is not a mathematics dictionary reoriented for engineers. The intent of this work is to take the most commonly used mathematical concepts and techniques and delineate their underpinnings. The process pulls together a great deal of primary literature in some cases. This makes the age of the work less noticeable and the utility of the work considerably greater.

TA402
.E5
Sci
Ref

1146. Encyclopedia/Handbook of Materials, Parts, and Finishes. Causer, Henry R., ed. Westport, CT: Technomic, 1976. 564p.
This source provides an encyclopedic view of the materials, forms, and parts used in modern finishing industries. Considerable detail is given on the entries. Because there is no other work which accomplishes this task, this is a good choice for technical and research collections.

1147. McGraw-Hill Encyclopedia of Engineering. New York: McGraw-Hill, 1983. 1264p.
This encyclopedia contains about 700 articles that analyze and explain the major engineering disciplines and current technology. It is a good dictionary for nonresearch collections, public and college libraries.

DICTIONARIES

1148. Acronyms, Initialisms, and Abbreviations Dictionary: A Guide to More Than 420,000 Acronyms, Initialisms, Abbreviations, Contractions, Alphabetic Symbols, and Similar Condensed Appellations. 12th ed. Towell, Julie E., and Helen E. Sheppard, eds. Detroit, MI: Gale Research, 1987. 2500p.

This work does precisely what the title and subtitle suggest. The editors have chosen to annotate the work via the subtitle; therefore, this is recommended for any collection interested in technology and abbreviations in that area.

1149. Compilation of ASTM Standard Definitions, 1986. 6th ed. Philadelphia: ASTM, 1986. 907p.

This is an excellent glossary and controlled vocabulary list used by the American Society for Testing and Materials. It is not, however, a true thesaurus, but is a working list compiled by consensus as opposed to fiat. This will be an excellent tool particularly for those libraries which own *Book of ASTM Standards* (see entry 1160).

1150. Comprehensive Dictionary of Engineering and Technology: With Extensive Treatment of the Most Modern Techniques and Processes. Dictionnaire General de la Technique Industrielle. Ernst, Richard E. Cambridge, England: Cambridge University Press, 1985. 2v.

Volume 1 covers French to English, and volume 2 English to French. Arranged alphabetically with the field specified, 160,000 entries are included. Subjects included are: farming, chemistry, electrical engineering, electronics, space travel, telecommunications, data processing, and microprocessors. Terms peculiar to the Belgian, Swiss, Canadian, and U.S. usage are included and indicated as to location. This is a good dictionary in two languages and is recommended for college and university general reference collections.

1151. Dictionary of Technology: German-English. Oxford, England: Elsevier, 1985. 1100p.

This is a re-elaboration of some specialist spheres such as production engineering, nuclear physics and nuclear technology, printing, agricultural engineering, shipping construction and navigation. A specialized dictionary, it is recommended for research and technical collections.

1152. Encyclopedic Dictionary of Mathematics for Engineers and Applied Scientists. Sneddon, I. N., ed. New York: Pergamon, 1976. 800p.

Arranged alphabetically, the terms defined are those used in math, math engineering, physics, and related fields. SI units are given. This is a well produced, single volume dictionary.

1153. Engineering Index Thesaurus. Engineering Index, Inc. New York: CCM Information Corp., 1972. 402p.

This thesaurus includes more than 11,800 terms or descriptors covering plastics, electrical/electronics, aeronautics, astronautics, chemical, civil, and mechanical engineering, fluid and solid mechanics, mathematics, nuclear, plasma and solid-state physics, optics, statistics, and systems engineering. The terms are listed in sets, each consisting of a main term followed by cross-reference to broader, narrower, or related terms. This is the thesaurus used by Engineering Index, Inc. in the maintenance of its database and is an excellent tool for any collection dealing with technology.

1154. English-Italian/Italian-English Technical Dictionary. Ragazzini, Giuseppe, and Adele Biagi. London: Longman, 1973. 1200p.

This is a middle-sized but exhaustive glossary of about 140 special languages (microlanguages) of industry, science and technology and also for particular sectors of industry, foodstuffs and footwear that are seldom to be found in micro-glossaries. It is recommended for college, university, and some public libraries.

1155. Gerrish's Technical Dictionary: Technical Terms Simplified. Gerrish, Howard H. South Holland, IL: Goodheart-Wilcox, 1982. 368p.

The purpose of this work is to clarify definitions and obscure meanings of technical words and phrases that form our vast technical vocabulary. Many are common words which have been given unusual meanings by industrial craftsmen. Each word is stated, identified by the type of trade, and then defined. It makes an excellent addition to any collection,

1156. McGraw-Hill Dictionary of Engineering. Parker, Sybil P., ed. New York: McGraw-Hill, 1984.

This dictionary consists of entries selected from the *McGraw-Hill Dictionary of Scientific and Technical Terms*, 1984 (see entry 229). Entries include concise definitions and indicate the main engineering field associated with the term. There is no particular reason to purchase both, though this is a good dictionary overall.

1157. Russian-English Polytechnical Dictionary: About 90,000 Terms. Kuznetsov, B. V., ed. Oxford, England: Pergamon, 1981. 722p.

Contains about 90,000 terms to be used as a "practical guide for those with an adequate language background and an understanding of the respective technical field." It encompasses words common to as many fields as practicable and applicable to mathematics, statistics, information theory, computers, electronics, chemical engineering, and metallurgy. Highly recommended for college and university collections.

1158. SHE: Subject Headings for Engineering. New York: Engineering Information, 1987. 218p.

This is the basic tool for controlling the vocabulary in *Engineering Index* (see entry 1135). SHE (Subject Headings for Engineering) is an alphabetical list of terms currently in use by *EI*. It includes many cross-references and scope notes and is of major importance to research and technical collections.

1159. Trilingual Dictionary for Materials and Structures. Dictionnaire trilingue des materiaux et des constructions. Dreisprachiges Wörterbuch der Werkstoffe und Konstruktionen. Holmstrohm, J. Edwin, Maurice Fickelson, and Danilo Jejiciic. New York: Pergamon, 1971. 947p.

Most multilingual dictionaries do not provide definitions. This dictionary, despite its age, is included here because it does give definitions that are still usable. It is recommended for research and specialized collections.

HANDBOOKS

1160. Book of ASTM Standards. Philadelphia: American Society for Testing Materials, 1939- . annual.

This is one of the major compilations of standards information in the world. The ASTM standards are concerned with the testing and recommended practice as they relate to products and are voluntary. Those that are also approved by or under consideration by the American National Standards Institute or the American Society of Mechanical Engineers are marked as such. The standards can be used by a variety of users for any number of reasons. This work is recommended for all types of libraries with the exception of school libraries.

1161.   CRC Handbook of Applied Thermodynamics. Palmer, David A. Boca Raton, FL: CRC Press, 1987. 304p.

This gives the reader an overview of the importance and interplay between physical properties and thermodynamics. It is a literature based handbook, taking from the published literature and offering the user a means to extrapolate from the data. This is a very well done handbook and is highly recommended for the professional and technical collection.

TJ265
P27
1987
Sci

1162.   CRC Handbook of Tables for Applied Engineering Sciences. 2nd ed. Bolz, Ray E., and George L. Tuve, eds. Boca Raton, FL: CRC Press, 1981. 1166p.

A comprehensive handbook, this is done in the excellent style and format of CRC and is a necessity for any library dealing with technology on a serious level. It contains the major tables and formulae necessary for the working engineer in most fields. Some subjects included are lasers, radiation, cryogenics, ultrasonics, semiconductors, high-vacuum techniques, eutectic alloys, and organic and inorganic surface coatings. Treated in greater depth are electrical science and radiation, chemistry and applications, nuclides and nuclear engineering, energy engineering and transport, mechanics structures and machines, environmental and bioengineering, environmental protection and human safety, communication and computation, measurement and instrumentation, and processes and control. This is a necessary addition to any working collection in technology.

TA151
C2
1973
Sci
Ref

1163.   Engineer-in-Training Review Manual: A Complete Review and Reference for the E.I.T. Examination. 6th ed. Lindeburg, Michael R. San Carlos, CA: Professional Engineering Registration Program, 1982. 643p.

Designed for engineers preparing for the engineer-in-training examination, this work contains information on all relevant subjects. It would make a valuable addition to college, university, and other technical information collections.

1164.   Engineering Formulas. 5th ed. Gieck, Kurt. New York: McGraw-Hill, 1986. 1v. (various paging).

This is an engineer's desk reference that is also an excellent choice for work in the field because of its small size. It covers most mathematical formulas and tables necessary to the practice of engineering, and is highly recommended for any technically oriented collections.

1165.   Engineering Manual: A Practical Reference of Design Methods and Data in Building Systems, Chemical, Civil, Electrical, Mechanical, and Environmental Engineering and Energy Conversion. 3rd ed. Perry, Robert H., ed. New York: McGraw-Hill, 1976. 971p.

This is a survey handbook that sets forth the concepts and formulas for most problems in engineering. It is a learning handbook as opposed to a desk manual or field handbook and is highly recommended for college, university, and some public library collections.

1166.   Engineering Mathematics Handbook: Definitions, Theorems, Formulas, Tables. 3rd ed. Tuma, Jan J. New York: McGraw-Hill, 1987. 498p.

This is a wide-ranging compendium of mathematical formulas and data for the practicing engineer. The organization of the work divides specific concepts into separate chapters. The particular relation to engineering is specifically noted. This is an excellent up-to-date work of interest to practicing engineers as well as engineering students and faculty.

1167. **Engineering Tables and Data.** Howatson, A. M., P. G. Lund, and J. D. Todd. London: Chapman & Hall, 1972. 167p.

This is a student's handbook included here because of its treatment of basic engineering concepts. While the concepts are mathematical, they are not overly so and make this work attractive to public, college, and university collections.

1168. **Guidebook for Technology Assessment and Impact Analysis.** Porter, Alan L., et al. New York: North Holland, 1980. 510p.

The processes of technology assessment and impact analysis are detailed in this guidebook which includes an annotated bibliography. A good source for general information, it is recommended for practicing engineers and practically oriented collections.

1169. **Handbook of Dimensional Measurement.** 2nd ed. Farago, Francis T. New York: Industrial Press, 1982. 524p.

This is directed to industrial production engineering on a general scale. Diagrammatic illustrations and synopses aid in the brief descriptions of topics. Topics covered include line-graduated instruments, fixed gauges, gauge blocks, comparative length measurements with mechanical indicators, pneumatic gauging, electronic gauges, engineering microscopes, optical projectors, angle measurements, the systems and application of measuring machines, profile measurements, the measurement of roundness and circular contours, and surface texture measurements. This is a good choice for highly technical collections and research collections.

1170. **Handbook of Engineering Management.** Ullman, J. E., et al. New York: Wiley, 1986. 848p.

This is a well done, comprehensive handbook covering the tools of managing projects in general engineering. It is highly recommended for all technical and technically oriented collections.

1171. **Household, Automotive, and Industrial Formulations.** 3rd ed. Flick, Ernest W. Park Ridge, NJ: Noyes Publications, 1986. 534p.

This collection of household/industrial chemical specialty formulations lists: (1) description of end use and most outstanding properties, (2) base chemical and modifier(s) in the heading, and (3) detailed chemical attributes.

1172. **Industrial Safety Handbook.** 2nd ed. Handley, William, ed. New York: McGraw-Hill, 1977. 480p.

This handbook emphasizes safety concepts, especially those used in handling hazardous materials. It is a specialized handbook for managers and engineering team leaders that is still of interest to a wide variety of persons in technology and research centers.

1173. **Maintenance Engineering Handbook.** 4th ed. Higgins, Lindley R., ed. New York: McGraw-Hill, 1987.

This is a basic reference tool covering more than the title might suggest. It covers quite well the maintenance engineering area and includes material on pollution control equipment, plant facility security, fuel conservation management, and the selection, installation, and upkeep of equipment and services. This handbook makes a worthwhile addition to any technical collection.

1174. **Material Handbook: An Encyclopedia for Managers, Technical Professionals, Purchasing and Production Managers, Technicians, Supervisors, and Foremen.** 12th ed. Brady, George S., and Henry R. Clauser. New York: McGraw-Hill, 1986. 1038p.

A well-used source, this handbook describes commercially available substances in terms of composition, properties, and uses. The work includes synthetic as well as naturally occurring materials and is an excellent addition to any process oriented engineering collection.

1175. **Practicing Scientist's Handbook: A Guide for Physical and Terrestrial Scientists and Engineers.** Moses, Alfred J. New York: Van Nostrand Reinhold, 1978. 1292p.

This comprehensive source provides information on all types of materials. Its scope is broader than *Material Handbook* (see entry 1174) and includes material from physics and chemistry, as well as engineering. This is also a handbook oriented to giving the engineer basic information in these areas. It is a welcome addition to most technically oriented collections.

1176. **Process Instruments and Controls Handbook.** 3rd ed. Considine, Douglas M., and Glenn D. Considine, eds. New York: McGraw-Hill, 1985. 1v. (various paging).

This is an excellent handbook, pulling together the contributions of over 140 experts in the field. Divided into broad categories, it assists those less familiar with the field, but over-simplifies for the expert. The overall result, however, is a first-rate handbook that is highly recommended for any technical library dealing with engineering control issues.

1177. **Standard Handbook of Engineering Calculations.** 2nd ed. Hicks, Tyler G., and S. David Hicks, eds. New York: McGraw-Hill, 1985. 1600p.

TA 151
H52
Sci
Ref

A handbook of calculation procedures for problems in engineering. The attraction of this work is that the calculations are done step-by-step. The work is broken into sections dealing with components of engineering. Solutions are given in an intelligible format. A very useful tool for both practicing and student engineers. Highly recommended for public, college, and university collections.

1178. **The Wiley Engineer's Desk Reference: A Concise Guide for the Professional Engineer.** Heisler, Sanford I. New York: Wiley, 1984. 567p.

Addresses practical problems as well as references to theoretical and derivative data. A practical and essential guide for engineers working in mechanics, materials, hydraulics, electronics, energy sources, and process control, it is not as basic as *Standard Handbook of Engineering Calculations* (see entry 1177).

DIRECTORIES

1179. **American Engineers of the Nineteenth Century: A Biographical Index.** Roysden, Christine, and Linda A. Khatri. New York: Garland, 1978. 247p.

This is an alphabetical listing of American engineers of the nineteenth century. References to obituaries or biographies are provided. This book would be of interest to major collections in the technology area only.

1180. **Biographical Dictionary of Scientists, Engineers and Inventors.** Abbott, David, ed. New York: P. Bedrick, 1986. 188p.

This biographical directory of scientists gives biographical accounts of both living and dead scientists, as well as their accomplishments. It contains a subject index and is an excellent first place to look for biographical information in this area.

1181. **Directory of Engineering Document Sources: Scientific and Management.** 2nd ed. Simonton, D. P., comp. Newport Beach, CA: Global Engineering Documentation Service, 1974. 1v. (various paging).

This work is a consolidated cross index to document initialisms assigned by governmental and industrial organizations to technical reports, specifications, standards, and related publications in engineering. Although dated, this is still a good source of information for technical collections.

1182. **Directory of Engineering Societies and Related Organizations.** 12th ed. Davis, Gordon, ed. New York: American Association of Engineering Societies, 1987. 217p.

This is a basic directory of Canadian and U.S. societies with a primary interest in engineering. The purpose of each group is given in addition to standard directory information. This is an excellent tool for public, special, and academic libraries.

1183. **Directory of Experts and Consultants in Science and Engineering.** 2nd ed. Woodbridge, CT: Research Publications, 1985. 2v.

Volume 1 contains consultant listings and volume 2 an expertise and name index. The two volumes list professional consultants who are technical specialists. Eighteen thousand consultants were selected from *Who's Who in Technology* (see entry 1192). Volume 1 is arranged by field, including electronics; mechanical technology; chemistry; civil engineering; energy technology and earth sciences; physics; and bio-technology. Each entry then includes, by state, the name, address, area of expertise, affiliations, education, and awards. Volume 2 is arranged by keyword then by person listed and page number. This can be an invaluable source in that all persons listed have indicated a willingness to serve as either an expert witness or consultant.

1184. **Directory of Industry Data Sources: The United States of America and Canada.** 2nd ed. Cambridge, MA: Ballinger, 1982. 3v.

This directory includes general reference sources, company data sources, publishers, and indexes, and reports material containing marketing data on 60 basic industries. The bibliographic indexing is detailed, making this a highly recommended source for technical and related collections.

1185. **Directory of Publishing Sources: The Researcher's Guide to Journals in Engineering and Technology.** Balachandran, Sarojini. New York: Wiley, 1982. 343p.

This directory covers approximately 300 journals, mostly English-language, in engineering and technology. It includes information about manuscript submission, style guide, and refereeing procedure, and is an interesting and useful tool for technical and academic collections emphasizing technology.

1186. **Directory of Testing Laboratories, Commercial-Institutional.** Philadelphia: American Society for Testing and Materials, 1982. 184p.

This directory lists U.S. laboratories primarily engaged in nondestructive testing. Arranged alphabetically, geographically, and by specific commodity tested, it is a necessity for technical production oriented collections.

1187. **Engineering College Research & Graduate Study.** Samaras, Patricia A., ed. Washington, DC: American Society for Engineering Education, 1986. 646p.

This is a separately published issue of *Engineering Education* (Washington, DC: American Society for Engineering Education, 1909-). The data were gathered by means of a questionnaire and include directory type information on 221 engineering schools offering graduate programs in engineering. Useful for academic collections in engineering provided no subscription to *Engineering Education* is held.

1188. **Engineering Research Centres: A World Directory of Organizations and Programmes.** Archbold, T., J. C. Laidlaw, and J. McKechnie, eds. Essex, England: Longman, 1984. 1031p.

Information for this tool was obtained by questionnaire, other directories, and buying guides. It profiles engineering research and development centers. There is a noticeable British slant to the entries, but overall it is international. A second edition is planned. This would be recommended for large technical collections with an international and preferably British strength.

1189. **High-Technology Market Place Directory.** Princeton Junction, NJ: Princeton Hightech Group, 1985- . irregular.

This is a directory of companies, primarily U.S., involved in high technology. Information on each company includes name, address, phone number, year established, area of specialization, revenues, number of personnel, and company officers. Serves as a good first-stop for locating market information.

HD9696
.A3
U515
1986
Sci
Ref

1190. **Kempe's Engineer's Year-book.** London: Morgan-Grampian. annual in 2v.

This handbook consists of a comprehensive account of the mathematics and practices inherent in engineering. It is an excellent tool and is highly recommended for any technical collection.

1191. **Who's Who in Engineering.** 6th ed. Davis, Gordon, ed. Washington, DC: American Association of Engineering Societies, 1985. 846p.

Formerly called *Engineers of Distinction*, this source provides good biographical data on engineers. A section on engineering societies and related organizations, a society index, and an awards index are provided. This is a good source for most technical libraries.

1192. **Who's Who in Technology.** 5th ed. Woodbridge, CT: Research Publications, 1986. 7v.

Dedicated to listing those who are at the pinnacle of technology, this work includes only individuals who have made outstanding contributions to the advancement of science, engineering, and/or technology. Each volume covers a different discipline such as electronic and computer science, mechanical engineering, chemistry, energy, and physics. The last volume is a master index of areas and names. This is an outstanding reference source and should be considered by any collection dealing even marginally with technology.

1193. **Who's Who of British Engineers.** 5th ed. London: Simon Books, 1980. 352p.

This is the British equivalent of *Who's Who in Engineering* (see entry 1191). Each entry lists name, title, publications, professional interests, address, birth date, and degrees. This is a good source for British engineers and is recommended for collections with an international focus.

12 Civil and Construction Engineering

Civil and construction engineering includes the planning, construction, and maintenance of structures. Site selection, foundation engineering, earthquake and hazard engineering, as well as materials engineering all play a role in the practice of civil and construction engineering.

Like all branches of engineering, civil and construction engineering is dependent on computational analyses. This requires extensive use of tabular data and handbook information. The availability and use of such materials is critical for the civil and construction engineer. This accounts for the large section on handbooks found here.

Civil and construction engineering also uses a number of other engineering fields. Transportation engineering, energy and the environment, and production engineering are three areas a civil engineer is likely to deal with at some point. This makes the information request in civil and construction engineering somewhat difficult to fill if the information provider is not aware of cross-field information. Like engineering in general, civil and construction engineering is expanding and becoming more interdisciplinary. While this chapter takes a narrow approach to the literature, the reader should be aware that literature use by the civil and construction engineer covers a wider area.

GUIDES TO THE LITERATURE

1194. **Bibliography on the Corrosion and Protection of Steel in Concrete.** Washington, DC: U.S. Government Printing Office, 1980.

This bibliography of papers, reports, and talks about steel in concrete and related subjects contains references indexed by subject and author. It is a basic bibliography of use to professional engineers and some research collections.

1195. **Bibliography on the Fatigue of Materials, Components, and Structures.** Mann, J. Y., comp. Elmsford, NY: Pergamon, 1978-83. 3v.

Chronologically and alphabetically organized, this bibliography covers fatigue of materials. Publication titles are abbreviated and English-language translations accompany foreign language article titles. Subject and author indexes are included. This well-conceived, well-done bibliography is recommended for most research collections.

1196. **Building Technology Publications.** Debelius, JoAnne R., ed. Washington, DC: U.S. Government Printing Office, 1979. with supplements.

This work catalogs all Center for Building Technology publications and includes titles and abstracts of all reports. Entries provide title, author, date of publication, key words, and abstracts. Author and key word indexes are included. Listed as well are non-National Bureau of Standards papers and reports. This source would be of interest to those involved in federal government building practices.

1197. **Construction Information Source and Reference Guide.** 4th ed. Ward, Jack W. Phoenix, AZ: Construction Publications, 1981.

Six color coded sections offer a variety of materials of interest to any student or professional concerned with construction or construction technology. The information provided relates to both standard reference tools and publications of professional institutes. A good choice for working collections in the construction trade.

1198. **Energy Conservation in Buildings 1973-1983: A Bibliography of European and American Literature on Government, Commercial, Industrial, and Domestic Building Energy Management and Technology.** Farmer, Penny. Sunnyvale, CA: Technical Communications, 1983. 107p.

Methods of energy conservation, such as insulation, design, construction, heat recovery, and costs are discussed for a variety of building types. This is a good, general bibliography.

1199. **Information Sources in Architecture.** Bradfield, Valerie J., ed. London: Butterworths, 1983. 419p.

A guide to the full range of sources on architectural information for those interested in the many aspects of the construction process. Sources such as organizations and their libraries, books and bibliographies, databases and data banks, and government literature, are all discussed in relation to the stages involved in the construction project. This is an excellent choice for academic and professional collections.

1200. **Sources of Construction Information: An Annotated Guide to Reports, Books, Periodicals, Standards and Codes.** Godel, Jules B. Metuchen, NJ: Scarecrow Press, 1977- . irregular.

One volume was published in this series. It describes books, reports, standards, and other publications of some interest to the architect, planner, engineer, contractor, and building official. The material is, in some cases, dated. This is a good source from which to begin a basic search and is recommended for public and college collections.

ABSTRACTS, INDEXES, AND BIBLIOGRAPHIES

1201. **ASCE Combined Index.** New York: The American Society of Civil Engineers, 1985- . annual.

A guide to material appearing in publications of the American Society of Civil Engineers, this excellent tool is recommended for research collections. Subject and author indexes are provided.

1202. **Concrete Abstracts.** Detroit, MI: American Concrete Institution, 1972- . bimonthly.

Covering primary literature, this source is of interest to practicing engineers and researchers. The coverage of the literature is good.

1203. **Earthquake Engineering Reference Index.** Ambraseys, N. N. London: Cementation Co., 1963. 1v. (various paging).

Although the imprint date is now over 20 years old, this is still an excellent bibliographic survey. It is in part a commentary on the lack of work in this important area. This is a source that would be of particular interest in research collections.

1204. **Engineering Geology Abstracts.** Alexandria, VA: American Geological Institute, 1984- . quarterly.

Arranged alphabetically by author under 22 subject headings, the geological information provided in this work is pertinent to engineering and the related areas. The scope is fairly broad, bringing together a great deal of information. Recommended only for research institutions.

1205. **Geotechnical Abstracts.** Essen: Deutsche Gesellschaft für Erd und Grundbau, (for) International Society for Soil Mechanics and Foundation Engineering, 1970- . monthly.

This is the English edition of *Dokumentation fuer Bodenmechanik und Grundbau* (Essen, West Germany: C. V. Kronprinzenstr, 1970-). The abstracts are in English regardless of the language of the original article. Coverage of the geotechnical literature is international in scope. This is an excellent source, though the lag time for publication is somewhat slow.

1206. **Highway Research Abstracts.** Washington, DC: U.S. Highway Research Board, National Research Council, National Academy of Sciences, National Academy of Engineering, 1931- . monthly.

This guide to current literature for the highway administrator and engineer has been superseded by *Transportation Research Abstracts* (see entry 1209).

1207. **HRIS Abstracts.** Washington, DC: Highway Research Information Service, 1968- . quarterly.

This classified arrangement of approximately 1,000 abstracts in each issue contains subject, source, and author indexes. Related publications include the less inclusive *Highway Research Abstracts* (see entry 1206), and its *Index to Publications* (1921-1949), updated by irregular supplements. This is an excellent source of information for the highway engineer.

1208. **International Civil Engineering Abstracts.** London: Telford, 1974- . monthly.

Until 1982 this was entitled *ICE Abstracts*, and until 1975, *European Civil Engineering Abstracts*. Published for the Institution of Civil Engineers in Great Britain, with the cooperation of the American Society of Civil Engineers, it provides informative abstracts of articles appearing in journals received in the International Civil Engineering Library. It contains a keyword index and is a good source for international information.

1209. **Transportation Research Abstracts.** Washington, DC: National Research Council, 1931- . monthly.

Until 1974 this was published as *Highway Research Abstracts* (see entry 1206). It contains abstracts from books, reports, and articles on various topics of transportation, and serves as a primary source of information for highway engineers and highway research.

1210. **WATERNET.** American Water Works Association, 1971- .
This database provides an index to the publications of the American Water Works Association and the WWA Research Foundation. Available from DIALOG.

ENCYCLOPEDIAS

1211. **Builders Encyclopedia.** Ulrey, Harry F. Indianapolis, IN: T. Audel, 1970. 593p.
This is not a list of trade names, per se, but is a standard dictionary of the building trade and its terminology. It contains a good introduction and is recommended for public and some academic institutions, especially colleges and trade schools.

1212. **Composite Materials.** Broutman, L. J., et al. New York: Academic Press, 1974. 465p.
This is a very comprehensive work dealing with interfaces in metal matrix composites, mechanics of composite materials, engineering applications of composites, metallic matrix composites, fracture and fatigue, interfaces in polymer matrix composites, and structural design and analysis. The age of the material is compensated, in part, by the depth of the treatment. It is recommended for academically oriented collections.

1213. **Encyclopedia of Architectural Technology.** Guedes, Pedro, ed. New York: NA31
McGraw-Hill, 1979. 313p. E58
An encyclopedia of structural, mechanical, and technical aspects of architecture, com- Main
piled by distinguished practicing architects, this is a good, general introduction to the engineering side of architecture.

1214. **Encyclopedia of Energy-Efficient Building Design: 391 Practical Case Studies.** Lee, Kaiman. Boston: Environmental Design and Research Center, 1977. 1023p.
Containing abstracts of projects that supply innovative methods of natural and renewable energy, this source is included because of the case study approach of the work. It provides a good conceptual design of both the projects and the work.

1215. **Encyclopedia of Wood: Wood as an Engineering Material.** U.S. Department of Agriculture. New York: Sterling Publishing, 1980. 376p.
A reprint of the *Wood Handbook* (Washington, DC: U.S. Government Printing Office, 1974), this reference provides information on the mechanical and physical properties of wood. It is pertinent to the work of engineers, builders, architects, and hobbyists, and makes a good addition to public and college libraries.

1216. **Foundation Engineering.** Leonards, G. A., ed. New York: McGraw-Hill, 1962. 1136p.
This work is a classic and will never go out of style. Its major flaw is that it does not deal with topics such as embankments, cut and natural slopes, and tunnels; however, it is still a required component of most good engineering collections.

1217. **Illustrated Encyclopedic Dictionary of Building and Construction Terms.** Brooks, TH9
Hugh. Englewood Cliffs, NJ: Prentice-Hall, 1976. 366p. B76
Including commonly used formulas, tables, and charts, this work is more complete Sc
than *Builders Encyclopedia* (see entry 1211). It is a concise, but well-done encyclopedia
suitable for any type of library.

1218. Planning and Estimating Underground Construction. Parker, Albert D. New York: McGraw-Hill, 1970. 300p.

A good discussion of tunnel construction is found in this source, and linings and shaft construction are covered in detail. This is a very practical encyclopedia with estimates of cost as a primary focus. It is a good overall reference source in an area with few good source books.

DICTIONARIES

1219. Architectural and Building Trades Dictionary. 3rd ed. Putnam, R. E., and G. E. Carlson. New York: Van Nostrand Reinhold, 1982. 510p.

In addition to 7,500 definitions and many illustrations, this dictionary provides some tips on construction and installation. It is a very good desk reference for those in the building trades.

1220. Complete Dictionary of Wood. Corkhill, T. New York: Stein & Day, 1980. 655p.

This standard reference covers all aspects of timber, but focuses primarily on the fabrication of wood. It includes 10,000 terms, of which some 1,000 are illustrated. It is highly recommended for any technical collection.

1221. Construction Regulations Glossary: A Reference Manual. Stein, J. Stewart. New York: Wiley, 1980. 930p.

This extensive glossary contains varied definitions of terms in the construction industry. It includes code interpretations, standard uses, historic references, technical and scientific data, and professional services. A section of reference data sources and an extensive index are also provided, making this a good reference for engineers and contractors.

1222. Dictionary of Building. 3rd ed. Scott, John S. New York: Halsted, 1984. 382p.

This updated edition of a British dictionary includes cross references, Imperial to metric (mainly SI) conversion factors, and abbreviations of units. Some terms are listed with U.S. synonyms. It is recommended only for research and internationally oriented collections.

1223. Dictionary of Civil Engineering. 3rd ed. Scott, John S. London: Collins, 1985. 308p.

An excellent dictionary in the area. It lists competing and variants of meaning for terms used in civil engineering. The approach is to relate the definition of terms to the practice of engineering. Some illustrations are provided. It is highly recommended for any engineering collection or collection dealing with engineering.

1224. Dictionary of Concrete. Barker, John A. London: Construction Press, 1983. 111p.

Entries give definitions and supplementary information on each term. This is a vital tool for students and practitioners of architecture, building, concrete construction, civil engineering, and quantity surveying.

1225. Dictionary of Geotechnics. Somerville, S. H., and M. A. Paul. London: Butterworths, 1983. 283p.

For use by practicing engineers and advanced students, this dictionary includes terms in everyday use by geotechnical engineers concerning soil and rock mechanics, soil and rock engineering, site investigation, hydrology, dewatering, ground stabilization, earthmoving and compaction, trenching, and excavation.

1226. **Dictionary of Soil Mechanics and Foundation Engineering.** Barker, John A. New York: Longman, 1981.

TA710
.A15
B37
Sci
Ref

The dictionary consists of approximately 2,500 brief entries and is intended for use by a broad audience. Although the emphasis is British, there are definitions of some terms with American applications. It is recommended only for academic collections.

1227. **Illustrated Dictionary of Building.** Marsh, Paul. London: Construction Press, 1982. 256p.

Some 4,000 definitions of terminology used in British building trades are included in this dictionary. The definitions are clear and concise, but the sketches prove to be very confusing. It is recommended only for large academic collections.

1228. **Illustrated Encyclopedic Dictionary of Building and Construction Terms.** Brooks, Hugh. Englewood Cliffs, NJ: Prentice-Hall, 1976. 366p.

This dictionary of construction terms is divided into 3 sections: alphabetical list, list by function, and commonly used formulas. It contains concise, understandable terms, usable by both the layperson and the specialist.

1229. **Means Illustrated Construction Dictionary.** Smit, Kornelius, ed. Kingston, MA: R. S. Means Co., 1985. 577p.

Written in simple everyday language, this work includes slang, regional, and colloquial terms used in the construction trades and professions in the United States. It serves as a very valuable tool to those involved in the construction fields.

1230. **Plumbing Dictionary.** 3rd ed. Jacobson, I. D., ed. Cleveland, OH: American Society of Sanitary Engineering, 1979. 151p.

Trade names and brand names are not found in this dictionary. However, over 2,500 terms related to plumbing and the plumbing trade are defined. This is a good source for specific trade definitions.

HANDBOOKS

1231. **ACI Manual of Concrete Practice.** Detroit, MI: American Concrete Institute, 1987. 5v.

This manual discusses materials and general properties of concrete; construction practices and inspection, pavements; use of concrete in buildings—design, specifications, and related topics; bridges, substructures, sanitary and other special structures; and masonry, pre-cast concrete, and special processes. This is a major source for information on concrete and concrete technology.

1232. **AIA Metric Building and Construction Guide.** Braybrooke, S., ed. New York: Wiley, 1980. 154p.

Containing essential information on the International System of Measurement (SI), this source includes charts, tables, drawings, and conversion factors. It is an informational handbook produced by the American Institute of Architects and is recommended for any working collection in the construction industry.

1233. **American Metric Construction Handbook.** Lytle, R. J. New York: McGraw-Hill, 1983.

This is a reprint of the 1976 edition. The work covers the metric system and conversion factors, discussing metrification at length. It is recommended for professional collections and academic collections. Other handbooks cover the SI unit conversion more thoroughly, though this work gives considerably more background information.

1234. **Architects' Data.** 2nd ed. Neufert, Ernst. London: Collins, 1985. 433p.

A classic handbook on guidelines in the planning and design of building projects, it provides data on user requirements, site selection, and planning criteria. Each section is composed of illustrations and layouts. SI units are used, but conversion tables are included. This is a good reference source for any architect, designer, contractor, or student.

1235. **Architectural Handbook: Environmental Analysis, Architectural Programming, Design and Technology, and Construction.** Kemper, Alfred M. New York: Wiley, 1979.

Describes a complete range of architectural processes in building design, construction, and environmental architecture. It is a good basic source, especially for the construction engineer.

1236. **ASTM Standards in Building Codes: Specifications, Test Methods, Practices, Classifications, Definitions.** 22nd ed. Philadelphia: American Society for Testing and Materials, 1985. 2v.

This listing of standards is published by the ASTM. It is from these standards that the building codes for cities and states are drawn, making this work a prime candidate for any collection with an interest in construction.

1237. **Builder's Complete Guide to Construction Business Success.** Reiner, L. New York: McGraw-Hill, 1978. 429p.

This comprehensive volume details the fundamentals of building small residential and office buildings. It explains business organization; reading plans and specifications; estimates and purchasing decisions; and cost and progress control; and serves as a reference on the building industry for those interested in starting a construction business.

TH145
H8
Sci

1238. **Building Construction: Materials and Types of Construction.** 6th ed. Ellison, Donald C., W. C. Huntington, and R. E. Mickadeit. New York: Wiley, 1987. 434p.

Materials in building construction are covered and a chapter on acoustics is included in this very well done handbook. It is highly recommended for any technical collection.

1239. **Building Construction Handbook.** Adrian, James J. Reston, VA: Reston Publishing Co., 1983. 591p.

Topics ranging from insurance and bonds to water supply and purification are covered in this handbook, and references to other more comprehensive works are provided. This is a good first-source handbook, but not an in-depth source.

1240. **Building Design Construction Handbook.** 4th ed. Merritt, Frederick S. New York: McGraw-Hill, 1982. 1472p.

This handbook contains excellent sections on building systems and protection of structures and occupants against hazards and lightning. The source of most information is cited. It is a highly recommended handbook.

1241. **Building Systems Integration Handbook.** Rush, Richard D. New York: Wiley, 1986. 445p.

Organized in four building systems (structure, envelope, mechanical, interior) and five levels (remote, touching, connected, meshed, and unique), this reference sets standards for the building professions. It contains contributions by over 100 building and design experts and was produced under the auspices of the American Institute of Architects. It is highly recommended for its holistic approach to construction.

1242. **Chemical Materials for Construction: Handbook of Chemicals for Concrete, Flooring, Caulks and Sealants, Epoxies, Latex Emulsions, Adhesives, Roofing, Waterproofing, Technical Coatings, and Heavy Construction Specialties.** Maslow, Philip. New York: McGraw-Hill, 1982. 570p.

A reference containing information on chemical materials used in construction. It includes a bibliography, appendix, and index, and is useful to architects, civil engineers, contractors, and technologists.

1243. **Civil Engineering Handbook.** 4th ed. Urquhart, Leonard C., ed. New York: McGraw-Hill, 1962. 1v. (various paging).

This is a standard handbook for civil engineers. The work is made up of contributions from specialists in several fields of civil engineering and is a necessity for any collection dealing with civil engineering on any level.

1244. **Civil Engineer's Reference Book.** 3rd ed. Blake, L. S., ed. London: Butterworths, 1975. 1v. (various paging).

Designed specifically to meet the needs of the recently graduated professional, and the experienced engineer, geologist, and mining engineer, this book includes data on civil engineering site management. Extensive bibliographies are provided.

1245. **Complete Concrete, Masonry, and Brick Handbook.** Adams, J. T. New York: Van Nostrand Reinhold, 1983. 1130p.

A good book, written in a comprehensive manner, for anyone who wants to use tools and materials in a productive way. It is recommended for personal or public libraries.

1246. **Component and Modular Techniques: A Builder's Handbook.** 2nd ed. Lytle, Robert, and Robert C. Reschke. New York: McGraw-Hill, 1982. 322p.

This is a reference handbook on construction techniques for three popular types of wood frame residential and light commercial buildings. It covers panelized home packages, structural framing components, and construction ideas, and includes over 250 illustrations and diagrams. A manufacturing list and a glossary are provided. This proves to be a welcome addition to civil engineers' and builders' collections.

1247. **Concise Soil Mechanics.** Smith, M. J. Plymouth, MA: McDonald & Evans, 1977. 146p.

This introductory handbook provides classification procedures and standard definitions in soil mechanics. It is recommended for working collections in the construction industry.

1248. **Concrete Bridge Designer's Manual.** Pennells, E. London: Cement and Concrete Association, 1978. 164p.

This generously illustrated manual on concrete bridge design is of interest to researchers and those involved in bridge design.

1249. **Construction Dewatering: A Guide to Theory and Practice.** Powers, J. P. New York: Wiley, 1981. 484p.

This helpful guide to problems in groundwater control uses knowledge from geology, chemistry, and soil mechanics. It covers such topics as soil and water interrelationships, permeability of soils, and design of pumping tests. A useful guide for civil engineers.

1250. **Construction Inspection: A Field Guide to Practice.** 2nd ed. Clyde, James E. New York: Wiley, 1983. 411p.

Dealing with ground construction, this field guide features a detailed list of nearly 500 matters related to civil engineering projects. Helpful data is included. Recommended for academic and working collections in construction.

1251. **Construction Materials for Architecture.** Rosen, Harold J. New York: Wiley, 1985. 23p.

A single reference source for new innovations in building materials. Features excellent, architectural quality illustrations, photographs, tables, and a comprehensive bibliography. It is highly recommended.

1252. **Consulting Engineer.** 2nd ed. Stanley, Claude Maxwell. New York: Wiley, 1982. 303p.

This source covers all aspects of the practice and functions of a consulting engineer, including relationships with clients, the organization, management and problems, and other information. It is useful for engineers, architects, managers, and anyone involved in this field.

1253. **Cutting for Construction: A Handbook of Methods and Applications of Hard Cutting and Breaking on Site.** Lazenby, David, and Paul Phillips. New York: Wiley, 1978. 116p.

Highly detailed, this handbook covers methods of onsite construction demolition which eliminate hazards to personnel and the environment. Necessary materials, safety precautions, and specifications are discussed, along with techniques such as cutting, explosives, and fire. Case studies are included. This is an important reference for engineers and construction workers.

1254. **Design Mix Manual for Concrete Construction.** Long, Leslie D., et al. New York: McGraw-Hill, 1982. 391p.

This self-teaching manual on the basics of concrete design examines the workability, durability, consistency, strength, and density of concrete mixes. It includes 270 tables, information sheets, procedures, computations, a glossary, and a bibliography. This is a valuable tool for engineers, contractors, lab technicians, and students.

1255. **Design Tables for Beams on Elastic Foundations and Related Structural Problems.** Iyengar, K. T. S. R., and S. A. Ramu. London: Applied Science Publishers, 1979. 141p.

Designed for structural engineers, this book provides data on elastically supported beams. It consists of two parts: theoretical background and a guide to the use of the tables. An excellent, but highly specialized tool.

1256. **Designer's Guide to OSHA: A Practical Design Guide to the Occupational Safety and Health Act for Architects, Engineers, and Builders.** 2nd ed. Hopf, Peter S. New York: McGraw-Hill, 1982. 301p.

A comprehensive working tool on the Occupational Safety and Health Act which uses a unique graphic format to illustrate the law. It provides hundreds of sketches, tables, and diagrams of common design problems to aid architects and engineers in conforming to the law and discusses the inspection process, safe working environments, and all OSHA changes since the early 1970s. It is essential for design professionals.

1257. **Domestic Water Treatment.** Lehr, Jay H., et al. New York: McGraw-Hill, 1980. 264p.

A detailed examination of domestic water sources, contaminants, treatments, and construction and maintenance of water supply systems. It includes coverage of analysis and treatment techniques, special types of water for specific uses, and allowable constituents in water. Appendices provide addresses of state agencies, handling advice of specific chemicals used in treatment, and a glossary. This source would be of interest to city administrators, homeowners, and construction specialists.

1258. **Efficient Electricity Use: A Reference Book on Energy Management for Engineers, Architects, Planners, and Managers.** 2nd ed. Smith, Craig B., ed. New York: Pergamon, 1978. 778p.

Divided into four parts: general introduction, description of specific uses of energy, political constraints, and specific technologies. It includes tables, charts, and graphs. Highly recommended, this is an excellent general treatment of the energy problem and potential solutions.

1259. **Environmental Science Handbook for Architects and Builders.** Szokolay, S. V. Lancaster, England: Construction Press, 1980. 532p.

Dealing with design systems that consider man-environment relationships, this handbook takes into account the physical sciences and social sciences necessary to have buildings meet human needs. A good social approach to construction, it is recommended for working and academic collections.

1260. **Excavation Handbook.** Church, Horace K. New York: McGraw-Hill, 1981. 1000p. TA730

A thorough treatment of the engineering aspects of soil and rock excavation methods C48 and equipment is provided in this handbook. Areas examined include geological aspects of Sci excavation, equipment, costs, rock fragmentation methods, and open cut mining. A glossary of excavation terms and extensive illustrations complement the text. This is a valuable aid for all engineering students and professionals, particularly those involved in construction or mining.

1261. **Field Engineer's Manual.** Parmley, Robert O., ed. New York: McGraw-Hill, 1981. 611p.

Handy, compact, and accurate, this is a quick reference to basic engineering data to assist preliminary surveys, solve field problems, and supplement technical materials shown or construction plans. Discusses construction materials, surveying, mechanical systems, electrical construction, drainage, and hydraulics. Designed for engineers and construction personnel.

1262. **Geotechnical Engineering Investigation Manual.** Hunt, Roy E. New York: McGraw-Hill, 1984. 983p.

Divided into investigation methods, characteristics of geologic materials and formations, and geologic hazards in such a way as to merge geology with civil engineering. The focus of the book makes it a prime candidate for technical and academic collections.

1263. **Ground Water Manual: A Guide for the Investigation, Development, and Manage-** TD403
ment of Ground-Water Resources. Washington, DC: U.S. Government Printing Office, U54 1985. 480p.

Covers all aspects of groundwater resources in their investigation, development, and 1986 management, and includes tables, graphs, illustrations, and bibliography. This is an ex- Sci cellent manual for the working engineer. Ref

1264. **Handbook of Applied Hydraulics.** 3rd ed. Davis, C., and K. Sorenson. New York: McGraw-Hill, 1984. 1611p.

An authoritative handbook on the design and construction of hydraulic structures which covers basic principles of hydrology and hydraulics, dams, water use, control, and disposal. It also contains practical examples and applications of interest to civil engineers.

1265. **Handbook of Composite Construction Engineering.** Sabnis, Gajanan M., ed. New York: Van Nostrand Reinhold, 1979. 380p.

While covering the basics of composite construction, this handbook stresses the concept of composite construction and the proper mixture of the materials. Though showing some age, this reference is still useful.

1266. **Handbook of Dam Engineering.** Golzbe, Alfred R., ed. New York: Van Nostrand Reinhold, 1977. 793p.

This handbook provides detailed guidance for dam construction and includes information on earthquake hazards, construction materials, and public safety controls. It is a highly recommended technical handbook.

1267. **Handbook of Geology in Civil Engineering.** Legget, Robert F., and Paul F. Karrow. New York: McGraw-Hill, 1983. 1308p.

This book focuses on the geologic interrelation with civil engineering and construction and deals with the major forms of engineering and special problems and environmental concerns. It is excellent for civil engineers and architects, as well as geologists.

1268. **Handbook of Heavy Construction.** 2nd ed. Havers, John A., and Frank W. Stubbs, Jr., eds. New York: McGraw-Hill, 1971. 1v. (various paging).

A favorite reference tool for heavy construction, it presents sections on management, equipment, and applications. Supporting literature is referenced; however, the age of the references makes this component suspect. Overall, this is good background information for the construction trade and is recommended for working collections and some large research collections.

1269. **Handbook of Highway Engineering.** Baker, Robert F., ed. Malabar, FL: Krieger, 1982. 894p.

This reprint of a 1975 edition was designed for the highway engineer. The reference provides principles, processes, and data necessary for the application of relevant technology. There are 26 sections complete with text, data, diagrams, and photographs. Among the topics covered are highway policies, administration, urban transportation planning, and geometric design standards.

1270. **Handbook of Hydraulics for the Solution of Hydraulic Engineering Problems.** 6th ed. Brater, Ernest F., and Horace Williams King. New York: McGraw-Hill, 1976. 1v. (various paging).

An illustrated handbook on the principles of hydraulics which contains considerable information and numerous tables, charts, and graphs. This is a handy reference for civil engineers and practicing engineers who seek solutions to on-the-job problems.

1271. **Handbook of Structural Concrete.** Kong, F. K., et al., eds. New York: McGraw-Hill, 1983. 1v. (various paging).

Intended as an international reference work, this handbook provides authoritative coverage of the principles, procedures, and data relating to fundamental behavior; design, analysis, construction, maintenance, and demolition; and design philosophies and their expression in codes of practice.

1272. **IES Lighting Handbook.** Kaufman, John E., ed. New York: Illuminating Engineering Society, 1984, 1987. 2v.

The 1984 volume is the reference volume; the 1987 volume is the applications volume. Together these two volumes make up the primary source of information on illumination in the world. Virtually any topic on illumination is covered in one of these volumes. A necessity for any serious collection on illumination or construction engineering.

1273. **Know Your Woods.** rev. ed. Constantine, Albert. New York: Scribner, 1987.

A thorough reference tool, it describes more than 300 principal woods and includes a detailed general index. An excellent addition to any collection.

1274. **Lineman's and Cableman's Handbook.** 7th ed. Kurtz, Edwin, and Thomas M. Shoemaker. New York: McGraw-Hill, 1986. 1v. (various paging).

A standard handbook on the fundamentals and procedures for the maintenance, operation, and construction of electric distribution and transmission lines. It includes material on transmission circuits, construction specifications, insulators, and grounding, and contains safety applications and self testing questions. Extensively illustrated by photographs and line drawings, it is a valuable reference for linemen, electricians, cablemen, field supervisors, apprentices, and other associate individuals. The sections cover general understanding of electricity, electrical terms, electric power systems, construction of overhead and underground distribution and transmission lines, and maintenance procedures.

1275. **Manual of Applied Geology for Engineers.** London: Institution of Civil Engineers, 1976. 378p.

A manual useful to both geologists and civil engineers, this covers soil and rock mechanics and contains input from governmental and industrial resources.

1276. **Manual of Energy-Saving in Existing Buildings and Plants.** Baron, Stephen L. Englewood Cliffs, NJ: Prentice-Hall, 1978. 2v.

Volume 1 is entitled *Operation and Maintenance*; volume 2, *Facility Modifications*. This handbook illustrates energy saving methods in commercial, industrial, and residential buildings, and shows how to reduce costs. Detailed checklists are provided. This is recommended for any collection except school libraries.

1277. **Manual of Geology for Civil Engineers.** Pitts, J. New York: Wiley, 1985.

A useful manual that treats the major aspects of descriptive geology, especially rock types and structural studies. It is recommended for academic and specialized collections.

1278. **Manual of Soil Laboratory Testing.** Head, K. H. London: Pentech, 1984- . irregular.

A practical manual on the technology of soil testing for civil engineering purposes. Topics covered include equipment; description of soils; testing and techniques; and safety. Chapters contain introduction; definitions; tests and procedures; and basic concepts. Suitable for undergraduate and community college students interested in soil testing, it is useful to laboratory technicians and civil engineers as well.

1279. **Manual of Steel Construction.** 8th ed. Chicago, IL: American Institute of Steel Construction, 1986. 808p.

A comprehensive handbook by any standard, its divisions include: "Dimensions and Properties," "Beam and Girder Design," "Column Design," "Connections," "Specifications," and "Miscellaneous." It is highly recommended for any collection which deals with steel construction in any form.

1280. **National Construction Estimator.** Los Angeles: Craftsman, 1985.

Building costs for both light and heavy construction are listed in this extremely useful handbook for anyone involved in construction, including laypersons. It is recommended for any public, academic, or specialized collection.

1281. **Practical Construction Equipment Maintenance Reference Guide.** Higgins, Lindley R., and Tyler G. Hicks. New York: McGraw-Hill, 1987.

This is a collection of 55 articles that examine various aspects of equipment maintenance. Subjects covered include engines, pumps, and compactors, and information is provided concerning personnel, facilities, budgeting, and basic tools. A valuable source for contractors and construction engineers.

1282. **Professional Handbook of Building Construction.** Allen, E. New York: Wiley, 1985. 743p.

A basic reference that deals with the common materials of building and the methods by which they are incorporated into buildings. Covers all of the most common construction systems and materials and is well illustrated with over 400 line drawings and 300 photographs. Highly recommended.

1283. **Road and Bridge Construction Handbook.** Lapinski, Michael. New York: Van Nostrand Reinhold, 1978. 156p.

Explains road building technology in simple, everyday terms while examining each phase of construction. It is recommended for all those engaged in bridge and road construction.

1284. **Standard Handbook for Civil Engineers.** 3rd ed. Merritt, Frederick S. New York: McGraw-Hill, 1983. 1v. (various paging).

An excellent handbook covering virtually all aspects of construction engineering including planning, design, and construction. Topics include computer operations; design management; construction management; structural theory; concrete design and construction; lightweight steel design and construction; and surveying. This is highly recommended for both professionals and research collections.

1285. **Structural Engineering for Professional Engineers' Examination: Including Statics, Mechanics of Materials, and Civil Engineering.** 3rd ed. Kurtz, Max. New York: McGraw-Hill, 1978. 375p.

Aims to help engineers pass the structural and civil engineering licensing examinations by reviewing basic theory, applications, and design codes. Designed primarily for professional engineers.

1286. **Structural Engineering Handbook.** 2nd ed. Gaylord, Edwin H., and Charles N. Gaylord, eds. New York: McGraw-Hill, 1979. 1v. (various paging).

Though this handbook covers the field of structural engineering the material used is still relevant to engineering. Topics covered include finite element analysis, reinforced concrete silos and bunkers, and steel poles for transmission lines. It is recommended for any civil engineering collection.

1287. **Structural Steel Designers' Handbook.** Merritt, Frederick, ed. New York: McGraw-Hill, 1972. 1v. (various paging).
This time proven handbook for structural design includes topics such as properties of structural steels, fabrication and erection, general structural theory, special structural theories, connections, criteria for building design, design of building members, floor and roof systems, lateral force design, criteria for bridge design, beam and girder bridges, truss bridges, arch bridges, and cable supported bridges. It is recommended for any working collection in construction engineering.

1288. **Timber Construction Manual.** 3rd ed. American Institute of Timber Construction. New York: Wiley, 1986.
Convenient reference for architects, engineers, contractors, teachers, and the laminating and fabricating industry. It contains design data and construction information, AITC recommended standards and specifications, new lumber grading requirements, and current timber design methods.

1289. **Tunnel Engineering Handbook.** Bickel, John O., and T. R. Kuesel, eds. New York: Van Nostrand Reinhold, 1982. 670p.
Contains valuable information of vital areas in the field of tunnel engineering including topics such as geological and geophysical investigations, materials handling, ventilation, lighting, and the like. A highly recommended source.

1290. **Water Treatment Handbook.** 5th ed. New York: Halsted Press, 1979. 1186p.
This comprehensive source covers a wide range of water treatment situations such as drinking water, swimming pool water, and industrial situations. Field experts have made contributions, and coverage includes analytical aspects, construction and design, and maintenance. This is highly recommended for civil engineering libraries.

1291. **Welding Handbook.** 7th ed. Weisman, Charlotte, ed. Miami, FL: American Welding Society, 1976- . irregular.
This well-respected handbook on welding contains information on all types of welding and materials handling for welding. The information in the handbook is taken from published literature, technical reports, and company reports. It is highly recommended for any reference collection in engineering.

DIRECTORIES

1292. **Directory of Construction Associations.** 2nd ed. MacDonald, Joseph A., ed. Huntington, NY: Professional Publications, 1979. 324p.
A quick and easy-to-use source listing contractor associations, professional and business societies, labor unions, government agencies, manufacturer and producer groups, and construction publications. Covers 87 specific categories, listing each organization alphabetically by official name.

1293. **Energy-Efficient Products and Systems: A Comparative Catalog for Architects and Engineers.** Energyworks. New York: Wiley, 1983- . 3-month updates. looseleaf.

A listing and description of product lines in conservation systems. Includes generic, brand name, and manufacturing indexes. Cross-referenced according to the Construction Specification Institute system.

1294. **Handbook of Construction Resources and Support Services.** MacDonald, J. A., ed. Huntington, NY: Professional Publications, 1979. 595p.

A directory of sources of information available to solve engineering and construction problems faced on construction projects. Contains a listing of consultants, reference libraries, government agencies, and professional societies.

13   Energy and Environment

Energy and environment is a loosely articulated area. Both science and engineering components are found more often in this field than in some other technical areas, making it clear that science and technology are moving closer together.

Energy is defined here as all types of energy, but because of the technological focus it concentrates on consumable (renewable and nonrenewable) energy and the transport of this energy to a market.

The environmental engineering component includes a great deal of material and is supplemented with a number of other chapters: geosciences, chemistry, botany and agriculture, and biology. The concentration here is the application of these tools to the interplay of humans and the environment in which they live.

The energy and environment chapter is a technology-oriented, that is, a tools-oriented chapter. This is a new area of interest for engineering and technology, but one that has a rich history. While this may appear contradictory, there is a long tradition in engineering of working to use technology in both efficient and effective ways. Engineering has not always been adept at the public relations component, but this chapter should indicate both a tradition and an increased awareness in the engineering community of the critical place both energy and the environment play in everyday life.

GUIDES TO THE LITERATURE

1295.   **Acid Rain Information Book.** 2nd ed. Bubenick, David V., ed. Park Ridge, NJ: TD196
Noyes Publications, 1984. 397p.   A25
    This is a greatly enlarged version of the 1982 edition. It is organized in logical progres-   R4
sion from sources of pollutants to mitigative measures and regulatory options. A discus-   1982
sion of uncertainties in the understanding of the subject is included along with a description of current and proposed research.

1296.   **Coal Information Sources and Data Bases.** Bloch, Caroline C. Park Ridge, NJ:
Noyes Data Corp., 1980. 128p.
    A guide to federal, state, and international agencies, departments, libraries, and universities that deal with coal data whether it be legal and regulatory data, assistance programs, or research and technology. This is a professional guide to the literature.

1297. **CRC Critical Reviews in Environmental Control.** Boca Raton, FL: CRC Press, 1970- . quarterly.

This work provides a concise and critical evaluation of literature in the environmental area. The articles focus on a predefined area and are written by specialists in the field. Bibliographies are included with each of the articles. This is an excellent state-of-the-art journal and is a must for any serious collection in environmental sciences.

1298. **Energy Information Guide.** Weber, R. David. Santa Barbara, CA: ABC-Clio, 1982-1984. 3v.

Each of the three volumes guides the user to organizations, government agencies, books, articles, and other printed and nonprint sources of information on energy in the United States. It is designed for students, researchers, government officials, those in business and others interested in America's energy present and future. Volume 1 covers general and alternate energy sources; volume 2, nuclear and electric power; and volume 3, fossil fuels. This is a complete, annotated bibliography covering over 9,000 items.

1299. **Energy Research Guide: Journals, Indexes, and Abstracts.** Viola, John, Newell B. Mack, and Thomas R. Stauffer, eds. Cambridge, MA: Ballinger, 1983. 284p.

This guide describes over 500 periodicals, indexes, and abstracts covering energy or related fields. It lists short annotations, price, address, and telephone number of the publisher, and is a good, quick answer source.

1300. **Energy Statistics: A Guide to Information Sources.** Balachandran, Sarojin. Detroit, MI: Gale, 1980. 272p.

Statistical sources on energy are provided in this guide. Part 1 is a listing of keyword and subject descriptions, part 2 is a list of 40 annotated sources, and part 3 is a list of 600 publications arranged by title. It is recommended for any public, academic, or special library.

1301. **Environment Index: A Guide to the Key Environmental Literature of the Year.** New York: Environment Information Center, 1971- . annual.

The bulk of each annual volume is devoted to a comprehensive index of recently published documents for journal articles, conference papers, academic reports, and corporate and government reports. Five separate indexes are provided: subject, industry code (SIC), geography, source, and author. The index is complemented by Enviroline, an online computer system that accesses EIC's database of more than 100,000 documents dating from 1970. A good state-of-the-art work, recommended for academic and special libraries.

1302. **Federal Energy Information Sources and Data Bases.** Bloch, Carolyn C. Park Ridge, NJ: Noyes Data Corp., 1979. 115p.

This directory is divided into four sections: "Cabinet Departments," "Administrative Agencies," "Quasi Government Agencies," and "Congressional Offices." A good, but aging, directory, it should be used with caution.

1303. **Gasohol Sourcebook: Literature Survey and Abstracts.** Cheremisinoff, Nicholas P., and Paul N. Cheremisinoff. Ann Arbor, MI: Ann Arbor Science Publishers, 1981. 221p.

This sourcebook presents a review of recent developments from 1965 and contains literature citations with selected abstracts. It appears in five sections: (1) biotechnology and bioconversion; (2) ethanol and methanol production; (3) automotive and other fuels; (4) production of chemical feedstocks; and (5) economics of alcohol production. This is a professional level text.

1304. **Guide to the Petroleum Reference Literature.** Pearson, Barbara C., and Katherine B. Ellwood. Littleton, CO: Libraries Unlimited, 1987. 193p.

This is perhaps the only guide which specifically treats the petroleum literature. The statistical information that one might expect to find is somewhat sparse, but the major pieces are covered. The literature may be considered by some to be too selectively chosen. The fact remains, however, that this is a good entry into the source literature. It is recommended for most libraries with an emphasis on energy.

1305. **How to Find Information on Canadian Natural Resources: A Guide to the Literature.** Pal, Gabriel. Ottawa, Canada: Canadian Library Association, 1985. 182p.

This is a significant contribution to the information resources dealing with the environment in North America. The majority of the book deals with chapters on specific areas of concern such as energy and climate. It is recommended for special collections.

1306. **Noise Pollution: A Guide to Information Sources.** Bragdon, Clifford R. Detroit, MI: Gale Research, 1979. 524p.

A good basic bibliography focusing on the following topics: physiological effects, behavioral effects, abatement, community noise, environmental impact, acoustics, and education. The material was gleaned from published and fugitive material as well as nonprint material. It is recommended because of its wide literature scope.

1307. **Nuclear Power Debate: A Guide to the Literature.** Mansfield, Jerry W. New York: Garland, 1984. 93p.

This is as balanced a bibliography on both sides of the debate as possible. The author acknowledges that much more has been written recently on the negative side of the issue than the positive, and this is reflected in the relative sizes of the two sections. There are two major drawbacks to this publication. First, it is too short. A much more extensive bibliography could have been developed and would have been more useful. The second problem is that the subject index is weak. In a short work such as this, this is a major failing. Still, the book should be considered by most libraries for general reference use.

1308. **Sourcebook on the Environment: A Guide to the Literature.** Hammond, Kenneth A., George Macinko, and Wilma B. Fairchild. Chicago, IL: University of Chicago Press, 1978. 613p.

Although ten years old, this is still a good bibliography because it gives the reader a background in three major areas: environmental perspectives, case studies, and major elements of the environment. The method is an essay format which is then followed by a bibliography. This would be a good addition to a retrospective collection.

1309. **Toxic and Hazardous Materials: A Sourcebook and Guide to Information Sources.** Webster, James K., ed. Westport, CT: Greenwood Press, 1987. 431p.

Over 1,600 information sources are included in this volume. Most of the material is annotated, and a series of eleven people contributed chapters which range in quality depending on the expertise of the writer. The clear bias is not only toward the English language, but toward U.S. materials as a whole. The overall effect is that of a balanced but not comprehensive work. The *Toxic Substances Sourcebook* (see entry 1310) is a more comprehensive work. Still, this volume should be seriously considered by most collections in the environmental science area.

1310. **Toxic Substances Sourcebook.** Ross, Steve, and Monica Pronen, eds. New York: Environment Information Center, 1980. 584p.

This is a good synthesis of the literature on toxic substances. It examines books, journal articles, and technical papers to provide a balanced description of the effect of toxic substances on the environment. An excellent addition to any library or information center.

1311. **Water Pollution: A Guide to Information Sources.** Knight, Allen W., and Mary Ann Simmons. Detroit, MI: Gale Research, 1980. 278p.

This comprehensive guide presents a compendium of reference material, case studies, and methodological ideas valuable to the scholar and practitioner. It contains a selected collection of periodical literature, government documents, professional journals, and teaching materials on water pollution. This is a professionally done work aimed toward professionals in the field.

1312. **World Energy: The Facts and the Future.** Hedley, Don. London: Euromonitor, 1981. 368p.

This is an assessment of present day world consumption of energy which forecasts how the world energy economy will have changed by the year 2000 and what is likely to happen beyond. It is an academic volume.

ABSTRACTS, INDEXES, AND BIBLIOGRAPHIES

1313. **Abstracts on Health Effects of Environmental Pollutants.** Philadelphia: BioSciences Information Service, 1972- . monthly.

This is a combination of two pre-existing databases, BIOSIS and MEDLARS. The result is a publication on occupational health and industrial medicine. This is a good source, but not as up-to-the-minute as BIOSIS or MEDLARS.

1314. **Acid Rain: A Bibliography of Research Annotated for Easy Access.** Stopp, G. Harry. Metuchen, NJ: Scarecrow, 1985. 174p.

This is a brief work considering the importance and the interest in acid rain. The work consists of 884 entries arranged by author, and the annotations are brief and usually descriptive. The author indicates a second edition will be forthcoming. A distinct bias toward U.S. and Canadian materials can be detected. The work is included here to complement *Acid Rain and the Environment* (see entry 1315). The two together come close to providing reasonable, though not complete, coverage.

1315. **Acid Rain and the Environment 1980-1984: A Select Bibliography.** Farmer, Penny, ed. Letchworth, Herts, England: Technical Communications, 1984. 108p.

Predominantly American references, the material here can be found elsewhere. The importance of this work is that it pulls together a reasonable sampling of that material and does so without a British slant.

1316. **APTIC.** Research Triangle Park, NC: Environmental Protection Agency, 1966-1976.

This database covers air pollution, including the social, political, legal, and administrative aspects. Produced by the Manpower and Technical Information Branch of the EPA, it is available from DIALOG.

1317. **AQUACULTURE.** Rockville, MD: National Oceanic and Atmospheric Administration, 1970- .
An online database providing information on the growing of marine, brackish, and freshwater organisms. Topics include disease, economics, engineering, food and nutrition, growth requirements, and legal considerations. Available from DIALOG.

1318. **AQUALINE.** Marlow, England: Water Research Centre, 1960- .
This online database provides information on all aspects of water, wastewater, and the aquatic environment. Topics include water resources, development and management, quality, water treatment, sewage, pollution, and environmental concerns. It is available from DIALOG.

1319. **Bibliography of the Urban Modification of the Atmospheric and Hydrologic Environment.** Griffiths, John F., and M. Joan Griffiths. Washington, DC: U.S. Environmental Data Service, 1974. 92p.
Although small and now over ten years old, this is still an interesting bibliography for the suggested solutions to the problems. Sections include information on: city, cloud, cooling power, dust and nuclei, electricity and ions, humidity, light, models, pollution, precipitation, radiation, temperature, visibility, wind, floods, ground water, runoff, sedimentation, stream temperature, and water quality. Recommended only for research collections with existing retrospective collections.

1320. **Biological Indicators of Environmental Quality: A Bibliography of Abstracts.** Thomas, William A., William H. Wilcox, and Gerald Goldstein. Ann Arbor, MI: Ann Arbor Science Publishers, 1973. 254p.
This is a very interesting source for information on testing living organisms in native habitats. In some cases techniques have been developed which go beyond the scope of this book. It remains a good source for general information because it pulls together a mountain of information. It is recommended with caution.

1321. **Canadian Energy Bibliography.** Armstrong, Jim. Toronto: Ontario Library Association, 1980. 146p.
Describes some 600 English language works in the field of energy, most published after 1975. Sources include journal articles, databases, government reports, films, books, and reference works. A wide variety of subjects within the energy field are covered, and more radical entries are balanced by opposing views. This is an important work for the researcher or activist.

1322. **Catalogues of the Library of the Marine Biological Association of the United Kingdom.** Boston: G. K. Hall, 1977. 16v.
This is a book catalog of one of the major environmental collections in the world. The collection includes materials related to marine biology, oceanography, fisheries, and related subjects. The subject index is somewhat unwieldy, classifying terms under overly broad headings. This is still a major collection, however, and this catalog is one potential checklist.

1323. **Chemical Regulations and Guideline System (CRGS).** Fairfax, VA: CRC Systems, Inc., 1981- .

This is an online index to U.S. federal regulatory material relating to the control of chemical substances. It is available from DIALOG.

1324. **Desalination and Recycling Abstracts.** Tel Aviv, Israel: National Center of Scientific and Technological Information, 1985- . quarterly.

Subject chapters include desalination-general, distillation, membrane processes, ion exchange, chemical and physical properties, effluent treatment, and energy sources and requirements. Subject, name, and patent indexes are provided.

1325. **DOE Energy.** Oak Ridge, TN: U.S. Department of Energy, 1974- .

A database of journal articles, report literature, conference papers, books, patents, dissertations, and translations. Available from DIALOG.

1326. **EBIB.** College Station, TX: Texas A&M, 1919- .

Contains worldwide literature on energy in an online database. Available from SDC.

1327. **EIS: Cumulative: The Year in Environmental Impact Statements.** Bethesda, MD: Cambridge Scientific Abstracts, 1977- . annual.

Divides the area of environmental impact statements into 12 subject areas. Contains subject, legal, geographical site, agency organization, EIS number and title, and EPA-EIS-agency indexes. Abstracts are formatted as to purpose, positive and negative aspects, legal mandates, and prior references. This is a solid reference work of great value.

1328. **Energy Abstracts for Policy Analysis.** Oak Ridge, TN: U.S. Department of Energy, 1975- . monthly with annual cumulative index.

A compendium drawn from publications of all levels of government, this is limited primarily to nontechnical or quasitechnical articles or reports in order to emphasize programmatic efforts.

1329. **Energy and the Social Sciences: A Bibliographic Guide to the Literature.** Yanarella, Ernest J., and Ann-Marie Yanarella. Boulder, CO: Westview Press, 1982. 347p.

Over 4,000 entries are arranged in major categories. Essays introduce each section, but no annotations are provided. The range of coverage is international, but the work has a distinct U.S. bias. This guide aims to assist social scientists, students, and librarians to become acquainted quickly with a wide variety of works from the technical and social sciences literature on energy.

1330. **Energy Index.** New York: Environment Information Center, 1971- . annual.

This is the cumulative index to *Energy Information Abstracts* (see entry 1331). In addition to being a tool for indexing, this is a stand-alone annual review to the major literature, events, legislation, and statistics in the energy field. It is an excellent addition to virtually any library dealing with environmental issues.

1331. **Energy Information Abstracts.** New York: Environment Information Center, 1976- . monthly.

This service abstracts energy-related journal articles, government reports, conference papers, and research reports. The scope of the publication is very broad, including the traditional as well as that which can be categorized, such as policy issues. The annual cumulation is published as *Energy Index* (see entry 1330). This is an excellent tool with material of interest to virtually anyone involved in the energy field.

1332. **Energyline.** New York: Environment Information Center, 1971- .
Covers over 200 core journals to produce an online database. Also covered are selected journals, reports, monographs, and newspapers. Available from DIALOG and SDC.

1333. **Energynet.**
An online database providing directory information on organizations and people in energy related fields.

1334. **Environline.** New York: Environment Information Center, 1971- .
An online database covering the environmental literature. Books, films, and reviews are included as well as extracts from the *Daily Federal Register.* Available from DIALOG and SDC.

1335. **Environment Abstracts.** New York: Environment Information Center, 1974- . monthly. v.4- .
The first three volumes were published under the title *Environment Information Access.* This is a descriptive abstracting service using both scientific and popular literature to cover the area of environmental issues in a very broad sense. It is an excellent tool because of the mixture of material. The annual cumulation is titled *Environment Index* (see entry 1336). Recommended for virtually any collection with an interest in the environment.

1336. **Environment Index.** New York: Environment Information Center, 1971- . annual.
This is the cumulated index for *Environment Abstracts* (see entry 1335), which also acts as a literature review and overall review of environment and related topics for the year. It specifically covers not only journals, but popular material, legislation, films, books, and patents, and makes an excellent addition to any library with an environment collection.

1337. **Environmental Bibliography.** Santa Barbara, CA: Environmental Studies Institute, 1973- .
Covers online the fields of general human ecology, atmospheric studies, energy, land resources, water resources, and nutrition and health. Available from DIALOG.

1338. **Environmental Impact Assessment: A Bibliography with Abstracts.** Clark, Brian D., Ronald Bisset, and Peter Wathern. New York: Bowker, 1980. 516p.
Over 1,100 references dealing with environmental impact assessment are included in this bibliography, though not all entries are annotated. This is a good beginning source for literature on the topic.

1339. **Environmental Quality Abstracts.** Louisville, KY: Data Courier, 1975- . quarterly.
This service examines the periodical literature for information in the environmental sciences. The focus is on scientific as opposed to popular material, although some popular material is included. This is a quality abstracting tool utilizing a descriptive approach and is recommended for serious collections in the environmental sciences.

1340. **EPA Index: A Key to U.S. Environmental Protection Agency Reports and Superintendent of Documents and NTIS Numbers.** Bower, Cynthia E., and Mary L. Rhoads, eds. Phoenix, AZ: Oryx Press, 1983. 385p.
Compiled to assist users in locating certain numbered EPA reports published prior to 1982, this work concentrates on EPA reports distributed to federal depository libraries or cited in the *Monthly Catalog of U.S. Government Publications* (see entry 357). SuDocs clas-

sification numbers are provided to aid in locating the report in depository libraries. Approximately 8,000 numbered EPA reports published from 1970-1981 are covered. Entries are arranged in two sequences: by report number and by title. Included is a notation of NTIS availability. This work centralizes often difficult to locate information in a single volume.

1341. **ERDA Energy Research Abstracts.** Oak Ridge, TN: ERDA Technical Information Center, 1976- . monthly.

Provides abstracting and indexing coverage to all scientific and technical works originating at the U.S. Department of Energy, its laboratories, research centers, and contractors. It also covers energy information in report form from domestic and foreign governments, universities, and research organizations. This is a good source for governmental information.

1342. **Freshwater and Terrestrial Radioecology: A Selected Bibliography.** Klement, Alfred W., and Vincent Schultz. Stroudsburg, PA: Dowden, Hutchinson & Ross, 1980. 587p.

This work contains 20,000 references to literature on radiocactive materials in the earth's ecosystem covering the period from 1898 to 1979. It is an excellent source for general through specific literature.

1343. **Geraghty and Millers Groundwater Bibliography.** 4th ed. Van der Leeden, Frits, ed. Plainview, NY: Water Information Center, 1987. 381p.

This bibliography contains approximately 4,600 references to publications in the groundwater field, though there are no annotations. Monographs, serials, and journal articles are included. This is not a guide to the literature, but is strictly a bibliography.

1344. **Global Marine Pollution Bibliography: Ocean Dumping of Municipal and Industrial Wastes.** Champ, Michael A., and P. Kilho Park. New York: IFI/Plenum, 1982. 399p.

This is an international work containing a great deal of information from many sources. Annotations are lengthy where provided. Includes subject and author indexes, and is recommended for research collections.

1345. **Pollution Abstracts.** Bethesda, MD: Cambridge Scientific Abstracts, 1970- . bimonthly.

An excellent abstracting service concentrating on air and water pollution, solid wastes, noise pesticides, radiation, and general environmental quality. This is a first-rate source for all types of materials related to pollution. Available online as well as in hard copy from DIALOG and SDC.

1346. **Selected Water Resources Abstracts.** Washington, DC: U.S. Government Printing Office, 1968- . semimonthly.

This is a primary source for material dealing with water in any form. Not restricted to the sciences, it contains material in the social sciences as well. The major drawback is the lag time, though this is still a necessary source for any serious collection in the environmental sciences. Available online as *Water Resources Abstracts* (see entry 1350) from DIALOG.

1347. **Solar Energy Index.** Machovec, George, comp. New York: Pergamon, 1982- .

This is a compendium of the Arizona State University Solar Energy Collection. The emphasis is on terrestrial solar thermal and photovoltaic applications of solar energy, and both theoretical and "how to do it" publications are covered. With less emphasis, wind energy, bioconversion, ocean thermal energy, and outer space applications of solar energy are covered. Material from the International Solar Energy Society is included. This is a reasonable checklist in this particular area.

1348. **Sun Power: A Bibliography of United States Government Documents on Solar Energy.** McAninch, Sandra, comp. Westport, CT: Greenwood Press, 1981. 944p.
    The multiple index approach of this work permits a wide range of inquiry. Each citation provides a complete record of all formats in which particular documents appear. Contains an excellent index. The scope of the work is broad enough to pull a wide variety of citations, making this a good choice for virtually any library.

1349. **Water Publications of State Agencies: A Bibliography of Publications on Water Resources and Their Management Published by the States of the United States.** Giefer, Gerald J., and David K. Todd. Huntington, NY: Water Information Center, 1976. 189p.
    This work is included here because it lists publications of state agencies. Although dated, this is one of the few attempts at pulling together state publications in the area of water. The arrangement is by state, then by issuing agency. It is to be used with caution, but not to be overlooked because of its age.

1350. **Water Resources Abstracts.** Washington, DC: U.S. Department of the Interior, 1968- .
    This comprehensive range of water related topics is available online from DIALOG. The hard copy equivalent is *Selected Water Resources Abstracts* (see entry 1346).

ENCYCLOPEDIAS

1351. **Encyclopedia of Environmental Science and Engineering.** 2nd ed. rev. Pfafflin, James R., and Edward N. Ziegler, eds. New York: Gordon & Breach, 1983. 3v. 1254p.
    A combination of an overview and a selected comprehensive treatment of some topics, this source bridges the gap between environmental sciences and engineering by comparing the techniques and issues of the two. It is an excellent tool for ongoing research in both fields, and is highly recommended for academic and research collections.

1352. **Environmental Planning: A Condensed Encyclopedia.** Gilpin, Alan. Park Ridge, NJ: Noyes Publications, 1986. 348p.
    This is a difficult book to annotate. The descriptions in some places are excellent. In others, they are simply not there. Data beyond 1981 are rarely used or mentioned. What it does well is to provide concise and pointed descriptions of specific points of history and law. The encyclopedia should be used with some caution because the data presented are, in more cases than not, six years old.

1353. **Grzimek's Encyclopedia of Ecology.** Grzimek, Bernhard, ed. New York: Van Nostrand Reinhold, 1976. 705p.
    Although somewhat dated, this is included because it is a translation of the Swiss work published in 1973. It gives an insight to the issues of Europe, some of which are much different from those of North America. This is to be used with care as a reference work, but is still an important tool.

1354. **Kaiman's Encyclopedia of Energy Topics.** Lee, Kaiman, and Jacqueline Masloff. Newtonville, MA: Environmental Design and Research Center, 1979. 2v. 800p.

Characterized best as a useful snapshot of current concepts and directions in the field of energy utilization and energy sources with an accent on the environment. It is highly recommended for any collection in the environmental sciences.

1355. **McGraw-Hill Encyclopedia of Energy.** 2nd ed. Parker, Sybil P., ed. New York: McGraw-Hill, 1981. 838p.

Leading international authorities from government, industry, and the academic community address the technological, environmental, economic, social, and political aspects of energy systems. This is a high-level, academic work.

DICTIONARIES

1356. **Dictionary of Dangerous Pollutants, Ecology, and Environment.** Tver, David F. New York: Industrial Press, 1981. 347p.

This one-of-a-kind dictionary includes a list of abbreviations and acronyms. An important addition to a research collection, it covers noise, air, and water pollution; nuclear energy; geothermal energy; solar energy, design, and construction; coal; waste control; biomass conversion; recycling; ecology; meteorology and climatology.

1357. **Dictionary of Energy.** Hall, Carl W., and George W. Hinman. New York: Dekker, 1983. 286p.

Words are drawn from a wide range of specialized fields working on energy related problems and definitions range from simple to complex. This is a good general dictionary for the area and is recommended for college and public collections.

1358. **Dictionary of Energy Technology.** Gilpin, Alan, and Alan Williams. London: Butterworths, 1982. 392p.

This first appeared as *Dictionary of Fuel Technology* (1969). It has been updated to include other sources of energy and political, economic, and environmental aspects of the subject of energy. This is a good desk top reference for professionals in the field.

1359. **Dictionary of the Environment.** 2nd ed. Allaby, Michael. New York: Van Nostrand Reinhold, 1983. 529p.

This is an updated dictionary, first published in 1977. It pulls together terms from a variety of intellectual pursuits within the broad umbrella of the environmental sciences. A good general purpose dictionary suitable for academic and some special libraries.

1360. **Dictionary of Waste and Water Treatment.** Scott, John S., and Paul G. Smith. London: Butterworths, 1981. 359p.

Explains the terminology within the field and aids in the understanding of the literature. Follows the convention for biological Latin where necessary. This is more a British publication and should find excellent use there.

1361. **Elsevier's Dictionary of Solar Technology: In Five Languages—English, German, French, Spanish, and Italian.** Nentwig, K., comp. Amsterdam, Netherlands: Elsevier, 1985. 213p.

Specialized terms from the field of solar technology are treated to help prevent "unfortunate" translations found in published papers. This will be a very useful work in an academic or research oriented collection with foreign language material.

1362. **Energy Terminology: A Multilingual Glossary: A Glossary for Engineers, Research Workers, Industrialists and Economists Containing over 1000 Standard Energy Terms in English, French, German and Spanish.** rev. ed. Oxford, England: Pergamon, 1983. 270p.

Contains about 1,000 terms relating to energy which are presented in English, German, French, and Spanish. The glossary is fully indexed. This is highly recommended for any collection with foreign language material in the environmental sciences.

1363. **Environmental Glossary.** 4th ed. Frick, G. William, ed. Rockville, MD: Government Institutes, 1986. 360p.

Definitions are gathered from EPA regulations, federal statutes, and from other governmental and private sources. The definitions primarily reflect congressional or EPA usage of terms for specific regulatory purposes. Contains explanatory material to assist in the clarity of definitions. Each definition has a code letter referring to the source. This is devised as a tool for those who deal with local, state, and federal environmental regulations.

1364. **Environmental Impact Statement Glossary: A Reference Source for EIS Writers, Reviewers and Citizens.** Landy, Marc, ed. New York: IFI/Plenum, 1979. 537p.

This is not a technical glossary or the standard glossary, but an effort to assemble the translation of complex EIS language into a vocabulary aimed at the lay reader. Aims to help people understand and communicate more effectively by presenting, analyzing, and comparing terminology used by various EIS organizations.

1365. **Glossary: Water and Wastewater Control Engineering.** 3rd ed. Washington, DC: American Public Health Association, 1981. 441p.

The goals of the new edition are to eliminate obsolete terms, to portray the great impact that chemistry and chemical engineering has in the field, to provide metric unit equivalents, and to improve usefulness through format changes. It is generally successful in its goals.

1366. **Renewable Energy Dictionary.** Arlington, VA: Volunteers in Technical Assistance, 1982. 484p.

This encyclopedic dictionary is composed of up-to-date and authoritative definitions of terms used in renewable energy fields. Terms are thoroughly cross-referenced and translations are made into French and Spanish. This is an excellent source for the layperson using renewable resources.

1367. **Solar Energy Dictionary.** Hunt, V. Daniel. New York: Industrial Press, 1982. 411p.

Definitions of over 3,000 solar energy terms are provided in this work, and subjects include passive/active solar energy, photovoltaic energy, biomass, alcohol fuels, wind energy, solar thermal energy, ocean energy, satellite power systems, industrial process heat, and waste energy conversion. Designed for the professional or academic.

HANDBOOKS

1368. **Bioenvironmental Systems.** Wise, Donald L., ed. Boca Raton, FL: CRC Press, 1987. 4v.

A comprehensive overview of bioenvironmental research and development programs worldwide. The focus is on bioconversion of organic residues, and anaerobic methane fermentation is stressed. Each chapter is the work of an expert or group of experts in the field. This is an excellent reference tool with state-of-the-art data. It is highly recommended for major research collections.

1369. **Changing Structure of American Industry and Energy Use Patterns.** Broehl, J., and A. Faruqui, eds. Columbus, OH: Battelle, 1987. 512p.

A compendium of views from experts in several varied fields, including automotive, electronics, aerospace, and chemistry. The overriding theme is the coupling of industry with energy use. This should be of great interest to energy economists as well as those involved in strategic planning in the energy sector.

1370. **Consumer's Energy Handbook.** Norback, Peter, and Craig Norback. New York: Van Nostrand Reinhold, 1981. 362p.

A layperson's guide to how to conserve energy and money in the consumer market. Interesting and very practical, it is highly recommended for any public library collection.

1371. **CRC Handbook of Biosolar Resources.** Zaborsky, Oskar R., ed. Boca Raton, FL: CRC Press, 1982- . irregular.

Serves as a reference source for the most pertinent information on biosolar resources ultimately intended for utilization. Arranged on the natural flow of events from production to utilization, its focus is on data of present or potential commercial significance. This is a professional source book.

1372. **CRC Handbook of Management of Radiation Protection Programs.** Miller, Kenneth L., ed. Boca Raton, FL: CRC Press, 1986. 536p.

Predominantly of interest to those involved with radiation litigation and public relations, this work also contains material dealing with the transportation of radioactive materials and the attendant rules and regulations. While not technical, some expertise is necessary to use the handbook. Recommended for serious collections in the environmental sciences.

1373. **CRC Handbook of Mass Spectra of Environmental Contaminants.** Hites, Ronald A. Boca Raton, FL: CRC Press, 1985. 433p.

A collection of the electron impact of mass spectra of 394 commonly encountered environmental pollutants. The author states, "mass spectra is the single most useful technique for the analysis of organic compounds in environmental samples." Included compounds were selected by an analysis of several U.S. Environmental Protection Agency and World Health Organization databases accessed through the Chemical Information System. In general, compounds with fewer than four carbon atoms or those not found in the Merck Index were excluded. This is a very comprehensive, timely source.

1374. **CRC Handbook of Radiation Measurement and Protection.** Brodsky, Allen, ed. Boca Raton, FL: CRC Press, 1979- . 2v.

Currently in two volumes: volume 1, *Physical Science and Engineering Data* and volume 2, *Biological and Mathematical Data.* The first volume provides the basic data utilized in radiation protection. Most of the data are presented in tabular form with little discussion. The second volume covers basic anatomical, physiological, and ecological data, and includes a good discussion on radiation toxicity. The second volume continues the format of the first in terms of presentation of data. This is a professional source for use by professionals and researchers.

1375. **Dangerous Properties of Industrial Materials.** 6th ed. Sax, N. Irving. New York: Van Nostrand Reinhold, 1984. 3124p.

T55.3
H3
S3
1989
Sci
Ref

This is a new edition of a classic in the field. Previously titled *Handbook of Dangerous Materials* (1951), this will remain as a chief desk reference for a whole range of researchers. Considered an invaluable reference source, it should be a prerequisite for any collection covering environmental issues as they relate to industry.

1376. **Energy Factbook.** Dorf, Richard C. New York: McGraw-Hill, 1981. 227p.

Provides information about the uses of energy, supplies of fossil fuels, alternative energy sources, and policy alternatives. The book is for the professional manager, engineer, and planner, though the material seems somewhat lower level than expected for a practicing engineer's handbook.

1377. **Energy Handbook.** 2nd ed. Loftness, Robert L. New York: Van Nostrand Reinhold, 1984. 763p.

An excellent handbook in terms of graphics as well as text. This has become a standard and continues the quality of the first edition. Not only is the material comprehensive, but it is well presented. Highly recommended for any serious collection in the energy field.

1378. **Energy Information Guide.** Weber, R. David. Santa Barbara, CA: ABC-Clio, 1982-84. 3v.

This entire series is excellent. Volume 1 covers general and alternative energy sources, volume 2 covers nuclear and electric power, and volume 3 covers fossil fuels. Each of the volumes is further subdivided into categories which discuss specific topics within the overall focus of the volume. Each individual section contains a full bibliography. This outstanding piece of work should be in any collection with an interest in energy information.

1379. **Energy Reference Handbook.** 3rd ed. Sullivan, Thomas F. P., and Martin L. Heaner. Rockville, MD: Government Institutes, 1981. 417p.

A glossary of key terms used in a rapidly changing area of the energy field. Tables and charts on energy which forecast reserves of various fuel resources are included, as well as conversion tables. This is a good source for both general and specific information in the energy area.

1380. **Energy Source Book.** McRae, Alexander, and Janice L. Dudas, eds. Germantown, MD: Center for Compliance Information, 1977. 724p.

Covers all forms of energy, describing the processes and economics of utilization. This particular source discusses in detail the energy crisis of the mid-1970s and various methods used to combat the crisis. It is important for an energy history as well as potential future reference.

1381. **Energy User's Databook: Basic, Derived and Related Data for Energy Users.** Locke, H. B., ed. London: Graham & Trotman, 1981. 130p.

Contains practical data now difficult or impossible to find elsewhere by practicing energy engineers. The data applies to plants still in service but no longer built. At the same time, the text is brought up to date to provide for the needs of the person on the job. This is a professional source.

1382. **Environment Regulation Handbook.** Ross, Steven S., ed. New York: Environment Information Center Special Studies Division, 1976- . monthly updates.

This tool provides the most current set of federal regulations and laws plus an interpretative section which guides the user with a variety of techniques, such as flow charts. This is a particularly valuable tool for anyone coming into contact with federal environmental law.

1383. **Environmental Exposure from Chemicals.** Neely, W. Brock, and Gary E. Blau, eds. Boca Raton, FL: CRC Press, 1985. 2v.

Provides state-of-the-art information for environmental exposure analysis including movement, distribution, and fate of chemicals in the environment. Experts in the field contributed to the volumes, which are well done and very technical. The set is recommended for research and working collections in chemistry and environmental science.

1384. **Environmental Impact Data Book.** Golden, Jack, et al. Ann Arbor, MI: Ann Arbor Science Publishers, 1979. 864p.

This source pulls together the requirements and issues surrounding the preparation of an environmental impact statement. It deals with a variety of potential issues such as models, legal framework, air quality, water resources, noise, physical resources, ecosystems, toxic chemicals, cultural, energy, and transportation. An important reference tool for public through professional and academic libraries.

1385. **Environmental Management of Water Projects.** Gangstad, E. O., and R. A. Stanley, eds. Boca Raton, FL: CRC Press, 1987. 176p.

This brief, but good, discussion of aquatic vegetation control for water resource management is divided into three parts: environmental engineering assessments, evaluation of selected aquatic herbicides, and evaluation of vegetation management programs. A practically oriented handbook, it is recommended for specific collections in aquatic environmental control.

1386. **Environmental Statutes.** 1985 ed. Rockville, MD: Government Institutes, 1985. 731p.

A comprehensive reference text in the realm of environmental law. The intended audience runs the gamut from the layperson to the expert. The volume brings together both the *U.S. Code, Statutes at Large,* and slip law. Few libraries have all these in one location, and this work brings the information together. No annotations are given, but the value of the work is found in its synthesis. This is a good source for a variety of users and should be considered for purchase by a wide variety of libraries and special collections.

1387. **Global Bioconversions.** Wise, Donald L., ed. Boca Raton, FL: CRC Press, 1987. 4v.

The emphasis of this work is on description of worldwide bioconversion research and development. Conversion of organic residues to useful products is the major focus of the set. Careful consideration must be made as to whether to purchase this set or *Bioenvironmental Systems* (see entry 1368). The present set is more practically oriented, and volume 4 is identical in both sets. It is recommended for less research oriented collections.

1388. **Ground Water Manual: A Guide for the Investigation, Development, and Management of Ground-Water Resources.** New York: Wiley, 1981. 480p.

This revision of the 1977 work by the same title is a guide for field personnel involved in the more practical aspects of ground-water resources. This professional source includes a bibliography.

1389. **Handbook of Energy Technology and Economics.** Meyers, Robert A., ed. New York: Wiley, 1983. 1089p.

Energy technology theory, engineering, and economic data for scientists, engineers, economists, planners, and managers are provided in this handbook which includes grounds for evaluation and comparison of energy technologies. The common denominator of these areas is economics. This is an academic or professional source.

1390. **Handbook of Environmental Control.** Bond, Richard G., and Conrad P. Straub, eds. Boca Raton, FL: CRC Press, 1972- . 6v.

The emphasis of this handbook is on data rather than discussion or analysis. Presently in six volumes, this is a massive and impressive collection of data on topics ranging from air pollution to health care. A working knowledge of chemistry is helpful in accessing the information. Highly recommended for academic and professional collections.

1391. **Handbook of Environmental Data on Organic Chemicals.** 2nd ed. Verschueren, Karel. New York: Van Nostrand Reinhold, 1983. 1310p.

The information included in this second edition includes physical and chemical data, air pollution data, water pollution information, and biological effects of organic chemicals on plants, animals, and man. This is an excellent tool for research and academic collections.

1392. **Handbook of Hazardous Waste Management.** Metry, Amir A. Westport, CT: Technomic Press, 1980. 446p.

Designed to give the reader a detailed understanding of the elements of hazardous waste management, the book is divided into generalized management concepts, treatment concepts, and ultimate disposal concepts. It is primarily an academic source.

1393. **Handbook of Toxicity of Pesticides to Wildlife.** Tucker, Richard K., Rick H. Hudson, and M. A. Haegele. Washington, DC: U.S. Department of the Interior, 1984. 90p.

This is a small listing of toxicity levels for various wildlife species arranged by the pesticides' common name. It serves as a good source for public and nonresearch organizations.

1394. **Handbook of Water Resources and Pollution Control.** Gehm, Harry W., and Jacob I. Bregman. Malabar, FL: Krieger, 1983.

A reprint of a 1976 handbook, this contains good, but sometimes dated, data on municipal and industrial water supply engineering. It should be used with care, but is still a good source for basic information. Recommended for university and research collections.

1395. **Heavy Metals in Wastewater and Sludge Treatment Processes.** Lester, J. N., ed. Boca Raton, FL: CRC Press, 1987. 2v.

Provides a comprehensive account of metallic contaminants by tracing the behavior, fate, and environmental significance of heavy metals through the waste treatment process. Extensive bibliographies refer to the primary literature. This is a well done technical handbook for the research and professional collection.

1396. **International Bio-Energy Directory and Handbook.** Bente, Paul F., ed. Washington, DC: Bio-Energy Council, 1984. 610p.

This thoroughly professional source reports only new technical information with references back to previous handbooks and directories. Contains essays concerning state of the art practices, much quantitative data, a bibliography of technical works, and a table of energy conversion units to aid in calculation.

1397. **International Environment Reporter.** Washington, DC: Bureau of National Affairs, 1978- . irregular.

Technically this is not a handbook, but is used as such. It is a looseleaf report divided into areas of current developments, monographs, federal regulations, decisions, mining, state water laws, state air laws, state solid waste, and land use. Individual articles are in-depth chronicles and analyses of particular environmental issues. This is an excellent source for anyone from the layperson through the expert in the field.

1398. **Optimizing Performance of Energy Systems.** Stricker, Paul. Columbus, OH: Battelle, 1984. 153p.

Written for the engineer involved in design, evaluation, and optimization of energy systems, this appears to be the only book of its type which focuses on simplicity, low cost, and reduction in data handling to achieve efficiency. An excellent, though technical book, the small size is not an indication of the intellectual content of the book. It is a clear choice for any research and technical collection dealing with energy.

1399. **Passive Solar Design Handbook.** New York: Van Nostrand Reinhold, 1984. 750p.

Provides a complete introduction to the concepts and terminology of passive solar energy design. Also presents much quantitative data for fast, simple analytical methods for gauging the relative performance of various types of systems. It is intended as a guide for architects, engineers, and researchers.

1400. **PCBs and the Environment.** Waid, John S., ed. Boca Raton, FL: CRC Press, 1986- . 3v.

Currently in three volumes, the last volume was published in 1987. This is basically a collection of reviews by a panel of experts in the current knowledge of PCBs in the environment. Only partly discussion, the majority of the volumes consists of tabular data. There are descriptions of research methodologies and some case studies. This is an excellent piece of work and highly recommended for any serious environmental chemistry or environmental sciences collection with a research focus.

1401. **Promoting Energy Conservation: An Analysis of Behavioral Research.** Katzev, Richard D., and Theodore R. Johnson. Columbus, OH: Battelle, 1987. 218p.

This work focuses less on technical and "hard" science analysis of energy conservation and examines more the considerable body of behavioral research which exists in the area of promotion of energy conservation. The evidence and the conclusions reached by the authors should lay the groundwork for future systems design. Highly recommended for any collection involved in research and development of energy and energy related areas.

1402. **Regulatory Chemicals of Health and Environmental Concern.** Leder, William H. New York: Van Nostrand Reinhold, 1985. 304p.

In a dictionary-style format, this work lists by chemical name chemicals from the *Federal Register, Code of Federal Regulations,* and voluntary standards and consent degrees. For each chemical, the CAS number is included along with citations to regulations and an abbreviated list of the effects of the chemical on health and environment. This should be a good source for initial information. The regulations and standards to which the work refers should be checked closely due to the fast changing nature of the area.

1403. **Solar Energy Handbook.** Kreider, Jan F., ed. New York: McGraw-Hill, 1981. 1100p.

Collects into one volume all the archival data and procedures available for solar system assessment and design. It is current as of the preparation date. The emphasis is on applications, not theories, and the information provided is expected to last the life of this book. The many forms of solar energy conversion are the main topic of this work. This is a handy and well done one-volume source.

1404. **Solid Waste Disposal and Reuse in the United States.** Murarka, Ishwar P., ed. Boca Raton, FL: CRC Press, 1987. 2v.

Presents information describing the sources, amounts, and composition of various solid wastes in the U.S. Trends are discussed in terms of areas of interest: electrical utilities, mining, and municipal refuse. The focus is on disposal and reuse. This is a timely and well-done handbook which contains much information on the subject presented via tables and discussion of various techniques. Recommended for professional and research collections.

1405. **Toxicological Aspects of Energy Pollution.** Sanders, Charles L. Columbus, OH: Battelle, 1985. 310p.

Presents a broad overview of known and potential human health hazards associated with major energy technologies. The book is a professional level source requiring some knowledge in both biomedical sciences and toxicology. It is recommended for collections in either biomedical or energy engineering with a research focus.

1406. **Transportation Energy Data Book.** 6th ed. Kulp, G., and M. C. Holcomb. Park Ridge, NJ: Noyes Publications, 1983. 205p.

This is an assembly and display of statistics that characterize transportation activity. It also presents data on other factors that influence transportation energy use. A good source of basic information and data on transportation, it is recommended for research and some public library collections.

1407. **Understanding Radioactive Waste.** 2nd ed. Murray, Raymond L. Columbus, OH: Battelle, 1985. 128p.

Presents information on all aspects of radioactive wastes in a clear and unbiased manner. The level of presentation is suitable for laypersons as well as the specialist seeking additional information. Recommended for public, academic, and special collections.

1408. **United States Energy Atlas.** 2nd ed. Cuff, David J., and William J. Young. New York: Macmillan, 1986. 1v. (various paging).

This atlas of energy sources and consumption for the United States contains many maps, graphs, and charts. It is arranged by type of energy. Part 1 covers nonrenewable resources, and part 2 covers the renewable. This is an excellent graphic source of information and is highly recommended for any collection.

1409. **Water and Water Pollution Handbook.** Ciaccio, Leonard L., ed. New York: Dekker, 1971-73. 4v.

This is more of a treatise than a handbook. It contains in-depth information on an entire range of problems in water pollution. The intent of the work is to aid those interested in water environment, including personnel in waste treatment and water purification plants; the transportation industry; service industries; government enforcement agencies; government, industrial, and university research laboratories; and sanitary, civil, and consulting engineers. Although it is dated, it is included because it contains in-depth material which is still relevant. Should be used with some caution due to its age.

DIRECTORIES

1410. **AEE Directory of Energy Professionals.** Atlanta, GA: Fremont Press, 1980- . annual.

A listing of members with a profile including home address. Provided also is a geographical listing broken down by state or country. This is a good source for directory-type information on those active in the energy area and is recommended for all types of collections with an energy interest.

1411. **Canadian Energy Directory.** Toronto: Ontario Library Association, 1980. 476p.

This directory offers broad coverage of energy information for Canada as a whole and lists individuals, government bodies, associations, colleges, companies, and organizations involved in technology and policy with respect to energy, past and present. Individuals' willingness to speak locally is also indicated.

1412. **Citizen's Energy Directory.** 2nd ed. rev. Simpson, Jan, and Ken Bossong. Washington, DC: Citizen's Energy Project, 1980. 59p.

Businesses and organizations involved in energy policy and energy conservation construction are listed by state. A list of state energy offices and a bibliography by subject is also included. This is a good, but brief, source for policy activists and consumers.

1413. **Conservation Directory: A List of Organizations, Agencies, and Officials Concerned with Natural Resource Use and Management.** Washington, DC: The National Wildlife Federation, 1956- . annual.

Covers the major organizations and agencies in the field of conservation. For each agency, the address, telephone, and names of the officials are included, though the list of officials needs to be used with some caution. This is recommended for any collection with an interest in the environment.

1414. **Directory of Consultants in Energy Technologies.** Westport, CT: Research Publications, 1985. 140p.

This directory lists 1,100 consultants in the energy field by area of expertise, name, and state of residence. It is also a reference for the analysis and implementation of energy research and development. This is a good source for a list of persons willing to consult or act as expert witnesses.

1415. **Energy Directory.** New York: Environment Information Center, 1974- . quarterly.

This is an excellent source in that it covers not only federal, but state, professional, and trade organizations. Entries provide names, titles, addresses, phone numbers, statements of purpose, programs, projects, publications, advisory board members, and maps and organization charts. A worthy addition to any collection.

1416. **Energy Products Specifications Guide: Conservation, Solar, Wind and Photovoltaics.** Harrison, NH: SolarVision, 1984. 757p.

An excellent guide for anyone interested in sources of alternative energy products, this work is basically a directory of suppliers of such products. It is intended for builders, architects, and engineers involved in the alternative energy field.

1417. **Energy Research Programs.** New York: Bowker, 1980- . annual.

A multidisciplinary directory of energy related programs, services, and industries, it lists 3,675 parent organizations having 5,900 research facilities. Coverage includes the

United States and Canada and select professional societies and agencies of the Government of Mexico. This is an excellent tool for any energy oriented collection.

1418. **Environmental Impact Statement Directory: The National Network of EIS-related Agencies and Organizations.** Landy, Marc, ed. New York: IFI/Plenum, 1981. 367p.
 A useful directory for writers, reviewers, and citizens, it contains 4,000 U.S. entries. Separate sections for physical and cultural directories are provided along with an appendix, bibliography, and index.

1419. **International Directory of New and Renewable Energy Information Sources and Research Centres.** 2nd ed. Paris: UNESCO, 1986. 661p.
 Lists 2,955 entries representing 136 countries. Included are major organizations and publications concerned with new and renewable energy resources with expertise in areas such as science, economics, and politics. This is a good international directory.

1420. **International Who's Who in Energy and Nuclear Sciences.** Essex, England: Longman Group, 1983. 531p.
 Arranged by name, this source contains professional biographical profiles of over 3,800 individuals. Coverage is worldwide and a country and topic list is included. This is a good source, though it misses a great deal.

1421. **Publishing Opportunities for Energy Research: A Descriptive Guide to Selective Serials in the Social and Technical Sciences.** Scull, Roberta A., comp. Westport, CT: Greenwood Press, 1986. 402p.
 The guide presents viable opportunities for publishing in the energy field other than the common publications. The focus is on English language sources. Two criteria for inclusion were used: (1) the publication must accept unsolicited manuscripts in English; and (2) the publication must be at least partially in English. The result is a good collection of alternative sources. The astute researcher will have already developed his or her own list; however, the utility for a new or first-time author will be reasonably high. Some care should be taken to verify the information due to changes in editorial policy, editors, and cessation.

1422. **Solar Energy Directory.** Oddo, Sandra, ed. New York: Grey House, 1983. 312p.
 A comprehensive guide to the field of solar energy, it provides materials for a wide range and number of levels of interest from the casual browser or beginning learner to the professor who needs information about colleagues or sources of hardware. Contains 3,000 listings with names, phone numbers, descriptions and concrete details for U.S. organizations, agencies, institutions, and industries working with the direct use of solar energy. Very comprehensive, it unifies information that would otherwise be very scattered.

1423. **Synthetic Fuels and Alternate Energy Worldwide Directory.** Tulsa, OK: Pennwell Publishing, 1981- . irregular.
 Provides a complete list of companies, organizations, individuals, government agencies, and educational institutions involved in the development and application of synthetic fuels and alternate energy sources. Subject and company indexes are provided.

1424. **U.S.A. Oil Industry Directory.** 26th ed. Tulsa, OK: Pennwell Books, 1987. 553p.
 Contains information on companies and associations involved in the oil industry. The data on each includes basic directory information and in some cases detailed company histories and personnel lists. The coverage, while broad, is uneven in terms of information

supplied. It is recommended as a directory, but not for any in-depth information on a consistent basis.

1425. **World Directory of Energy Information.** Swin, Christopher, and Andrew Buckley, eds. New York: Facts on File, 1981- . irregular.

Presently in three volumes spanning 1981-1984, this directory profiles energy information sources in 105 countries outside of the Soviet block. Areas of focus include energy production, resources, consumption, trade, and alternative energy. This is a good overview of world energy concerns recommended for all collections.

1426. **World Energy Directory: A Guide to Organizations and Research Activities in Nonatomic Energy.** 2nd ed. Smith, Wendy M., ed. Harlow, Essex, England: Longman, 1985. 582p.

A comprehensive guide to energy research and development projects throughout the world. It includes brief country profiles of energy resources, needs, and achievements, and is an excellent choice for any collection.

1427. **World Environmental Directory.** 4th ed. Silver Spring, MD: Business Publishers, 1980. 965p.

This is a directory of the worldwide environmental community. The fourth edition has been revised 49 percent over the third edition of 1977-78. It is divided into two parts covering the United States and foreign countries. Contains product, category, and geographical indexes. This is a comprehensive resource for information that otherwise would be difficult to locate.

1428. **World Nuclear Directory: A Guide to Organizations and Research Activities in Atomic Energy.** Wilson, C. W. J., ed. Harlow, England: Francis Hodgson, 1981. 975p.

Organizations in all countries with nuclear energy programs are listed. Individual statistics for each plant are given, where known and available. Serves as a good source in the area and is probably the only source of its kind with international coverage.

14 Mechanical and Electrical Engineering

These two large areas of engineering are in some ways the oldest. Mechanical engineering is concerned with machinery and the study of mechanics as an applied field. Mechanics is also an area of concentration in physics, but under that category is more a theoretical concern. The mechanical engineer deals with both large and small scale mechanics. Microscopic mechanisms to giant machines are all a part of this world. To some degree one of the most common thoughts of a layperson in describing an engineer is of a person dealing with machinery.

Electrical engineering is much like mechanical engineering in terms of its scope. Microelectronics to the heaviest high tension transmission lines are within the area defined by electrical engineering. The electrical engineer, perhaps more than any other engineer, can run the gamut between a lab-coated researcher to a field-oriented technician.

The scope of these fields is one reason there is a large section on encyclopedias and dictionaries. The handbook section, however, is the largest from necessity. These are fields with a great deal of movement in terms of research and a long history of data gathering. Both of these components must be used by the mechanical and electrical engineer in the performance of their professional duties. The information must be both specific and current. The sources here attempt to meet these criteria.

GUIDES TO THE LITERATURE

1429. **Robotics and CAD/CAM Market Place: A Worldwide Guide to Information Sources.** New York: Bowker, 1985. 242p.

A listing of reference materials, organizations, industrial research laboratories, manufacturers, and scientific and technical specialists, including handbooks, monographs, conference proceedings, online databases, and more. It covers the technical aspects of automation as well as the social, economic, political, and human factors involved. Designed for laypersons to professionals, it is a source of answers to questions about the mechanization of work. This is an essential guidebook for nearly everyone seeking information in this area.

1430. **World Yearbook of Robotics Research and Development.** 2nd ed. Aleksander, Igor, ed. London: Kogan Page, 1986. 583p.

This overview of current research in robotics also contains a world directory of organizations involved in robotics and robotics related research. A very good but brief overview, it is recommended for any serious research collection.

ABSTRACTS, INDEXES, AND BIBLIOGRAPHIES

1431. **Applied Mechanics Reviews.** New York: American Society of Mechanical Engineers, 1948- . monthly.

This excellent source contains reviews of advances in a broad range of the mechanical engineering sciences. The arrangement is by subject with abstracts, mostly short, within the subject area. Some abstracts for monographs may be longer. This is a classic source because it succeeds at what it was designed to do.

1432. **Bibliography on Engine Lubricating Oil.** Fox, M. F., M. J. Hill, and Z. Pawlak. Brookfield, VT: Gower, 1987. 223p.

This specialized bibliography on an increasingly important topic would be of particular interest to special collections or professionals in the field.

1433. **Computer Data Base.** Northbrook, IL: Management Contents, 1983- . updated every 2 weeks.

Available from DIALOG, this online database contains abstracts from journals, newsletters, tabloids, proceedings, and meetings.

1434. **Current Papers in Electrical and Electronics Engineering.** London: Institution of Electrical Engineers, 1969- . monthly.

This is not precisely an abstracting service; it is more of a listing which aids in the timeliness of the material. The references are to the material abstracted in *Electrical and Electronics Abstracts* (see entry 1437). This is a good source for current awareness.

1435. **Digest of Literature on Dielectrics.** Washington, DC: National Research Council, 1946- . annual.

A critical bibliography of the previous year's literature in all phases of dielectrics, this work contains specialized material which will be of interest only to those involved in this particular area.

1436. **Electric Power Data Base.** Palo Alto, CA: Electric Power Research Institute, 1972- . updated monthly.

Provides references to research and development projects of interest to the electric power industry. Available from DIALOG.

1437. **Electrical and Electronics Abstracts.** London: Institution of Electrical Engineers, 1898- . monthly.

This is a part of *Science Abstracts*. For each entry, complete bibliographic data are given. Author and subject indexes and subsidiary indexes are provided, including a bibliography index, book index, and corporate author index. This is a classic, excellent source of material in the area.

1438. **Electronic Inventions and Discoveries: Electronics from Its Earliest Beginnings to the Present Day.** 3rd ed. rev. Dummer, G. W. A. Oxford, England: Pergamon, 1983. 233p.

The book is a concise overview of inventions in electronics over the spectrum of subfields from the beginning of Michael Faraday's discovery of electromagnetics to the present day. This volume would be helpful not only to the student and professional in electronics, but to the hobbyist and general public as well.

1439. **Engineering Eponyms: An Annotated Bibliography of Some Named Elements, Principles, and Machines in Mechanical Engineering.** 2nd ed. rev. Auger, C. P. London: Library Association, 1975. 122p.

This work covers mechanical eponyms, with the exception of those from the textile industry. Arranged alphabetically by eponym, it includes discussion and references. This annotated bibliography pertains to various aspects of mechanical engineering, such as selected elements, principles, and machines, and is useful in all those areas.

1440. **EPIA.** Washington, DC: Utility Data Institute, 1975- . updated bimonthly.

This database accesses literature on electric power plants and related facilities. It contains material from some government reports, industrial research reports, and contractor reports. Available from SDC.

1441. **Fluid Power Abstracts.** Cranfield, England: BHRA Fluid Engineering, 1960- . monthly.

The material abstracted is taken solely from technical journals. This is a practical source for working engineers or those who specify materials.

1442. **Fluidics Feedbacks: Abstracts, Reviews, Industrial News, Products, Patents: A Monthly Review of the World of Fluidics.** Cranfield, England: British Hydromechanics Research Association, 1967- . monthly.

This is a specialized source in that it only covers materials related to hydraulic engineering. It is divided into sections which cover topics such as circuits and circuit components, general topics, devices of moving parts, devices of nonmoving parts, applications, and new products. Recommended for working mechanical engineering collections.

1443. **Index to IEEE Publications.** New York: Institute of Electrical and Electronics Engineers, 1971- . annual.

Provides extensive coverage of abstracts, book reviews, conference papers, articles, and communications originally published in the IEEE publications. It also contains complete bibliographic information and various user's aids.

1444. **Index to Place of Publication of ASME Papers, 1950-1977.** Schenectady, NY: General Electric Company, 1981. 76p.

This serves as an aid for librarians and others faced with ascertaining the journal references for ASME papers when provided with only the preprint numbers of the papers. It is highly recommended for technical collections.

1445. **INSPEC.** Piscataway, NJ: Institution of Electrical Engineers, 1969- . updated monthly.

A database corresponding to *Physics Abstracts* (see entry 979), *Electrical and Electronics Abstracts* (see entry 1437), and *Computer and Control Abstracts* (see entry 889). Available from BRS, DIALOG, and SDC.

1446. **Ion Implantations in Micro-Electronics: A Comprehensive Bibliography.** Agajanian, A. H. New York: IFI/Plenum, 1981. 255p.

This bibliography of literature from 1976-1980 includes journals and theses. Citations are grouped under subject headings arranged within categories, and detailed author and subject indexes appear. Appropriate for a technical library, this source is best put to use by those with some prior knowledge.

1447. **ISMEC.** Louisville, KY: Institution of Mechanical Engineers, 1973- . updated monthly.

This database of information in mechanical engineering is available from BRS and DIALOG.

1448. **ISMEC Bulletin.** London: Institution of Mechanical Engineers, 1973- . monthly.

One original intent of this publication was speed of publication. The listing of papers is done in a classified arrangement, which is sometimes a drawback, and the classification can be unwieldy in some new areas of interest. The coverage is worldwide for mechanical engineering, however, which makes this a very good source for any research collection.

1449. **Jet Pumps and Ejectors: A State of the Art Review and Bibliography.** 2nd ed. rev. Bonnington, S. T., and A. L. King. Cranfield, England: BHRA Fluid Engineering, 1976. 110p.

This useful tool for plant designers and users features a chronological arrangement of approximately 400 references. Detailed subject and author indexes are included.

1450. **Key Abstracts: Electrical Measurements and Instrumentation.** London: Institution of Electrical Engineers; New York: Institute of Electrical and Electronics Engineers, 1976- . irregular.

1451. **Key Abstracts: Physical Measurements and Instrumentation.** London: Institution of Electrical Engineers; New York: Institute of Electrical and Electronics Engineers, 1976- . irregular.

1452. **Key Abstracts: Systems Theory.** London: Institution of Electrical Engineers; New York: Institute of Electrical and Electronics Engineers, 1978- . monthly.

These three titles were designed for use by research and development specialists and for smaller specialized companies and libraries. Each *Key Abstract* is drawn from the INSPEC database (see entry 1445) and covers only the most important worldwide developments within its specific subject discipline. This is an excellent tool for important literature chosen by experts in the field.

1453. **Laser Literature: An Annotated Guide.** Tomiyasu, Keyo. New York: Plenum, 1968. 172p.

This is a derivative work, originating from a series of bibliographies published in the *IEEE Journal of Quantum Electronics* (Piscataway, NJ: Institution of Electrical and Electronics Engineers, 1965-). The work lists about 4,000 papers, reports, articles, and monographs. Its main use now is retrospective.

1454. **Literature Survey of Communication Satellite Systems and Technology.** Unger, J. H. W., comp. New York: IEEE Press, 1976. 409p.

This good retrospective bibliography is still useful for describing the satellite systems now in operation. It is arranged in three sections: permuted title index, author index, and list of references.

1455. Micro-Electronic Packaging: A Bibliography. Agajanian, A. H., comp. New York: IFI/Plenum Press, 1979. 243p.

Includes references taken from various abstracts and indexes between 1976 and 1978 covering the field of microelectronic packaging. Entries are alphabetically organized by author and categorized into subject headings and subheadings. Contains a subject index. This is a professional reference.

1456. MOSFET Technologies: A Comprehensive Bibliography. Agajanian, A. H., comp. New York: IFI/Plenum Press, 1980. 377p.

A compilation of references to MOSFET technologies literature from 1976 to 1980. Three chapters cover literature on technologies, properties, characterization, and dielectric and thin films. Primarily intended for researchers and circuit designers, this is an excellent source in semiconductor technology.

1457. Robotics: An International Bibliography with Abstracts. Gomersall, Alan, and Penny Farmer. Bedford, England: IFS, 1984. 209p.

Contents include general literature, research and industrial practice, design and performance, operating components and sensors, control theory and systems, and applications (30 percent of listing). The listing of articles is restricted to those readily accessible from university and major library collections. As such, it is recommended for university and major libraries.

1458. Robotics, 1960-1983: An Annotated Bibliography. Garoogian, Andrew. Brooklyn, NY: CompuBibs, 1984. 119p.

Comprised of mostly nontechnical magazine and newspaper articles and references to several current U.S. government publications, this bibliography is arranged under a variety of subjects. It seeks to engender a historical perspective through presentation of a variety of viewpoints and is a good source for public and college collections.

1459. SAE Transactions. Warrendale, PA: Society of Automotive Engineers, 1905- . annual.

A major source of information of interest to the Society of Automotive Engineers. This is a critical source for both technical and trade information in the automotive engineering field. A necessary tool for most research collections.

1460. Solid-State Abstracts Journal. Bethesda, MD: Cambridge Scientific Abstracts, 1967- . bimonthly.

SSAJ is devoted to complete and comprehensive coverage of world literature on the theory, production, and application of solid state materials and devices. It is an excellent abstracting tool of interest to any electrical engineer.

ENCYCLOPEDIAS

1461. Encyclopedia of Electronic Circuits. Graf, Rudolf F. Blue Ridge Summit, PA: TAB Books, 1985. 760p.

This is a compilation of schematic diagrams for analog and digital circuits. The schematics are pulled from a variety of electronics publications and are complete with a bibliographic citation to the original literature. The drawings are clear and distinct, and some have parts inventories. This is recommended for almost all types of libraries and will be used by hobbyists as well as electrical engineers.

1462. **Encyclopedia of Electronics.** Gibilisco, Stan, ed. Blue Ridge Summit, PA: TAB Books, 1985. 983p.

This is a complete source of information on all aspects of electricity, electronics, and communications technology. It is intended as a permanent reference source for students, hobbyists, and professionals, and contains more than 3,000 articles. A categorized list of articles at the beginning of the book supplements the index as a thesaurus of terms. Useful as a reference source for graduates and those advanced in the field, it is also useful as a textbook for undergraduates, those new to the field, and librarians. No bibliography is provided at the end of articles, but many of the terms and items are very specific.

1463. **Encyclopedia of Fluid Mechanics.** Cheremisinoff, Nicholas P., ed. Houston, TX: Gulf Publishing, 1986- . irregular.

Composed of several volumes in a continuing series, volume 1 covers flow phenomena and measurement; volume 2, dynamics of single-fluid flows and mixing; and volume 3, gas-liquid flows. This is an excellent series in a very difficult area of engineering and is highly recommended for all research collections in technology.

1464. **Encyclopedia of Hydraulics, Soil, and Foundation Engineering.** Vollmer, Ernst. Amsterdam, Netherlands: Elsevier, 1967. 398p.

A testament to its durability, this work is over 20 years old and is still being used by engineers in the field. It deals with a variety of foundation engineering problems including hydraulic engineering, hydromechanics, river training weirs and dams, water resources, soil engineering, soil mechanics, soil excavation, soil deposition, foundation excavation in dry soil, foundation materials behavior in soil symbols, abbreviations, and conversion factors. This is a working reference book as opposed to one containing the latest technical data.

1465. **Encyclopedia of Instrumentation and Control.** Considine, Douglas M., ed. Huntington, NY: Krieger, 1981. 788p.

Considine is a prolific author who is a first-rate editor. In this work he has taken the level of current knowledge of instrumentation and control, described it, and used it within the context of projected developments. This is an excellent piece of work for any serious research collection.

1466. **Encyclopedia of Integrated Circuits: A Practical Handbook of Essential Reference Data.** 2nd ed. Buchsbaum, Walter H. Englewood Cliffs, NJ: Prentice-Hall, 1987. 530p.

The purpose of the book is to describe how integrated circuits function. They are divided into four categories: analog, consumer, digital, and interface. Each entry has a description, logic diagram, and key parameters. Good for both the hobbyist and engineer.

1467. **Encyclopedia of Semiconductor Technology.** Grayson, Martin, ed. New York: Wiley, 1984. 941p.

A useful reference work for most purposes, this encyclopedia provides a good general overview of semiconductor technology.

1468. **Illustrated Encyclopedia of Solid-State Circuits and Applications.** Mackenroth, Donald R., and Leo G. Sands. Englewood Cliffs, NJ: Prentice-Hall, 1984. 353p.

A book suitable for vocational schools or young adult technology collections because of its general descriptions of various circuits and their function.

1469. **Illustrated Encyclopedic Dictionary of Electronic Circuits.** Douglas-Young, John. Englewood Cliffs, NJ: Prentice-Hall, 1983. 444p.

A reference tool with a useful appendix that includes conversion factor tables, graphic symbols, and mathematical tables. Though mostly for the beginning electronics buff, some sections are technical and complicated.

1470. **TAB Handbook of Hand & Power Tools.** Graf, Rudolf F., and George J. Whalen. Blue Ridge Summit, PA: TAB Books, 1984. 501p.

Although the title suggests this is a handbook, it is an encyclopedia covering virtually everything one would wish to know about tools. The coverage is expansive, touching on tools for work, hobbies, and home use. This is an excellent work for most public and nonresearch collections.

1471. **Water Supply Engineering.** 6th ed. Babbit, Harold. New York: McGraw-Hill, 1962. 672p.

Contains a wealth of information that should not be overlooked because of the imprint date. Although some of the material may be somewhat dated, the work has considerable staying power. The breadth of material and the variety of users makes this still a good choice for most collections. Chapters deal with topics ranging from methods of water analysis to the management of water works.

DICTIONARIES

1472. **Air-Conditioning, Heating, and Refrigeration Dictionary.** Zurick, Timothy. Birmingham, MI: Business News Publishing, 1977. 126p.

Entries pertain to the fields of air conditioning, heating, and refrigeration. Succinct and easy to use, it is a good choice for technical or college collections.

1473. **CAD/CAM Dictionary.** Preston, Edward J., George W. Crawford, and Mark E. Coticchia. New York: Dekker, 1985. 210p.

This is a ready-reference guide for those not familiar with CAD/CAM technology. Containing no illustration and no bibliography, its stark format detracts from the overall work.

1474. **Computer Graphics Glossary.** Hubbard, Stuart W. New York: Van Nostrand Reinhold, 1984. 94p.

A descriptive glossary, it lists the most common meaning of the word followed by other contending definitions plus usage notes. This is good for a general collection in a public or college library.

1475. **Concise Illustrated Russian-English Dictionary of Mechanical Engineering: 3795 Terms.** Shvarts, Vladimir V. New York: State Mutual Book, 1980. 224p.

Symbols and drawings are matched with words of both languages. The contents are by subject area in both languages, though the index is in Russian only. This dictionary contains a supplement to many of the terms with notes given on the internationally accepted symbols, formulas, diagrams, engineering drawings, and sketches. It is recommended for research collections only because of the strictly Russian index.

1476. **Dictionary of Computer Graphics.** Vince, John. White Plains, NY: Knowledge Industry Publications, 1984. 132p.

Describes some of the words and concepts often employed in technical literature. Some explanations are as lengthy as two paragraphs. The format and the definitions are good.

1477. **Dictionary of Electrical, Electronics, and Computer Abbreviations.** Brown, Phil R. London: Butterworths, 1985.

A mix of subject resources has been selected to provide a comprehensive and broad view of "electronics" and all that is associated with it. At times the breadth of this dictionary necessitates a shorter definition than is desirable, but overall it is well done.

1478. **Dictionary of Electrical Engineering.** 2nd ed. Jackson, K. G., and R. Feinberg. London: Butterworths, 1981. 350p.

This edition takes into account the revision of international electrotechnical vocabulary and universal acceptance and practice of SI units. It is a good electrical engineering dictionary, though the definitions are sometimes a bit cursory.

1479. **Dictionary of Electrical Engineering and Electronics: English, German.** Budig, Peter-Klaus, ed. New York: Elsevier, 1985. 724p.

Contains over 60,000 terms, both traditional and new. The overall intent is to provide a useful tool for the comprehension of technical English-language literature. This is a very good dictionary worthy of consideration by almost any technically oriented collection.

1480. **Dictionary of Electrical Engineering, Telecommunications, and Electronics.** Goedecke, Werner. London: Pitman, 1966. 3v.

A multilingual dictionary which covers the areas of electrical engineering, telecommunications, and electronics. The age of the dictionary is an important consideration; however, it is overridden by the German-French-English component. This is a good multilingual dictionary, but not necessarily current. Recommended for translation work but not for ready reference.

1481. **Dictionary of Electronics.** 2nd ed. Amos, S. W. London: Butterworths, 1987. 324p.

This is a good, elementary dictionary in basic electronics. It is not a comprehensive work, however, and the definitions are somewhat lacking in consistency and content. Most entries are short (six lines), with some entries taking as much as a quarter of a page. The brevity of most of the definitions in the computer area makes the work somewhat suspect. It is recommended for public and nontechnical libraries.

1482. **Dictionary of Mechanical Engineering.** 3rd ed. Nayler, G. H. F. London: Butterworths, 1985. 394p.

Approximately 6,000 of the most commonly used terms in the literature of mechanics are chosen for precise definition in this amply illustrated dictionary. Emphasis is on British terms. The terms have been expanded to include both mechanical engineering design and manufacture, typified by the field of robotics.

1483. **Dictionary of Refrigeration and Air-Conditioning.** Booth, K. M., ed. Amsterdam, Netherlands: American Elsevier, 1970. 315p.

This is a basic set of definitions in refrigeration and air conditioning. It should be noted that references are usually to United Kingdom Imperial units and not to American units. This is a good source of basic information, but is recommended with caution because of the UK slant.

1484. **Dictionary of Robot Technology.** Burger, Erich, comp. Amsterdam, Netherlands: Elsevier, 1986. 300p.

This dictionary is in four languages: English, French, German, and Russian. Given the change-by-the-minute nature of this field, a multilingual dictionary of this currency is an excellent addition to any collection.

1485. **Dictionary of Robotics.** Waldman, Harry. New York: Macmillan, 1985. 303p.

More than 2,000 terms and 100 illustrations related to robotics and allied disciplines are listed here. This is a good reference aid, suitable for the student or researcher, and contains more entries than does the *Dictionary of Robot Technology* (see entry 1484), but without the multilingual component.

1486. **Dictionary of Telecommunications.** Aries, S. J. London: Butterworths, 1981. 329p.

Definitions are concise, and except where necessary consist of short essays. North American usage is given careful attention. As an aid in keeping up with this fast moving field, this is a highly recommended dictionary.

1487. **Dictionary of Terms Used in the Safety Profession.** 2nd ed. Abercrombie, Stanley A., comp. Park Ridge, IL: American Society of Safety Engineers, 1981. 58p.

This is an alphabetical listing of terms used in the areas of construction safety, fire protection engineering, toxicology, and industrial hygiene which provides addresses of professional and governmental agencies involved with the safety profession. It is a specialized dictionary for students in the occupational safety and health area.

1488. **Dictionary of Water and Sewage Engineering.** Meinck, Fritz, and Helmut Mohle. Munich: R. Oldenbourg, 1983. 937p.

This is very much a translation dictionary. It contains no definitions, but does an admirable job of matching German terms with terms in English, French, and Italian. There is also an index which is arranged by English, French, and Italian terms. This is highly recommended for research collections.

1489. **Electronics Dictionary.** 4th ed. Markus, John. New York: McGraw-Hill, 1978. 745p.

This well illustrated, comprehensive dictionary includes approximately 17,000 terms in electronics and presents the current language of electronics with clear, concise terms accompanied by detailed illustrations. The "Electronic Style Manual," which simplifies troublesome spelling and grammatical problems, is also featured.

1490. **Electro-Optical Communications Dictionary.** Bodson, Dennis, and Dan Botez, eds. Rochelle Park, NJ: Hayden Book Co., 1983. 168p.

Intended for use by those involved in fiber optic and lightwave communications systems, this dictionary contains entries that are complete with inversions and cross references. It is a very good source for highly technical information.

1491. **Elsevier's Dictionary of Electronics: English/French.** King, G. G. New York: Elsevier, 1986. 619p.

This is a dictionary of nonstandard terms covering electronics in the broadest sense. Each entry was thoroughly investigated for accuracy. Multiple word entries are arranged by the keyword in the phrase, regardless of placement in the phrase. Recommended for all libraries with collections in electronics.

1492. **Elsevier's Dictionary of Water and Hydraulic Engineering.** van der Tuin, J. D., comp. New York: Elsevier, 1987. 449p.

Water engineering is a common problem in most countries. There are over 5,000 basic terms listed which are then translated into over 32,000 equivalent terms in French, Spanish, Dutch, and German. This will be a very useful tool in any multilingual environment or research center.

TK7804
TM
1984
Sci
Ref

1493. **Encyclopedic Dictionary of Electronic Terms.** Traister, John E., and Robert J. Traister. Englewood Cliffs, NJ: Prentice-Hall, 1984. 604p.

This comprehensive dictionary of terms in the electronics industry and research areas contains many newer terms not found in older dictionaries. It is a good choice for any collection.

1494. **Glossary: Water and Wastewater Control Engineering.** 3rd ed. American Public Health Association. Washington, DC: American Public Health Association, 1981. 398p.

This comprehensive, authoritative dictionary provides multiple definitions where applicable. It is highly recommended for any serious collection in water engineering.

TK9
I478
1993
Sci
Ref

1495. **IEEE Standard Dictionary of Electrical and Electronics Terms.** 3rd ed. Jay, Frank, ed. New York: Institute of Electrical and Electronics Engineers, 1984. 1173p.

This is a first-rate dictionary containing technical terms from across the broad range of electrical and electronic technology. In each definition, the official standard of the IEEE is noted. Usually there is a reference to other standards, such as ANSI and IEC. The current edition includes terms that have been standardized by the American Standards Association since 1977. Includes 140 drawings and diagrams and an appendix of 15,000 common acronyms. Indispensable for engineers, technicians, students, editors, writers, and publishers, it is recommended for all science libraries.

TK7804
T87
1990
Sci
Ref

1496. **Illustrated Dictionary of Electronics.** 3rd ed. Turner, Rufus P., and Stan Gibilisco. Blue Ridge Summit, PA: TAB Books, 1985. 595p.

Covers a broad range of topics including computers, microcircuitry, cyclotrons, physics, chemistry, and audio electronics. Includes concise definitions, hundreds of abbreviations and acronyms, line drawings, circuit diagrams, tables and charts. Features cross-references for additional information or a contrasted definition. Also, a schematic symbols chart is provided to assist in interpreting the schematics appearing throughout the book. The definitions are supplemented by the basic information in the appendix on symbols, charts, and data. No introduction stating the focus and methods used in writing this dictionary is available. However, as a reference source for the hobbyist and professional alike, this should be helpful. It is a welcome addition to any library providing information on current technological developments and discoveries in electronics.

1497. **Illustrated Dictionary of Mechanical Engineering.** Schwartz, Vladimir V. The Hague: Nijhoff, 1984. 416p.

In English, German, French, Dutch, and Russian, this is for persons just starting the study of mechanical engineering in a foreign language. It is a picture book of illustrations matched with the word equivalent in several languages. Recommended for students of different nationalities.

1498. **International Dictionary of Heating, Ventilating, and Air-Conditioning.** New York: Methuen, 1982. 416p.

Compiled by the representatives of an international association of heating engineers, this dictionary contains a list of terms in English, followed by the equivalent term in German, French, Hungarian, Italian, Dutch, Polish, Russian, Spanish, and Swedish. There is also an index for each of these languages, referring back to the English.

1499. **Macmillan Dictionary of Data Communications.** 2nd ed. Sippl, Charles J. London: Macmillan Press, 1985. 532p.

This dictionary of terms relating to electronic data processing is a good beginning source for definitions in the area. The definitions are up-to-date and reflect current jargon and usage. It is recommended for any good engineering collection.

1500. **McGraw-Hill Dictionary of Electrical and Electronic Engineering.** Parker, Sybil P., ed. New York: McGraw-Hill, 1984. 488p.

This is yet another spinoff from the *McGraw-Hill Dictionary of Scientific and Technical Terms* (see entry 229), with adequate but sparse definitions. The electronics field is covered by this dictionary, *McGraw-Hill Dictionary of Electronics and Computers* (see entry 1501), and the parent dictionary. There is serious question as to whether a collection needs all three.

1501. **McGraw-Hill Dictionary of Electronics and Computers.** Parker, Sybil P., ed. New York: McGraw-Hill, 1984. 582p.

Many of these articles were taken from the *McGraw-Hill Dictionary of Scientific and Technical Terms* (see entry 229). Others were written exclusively for this book. The discipline of electronics and the manifold applications of electronic devices are explored, with particular emphasis on computer science and engineering. Bibliographies are included at the end of articles. This is useful as an entree into electronics and would be good in a technical college or four-year college/university collection.

1502. **McGraw-Hill Dictionary of Mechanical and Design Engineering.** Parker, Sybil P., ed. New York: McGraw-Hill, 1984. 387p.

The brevity of this work, as compared with the parent dictionary, *McGraw-Hill Dictionary of Scientific and Technical Terms* (see entry 229), is its major contribution. This will find good utilization in the field and as a desk reference. Collections which have the larger dictionary should approach purchase of this title with caution.

1503. **Modern Dictionary of Electronics.** 6th ed. Graf, Rudolf F. Indianapolis, IN: H. W. Sams, 1984. 1152p.

The major contribution of this work is its clear and concise definitions in the fields of communication, microelectronics, fiber optics, semiconductors, reliability, computers, and medical electronics. It is highly recommended for an electrical engineering collection.

HANDBOOKS

1504. **American Electrician's Handbook.** 11th ed. Summers, Wilford I., ed. New York: McGraw-Hill, 1987. 1v. (various paging).

TK 151
C8
1992
sci
Ref

This is a complete revision of a classic handbook on the design, operation, selection, installation, and maintenance of electrical equipment. It is both a professional reference tool and a guide for the "practical electrical person," according to the preface. Containing new coverage in several areas, it complies with the National Electrical Code® and other standards, and is an impressive work in terms of size and scope. It goes far beyond the knowledge or skill of the "practical electrical person." The revision of the text is well done with clear, concise prose. The classic, one-stop source for electrical and electrical engineering information. Overall, the book contains a wealth of information, probably more than the general electrician or electrical engineer will use. This work is best suited to the field engineer or electrician but is also a good reference tool in an engineering collection.

TH720I
A83
Sci Ref

1505.   **ASHRAE Handbook. Applications.** New York: American Society of Heating, Refrigeration, and Air-Conditioning Engineers, 1982- . every 4 years.

1506.   **ASHRAE Handbook. Equipment.** New York: American Society of Heating, Refrigeration, and Air-Conditioning Engineers, 1983- . every 4 years.

1507.   **ASHRAE Handbook. Fundamentals.** New York: American Society of Heating, Refrigeration, and Air-Conditioning Engineers, 1981- . every 4 years.

TH7011
A45
Sci

1508.   **ASHRAE Handbook. Systems.** New York: American Society of Heating, Refrigeration, and Air-Conditioning Engineers, 1984- . every 4 years.
These four titles provide a wealth of reference data in heating, air-conditioning, refrigeration, and ventilation. They cover basic theory, general engineering data, basic materials, basic and advanced tables, and terminology. They are required material for any collection in mechanical engineering.

TA332
A79
1983
Sci Ref

1509.   **ASM Handbook of Engineering Mathematics.** American Society for Metals. Metals Park, OH: American Society for Metals, 1983. 697p.
A practical reference for practicing engineers and engineering students which focuses on mathematics of mechanical engineering. A solid reference work, it is highly recommended.

TJ233
A572
Sci

1510.   **ASME Handbook.** American Society of Mechanical Engineers. New York: McGraw-Hill, 1983. 4v.
This is a standard handbook in mechanical engineering. Like most standards, the reason for its popularity is that it works. It covers metals engineering design, engineering tables, metals engineering processes, and the properties of metals. An excellent source of highly technical information.

1511.   **Beginner's Handbook of Electronics.** Olsen, George H., and Forrest M. Mims. Englewood Cliffs, NJ: Prentice-Hall, 1980. 305p.
Describes the use of capacitors, transistors, resistors, and other basics of modern electronics such as circuitry, components, and semiconductors. It is a useful reference for both the amateur and the professional.

1512.   **Changes in the 1984 National Electrical Code.** Flach, George W. Englewood Cliffs, NJ: Prentice-Hall, 1984. 150p.
The book includes the latest changes in the National Electrical Code. It includes tables and examples, and is highly recommended if the *National Electrical Code Handbook* (see entry 1577) is also a part of the collection.

1513.   **Complete Handbook of Practical Electronic Reference Data.** 3rd ed. Buchsbaum, Walter H. Englewood Cliffs, NJ: Prentice-Hall, 1987. 635p.
An excellent use of graphs and tables makes this a reliable basic information source. Fundamental engineering knowledge is sufficient for use.

1514. **CRC Handbook of Laser Science and Technology.** Weber, Marvin J., ed. Boca Raton, FL: CRC Press, 1982- . (currently 5v.).

An excellent overview of the laser and its application to engineering and science in general. Volume 1 is entitled *Lasers and Masers*, 1982; volume 2, *Gas Lasers*, 1982; volume 3, *Optical Materials* (part 1), 1986; volume 4, *Optical Materials* (part 2), 1986; and volume 5, *Optical Materials* (part 3), 1987.

1515. **CRC Handbook of Lubrication (Theory and Practice of Tribology).** Booser, E. R., ed. Boca Raton, FL: CRC Press, 1984. 2v.

TJ1075
C7
1983
Sci

The handbook covers the general area of lubrication and tribology in all its facets. Both metric and English units are provided throughout. It is an excellent source for specific information.

1516. **Data Book for Pipe-Fitters and Pipe-Welders.** Williamson, E. M. Folkestone, England: Bailey Brothers & Swinfen, 1984. 160p.

A pocket-sized reference that contains data on fitting and welding pipes. It includes tables and diagrams and is highly useful for the engineer in the field and as ready reference in a collection.

1517. **Design Manual for High-Temperature Hot-Water and Steam Systems.** Cofield, Rogers E. New York: Wiley, 1983. 340p.

A one-volume technical engineering source demonstrating a most practical hands-on approach for solving problems in the design and analysis of high temperature hot water and steam energy systems. It is technical information for use by technicians.

1518. **Electric Cables Handbook.** McAllister, D., ed. London: Granada, 1982. 880p.

TK3301
E43
Sci

A valuable reference and technical book for those involved with power cable. It includes tables, charts, photographs, and appendices that prove to be useful sources of information.

1519. **Electrical Engineer's Reference Book.** 14th ed. Laughton, M. A., and M. G. Say, eds. Guildford, England: Butterworths, 1985. 1100p.

Subheadings are: "Fundamentals," "Energy Supply," "Power-Plant," "Application," and "Standards." This reference serves as a practical complement to academic studies. It uses SI units and is an excellent choice for academic and technically oriented collections.

1520. **Electronic Circuits Note Book: Proven Designs for Systems Applications.** Weber, Samuel, ed. New York: McGraw-Hill, 1981. 344p.

This work covers the most common electrical engineering problems and their solutions. It contains 268 circuits, organized alphabetically by function, and is a valuable aid for working engineers.

1521. **Electronic Data Reference Manual.** Mandl, Matthew. Reston, VA: Reston Publishing Co., 1979. 323p.

TK7825
M26
Sci

Designed for engineers and repair persons, this manual provides essential information on current developments in electrical communications. It covers integrated circuits, AM, FM, and is also useful for reference on service and construction design. It contains concise illustrations.

1522. **Electronic Filter Design Handbook.** Williams, Arthur B. New York: McGraw-Hill, 1981. 541p.

Provides treatment of numerous aspects of filter design. It is intended for upper level undergraduate students interested in communications hardware and communications.

1523. **Electronic Imaging Techniques: A Handbook of Conventional and Computer-Controlled Animation, Optical, and Editing Processes.** Levitan, Eli L. New York: Van Nostrand Reinhold, 1977. 195p.

This handbook is devoted to electronic imaging techniques and discusses computer animation, digital, online/off-line systems, optical effects, and video. Extremely well illustrated, it is still a good source for basic techniques but should not be used for state-of-the-art information.

1524. **Electronics Engineer's Handbook.** 2nd ed. Fink, Donald G., ed. New York: McGraw-Hill, 1982. 251p.

This is an applications oriented approach to "the essential principles, data, and design information on the components, circuits, equipment, and systems of electronics engineering as a whole." It is a valuable addition to any electrical engineering collection.

1525. **Electronics Engineer's Reference Book.** 5th ed. Mazda, F. F., ed. London: Butterworths, 1983. 1v. (various paging).

Topics include semiconductor memories, microprocessors, fiber optic communications, office communications, attenuators, filters, and telephone systems. Extensively rearranged and revised, it is recommended because of its breadth of coverage.

1526. **Fiber Optics.** Daly, James C., ed. Boca Raton, FL: CRC Press, 1984. 256p.

This is both a practical and a theoretical handbook for the design of fiber optics communications systems. Each chapter was written by an expert in the particular field addressed by the chapter. This is a good choice for upper level academic collections and research and development collections.

1527. **Flow Measurement Engineering Handbook.** Miller, R. W. New York: McGraw-Hill, 1983. 934p.

A well written and organized handbook on flow measuring devices and equations, analysis techniques, and standards. Most helpful to the practicing engineer interested in a working tool and reference guide to aid in the selection, design, and application of flow meters and flow measurement systems.

1528. **Fundamentals Handbook of Electrical and Computer Engineering.** Chang, Sheldon S. L. New York: Wiley, 1982-83. 3v.

A handbook covering the field of electrical and computer engineering in three volumes, it emphasizes active applications of engineering design and the ever increasing tie between electrical engineering, mathematics, and physics.

1529. **Giant Handbook of Electronic Circuits.** Collins, Raymond A., ed. Blue Ridge Summit, PA: TAB Books, 1980. 880p.

This handbook for designers and hobbyists provides schematic diagrams for a number of electronic circuits. Contents include AM and FM broadcast receivers, automatic circuits, computer related circuits, music related circuits, and more.

1530. **Guide to the 1984 National Electrical Code.** Palmquist, Roland E. Indianapolis, IN: T. Audel, 1984. 655p.

Details the rules necessary for installing electrical wiring, but emphasizes questions that appear on the master electrician's examination. Wiring systems, installation, and theory are covered. Extensive, illustrative tables and circuit diagrams support the text and are easily understood. This is supplemented by an adequate index and a short bibliography. For practicing engineers and contractors, as well as students.

1531. **Handbook for Electronics Engineering Technicians.** 2nd ed. Kaufman, Milton, and Arthur H. Seidman, eds. New York: McGraw-Hill, 1984. 1v. (various paging).

TK7825
H37
Sci

The format for this handbook is tutorial. Definitions of terms and parameters are given first, followed by a breakdown of the types or characteristics of components, an analysis of basic and special functions, detailed practical problems, working solutions, and various clarifying tables, charts, or illustrations. The work does not require technical knowledge until the user delves more deeply into the examples. This is an excellent handbook for a range of users.

1532. **Handbook of Active Filters.** Johnson, D. E., Ray Johnson, and H. P. Moore. Englewood Cliffs, NJ: Prentice-Hall, 1980. 244p.

This thorough presentation of practical active filter designs contains numerous design examples and tables, and contains an extensive bibliography. Researchers and academic collections will find this title attractive.

1533. **Handbook of Advanced Robotics.** Safford, Edward L. Blue Ridge Summit, PA: TAB Books, 1982. 468p.

This simplified text is suitable for beginning students of robotics or the hobbyist. It would be useful as an introductory manual for the layperson.

1534. **Handbook of Basic Electronic Troubleshooting.** Lenk, John D. Englewood Cliffs, NJ: Prentice-Hall, 1979. 239p.

Provides both an introduction for beginners and a complete reference for advanced technicians to basic electronic troubleshooting. Outlines procedures for locating faulty circuits and defective components in equipment, and contains more than 160 wiring diagrams and voltage and resistance data.

1535. **Handbook of Batteries and Fuel-Cells.** Linden, David, ed. New York: McGraw-Hill, 1984. 1v. (various paging).

This is a useful volume for general public and academic libraries. It consists of text with tables and illustrations. References are not extensive.

1536. **Handbook of Chlorination for Potable Water, Waste Water, Cooling Water, Industrial Processes, and Swimming Pools.** White, George Clifford. New York: Van Nostrand Reinhold, 1972. 744p.

TD462
W47
Sci

This handbook is directed to designers, operators, students, and regulatory agencies working with systems that utilize chlorine. Twelve chapters are written by experts and amount to a literature review. The age of the handbook precludes it being used as a critical bibliography, but the data presented are still useful to a variety of users. The chapters cover history, facilities design, operation and maintenance, chemistry, determination of chlorine residuals in water treatment, chlorination of potable water, wastewater, swimming pools and cooling water, other applications, chlorine dioxide, hypo chlorination, and other methods of disinfection.

1537. **Handbook of Electronic Communications.** Miller, Gary M. Englewood Cliffs, NJ: Prentice-Hall, 1979. 338p.

Written for working technicians, this handbook contains extensive information on electronic communications systems. It is well illustrated and provides helpful data sheets.

1538. **Handbook of Electronic Formulas, Symbols, and Definitions.** Brand, John R. New York: Van Nostrand Reinhold, 1979. 359p.

This is a dictionary-style handbook where the symbols are arranged alphabetically. It is internally arranged into seven categories: passive circuits; English letters, passive circuits; Greek letters, transistors; static conditions, transistors; small signal conditions; operational amplifiers; symbols and definitions, and operational amplifiers; formulas and circuits. The main flaw in this handbook is the seven categories which sometimes impede rather than aid in finding information.

1539. **Handbook of Electronics Calculations for Engineers and Technicians.** Kaufman, Milton, and Arthur H. Seidman, eds. New York: McGraw-Hill, 1979. 550p.

This practical guide to electronics problems and their solutions covers DC and AC circuit analysis, power supplies, microprocessors, tuned amplifiers, and computer aided circuit design. This is a helpful reference to practicing electrical engineers and technicians.

1540. **Handbook of Electronics Industry Cost-Estimating Data.** Taylor, T. New York: Wiley, 1985. 410p.

A particularly interesting handbook for estimating project costs as well as component costs for the electronics industry. This will be of interest to a variety of people from contractors to research and development organizations.

1541. **Handbook of Electronics Packaging Design and Engineering.** Matisoff, Bernard S. New York: Van Nostrand Reinhold, 1982. 471p.

An easy reference source on choosing the most effective packaging technique for on-the-job applications. It also contains formulas and information on thermal control and enclosures. This is a good source for decision-making in the packaging field.

1542. **Handbook of Industrial Robotics.** Nof, Shimon Y., ed. New York: Wiley, 1985. 1385p.

Signed chapters and extensive bibliographies make this a particularly valuable reference work. Coming very close to being a handbook and a critical literature review, this is a clear choice for any research oriented collection.

1543. **Handbook of Machinery Adhesives.** New York: Dekker, 1985. 336p.

A comprehensive, up-to-date reference source dealing with adhesives and their use in and with machinery. A narrow topic, but covered well and concisely here. Recommended for specific technical collections only.

1544. **Handbook of Measurement Science.** Sydenham, Peter H., ed. New York: Wiley, 1982-83. 2v.

Volume 1 is entitled *Theoretical Fundamentals*; volume 2, *Practice Fundamentals*. This is a catalog and description of the principles underlying the measurement process and measurement systems. Volume 1 is mainly a summary of the basic theory of the nature and behavior of this design and system. Written by experts, this is an excellent technical handbook.

1545. **Handbook of Mechanical and Electrical Systems for Buildings.** Bovay, H. E., ed. New York: McGraw-Hill, 1981. 800p.

TH6010
H29
Sci Ref

A survey of methods in the design of electrical and mechanical building systems, its chapters discuss air conditioning systems, plumbing, alarm systems, and communications systems. This is a good reference for engineers, architects, and builders.

1546. **Handbook of Mechanics, Materials, and Structures.** Blake, A., ed. New York: Wiley, 1985. 710p.

A consistently well done handbook dealing with structures and the engineering necessary to erect any structure. Highly recommended for any engineering collection.

1547. **Handbook of Modern Electrical Wiring.** 2nd ed. Traister, John E. Carlsbad, CA: Craftsman, 1985. 293p.

This complete practical guide outlines the basic principles and actual installation of electrical writing. It provides many applications and praiseworthy illustrations. This is a reference for beginning workers in the electrical construction field, but also for students, contractors, and the general public.

1548. **Handbook of Modern Electronics and Electrical Engineering.** Belove, C., ed. New York: Wiley, 1986. 2401p.

An extremely useful and current handbook covering the field of electrical and electronic engineering. This is a first-rate choice for handbook information in electronics of any sort.

1549. **Handbook of Power Generation: Transformers and Generators.** Traister, John E. Englewood Cliffs, NJ: Prentice-Hall, 1983. 246p.

The focus of this work is on the practical, on-the-job dealings for a broad spectrum of applications in electrical power generation and distribution with a slight mention of theories. It is a helpful aid for electrical engineering texts.

1550. **Handbook of Practical Electrical Design.** McPartland, J. F., ed. New York: McGraw-Hill, 1984. 1v. (various paging).

TK3271
M35
1984
Sci

This is a thorough reference work on the design aspects of electrical systems for commercial, industrial, and residential buildings. Specific emphasis is on the National Electrical Code (NEC), but also includes Occupational Safety and Health Administration regulations and other codes, such as those of the National Fire Protection Association. It is suitable for both academic libraries with electrical engineering programs and libraries serving the general public.

1551. **Handbook of Precision Engineering.** Davidson, A., ed. New York: McGraw-Hill, 1971- . irregular.

Practically a treatise on precision engineering, the one intention of the work is to act as a last stop reference for information on precision engineering. It has earned a deserved reputation as an excellent handbook series and should be a part of any mechanical engineering collection which deals with precision engineering.

1552. **Handbook of Simplified Electrical Wiring Design.** Lenk, John D. Englewood Cliffs, NJ: Prentice-Hall, 1979. 332p.

Contains step-by-step procedures in solid-state design. As such, it is an excellent tool for some public, college, and technical collections.

1553. Handbook of Transformer Applications. Flanagan, W. M. New York: McGraw-Hill, 1985. 1v. (various paging).

A good source for technical information in the transformer design area, this source contains good tables and illustrations to complement the text. It is recommended for technical collections or highly specialized collections.

1554. Handbook of Valves, Piping, and Pipelines. Warring, R. H. Houston, TX: Gulf Publishing, 1982. 434p.

Describes in detail more than 20 different types of valves and thoroughly examines all aspects of piping and pipelining. This is an excellent source in a highly technical area.

1555. Heat-Transfer Pocket Handbook. Cheremisinoff, Nicholas P. Houston, TX: Gulf Publishing, 1984. 240p.

A compact reference work that provides a short and concise guide to solving heat transfer problems. It is not a reference text, but is a guide to calculations, formulas, data, and design practices. Glossary, unit conversion factors, and a simple index are included.

1556. Hydraulic Pumps and Motors: Selection and Application for Hydraulic Power Control Systems. Lambeck, Raymond P. New York: Dekker, 1983. 154p.

A concise reference guide that provides a general overview of various types of pumps, motors, and controls. Recommended to all libraries with engineering collections.

1557. IC Master. Garden City, NY: United Technical Publications, Inc., 1977- . annual.

The most complete guide to integrated circuits available. It includes a part index arranged by part number and a military parts directory. This is a necessary source for integrated circuit information.

1558. IES Lighting Handbook. 6th ed. Kaufman, John E., ed. New York: Illumination Engineering Society of North America, 1981. 2v.

Contains technical and illustrative information on lighting principles. Several different standards are also referenced as a guide for the illumination engineer. This is a very specific work, but excellent in its presentation.

TK7825
L83
1984
Sci
Ref

1559. Illustrated Handbook of Electronic Tables, Symbols, Measurements, and Values. 2nd ed. Ludwig, Raymond H. Englewood Cliffs, NJ: Prentice-Hall, 1984. 430p.

Useful to anyone solving problems in electronics, this is a directory of electronic symbols, tables, conversion factors for technical applications, formulas, and methods of problem solving. The print is clear and larger than usual and the illustrations are easy to read. Users would include students from the technical programs to the graduate level, technicians, and engineers. The information is encapsulated, allowing for one to read just the section with the information sought. This is a good, practical reference book.

1560. Industrial Robotics Handbook. Hunt, V. Daniel. New York: Industrial Press, 1983. 432p.

This handbook incorporates a broad overview of industrial robots with information on the applications for robots, procedures for system selection, technical characteristics for some 80 systems, and various discussions on robot related topics.

1561. Instrument Engineers' Handbook. rev. ed. Liptbak, Bbela G., ed. Radnor, PA: Chilton, 1985. 1110p.

A comprehensive work covering level, pressure, density, temperature, flow, viscosity, weight and analytical measurement, sensors and safety instrumentation, control valves, other types of final control elements, regulators, controllers and logic components, control boards and receiver displays, transmitters and telemetering, control theory, process computers, analog and hybrid computers, process control systems, reports of the new developments in process sensors and computers, and data transmission.

1562. **International Countermeasures Handbook: 1978-79.** 4th ed. Eustace, Harry F. Palo Alto, CA: EW Communications, 1978. 496p.
A thorough presentation on electronics warfare systems including microwave and infrared/electro-optical technology, tactical and airborne systems, flares, and aerosols. Contains information on U.S. expenditures, Soviet systems, and companies that produce electronic warfare equipment. Provides tables, diagrams, charts, and an index. More technical language makes this reference suitable for those involved in the electronic warfare industry.

1563. **Linear and Interface Circuits Applications.** Pippenger, D. E., E. J. Tobaben, and C. L. McCollum. New York: McGraw-Hill, 1985. 1v. (various paging).
Written by staff members of the Texas Instruments company, this volume covers nonlogic linear and interface circuits. The authorship is very clear in that TI and TI-compatible circuits are the true focus of the book. Other than this caveat, this is an excellent handbook for illustration of circuits and problem solving for nonlogic circuits. It is highly recommended for research and development collections.

1564. **Mark's Standard Handbook for Mechanical Engineers.** 9th ed. Avallone, Eugene A., and Theodore Baumeister, eds. New York: McGraw-Hill, 1987. 1v. (various paging).
This is a classic and well-known reference in mechanical engineering. It covers the properties and handling of materials, machine elements, fuels and furnaces, power generation, pumps and compressors, instrumentation, and environmental conrol. This is a good source for basic information in mechanical engineering.

1565. **Master Semiconductor Replacement Handbook—Listed by Industry Standard Number.** Blue Ridge Summit, PA: TAB Books, 1982. 684p.
This giant index lists parts by ISN and shows the replacement parts produced by five leading semiconductor suppliers: Sylvania, RCA, General Electric, Radio Shack, and Motorola. Especially when used with a companion index of parts by manufacturer's number, this is useful to anyone troubleshooting an electronic circuit and seeking replacement parts. Users include the student, the technician, the engineer, and the hobbyist.

1566. **McGraw-Hill's Compilation of Data Communications Standards.** 3rd ed. Folts, Harold C., ed. New York: McGraw-Hill, 1986.
Six groups working in the communications field have reproduced in their entirety the most often used data communications standards. The groups are the U.S. federal government, the International Telegraph and Telephone Consultative Committee (CCITT), the International Organization for Standardization (ISO), the American National Standards Institute (ANSI), and the Electronics Industries Association (EIA) and ECMA. All of the standards are cross-indexed. Emphasis is on the international scene.

1567. **McGraw-Hill's National Electrical Code Handbook.** 19th ed. McPartland, J. F., ed. New York: McGraw-Hill, 1987. 1212p.

TK260
N2
1993

A popular handbook that explains various provisions of the National Electrical Code. Contains new specifications and changes in design, sizing, and grounding. This is a useful reference for electricians, electrical engineers, and technicians.

1568.   **Mechanical Design and Systems Handbook.** 2nd ed. Rothbart, Harold A., ed. New York: McGraw-Hill, 1985. 1v. (various paging).

This comprehensive, updated work includes computer assisted design and manufacturing, and other topics. There is a significant expansion of treatment of practical and theoretical design of mechanisms and machinery.

1569.   **Mechanical Engineer's Handbook.** Kutz, Myer, ed. New York: Wiley, 1986. 2316p.

The emphasis of this handbook is on digital computers and energy and power systems. This is a very comprehensive handbook which is being well received. The size of the book makes it more complete than most. It is highly recommended.

1570.   **Mechanical Hands Illustrated.** rev. ed. Ichiro, Kato, and Kuni Sadamoto, eds. Washington, DC: Hemisphere Publishing, 1985. 216p.

This is a translation of the first edition originally published in Japan in 1977. This American edition does not appear to be a revised edition, but rather a translation of the textual material. Nonetheless, this is still the only reference book of its type in Japanese or in English. A reference book for the professional robotics design engineer, the text is divided into three main areas: (1) design and engineering concerns related to mechanical arms, especially robotic and prosthetic devices; (2) diagrams, drawings, and photographs of existing mechanical arms (industrial and R&D devices) suitable to illustrate design concept and arm-function; and (3) patents illustrated by line drawings with a listing of applicable patent numbers and manufacturer's name. An appendix shows various arms in operation but without commentary or description other than minor captions. The index is a major weakness in that it is arranged by manufacturer only. A second major weakness is the lack of post-1977 devices. This is recommended for its singular contribution as the only work of its kind in English, not for its timeliness.

1571.   **Mechanical Technician's Handbook.** Webb, Maurice J., ed. New York: McGraw-Hill, 1983. 467p.

This book covers building models and apparatus from instructions; selection components and instruments for the assembly of apparatus; and safety conduction tests. Also contains tables and illustrations. It is good for technicians who make and test new products.

1572.   **Mechanisms and Dynamics of Machinery.** 4th ed. Mabie, Hamilton H., and Charles F. Reinholtz. New York: Wiley, 1987. 644p.

This source provides data on force, gravitational preference of machinery, and mass. It expresses all dimensions in SI units and is a very good source for the designing of machinery and placement of heavy machinery.

1573.   **Microprocessor Source Book.** Loveday, George. London: Pitman, 1986. 247p.

This work was designed to serve as a good reference source for students and those working in industry. Since it was designed for this purpose rather than for the general audience, the "state-of-the-art" has been avoided. The microprocessor article contains extensive information on the microprocessors in production today. Though it has no page numbers, the table of contents acts as an index. An appendix of program examples is provided. This volume will be an excellent reference source in an undergraduate program or vocational-technical program, as it is probably too elementary for advanced researchers and graduate students.

1574. **Modern Electronic Circuits Reference Manual.** Markus, John. New York: McGraw-Hill, 1980. 1238p.

Includes circuits utilizing a range of different transistors and integrated circuits. Circuits are referenced to original publication sources. Lists of addresses of publications, abbreviations, and an index are provided. This is a worthwhile purchase for any technical library.

1575. **National Electrical Code Reference Book.** Garland, J. D., ed. Englewood Cliffs, NJ: Prentice-Hall, 1988. 1v. (various paging).

This is a reference guide for electricians, electrical contractors, and inspectors, as well as a reference for vocational students and individuals. The overall intent of the work is to provide a clear understanding of the rules as prescribed in the *National Electrical Code Handbook* (see entry 1577). This is a necessary publication for any technical collection which deals with electrical concerns.

1576. **National Electrical Safety Code.** New York: Institute of Electrical and Electronics Engineers, 1984. 384p.

Provides information on overhead and underground lines and supply stations, covering such topics as safe installation and maintenance of electric supply stations, and supply and communication lines.

1577. **NFPA Handbook of the National Electrical Code.** Summers, Wilford L. Boston: National Fire Protection Agency, 1978. 1v. (various paging).

This is a reproduction of the most recent National Electrical Code with diagrams, illustrations, and commentary. It is a necessity for electrical engineers, contractors, librarians, and legal collections.

1578. **Nomograms for Steam Generation and Utilization.** Ganapathy, V. Atlanta, GA: Fairmont, 1985. 176p.

Designed to be used by mechanical engineers on the job as well as in design. The graphs are clear and concise as are the instructions for their use. This is highly recommended for technology collections in special and academic libraries.

1579. **Noncrystalline Semiconductors.** Pollak, Michael, ed. Boca Raton, FL: CRC Press, 1987. 3v.

This source deals with the various phenomena and properties of general applicability to all nonmetallic and noncrystalline systems. This is an excellent state-of-the-art discussion of the semiconductor technology. It is an in-depth review of current research. This is a clear choice for any research collection in electrical engineering.

1580. **Plant Engineer's Handbook of Formulas, Charts, and Tables.** 2nd ed. Moffat, Donald W. Englewood Cliffs, NJ: Prentice-Hall, 1982. 397p.

A one-volume source combining the important formulas and tables needed by the practicing plant engineer. Data are divided according to type of materials, such as concrete blocks, wood, steel, and aluminum. This is a good short answer reference source.

1581. **Practical Electrical Wiring: Residential, Farm, and Industrial.** 13th ed. Richter, Herbert P., and W. Creighton Schwann. New York: McGraw-Hill, 1984. 685p.

This is a simple presentation on electrical wiring that provides details on theory and basic principles and wiring for residential, non-residential, and farm areas. Provides tables, examples, and a bibliography. Useful to both professional and novice electricians.

1582. **Printed Circuits Handbook.** 3rd ed. Coombs, Clyde F., ed. New York: McGraw-Hill, 1988. 1v. (various paging).

This handbook includes illustrations and provides data, guidelines, and proven troubleshooting techniques. Contains detailed information on environmental protection and computer-assisted design processes.

1583. **Pump Handbook.** 2nd ed. Karassik, Igor J., et al., eds. New York: McGraw-Hill, 1986. 1v. (various paging).

This work deals with types of pumps by discussing theory, construction, and performance characteristics. Centrifugal, power, steam, screw and rotary, jet, and other types are discussed within the framework above. It also covers pump components such as couplings, controls, valves, and the instruments used in pumping systems. Evaluation and maintenance are also discussed. This is highly recommended for any collection that is a working technical collection or a research collection in mechanical engineering.

1584. **Radio Amateur's Handbook.** 15th ed. rev. Collins, A. Frederick, and Robert Hertzberg. New York: Harper & Row, 1983. 387p.

This is a standard handbook for radio engineering. The fundamental theories of radio are discussed in a format and manner suitable for a novice. This makes the work a natural for purchase by public and nonspecialized collections.

1585. **RC Active Filter Design Handbook.** Stephenson, F. W. New York: Wiley, 1985. 418p.

A very technical handbook covering filter design, it is recommended only for collections deeply involved in the design or utilization of filter devices. Data and diagrams are included.

1586. **Reference Manual for Telecommunications.** Freeman, Roger L. New York: John Wiley & Sons, 1985. 1504p.

Provides a central source of basic information that will have repeated application. Basic disciplines of transmission and switching in 26 subject areas are covered, and a subject index is included. Given the currency of the telecommunications area, this should be a welcome addition to virtually any engineering collection.

1587. **Shock and Vibration Handbook.** 3rd ed. Harris, Cyril M., ed. New York: McGraw-Hill, 1987. 1v. (various paging).

Covers the theoretical and practical aspects of shock and vibration engineering. The basic divisions of the handbook cover instrumentation and measurements, standards, analysis and testing, concepts in the treatment of data, procedures for analyzing, isolation, damping, balancing, equipment design, packaging, and the effects of shock and vibration on man. It is highly recommended for technical collections.

1588. **Spring Designer's Handbook.** Carlson, Harold. New York: Dekker, 1978. 350p.

Covers practical application of spring design principles. Includes step-by-step design procedures, data, and graphic material. Useful to engineers at all levels of training.

1589.   **Standard Applications of Mechanical Details.** Mueller, Jerome F. New York: McGraw-Hill, 1985. 331p.

This is a compilation of mechanical details related to building design. There is a considerable amount of text, unlike the author's previous work, *Standard Mechanical and Electrical Details* (New York: McGraw-Hill, 1981). Not as complete as *Architectural Graphics Standards* (New York: Wiley, 1981), its scope is much more narrow and deep. It is highly recommended for professional collections and those associated with engineering and architectural schools.

1590.   **Standard Handbook for Electrical Engineers.** 12th ed. Fink, Donald G., and H. Wayne Beatty, eds. New York: McGraw-Hill, 1987. 1v. (various paging).

A single-volume handbook with data on transmission, distribution, and application of power. The treatment of the subject is very technical, precluding use by nonengineers. This is a technical source for technicians and researchers.

1591.   **Standard Handbook of Machine Design.** Shigley, J. E., and C. R. Misckhe, eds. New York: McGraw-Hill, 1986. 1v. (various paging).

This is a good desk reference for the machinist and engineer involved directly in the design of heavy machinery. It is specialized, but written at a level that other engineers will understand.

1592.   **Switchgear and Control Handbook.** 2nd ed. Smeaton, Robert W., ed. New York: McGraw-Hill, 1987. 1v. (various paging).

This is a comprehensive, up-to-date, and authoritative guide to switchgear design, for use by engineers involved in electrical power applications.

1593.   **Thermal Insulation Handbook.** Turner, William C., and John F. Malloy. New York: McGraw-Hill, 1981. 629p.

Of interest to engineers and contractors, this is a practical reference source on the techniques and information needed to solve insulation problems. It describes heat transfer, equipment, proper insulation, weather barriers, inspection, and maintenance.

1594.   **Transistor Substitution Handbook.** 23rd ed. Indianapolis, IN: Sams, 1984. 1v. (various paging).

This computer generated handbook of American and foreign transistors is listed in numerical and alphabetical order. It is an excellent source of information for substitution and is highly recommended for electronics laboratories and research collections.

1595.   **Tube Substitution Handbook.** Indianapolis, IN: Sams, 1960- . annual.

Although the vacuum tube is no longer the electronic component of choice for most applications, this handbook pulls together valuable information on substitution tubes. It is an extremely valuable source when needed.

DIRECTORIES

1596.   **Directory of Foreign Manufacturers in the United States.** 3rd ed. Arpan, Jeffrey S., and David A. Ricks. Atlanta, GA: Georgia State University, Business Publications, 1985. 384p.

This directory lists 3,400 firms alphabetically and indexes them by parent company. As a list of foreign owned domestic businesses it can be a very useful tool given the spread of multinational corporations.

1597. Directory of Industrial Heat-Processing and Combustion Equipment. Atlanta, GA: Fairmont Press, 1984- . biennial.

A directory of processing and combustion equipment manufactured by 37 companies, and an expanded list of manufacturers, followed by a production classification section of types of equipment.

1598. Directory of Microcomputer Software for Mechanical Engineering Design. O'Connell, Colette, et al., eds. New York: Dekker, 1985- . annual.

Appropriate for both new and experienced microcomputer users, this directory provides information on a wide variety of programs from many sources.

1599. Electronic Engineers Master. Garden City, NY: United Technical Publications, 1976- . annual.

The first three volumes contain a product index and directory, a manufacturers and sales office directory, and a distributor directory. Volume 4 serves as the index to the first three volumes.

1600. Electronic Market Data Book. Washington, DC: Electronic Industries Associations, 1970- . annual.

Based on data supplied by several hundred companies, governmental, and private sources, this is a statistical compilation of the directions and trends in the electronics industry. It is an excellent addition to a large variety of libraries.

1601. Electronics Buyer's Guide. New York: McGraw-Hill, 1945- . annual.

Listing over 4,000 products and services in electronics technology, this buyer's guide includes a directory of trade names and an index to advertisers.

1602. Electronics Research Centres: A World Directory of Organizations and Programs. Harlow, England: Longman, 1986. 546p.

Entries are arranged by country and then by institution and subsidiary, if any. The length and completeness of the entries varies considerably. This work should be used with care, as much of the information can be found elsewhere and fairly readily. It is recommended for some specialized collections, but with some caution.

1603. IEA: The Directory of Instruments, Electronics, Automation. 13th ed. London: Morgan-Grampian Publishing, 1979. 6v.

This directory of instruments, electronics, and automation includes manufacturers' addresses and UK agents. This is a good buyer's guide for UK products.

1604. IEEE Membership Directory. New York: Institute of Electrical and Electronics Engineers, 1966- . irregular.

Includes history, officers, members, biographies of selected members, and awards. As the largest electrical and electronics organization in North America, this is an excellent place for directory information on persons in these fields.

1605. International Programmable Controllers Directory. Flora, Philip C., ed. Conroe, TX: Technical DataBase Corp., 1985. 123p.

This is a product directory generated from data gathered by questionnaires returned by manufacturers. It is not verified by author. Subject headings include: adaptive control systems, computer numerical control, data acquisitions, direct numerical control, motion control systems, peripheral devices, positioning systems, process control systems, and programmable controllers.

1606. **International Robotics Yearbook.** Cambridge, MA: Ballinger, 1984- . annual.

This is the first single reference source to provide summary information on robotics. It is divided into three parts. Part 1 is a worldwide directory of manufacturers, suppliers, and services of robots and robot systems; part 2 is a directory of world research and development activities; and part 3 is a directory of grants and funding sources for robotics research and development, and a directory of robot associations. A subject index to research activities is available. This is an excellent tool for special and research libraries in the field.

1607. **Marquis Who's Who Directory of Computer Graphics.** Chicago, IL: Marquis Who's Who, 1984- . annual.

Profiles computer graphics specialists and major industrial and academic users by describing their current job function, computer graphics function, and areas of expertise.

1608. **Mechanical Engineer's Catalog and Product Directory.** American Society of Mechanical Engineers. New York: American Society of Mechanical Engineers, 1962- . annual.

This catalog is divided into three sections: a full line section, including 4,000 leading manufacturers; a product directory section, including 50,000 listings of products; and an ASME publications section, including all available ASME publications codes, standards, and periodicals with ordering instructions.

1609. **Robotics Technical Directory.** Research Triangle Park, NC: I.S.A. Services, 1984- . annual.

A listing of reference materials, products, organizations, online databases, educational institutes, research laboratories, publishers, manufacturers, and scientific and technical specialists dealing with all aspects of robotics, industrial automation, computer aided design (CAD), and computer aided manufacturing (CAM).

1610. **Telecommunications Systems and Services Directory.** Schmittroth, John, and Martin Conners, eds. Detroit, MI: Gale Research, 1983- . irregular.

A comprehensive directory of both established and newly developed telecommunications systems which include 150 long distance telephone services, 125 data communications services; over 100 electronic mail services, 75 videotext and teletext services, 150 teleconferencing services, 200 telex and telegram services, 70 local area networks, 50 satellite services, and more. A detailed glossary and four detailed indexes are provided which include a master index listed by names, function/service-type index, personal name index, and a geographic index. This is a major tool.

1611. **Teleconferencing Resources Directory.** White Plains, NY: Knowledge Industry Publications, 1983- . annual.

A comprehensive guide to the wide variety of equipment, facility, and services suppliers in the teleconferencing business. It is divided into two parts: (1) alphabetical listing, and (2) 10 indexes.

1612. **Who Knows? Selected Information Resources on Electronics.** Feulner, John A., comp. Washington, DC: U.S. Library of Congress, 1984. 59p.

A directory of organizations, government laboratories, societies, and research centers that provide assistance and information on topics in electronics. Covers such fields as telecommunications, high fidelity, and systems engineering, and includes facts such as names, addresses, and telephone numbers. Recommended for science and engineering libraries.

1613.   **Who's Who in Electronics.** Graeser, Kathi, ed. Cleveland, OH: Harris, 1949- . annual.

This is a listing of electronics firms, distributors, and representatives in alphabetical and geographic sequences. Also provided are names and addresses, names of executives or key personnel, number of employees, products, major SIC code, annual sales volume, and the year the company was established. It is an excellent directory for electronics industry directory type information.

CHAPTER

15 Production and Processing Engineering

Production and processing engineering deals with areas commonly defined as chemical engineering, petroleum engineering, metallurgical engineering, paints and coatings, and textile engineering. While these are diverse areas, there is a commonality: each involves the production or the processing of an element and the technology inherent in that processing.

There are overlaps in engineering and in the chapters here. An example of one of the less distinct divisions is between petroleum engineering as process and production engineering, and petroleum engineering as distinct from energy engineering. The choice as to which chapter was best suited for an individual work was based on their intent and content. Like other engineering chapters, this one is composed mostly of handbook material. The materials here were chosen for their currency as well as their thoroughness.

GUIDES TO THE LITERATURE

1614. **Brief Guide to Sources of Metals Information.** Hyslop, Marjorie R. Washington, DC: Information Resources, Press, 1973. 180p.

This guide contains a wealth of information primarily of use to metallurgists. The book covers information sources, major libraries, societies, and secondary literature sources. United States and Canadian sources are emphasized. Although the material here is somewhat dated, there is no other book which does what this one does. It is recommended with some care.

1615. **Chemical and Process Engineering Unit Operations: A Bibliographical Guide.** Bourton, Kay. New York: IFI/Plenum, 1968. 534p.

This bibliography with annotations concentrates on chemical engineering. The material should be used with some care, given its age. This is still useful, however, for its listings of major reference works still used by those in the field.

1616. **Guide to the Petroleum Reference Literature.** Pearson, Barbara C., and Katherine B. Ellwood. Littleton, CO: Libraries Unlimited, 1987. 193p.

Included in this guide is a selected list of reference tools chosen from major petroleum company and university library collections. In addition, materials sent from scientific publishers for review and from the Special Libraries Association and Geoscience Information Society are listed. The literature included is international in scope, primarily in English, and for the most part, published after 1978.

1617. **History of Chemical Technology: An Annotated Bibliography.** Multhauf, Robert P. New York: Garland, 1984. 299p.

The scope of this particular work is too broad to allow adequate coverage. Most of the items are annotated; however, the lack of several important items is a definite problem. On the positive side, this is one of the better attempts to control the literature in this area. It is recommended in spite of its flaws.

1618. **Industrial Minerals and Rocks: (Nonmetallic Other Than Fuels).** 5th ed. Lefond, Stanley J., ed. New York: Society of Mining Engineers, American Institute of Mining, Metallurgical, and Petroleum Engineers, 1983. 2v.

This comprehensive survey of the industrial minerals industry is generally divided by industrial minerals grouped by uses, sources of information for industrial materials, and commodities.

1619. **Information Resources in Toxicology.** 2nd ed. Wexler, Philip. New York: Elsevier, 1987. 531p.

Rather than leading to a source, this work provides answers to reference questions. It is a good source for ready reference questions related to food science and technology.

1620. **Information Sources in Biotechnology.** 2nd ed. Crafts-Lighty, A. New York: Stockton Press, 1986. 403p.

Only English-language sources published up until March 1986 are listed. No journal articles are included. This work describes the business and science of biotechnology, and provides a brief critical review of the most important information sources.

1621. **Offshore Petroleum Engineering: A Bibliographic Guide to Publications and Information Sources.** Chryssostomidis, Marjorie. New York: Nichols Publishing, 1978. 367p.

This bibliography has a three-fold purpose: to assist the neophyte, to provide the involved professional with additional, hard-to-locate references, and to identify the basic information sources in offshore petroleum engineering. Books, articles, reports, and conference papers are among the pertinent information cited. The annotations are arranged by subject, and author, title, and permuted topic indexes are provided.

1622. **Plastics and Rubbers: World Sources of Information.** Yescombe, E. R. London: Applied Science Publishers, 1976. 547p.

This listing of literature and other information sources on rubber and plastics includes references up to 1975. Directory information on related worldwide organizations is featured. This is a useful guide to students, researchers, and engineers.

1623. **Textiles in America: 1650-1870.** Montgomery, Florence M. New York: Norton, 1984. 412p.

The first half of the book is an illustrated history of textile uses in America. It is arranged by application to include window curtains, upholstery, and bed hangings. The second half is a well illustrated dictionary. This is highly recommended for any collection dealing with textiles.

ABSTRACTS, INDEXES, AND BIBLIOGRAPHIES

1624. **AGRICOLA.** Beltsville, MD: National Agriculture Library, 1970- . monthly.

Produced by the NAL, this database includes in its coverage international journal and monographic literature in agriculture and related fields. The material for 1970-78 was known as CAIN. Available from a variety of vendors.

1625. **APILIT.** New York: American Petroleum Institute, 1964- . monthly.

Prepared by the Central Abstracting and Indexing Service of the API, this database covers the refining literature on a worldwide basis. Available from SDC.

1626. **APIPAT.** New York: American Petroleum Institute, 1964- . monthly.

This online database covers both U.S. and non-U.S. refining patents. Prepared by the Central Abstracting and Indexing Service of the API, it is available from SDC.

1627. **Chemical Vapor Deposition, 1960-1980: A Bibliography.** Hawkins, Donald T., ed. New York: IFI/Plenum, 1981. 737p.

Citations pertaining to chemical vapor deposition and vapor transport processes are contained in this computer produced bibliography of documents. It is suitable for any technical library involved with research of chemical vapor deposition.

1628. **COMPENDEX Chemical Engineering.** New York: Engineering Information, Inc., 1983- . quarterly.

This database is available on CD-ROM and covers the major aspects of chemical and agricultural engineering. Specific areas include mining and petroleum engineering, optical technology, and food technology.

1629. **Fluidex.** Cranfield, England: BHRA Fluid Engineering, 1974- . quarterly.

A database providing indexing and abstracting of fluid engineering, including theoretical research. It is available from DIALOG.

1630. **Food and Nutrition Bibliography.** 11th ed. Phoenix, AZ: Oryx Press, 1984. 557p.

Compiled from data provided by the National Agricultural Library, this is a comprehensive annotated guide to print and audiovisual materials covering all areas related to human nutrition. It is indexed and would be useful to researchers, educators, and librarians.

1631. **Food Science and Technology Abstracts.** Shinfield, England: International Food Information Service, 1969- . monthly.

This service abstracts over 1,000 journals and is considered a major source for food science materials. It is available from DIALOG as an online database.

1632. **IMM Abstracts.** London: Institution of Mining and Metallurgy, 1950- . bimonthly.

A survey of the literature on mining of minerals, mineral dressing, and metallurgy other than ferrous metals. The scope is worldwide. This is a good source for particular information and is recommended for specific applications in research collections.

1633. **International Petroleum Abstracts.** Chichester, England: Wiley, 1973- . quarterly.
   An internationally respected abstracting service which concentrates on all aspects of petroleum and petroleum products and services. Though its broad subject arrangement makes it somewhat difficult to use, this is still a necessity for any research collection.

1634. **Master Index to Materials and Properties.** Touloukian, Yeram Sarkis, and C. Y. Ho. New York: IFI/Plenum Press, 1979. 178p.
   Presented in tabular form, the material covers substance name and physical properties, as well as volume number and page for relevant items. It is invaluable to any scientific library involved in materials science.

1635. **METADEX.** Metals Park, OH: ASM International, 1966- . monthly.
   The database corresponds to *Metals Abstracts and Index* (see entry 1636), *Alloys Index* (Metals Park, OH: ASM International, 1974-), and two other sources which have now ceased publication. It is available from BRS, DIALOG, and SDC.

1636. **Metals Abstracts and Index.** Metals Park, OH: ASM International, 1968- . monthly.
   This is an internationally respected abstracting tool covering a wide variety of metallurgical information. It is a classic work and deserves its reputation as an excellent source of information. Available online as *METADEX* (see entry 1635).

1637. **Mineral Exploration, Mining, and Processing Patents, 1975.** North, Oliver S. Arlington, VA: The Author, 1976. 295p.
   Included in this work are items published since 1971 about patents from 1964-1971. Most of the significant U.S., Canadian, and British patents on the exploration and mining of metallic and nonmetallic minerals, beneficiation and concentration, extractions, and refining of ores are covered. Although dated, this is a valuable source of patent information in the area. Recommended, but with caution.

1638. **Multicomponent Alloy Constitution Bibliography 1974-1977.** Prince, Alan. London: The Metals Society, 1981. 503p.
   This bibliography contains more than 18,000 document references. Only those systems with more than two components are included. Entries begin with ternary systems followed by quaternary systems, etc. Arrangement within each type of system is based on the components.

1639. **Offshore Abstracts.** London: Offshore Information Literature, 1974- . bimonthly.
   An extensive review of information for the offshore industry derived from a worldwide coverage of scientific and technical journals, conference papers, research reports, trade literature, standards and patents. Full bibliographic citations are provided.

1640. **Offshore Petroleum Engineering: A Bibliographic Guide to Publications and Information Sources.** Chryssostomidis, Marjorie. New York: Nichols Publishing, 1978. 367p.
   A bibliography on offshore petroleum engineering and related fields. Topics covered include offshore structures engineering, underwater and deep sea operations, sea floor engineering, and oceanography. Lists citations from U.S. and international books, reports, conference proceedings, and articles. Entries are grouped into 22 categories subdivided into 100 subsections. Subsections are coded alphanumerically and contain full bibliographic data. Appendices contain a list of sources, directory of publishers, and tips

on locating and obtaining publications. Author, title, and permuted topics indexes are provided. This is a valuable reference work for petroleum engineers and academic libraries.

1641. **Paperchem.** Appleton, WI: Institute of Paper Chemistry, 1966- . monthly.

Database covering over 1,000 periodicals and patents related to the paper industry. Available from DIALOG and SDC.

1642. **P/E News.** New York: American Petroleum Institute, 1975- . weekly.

Covers five major publications in the petroleum and energy fields. Available from DIALOG and SDC.

1643. **Textile Technology Digest.** Charlottesville, VA: Institute of Textile Technology, 1944- . monthly.

This digest contains international coverage of all aspects of textile technology. An author index is included in individual issues. In 1972, cumulative author, patent concordance, and subject indexes were published. This has been available from DIALOG since 1978.

1644. **TULSA.** Tulsa, OK: University of Tulsa, 1965- . weekly.

A database of oil and gas exploration, development, and production. Available from SDC.

1645. **WELDASEARCH.** Cambridge, England: The Welding Institute, 1967- . monthly.

This database provides primary coverage of the international literature on all aspects of the joining of metals and plastics and related areas. Available from DIALOG.

1646. **World Aluminum Abstracts.** Metals Park, OH: ASM International, 1968- . monthly.

Formerly *Aluminum Abstracts* (1963-1969), this service covers over 1,600 journals. It is arranged under broad subject headings and is available as an online database from DIALOG.

1647. **World Textiles.** Manchester, England: Shirley Institute, 1970- . monthly.

This database indexes the world literature of the science and technology of textile and related materials. It is available from DIALOG.

ENCYCLOPEDIAS

1648. **Chemical Engineering Practice.** Cremer, Herbert W., ed. New York: Academic Press, 1956-1965. 12v.

660.28
C91c
Sci

This is perhaps the definitive encyclopedia for chemical engineering and is widely respected and used by chemical engineers. Each article is written by an expert in the field. A necessity for serious collection in chemical engineering.

1649. **Chemical Technology: An Encyclopedic Treatment: The Economic Application of Modern Technological Developments.** New York: Barnes & Noble, 1968- .

This is a curious publication in that it can be used both by a novice and by the expert in the field. It examines all phases of chemical engineering and technology. Bibliographies lead to the primary literature. This is an excellent source of information more in the form of a treatise. Some consider this a successor to J. F. Van Oss's *Warenkennis en Technologie* (Amsterdam, Netherlands: Elsevier, 1948-1950).

1650. **Corrosion and Corrosion Control: An Introduction to Corrosion Science and Engineering.** 3rd ed. Uhlig, Herbert H., and R. Winston Revie. New York: Wiley, 1985. 441p.

This is a state-of-the-art analysis of corrosion and control. It is encyclopedic in coverage and is intended for use by experts in the field. Highly recommended for research collections or specialized research and development collections.

1651. **Encyclopedia of Chemical Processing and Design.** McKetta, John J., ed. New York: Dekker, 1976- . 25v. irregular.

Currently in 25 volumes, this is a comprehensive treatise and encyclopedia on all aspects of chemical processing and design. The emphasis is on the area of plant design and an unusually large amount of bibliographic material accompanys each article. It is highly recommended.

1652. **Encyclopedia of Chemical Technology.** 3rd ed. Kirk, Raymond E., and Donald F. Othmer, eds. New York: Wiley, 1978- . irregular.

A classic encyclopedia, each volume in the series is self-contained. The general intent is to cover chemical technology, industrial processes, uses of materials, unit operation, processes, and fundamentals of chemistry. It is available online from BRS.

1653. **Encyclopedia of Composite Materials and Components.** Grayson, Martin, ed. New York: Wiley, 1983. 1161p.

Consists of carefully selected reprints from the world renowned Kirk-Othmer *Encyclopedia of Chemical Technology* (see entry 1652). Useful as a handy reference tool, teaching aid, or research reference, it contains 50 main entries, each averaging 10,000 words in length.

1654. **Encyclopedia of Fluid Mechanics.** Cheremisinoff, N. P., ed. Houston, TX: Gulf Publishing, 1986-87. 6v.

This work is planned for eight volumes, but only six are currently available. Each volume attempts to stand on its own and does a credible job. The indexing is very good for each of the volumes. What is presently missing is a combined index, which would tie together the theories and applications covered in the separate volumes. This is an excellent work and should be included in any serious academic collection.

TX 349
M2
Sci
Ref

1655. **Encyclopedia of Food & Nutrition.** Adams, Catherine F. New York: Drake Publishers, 1977. 175p.

This is an alphabetically arranged compendium of data on the nutritional value of foods. It includes water content; calories; and protein, fat, carbohydrate, and vitamin value per portion. A metric conversion table is included.

1656. **Encyclopedia of Food Engineering.** 2nd ed. Hall, Carl W., A. W. Farrall, and A. L. Rippen. Westport, CT: AVI Publishing Co., 1986. 882p.

This edition has been changed in style and format. New entries have been added and existing entries have been updated. Subject headings were selected on the basis of use in the field. A reference reading list is provided.

TP 368.2
E6
Sci
Ref

1657. **Encyclopedia of Food Science.** Peterson, Martin S., and Arnold H. Johnson. Westport, CT: AVI, 1978. 1005p.

Contains more than 250 articles on food science. Provides composition, attributes, and manufacturing processes of various foodstuffs. It is comprehensive and well arranged for ready reference. A valuable tool.

1658. **Encyclopedia of Industrial Chemical Additives.** Ash, Michael, and Irene Ash, comps. New York: Chemical Publishing Co., 1984. 454p.

TP9 E688 1984 Sci Ref

A comprehensive compilation of trade name products that function as additives in enhancing the properties of various major industrial products. It is divided alphabetically into sections based on principal function and contains a cross-referenced index to all trade name products.

1659. **Encyclopedia of Industrial Chemical Analysis.** Snell, Foster Dee, and Clifford L. Hilton, eds. New York: Interscience, 1966-1974. 20v.

This is a massive work and should be used despite its age. The first three volumes cover general techniques, with the actual encyclopedia beginning with volume 4. This is a very complete source, especially given its scope as an international encyclopedia of techniques and methodologies in laboratories around the world. It is recommended, but with some caution.

1660. **Encyclopedia of Materials Science and Engineering.** Bever, Michael B., ed. Oxford: MIT Press, 1986. 8v.

Features articles by over 1,200 distinguished authors and Nobel laureates. Includes articles, bibliographic references of key sources in the literature, diagrams, photographs, and many tables.

1661. **Encyclopedia of Metallurgy and Materials.** Tottle, C. R. Plymouth, England: MacDonald & Evans, 1984. 380p.

X

Tables of the numeric data and electronic structure of the atom are included in this work, along with a periodic table. Illustrations accompany entries as needed. The author provides a table to compare SI units with English units.

1662. **Encyclopedia of Plastics, Polymers, and Resins.** Ash, Michael, and Irene Ash, comps. New York: Chemical Publishing, 1982- . 2v.

TP986 .A1 A83 1982 Sci Ref

Currently in two volumes, this encyclopedia coordinates and unifies practical information on plastic, polymer, and resin trademark products. The compilers provide an abbreviation key; chemical description; applications; form and color; and mechanical, thermal, and electrical properties of each product.   *TP1130 .A84 1992 Sci Ref*

1663. **Encyclopedia of Polymer Science and Engineering.** 2nd ed. Mark, Herman F., et al., eds. New York: Wiley, 1985- .

This second edition of *Encyclopedia of Polymer Science and Technology* is currently in seven volumes, with more to come. It is an illustrated general work covering the field. A separate index is provided. The first edition was a widely used handbook; the second edition will be just as popular.

1664. **Encyclopedia of Surfactants.** Ash, Michael, and Irene Ash. New York: Chemical Publishing, 1980-85. 4v.

QD549 .A75 1980 Sci Ref

Covering U.S. and foreign manufacturers of surfactants, this fourth volume is a supplement. A highly technical and specific source, it is still well done and highly recommended for specific collections.

1665. **Encyclopedia of Textiles.** 3rd ed. Englewood Cliffs, NJ: Prentice-Hall, 1980. 636p.

This abundantly illustrated work contains simplified explorations of all processes and fibers. Production and consumption tables with flowsheet diagrams are included.

1666.   **Encyclopedia of Textiles, Fibers, and Non-Woven Fabrics.** Grayson, Martin, ed. New York: Wiley, 1984. 581p.

This is no more than a carefully selected collection of articles from the Kirk-Othmer *Encyclopedia of Chemical Technology* (see entry 1652). If the larger set is held, there is no reason to purchase this encyclopedia. However, this is a good compilation of selected information and is recommended for specific collections.

1667.   **Foods and Food Production Encyclopedia.** Considine, Douglas M., and Glenn D. Considine, eds. New York: Van Nostrand Reinhold, 1982. 2305p.

This encyclopedia covers three fundamental stages: (1) the start of the food growth cycle; (2) the nurturing of growing plants and animals; and (3) the processing of raw foods. The book emphasizes fundamental principles. Unfortunately, the topic is much too large. In-depth reporting would be impossible within the existing constraints.

1668.   **Foods & Nutrition Encyclopedia.** Ensminger, A. H., et al. Clovis, CA: Pegus Press, 1983. 2v.

Format, illustrations, and text are patterned after styles common to the 1950s. This is suitable for the interested layperson and is recommended for public and school collections.

HD9560.5
I59
Main
Ref

1669.   **International Petroleum Encyclopedia.** Weber, George, ed. Tulsa, OK: Pennwell Publishing Co., 1968- . annual.

This is an annotated listing of petroleum activity for the previous year. It consists of maps and tables imparting information on the world petroleum trade. Partly a directory and partly a handbook, it is listed here because it receives its greatest usage as a handbook. It is a required source of information for any collection dealing with petroleum engineering.

1670.   **Kirk-Othmer Concise Encyclopedia of Chemical Technology.** New York: Wiley, 1985. 1318p.

This self-contained encyclopedia of chemical technology provides access to information contained in the third edition of the *Encyclopedia of Chemical Technology* (see entry 1652). It is useful to both students and specialists.

TN671
.S55
1992
Sci
Ref

1671.   **Metals Reference Book.** 5th ed. Smithells, Colin J., ed. London: Butterworths, 1976. 1566p.

This is the world-class, authoritative handbook on metals and metallurgy. The areas covered in the sections are: introductory tables; general physical and chemical constants; x-ray crystallography; crystallography; crystal chemistry; metallurgically important minerals; thermochemical data; physical properties of molten salts; metallography; equilibrium diagrams; gas metal systems; diffusion in metals; general physical properties; elastic properties and damping capacity; temperature measurement and thermoelectric properties; radiating properties of metals; electron emission; electrical properties; steels and alloys with special magnetic properties; mechanical testing; mechanical properties of metals and alloys; hard metals; lubricants; friction and wear; casting alloys and foundry data; refractory materials; fuels; controlled atmospheres for heat treatment; masers and lasers; guide to the corrosion resistance of metals; electroplating and metal finishing; welding; and solders and brazing alloys. This is a necessity for any collection dealing with metals or materials science.

1672.   **Ullmann's Encyclopedia of Industrial Chemistry.** 5th ed. rev. Gerhartz, Wolfgang, et al., eds. Weinheim, West Germany: VCH Verlagsgesellschaft, 1985. 594p.

The fifth edition is the first edition of *Ullmanns Encyklopaedie der Technischen Chemie* (see entry 1673) translated and printed in English. More emphasis has been placed on the topics of biotechnology, microelectronics, pharmacology, materials science, and the need to protect the environment, workers, and the present and future generations from hazardous chemicals and processes. It is highly recommended even if the German version is also owned.

1673. **Ullmanns Encyklopaedie der Technischen Chemie.** 4th ed. Weinheim, West Germany: Verlag Chemie, 1982. 25v.
This is an outstanding encyclopedia which covers all areas of chemical technology. Each of the volumes is a complete encyclopedia of a particular segment of chemical technology. It is highly recommended for research and other collections where professionals and researchers are the primary users.

1674. **Wiley Encyclopedia of Packaging Technology.** Bakker, Marilyn, and David Eckroth, eds. New York: Wiley, 1986. 746p.
Signed articles on a broad range of packaging technology are contained in this illustrated encyclopedia. Bibliographies are provided. Overall, this is a very good encyclopedia with good technical detail.

DICTIONARIES

1675. **Chemical Synonyms and Trade Names: A Dictionary and Commercial Handbook Containing over 35,500 Definitions.** 8th ed. rev. Gardner, William, and Edward I. Cooke. Oxford, England: Technical Press, 1978. 769p.
This is an alphabetical listing of chemical terms and proprietary trade names. This work accomplishes two things: first, it serves as a dictionary of terms relating to chemical technology; second, it acts as an index to trade names, relating them to companies. This work will find use by a wide range of persons needing information on chemical technology both in general and in particular.

1676. **Dictionary of Ceramic Science and Engineering.** O'Bannon, Loran S. New York: Plenum, 1984. 302p.
A comprehensive overview of the terminology in the field, including such areas as white wares, structural clay products, refractories, cement and concrete, glass, ceramic-metal systems, piezo-electrics, electronics, nuclear energy, aerospace, and lasers.

1677. **Dictionary of Drying.** Hall, Carl W. New York: Dekker, 1979. 350p.
This dictionary is based on the literature in the field and the experience of the author. It is cross-referenced with 4,000 entries and contains a list of 75 English-language monographs published since 1950. Among key features are tables, charts, line drawings, evaluations of energy use, descriptions of drying processes, and conversion tables.

1678. **Dictionary of Nutrition and Food Technology.** 5th ed. Bender, Arnold E. London: Butterworths, 1982. 309p.
Contains approximately 3,000 briefly defined terms for food chemists and public health workers. It is recommended for academic and research collections, though some public collections will find this useful as well.

1679.   **Elsevier's Dictionary of Chemical Engineering.** Clason, W. E. Amsterdam, Nether-lands: Elsevier, 1968. 2v.

This multilingual dictionary is arranged by the English term followed by correspond-ing French, Spanish, Italian, Dutch, and German terms. The coverage of the work is very broad, including fields such as agricultural chemistry, inorganic industrial chemistry, bacteriological chemistry, chromatography, conserving industry, dairy industry, dyeing and printing, electrochemistry, fuels, and the petroleum industry. It is recommended for most collections. Care should be taken not to use this as a state-of-the-art reference source, however.

1680.   **Elsevier's Dictionary of Metallurgy and Metal Working in Six Languages: English/ American, French, Spanish, Italian, Dutch, and German.** Clason, W. E., comp. Amster-dam, Netherlands: Elsevier, 1978. 848p.

This is an admirable attempt to standardize the nomenclature in the metallurgical world. It is arranged by the English terms with the other languages following. This is a good dictionary and one which will be well used by a variety of persons from the novice through the professional engineer.

1681.   **Encyclopedic Dictionary of Industrial Technology: Materials, Processes, and Equipment.** Tver, David F., and Roger W. Bolz. New York: Chapman & Hall, 1984. 353p.

The short entry dictionary format of this source makes it suitable for ready reference. A select bibliography concludes the work. Recommended for virtually any collection with an interest in technology.

1682.   **Fairchild's Dictionary of Textiles.** 6th ed. Wingate, Isabel B. New York: Fairchild, 1979. 691p.

This updated edition provides expanded coverage and includes definitions relating to textile technology, electronic equipment, methods of dyeing, printing, and finishing fabrics. It also contains an annotated list of trade associations and institutes. Recom-mended for all types of libraries.

1683.   **Handbook of Oil Industry Terms and Phrases.** 4th ed. Langenkamp, R. D., ed. Tulsa, OK: Pennwell Publishing, 1984. 347p.

A listing of oil industry terms from the areas of personnel, equipment, and techniques, along with terms from other areas. This work provides a basic limited knowledge of the oil industry. It is an excellent dictionary, misnamed as a handbook.

1684.   **Illustrated Petroleum Reference Dictionary.** 3rd ed. Langenkamp, Robert D., ed. Tulsa, OK: Pennwell Books, 1985. 695p.

Included in the more than 3,000 entries are Gerolde's Universal Conversion Factors and Club's Abbreviations. This is an excellent source of information and is highly recom-mended for technology collections of all sorts.

1685.   **Industrial Engineering Terminology: A Revision, Consolidation, and Redesigna-tion of ANSI Z94 Index and ANSI Z94.1-12.** Norcross, GA: Institute of Industrial Engineers, 1983. 398p.

This is the official compilation of the definitions adopted by the Z94 Committee of the American National Standards Institute (ANSI). Though there may be some difficulty in using it, all libraries with an interest in industrial engineering should consider it a necessity.

1686. **Macmillan Dictionary of Biotechnology.** Coombs, J. London: Macmillan, 1986. 330p.

Cross-referenced and illustrated, this is a very well done dictionary in a fast-moving field. It is highly recommended for most collections wishing to stay current in this field.

1687. **Paint Coatings Dictionary.** Philadelphia: Federation of Societies for Coatings Technology, 1978. 613p.

This is a highly recommended dictionary of paints and coatings. It is a professional source and will find greatest use in specific and specialized collections.

1688. **Textile Terms and Definitions.** 8th ed. Manchester, England: The Textile Institute, 1986. 297p.

Describes the ways terms are now used in the textile industry. It contains very short entries with illustrations but no bibliography. Recommended for specialized collections only because of the British slant.

1689. **Thesaurus of Metallurgical Terms.** 7th ed. Metals Park, OH: ASM International, 1986. 169p.

Serves as the vocabulary authority for *Metals Abstracts and Index* (see entry 1636). It includes some 9,000 terms and is also useful in the *Alloys Index* (Metals Park, OH: ASM International, 1974-) classification scheme. The vocabulary for indexing and retrieving technical information in metallurgy, particularly the appropriate databases, is contained within. This is a valuable tool for the online information searcher.

1690. **Whittington's Dictionary of Plastics.** 2nd ed. Whittington, Lloyd R. Westport, CT: Technomic, 1978. 344p.

Sponsored by the Society of Plastics Engineers, this work includes developments in polymers, processing methods, and applications. Terms are mostly related to toxicity, ecological impact, flammability, and other safety aspects. Not an overly technical work, it is recommended for all technical collections.

HANDBOOKS

1691. **Adhesives Handbook.** 3rd ed. Shields, J. London: Butterworths, 1985. 358p.

This handbook fills a need for locating information on adhesives. It describes processes of bonding and provides a glossary and a comprehensive reference. It is highly recommended for specific and specialized collections.

1692. **ASM Metals Reference Book.** 2nd ed. Metals Park, OH: ASM International, 1983. 560p.

An expansion of the first edition which was designed as a first-stop source for metals data. Data on the elements and the compositions and properties of the major industrial alloys were consolidated. The second edition has been expanded to include information on processing and on the elements and conversion factors, plus testing and inspection. This is a required source for any collection dealing with metallurgy or materials science.

1693. **Atlas of Fatigue Curves.** Boyer, Howard E., ed. Metals Park, OH: ASM International, 1986. 518p.

More than 500 fatigue curves are given for ferrous and nonferrous alloys, and complete references are given to the literature from which the curve was extracted. This will save the engineer considerable time and effort and is highly recommended for both research and development collections.

1694. **Case Hardening of Steel.** ASM International. Metals Park, OH: ASM International, 1987. 319p.

This work discusses various methods currently in use for case hardening of steel. The first part of the book gives some background information and data on the hardening process in general. The second half delves into specific topics. This is highly recommended as a technical source for heat treating of steel.

1695. **Chemical and Process Plant: A Guide to the Selection of Engineering Materials.** 2nd ed. Evans, Lee S. New York: Wiley, 1980. 190p.

A guide to materials useful in the construction and maintenance of process plants. It is recommended for technical collections and for working collections in the chemical engineering sector.

TP151
.P45
1984
Sci
Ref

1696. **Chemical Engineer's Handbook.** 6th ed. Perry, Robert H., and Cecil H. Chilton, eds. New York: McGraw-Hill, 1984. 1v. (various paging).

This is a handbook for experts, created by experts. The material in this handbook is broken into several sections, each complete in itself. This is a classic handbook for chemical engineers and is used both as a desk reference as well as a ready reference tool in engineering collections. A necessity for any engineering collection dealing with chemical engineering.

1697. **Chemical Formulary.** New York: Chemical Publishing, 1933- .

This is a classic source for chemical information. The information it contains spans the entire chemical engineering field. It touches on topics from the treatment of materials and products to the individual chemical compounds for a particular product. The introduction always contains information on chemical apparatus, methodologies, and cost factors. An especially interesting feature is the information on preparation of home products. This source will find use in any collection, including some school collections. It is highly recommended for virtually any collection.

1698. **Chemical Technicians' Ready Reference Handbook.** 2nd ed. Shugar, Gershon J., et al. New York: McGraw-Hill, 1981. 867p.

This is a reference handbook for chemical technicians. It contains formulas, equations, principles, and methods needed for all laboratory procedures, and provides materials and information on toxic vapors, compressed gases, and cleaning glassware. A recommended reference for all chemists and chemical laboratory technicians.

1699. **Compendium of Safety Data Sheets for Research and Industrial Chemicals.** Keith, Lawrence H., and Douglas B. Walters, eds. Deerfield Beach, FL: VCH, 1985. 3v.

This work provides in a single source the most commonly sought and useful information for safety oriented needs involving chemicals of both research and industry. It is listed alphabetically by compound followed by a description of characteristics.

1700. **Composite Materials Handbook.** Schwartz, M. M. New York: McGraw-Hill, 1984. 651p.

A practical handbook on the topics of resin and metal matrix materials, mostly at the macrostructure level. It contains extensive illustrations and charts, with a useful glossary and index as well. Valuable to working engineers.

1701. **Composites.** Metals Park, OH: ASM International, 1987. 925p.

This is a practical handbook. The focus is directed more toward problem solving and less toward theory. Beginning with constituent materials and ranging through the manufacturing process and applications, this is the largest single volume of information on composites published. It is an authoritative source and highly recommended for any technically oriented collection.

1702. **Condensed Silica Fume in Concrete.** Malhotra, V. M., et al., eds. Boca Raton, FL: CRC Press, 1987. 256p.

This is a balanced view of the effect of condensed silica fume on the range of concrete products such as concrete paste, mortar, and concrete. The nature and types of condensed silica fumes are discussed as well as handling and transportation problems. This is a very specific handbook for specific applications and is recommended for special collections.

1703. **Construction Materials: Types, Uses and Applications.** Hornbostel, Caleb. New York: Wiley, 1978. 878p.

Alphabetically arranged, this volume contains much information on construction materials. Aspects of construction materials are discussed under such topics as physical and chemical properties, history, and manufacturing.

1704. **Corrosion-Resistant Materials Handbook.** 4th ed. De Renzo, D. J., ed. Park Ridge, NJ: Noyes Data Corp., 1985. 965p.

This was designed as an aid in choosing suitable, commercially available corrosion resistant materials for a particular application. It contains 160 tables arranged by types of corrosion resistant materials. Corrosive material index, trade name index, and company name and address listing are included.

1705. **CRC Handbook of Food Additives.** 2nd ed. Furia, Thomas E., ed. Boca Raton, FL: CRC Press, 1980. 2v.

Covers various data on additives based on FDA standards. Each chapter, written by chemists, includes definitions, chemical properties and reactions, representative uses, and safety inhibitors. Also included is a guide to current regulations for frequently used additives. This is an excellent tool for those in food sciences and chemical engineering.

1706. **CRC Handbook of Materials Science.** Lynch, Charles T., ed. Boca Raton, FL: CRC Press, 1974- . 4v.

Volume 1 is entitled *General Properties*; volume 2, *Metals, Composites, and Refractory Materials*; volume 3, *Non-Metallic Materials and Applications*; and volume 4, *Wood*. This is a readily accessible guide to the physical properties of solid state and structural materials. Interdisciplinary in approach and content, it covers a broad variety of types of materials. This is a classic source of information and a necessity for any collection in materials engineering.

1707. **CRC Handbook of Nutritive Value of Processed Food.** Rechcigl, Miloslav, ed. Boca Raton, FL: CRC Press, 1982. 2v.

This two-volume set explores various processing methods and their effects on the nutritive value of food for human and animal feedstuffs. It contains extensive illustrations and tables, and is recommended for any food sciences collection as well as general reference collections in public and academic libraries.

1708.　**CRC Handbook of Solubility Parameters and Other Cohesion Parameters.** Barton, Allan F. Boca Raton, FL: CRC Press, 1983. 608p.

This is a comprehensive source on solubility parameter values and their application for a wide range of scientists and technologists concerned with polymers, plasticizers, solvents, pigments, paints, dyes, lubricants, adhesives, and biocompatible materials. It is a very complete source and is highly recommended for any research collection.

1709.　**Dangerous Properties of Industrial Materials.** 6th ed. Sax, N. Irving, et al. New York: Van Nostrand Reinhold, 1984. 3124p.

This is a highly recommended source for information on industrial and laboratory materials. In addition to the individual listings, information is given on the hazards each chemical may present to humans and animals. An alphabetical listing of compounds and formulas is provided. This is a useful source for any public or academic collection dealing with chemistry.

1710.　**Elementary Engineering Fracture Mechanics.** 4th ed. Broek, David. Norwell, MA: Martinus Nijhoff, 1986. 501p.

As the title suggests, this handbook concentrates on the application of fracture mechanics to simple and practical problems. This edition includes newer material such as the J-integral as an energy concept and fatigue crack propagation material. This will be useful to both the beginning engineer or engineering student as well as the professional. It is highly recommended.

1711.　**E/MJ Operating Handbook of Mineral Surface Mining and Exploration.** Hoppe, Richard, ed. New York: McGraw-Hill, 1978. 450p.

A reference handbook of the methods, applications, tools, discoveries, and problems of surface mining. Useful in a variety of settings, it is recommended for some public and most academic collections with an interest in mining engineering.

1712.　**Encyclopedia/Handbook of Materials, Parts, and Finishes.** Clauser, Henry R., ed. Westport, CT: Technomic, 1976. 564p.

This is a concise source of information on thousands of industrial materials. It lists generic name and describes chemical and engineering properties. Much information is brought together in one volume. Designed for engineers, designers, and chemists, this source should be used with care due to its age; however, it retains its value in those things in the industry which have not changed.

1713.　**Engineering Properties of Steel.** Harvey, Philip D., ed. Metals Park, OH: ASM International, 1982. 527p.

Presents data for carbon, alloy, stainless, and heat resisting, tool, ASTM structural, and managing steels. Also included are the chemical composition, general characteristics and uses, mechanical properties, and machining data for many steels used in industrial applications. This is an excellent tool for professional collections.

1714.　**Engineers' Guide to Composite Materials.** Weeton, John W., ed. Metals Park, OH: ASM International, 1986. 388p.

This is an essential reference tool for anyone engaged in materials science engineering. The primary format is tabular and graphic with a minimum of text. An excellent source for serious engineers.

1715. Equipment Design Handbook for Refineries and Chemical Plants. 2nd ed. Evans, Frank L. Houston, TX: Gulf Publishing, 1980. 2v.

Contains practical information for the design engineer interested in oil refining and chemical industries. It is broadly divided into five sections: drivers, compressors, ejectors, pumps, and refrigeration. Volume 2 covers nonrotating equipment. Consisting of very specific information for design engineers, this source is recommended for technical collections in academic and professional collections.

1716. Fabric Almanac. 2nd ed. Klapper, M. New York: Fairchild, 1971. 191p.

This almanac contains an introduction to textiles in the 1970s. It includes key industry statistics as well as fabric glossary, principal U.S. man-made fibers and their uses, natural fibers and their sources. Though this is a good source, it should not be used for state-of-the-art information. Included here because some fabrics have not changed.

1717. Field Metallography, Failure Analysis and Metallurgy. Blum, M. E., et al., eds. Metals Park, OH: ASM International, 1987. 600p.

The editors have gathered experts in a variety of fields related to microstructural topics. The result is a compendium of 42 papers covering a wide range of topics of interest to those actively engaged in research and development in microstructural components. This is a very technical series of papers of greatest interest to technicians and professional engineers.

1718. Finishing Handbook and Directory. 35th ed. Davies, M. A. S., ed. London: Sawell Publications, 1985. 519p.

A useful handbook and directory dealing with varied aspects of metal, wood, and plastic finishing; electroplating and processes; paint application; and drying equipment. Will be useful in public, academic, and technical collections.

1719. Fluid Flow Pocket Handbook. Cheremisinoff, Nicholas P. Houston, TX: Gulf Publishing, 1984. 199p.

A useful tool for engineers, technicians, and students on the flow of gas and liquids. It contains ten sections on physical properties, governing equations of flow, pipe flow calculations, gas flow calculations, discharge through variable head meters, flow through coils and around tubes, channel flows, two-phase flows, gas-solid flows, and pump calculations. Tables, figures, references, glossary, and a brief index are included. This is highly recommended for technical and professional collections.

1720. Food Industries Manual. 21st ed. Ranken, M. D., ed. Glascow, Scotland: Leonard Hill, 1984. 530p.

A comprehensive work of food processing and handling, this new edition adds coffee, tea, cocoa, and snack foods to the already established fields of meat products, fats, fruit juices, pickles and sauces, and nutrition. A standard work in Britain.

1721. Formulary of Paints and Other Coatings. Ash, Michael, and Irene Ash, comps. New York: Chemical Publishing, 1978- . irregular.

Deals with paints and finishes, providing specific lists of ingredients and formulas. It is well arranged for easy access to information, and is considered to be an important addition to the chemical literature. Recommended for all special, engineering, and research libraries.

1722.   **Guide to Materials Engineering Data and Information.** Metals Park, OH: ASM International, 1986. 1v. (various paging).
This is an excellent ready-reference guide to questions related to metals or materials science. It does not have the depth of *Metals Handbook* (see entry 1757), but it is easy to use with clear and concise information. Additional sections include a style manual, lists of reference works and journals, and a history of metallurgy. Highly recommended as a ready-reference tool in any collection dealing with metals or materials science.

1723.   **Handbook of Adhesives.** 2nd ed. Skeist, Irving, ed. New York: Van Nostrand Reinhold, 1977. 921p.
This is a broadly based handbook on all aspects of adhesives. It contains descriptions of important adhesive materials and their applications. A glossary and bibliography round out the work. This is recommended for most technical collections, but with some caution due to the date.

1724.   **Handbook of Analysis of Synthetic Polymers and Plastics.** Urbanski, Jerzy, et al. New York: Halsted, 1977. 494p.
Details the analysis of synthetic polymers and plastics. It is divided into two parts: instrumental and conventional methods of analysis, and analysis of individual polymers. Although it does not contain the most up-to-date information, it does bring together methodologies in one place.

1725.   **Handbook of Chemical Engineering Calculations.** Chopey, Nicholas P., ed. New York: McGraw-Hill, 1984. 1v. (various paging).
An extension of the *Standard Handbook of Engineering Calculations* (see entry 1177), this handbook is a helpful aid in solving the main process related problems that occur in chemical engineering practice. An excellent tool even if the larger handbook is also owned.

1726.   **Handbook of Chemistry Specialties: Textile Fiber Processing, Preparation and Bleaching.** Nettles, J. E. New York: Wiley, 1983. 467p.
This reference source contains a review of the chemistry and technology of compounds used in textiles processing. It is very logical and informative in its presentation. Recommended only for technical collections.

1727.   **Handbook of Composites.** Lubin, George, ed. New York: Van Nostrand Reinhold, 1982. 786p.
This handbook has been compiled to help the reader understand composite materials and their characteristics, design, and applications. It is arranged into four sections: raw materials, processing methods, design, and application. Highly recommended for any materials science collection.

1728.   **Handbook of Compressed Gases.** 2nd ed. New York: Van Nostrand Reinhold, 1981. 507p.
Provides basic information about compressed gases, their transportation, uses, safety considerations and rules, and regulations pertaining to them. It should be a very valuable tool for technical collections.

1729.   **Handbook of Dimensional Measurement.** 2nd ed. Farago, Francis T. New York: Industrial Press, 1982. 524p.
Contains practical information on the methods and equipment of measurement for modern industrial production. Numerous tables with diagrammatic illustrations facilitate ready reference. Highly recommended for virtually any collection with technical leanings.

1730. **Handbook of Essential Formulae and Data on Heat Transfer for Engineers.** Wong, H. Y. London: Longman, 1977. 236p.

A summary handbook of heat transfer data. This is an excellent handbook and one which will find great use in design and production engineering collections.

1731. **Handbook of Fillers and Reinforcements for Plastics.** Katz, Harry S., and J. V. Milewski, eds. New York: Van Nostrand Reinhold, 1978. 652p.

A compilation of useful and valuable information which contains contributions from 30 experts. Recommended for technical collections dealing with plastics.

1732. **Handbook of Industrial Engineering.** Salvendy, Gavriel, ed. New York: Wiley, 1982. 1v. (various paging).

Contains articles written by hundreds of experts in the application of theory of industrial engineering to real life situations. Provides a source of ideas for improvement in organization and design, planning and control, ergonomics, and performance measurements. This is an excellent handbook for any technical collection.

1733. **Handbook of Materials Handling.** Swedish Research Commission. New York: Halsted, 1985. 286p.

An excellent handbook outlining and detailing the handling of materials on both large and small scales. Recommended for any materials science collection.

TS180
M3413
1985
Sci

1734. **Handbook of Metal Forming.** Lange, Kurt, ed. New York: McGraw-Hill, 1985. 1232p.

Contains state-of-the-art information on metallurgy, tribology, material properties and process data, while concentrating on the metal forming process as a system. This is a thorough handbook and is highly recommended.

1735. **Handbook of Metal Treatments and Testing.** Ross, Robert B. New York: Wiley, 1977. 467p.

Describes and defines some 1,000 processes and testing methods in metallurgy. Due to the age, it is recommended with caution to practicing engineers and industrial libraries.

1736. **Handbook of Package Engineering.** 2nd ed. Hanlon, Joseph F. New York: McGraw-Hill, 1984. 1v. (various paging).

A one-volume handbook with extensive information on all types of materials used in packaging. Well indexed and illustrated, it is recommended for any engineering collection.

1737. **Handbook of Plastics and Elastomers.** Harper, Charles A., ed. New York: McGraw-Hill, 1975. 1v. (various paging).

This is a dated handbook which is still in wide use by a variety of engineers. Its ability to appear timeless is due to the encyclopedic manner in which the handbook approaches the plastics industry. Although an update is needed, this will continue to be of use to a wide variety of engineers involved in this industry.

1738. **Handbook of Powder Science and Technology.** Fayed, M. E., and L. Otten, eds. New York: Van Nostrand Reinhold, 1984. 850p.

Compiled from the contributions of experts in the field, this handbook consists of 19 chapters, each individually authored, covering particle size to production. It is highly recommended for collections in the materials science area.

1739. **Handbook of Reactive Chemical Hazards.** 3rd ed. Bretherick, L. London: Butterworths, 1985. 1852p.

Arranged by compound, this handbook gives the researcher prior knowledge of potentially dangerous situations either in the laboratory or elsewhere. It is not as well known or well used as *Dangerous Properties of Industrial Materials* (see entry 1709), but contains essentially the same information for a smaller subset of materials.

1740. **Handbook of Stainless Steels.** Peckner, Donald, and I. M. Bernstein, eds. New York: McGraw-Hill, 1977. 928p.

Presents data on corrosive metals, including areas such as metallurgy, physical characteristics, and machining. Extensive references are provided, as well as over 740 illustrations. This is a good source for the engineer involved in fabrication of stainless steels.

1741. **Handbook of Textile Fibers, Dyes, and Finishes.** Needles, Howard L. New York: Garland STPM Press, 1981. 170p.

This is an introductory reference to basic properties of textile fibers, dyes, and finishes. It is not as complete as *Handbook of Textile Fibres* (see entry 1742), but it was designed to be introductory and not to provide a full treatment of the field. Recommended as an introductory handbook for college and some academic collections.

1742. **Handbook of Textile Fibres.** 5th ed. Cook, J. Gordon. Shildon, England: Merrow, 1984. 2v.

Volume 1 is entitled *Natural Fibres*, and volume 2, *Man-made Fibres*. The emphasis is on production and use. Natural polymer fibers and fibers from synthetic polymers are discussed in detail. Included is a directory of man-made fibers in which general class and manufacturer are given. This is a very complete handbook in the textile area.

1743. **Handbook of Water-Soluble Gums and Resins.** Davidson, Robert L., ed. New York: McGraw-Hill, 1980. 700p.

Written by leading experts in the field of hydrogels, this handbook was designed as a supplement to the *Encyclopedia of Polymer Science and Engineering* (see entry 1663); each chapter covers one type of synthetic or natural gum or resin. Chapters include general information, uses, formulations, trade names, laboratory techniques, and supplementary reading lists. Graphs, tables, diagrams, black-and-white photographs, and an index are also provided. This is an excellent piece of work and is highly recommended.

1744. **Hardness Testing.** Metals Park, OH: ASM International, 1987. 200p.

This is a practical handbook dealing with all aspects of hardness testing. It consists of eight chapters which present an excellent guide for anyone working in this area. Recommended for working collections as well as research collections.

1745. **High-Temperature Property Data: Ferrous Alloys.** Rothman, M. F., ed. Metals Park, OH: ASM International, 1987. 550p.

Organizes information by alloy, then lists physical and mechanical properties from room temperature to 1000°C of the various alloys. The alloys are arranged in AISI order. This is an excellent technical source of information and will be highly regarded by technicians and scientists alike.

1746. **Identification of Textile Materials.** 7th ed. rev. Manchester, England: Textile Institute, 1975. 262p.

This is a working tool for the laboratory testing that leads to identification of unknown fibers. Also provided are a glossary and an introductory description of the textile fibers available commercially. This is an excellent source of information on techniques. It is, however, only a starting point due to its age.

1747. **Industrial Hazard and Safety Handbook.** 3rd rev. impression. King, Ralph W., and J. Magid. London: Butterworths, 1982. 793p.

A practical reference work for industrial and safety engineers, this handbook contains concise information and useful tables. The emphasis is British. Recommended for research collections.

1748. **Industrial Lubrication: A Practical Handbook for Lubrication and Production Engineers.** Billett, Michael. New York: Pergamon, 1979. 136p.

Contains practical information on lubrication. Stresses safety factors, selection, care, storage, and evaluation. Ample illustrations are provided. Suitable for engineers and practitioners.

1749. **Industrial Safety Handbook.** 2nd ed. Handley, William, ed. New York: McGraw-Hill, 1977. 480p.

The handbook contains important information on the prevention of accidents in the workplace. Covering all pertinent issues, it is an informative guide for anyone concerned with the health and safety of workers. This is supplemented by the British safety handbook, *Industrial Hazard and Safety Handbook* (see entry 1747).

1750. **Industrial Solvents Handbook.** 3rd ed. Flick, Ernest W., ed. Park Ridge, NJ: Noyes, 1985. 648p.

Contains tables of basic data on the physical properties of most solvents and on the solubilities of a variety of materials in these solvents. Data has been extracted from manufacturers' literature and deals with hydrocarbon solvents, halogenated hydrocarbons, nitroparaffins, organic sulfur compounds, monohydric alcohols, polyhydric alcohols, phenols, aldehydes, ethers, glycol ethers, ketones, acids, amines, and esters. Phase diagrams for multicomponent systems are included. The table of contents serves as an index and is organized by chemical group.

1751. **International Plastics Handbook.** 2nd ed. Saechtling, H. New York: Macmillan, 1987. 600p.

This well-organized and compact collection of information on plastics covers the entire area of the plastics industry. This is highly recommended for any technical collection.

1752. **Machinery's Handbook: A Reference Book of the Mechanical Engineer, Draftsman, Toolmaker, and Machinist.** 22nd ed. Obert, Erik, Franklin Jones, and Holbrook Horton. New York: Industrial Press, 1984. 2512p.

The emphasis is on practicality and the design and repair of production machinery. This edition stresses metric standards and is highly recommended for anyone specifying machinery or designing machinery for production purposes.

1753. **Maintenance Engineering Handbook.** 4th ed. Higgins, Lindley R., ed. New York: McGraw-Hill, 1987. 1152p.

A basic reference on general maintenance of industrial plants. Includes new material on pollution control equipment, fuel conservation, and plant security. Contains tables, charts, and graphs as well as topical glossaries and a detailed index. This is an excellent handbook, recommended for those in production engineering who deal with equipment maintenance.

1754. **Materials Handbook: An Encyclopedia for Managers, Technical Professionals, Purchasing and Production Managers, Technicians, Supervisors, and Foremen.** 12th ed. Brady, George S., and Henry R. Clauser. New York: McGraw-Hill, 1986. 1038p.

A standard handbook listing over 13,000 industrial materials and substances. Includes chemicals, fuels, minerals, textiles, foodstuffs, synthetics, and provides details on composition, characteristics, uses, and trade names. It is a recommended reference for engineers, technicians, and purchasing managers.

1755. **Materials Handling Handbook.** 2nd ed. Kulwiecv, Raymond A., ed. New York: Wiley, 1985. 1458p.

This comprehensive work on materials handling engineering is an excellent choice for a materials science collection.

1756. **Metallic Materials Specification Handbook.** 3rd ed. Ross, Robert B. London: Spon, 1980. 793p.

Classified according to chemical analysis, this handbook contains trade names, specifications, or symbols relating to metals. It assists in providing an alternative list of materials for consideration.

TN671
.A4
Sci Ref

1757. **Metals Handbook.** 9th ed. Metals Park, OH: ASM International, 1961- . 13v.

This is a definitive handbook on metals. First published in 1927, it continues to include all materials that a metallurgist would find necessary. The coverage is complete within the confines of metals. The emphasis of this edition is on SI units. This would be a necessity for any metallurgical collection.

1758. **Metals Handbook Comprehensive Index.** 2nd ed. Metals Park, OH: ASM International, 1987. 664p.

This is a quick and convenient index to the *Metals Handbook* (see entry 1757). It saves the user from checking in individual indexes for each of the volumes in *Metals Handbook*. If the *Metals Handbook* is a part of the collection, this index should be included as well.

1759. **Metals Handbook, Desk Edition.** Metals Park, OH: ASM International, 1985. 1376p.

This is an abbreviated form of *Metals Handbook* (see entry 1757). It is an excellent tool for those who have need of quick information or information that is less in-depth than that available in the *Metals Handbook*. Highly recommended for ready-reference collections.

1760. **Metals Reference Book.** 5th ed. Smithells, Colin J., ed. London: Butterworths, 1976. 1566p.

A good source, though not as complete in several areas as *Metals Handbook* (see entry 1757). This is in some ways a more manageable handbook. It is complete in terms of its scope, and therefore is recommended for any metallurgical collection.

1761. **Microemulsions: Structure and Dynamics.** Friberg, Stig E., and Pierre Bothorel, eds. Boca Raton, FL: CRC Press, 1987. 256p.

This is a state-of-the-art review of microemulsion systems. The international set of experts gathered by the editors have made this an excellent work. It is recommended for any collection in materials science and a number of other related areas.

1762. **Non-Ferrous Metals Data, 1983.** New York: American Bureau of Metal Statistics, 1984. 150p.

Consists of statistical tables relating to the production, consumption, imports, exports, and prices of nonferrous metals. Also includes miscellaneous tables on exchange rates, equivalents, and stockpile materials. This is a valuable addition for business and economics libraries.

1763. **Paint Handbook.** Weismantel, Guy E., ed. New York: McGraw-Hill, 1981. 1v. (various paging).

Contains practical information on specifying paints and coatings. The emphasis of this work is on industrial and architectural coatings. It does not deal with theory, and instead focuses on practical orientation. More information is contained here than in *Paints and Coatings Handbook* (see entry 1764). The basic information, however, is the same.

1764. **Paints and Coatings Handbook for Contractors, Architects, Builders, and Engineers.** 2nd ed. Banov, Abel. New York: McGraw-Hill, 1982. 432p.

A basic reference source on paints and coatings. It contains illustrations and an index. This is a practical handbook for use in the field and in writing specifications. It should be a part of any architectural and chemical engineering collection.

1765. **Pearson's Handbook of Crystallographic Data for Inter-Metallic Phases.** Villars, P., and L. D. Calvert. Metals Park, OH: ASM International, 1985. 3v.

Compiles data from the international literature from 1913-1982 and partially from 1983-1984, summarizing the contents of over 21,000 publications. The aim is simplicity. Arguments for inclusion of chemical information such as "Types" and "Anti-Types" have been resisted. This is an excellent technical handbook of use to professionals and technicians.

1766. **Perry's Chemical Engineers' Handbook.** 6th ed. Perry, Robert H., and Don W. Green, eds. New York: McGraw-Hill, 1984. 1v. (various paging).

Each of the 25 sections has been updated and revised. SI units have been featured alongside the conventional. Two new sections entitled "Bio-engineering" and "Waste Management" have been added. This is a good handbook and recommended for most chemical engineering collections.

1767. **Petroleum Processing Handbook.** Bland, William F., and Robert L. Davidson. New York: McGraw-Hill, 1973. 1v. (various paging).

Contains practical information on processing of crude petroleum into marketable commodities. The scope of the work is very broad, consisting of evaluation of crude oils through plant processes and environmental concerns. This is a handbook that, despite its age, is still in use. It should be revised, but also should be a part of any chemical engineering collection.

1768. **Plant Engineers' and Managers' Guide to Energy Conservation.** 3rd ed. Thumann, Albert. Lilburn, GA: Fairmount Press, 1986. 1v. (various paging).

A comprehensive, though not overly detailed, guide to energy management in plants. It contains much practical advice and suggests means of energy cost reduction.

1769. **Polymer Handbook.** 2nd ed. Brandrup, J., and E. H. Immergut, eds. New York: Wiley-Interscience, 1975. 1v. (various paging).

Gives basic data and references on the physical and chemical properties of polymers. Nomenclature, polymerization, solutions, and solid state properties and constants are included. This is a good reference work, but is not an up-to-date source.

TP1087
E46
1985
SciRef

1770. **Polymers: An Encyclopedia Sourcebook of Engineering Properties.** Kroschwitz, Jacqueline I., ed. New York: Wiley, 1987. 665p.

This is a reprint of entries from the *Encyclopedia of Polymer Science and Engineering* (see entry 1663). In effect, this reprint pulls together the data found throughout the larger work. It has a good subject index and the actual text has a large number of cross-references. Highly recommended both for professional and academic collections.

1771. **Pump Handbook.** 2nd ed. Karassik, Igor J., et al., eds. New York: McGraw-Hill, 1986. 1v. (various paging).

This work deals with types of pumps by discussing theory, construction, and performance characteristics. Centrifugal, power, steam, screw and rotary, jet, and other types are discussed within the framework above. In addition, pump components such as couplings, controls, valves, and the instruments used in pumping systems are covered. Evaluation and maintenance are also discussed. This is highly recommended for any collection that is a working technical collection or a research collection.

1772. **Rare Metals Handbook.** 2nd ed. Hampel, Clifford A., ed. Huntington, NY: Krieger, 1971. 715p.

This work deals with the 55 metals classified as rare. There is a good discussion of the availability, processing, and physical properties of these metals. Although the age of the work is a problem, the subject is not as volatile as other types of information. It is recommended for research collections in metallurgy.

TP145
.R54
1983
Sci
Ref

1773. **Riegel's Handbook of Industrial Chemistry.** 8th ed. Kent, James A., ed. New York: Van Nostrand Reinhold, 1983. 979p.

Though titled as a handbook, this is a review of the chemical processing industry. It is closer to a methodological review or treatise than a handbook. The topics include industrial chemistry, air pollution control, and wastewater technology. Written by experts in the field, this is a valuable source of information on current technologies in the chemical industry. It is highly recommended for either working or research collections.

1774. **Science and Technology of Tributyl Phosphate.** Schultz, Wallace W., and James D. Navratil, eds. Boca Raton, FL: CRC Press, 1986. 2v.

This source discusses the important applications and uses of tributyl phosphate (TBP). Special attention is paid to the hydro-metallurgical uses. The strength of the work is that it goes beyond the traditional uses of TBP in reprocessing of nuclear fuels. This is a technical handbook for technicians and experts in the field.

1775. **Smithell's Metals Reference Handbook.** 6th ed. Brandes, Eric A., ed. London: Butterworths, 1983. 1v. (various paging).

This is a convenient summary of data relating to metallurgy. It is one volume, packed with 36 chapters. SI units are used throughout. The chapter on vapor deposited coatings and the tables on superplasticity are especially good. This is highly recommended.

1776. **Source Book for Food Scientists.** Ockerman, Herbert W. Westport, CT: Avi, 1978. 926p.

A compilation of facts and data relevant to food science and technology. It is divided into two parts: alphabetic descriptions of foods and food terms, and tables illustrating food composition and properties. Recommended for public, academic, and some school libraries.

1777. **Source Book on Industrial Alloy and Engineering Data: A Comprehensive Collection of Alloy and Engineering Data in Tabular and Graphical Form.** Metals Park, OH: ASM International, 1978. 469p.

This source book is divided into 10 sections covering such topics as carbon and alloy steels, tool steels, aluminum and aluminum alloys, and powder metal parts. Data are arranged in tabular and graphical form. An additional section of conversion tables is included. This is recommended for ready reference collections in academic and special libraries.

1778. **SPI Plastics Engineering Handbook.** 3rd ed. New York: Reinhold Book Corp., 1968. 565p.

This handbook covers major plastics processing methods and details properties, processing methods, and performance data. It is dated, but is still useful as background material in the plastics industry. Not recommended for research collections, it would be useful only to some industrial collections.

1779. **Standard Handbook of Machine Design.** Shigley, Joseph E., and Charles R. Misckhe, eds. New York: McGraw-Hill, 1986. 1v. (various paging).

This handbook connects formal education and the practice of design engineering by including the general knowledge required by every machine designer. It is a desktop reference for working engineers.

1780. **Standard Handbook of Plant Engineering.** Rosaler, Robert C., and James O. Rice, eds. New York: McGraw-Hill, 1983. 1v. (various paging).

Contains proven methods for achieving efficient, cost effective operations for planning, construction, and maintenance of plant facilities. Techniques and uses in energy conservation, pollution control, and data processing are included. This is a good basic handbook suitable for a variety of collections.

1781. **Standard Handbook of Textiles.** 8th ed. Hall, A. J. Broadway, NJ: Textile Book Service, 1975. 440p.

A basic, nontechnical reference that includes information from the viewpoint of both the manufacturer and the user. Many photographs and illustrations bearing on the conversion of textile fibers into textile materials are included. Recommended for basic collections in textile technology.

1782. **Technician's Handbook of Plastics.** Grandilli, Peter A. New York: Van Nostrand Reinhold, 1981. 246p.

A well written, technically accurate handbook containing the theory, practical application, and problems of the basic plastic processes of injection molding, blow molding, extrusion, compression, transfer molding, and a number of thermoset processes. It is highly recommended.

1783. **Thermoplastic Elastomers: A Comprehensive Review.** Legge, N. R., and G. Holden, eds. New York: Macmillan, 1987. 600p.

Brings together into one volume the current state-of-the-art reviews. It deals with description of polymers, chemical structure of polymers, molecular weights, processing, physical properties, and applications. A section dealing with future trends is included. This is recommended for any collection with research and development interests in this area.

1784. **Tool and Manufacturing Engineers Handbook: Vol. 3, Materials, Finishing, and Coating.** 4th ed. Wick, Charles, ed. Dearborn, MI: Society of Manufacturing Engineers, 1985. 1v. (various paging).

This new edition of a classic handbook covers all phases of manufacturing, planning, control, design, and tooling. It presents detailed information and practical data and techniques, and also contains metric conversion charts and information on new technology. For all engineering libraries.

1785. **Underground Mining Methods Handbook.** Hustrulid, W. A., ed. New York: American Institute of Mining, Metallurgical and Petroleum Engineers, 1982. looseleaf.

Emphasizes principles, estimation, and design guidelines and illustration through the use of practical examples. Costs are presented where applicable. Its eight sections generally cover mining methods, design, equipment, finance, foundations, and ventilation. This is recommended for working collections.

1786. **Understanding How Components Fail.** Wulpi, Donald J. Metals Park, OH: ASM International, 1985. 262p.

This is a practical and useful source of information on metal failure. It replaces the classic *How Components Fail* (Metals Park, OH: ASM International, 1966). This is an excellent desk reference and should be considered by any technical collection.

1787. **Welding Data Book.** Cleveland, OH: Industrial, 1958/59- . irregular.

This data book is divided into five sections. Section A is a directory of products and manufacturers; section B contains trade names; section C covers manufacturers' catalogs/ outlets; section D provides engineering and application data; and section E tells where to buy locally. This is very specific information of interest to welding engineers and research organizations.

1788. **Woldman's Engineering Alloys.** 6th ed. Gibbons, Robert C. Metals Park, OH: ASM International, 1979. 1815p.

This handbook puts information on over 45,000 alloys into one place. It lists commercial and engineering alloys produced both in the U.S. and abroad. Chemical composition, uses, manufacturers, and specific properties of each alloy are listed. This is an excellent source of technical information and is recommended for engineering, technical, and special collections.

DIRECTORIES

1789. **Chemical Engineering Faculties.** New York: American Institute of Chemical Engineers, 1951-52- . annual.

Includes both U.S. and foreign schools in 55 countries. Standard educational directory information is given, which includes, when available, the names and telephone numbers of faculty and types of degrees awarded. This is an excellent ready reference tool for any collection in engineering.

1790. **Cryogenics Handbook.** Law, Beverly, ed. Guilford, England: Westbury House, 1981. 423p.

This directory of companies and equipment suppliers in the cryogenics industry provides name, address, contact person, and description of the company. It also has an index of products and a partial list of international research projects. This is a good source for a fast-moving area.

1791. Directory of Food and Nutrition Information Services and Resources. Frank, Robyn C., ed. Phoenix, AZ: Oryx Press, 1984. 287p.

A directory of information services and resources on the subject, with emphasis on nutrition education, food science management, and aspects of applied nutrition. The largest part is a listing of organizations, with additional listings of 60 databases on food and nutrition, and microcomputer software programs. It is indexed by type of organization and geographic location. This is a good listing, but makes no critical differentiation.

1792. Directory of Industrial Heat-Processing and Combustion Equipment, United States Manufacturers: 1984. 4th ed. Miller, Richard K., ed. New York: Information Clearinghouse, 1984.

A source of technical information on all kinds of equipment, including furnaces, ovens, and kilns. Industrial heating and combustion systems are also covered.

1793. Handbook of Manufacturing Software: A Comprehensive Directory. Miller, Richard K., Kenneth A. Kovaly, and Terri Walker, eds. Madison, GA: SEAI Technical Publications, 1985. 176p.

Includes a brief overview of hardware and software for manufacturing applications. Nonevaluative descriptions of 502 software packages with prices are included.

1794. Illustrated Guide to Textiles. 4th ed. Joseph, Marjory L., and Audrey Gieseking. Canoga Park, CA: Plycon Press, 1986. 192p.

Designed to provide textile executives with a guide to sources of equipment, supplies, and services required today for the manufacturing of textiles. Includes 2,500 headings, 1,800 suppliers of one or more products, and 170 advertisements. Can be an invaluable source of specific manufacturer or textile information.

1795. Resume 1985: The Complete Annual Review of Oil and Gas Activity in the United States. Denver, CO: Petroleum Information Corporation, 1986. 259p.

This has been published in various formats since the 1920s and assumed its present form in 1978. Narrative overviews of the year's activity are combined with statistical data and comparisons, and detailed discovery well data. Cost estimates are provided. This is a very complete annual survey and is recommended for ready reference in any technical collection.

1796. Woldman's Engineering Alloys. 6th ed. Gibbons, Robert C., ed. Metals Park, OH: ASM International, 1979. 1815p.

This compilation of industrial alloys is arranged alphabetically by trade name. A list of producers is also given, as are chemical compositions and major uses. This is an excellent reference source.

1797. World Index of Strategic Minerals: Production, Exploitation, and Risk. Hargraves, D., and S. Fromson. New York: Facts on File, 1983. 300p.

Access to the contents is by reference to the four broad sections: (1) assessing the strategic risks of the minerals and countries; (2) minerals; (3) countries; and (4) companies. Cross-referenced.

TA483
.W04
1990
Sci
Ref

TN12
H27
1983
Sci

16   Transportation Engineering

Transportation engineering involves the planning, design, and construction of means by which to transport people and objects. The scope includes all modes of transport from highways to space travel. Components of aerospace engineering, civil engineering, mechanical engineering, and some electrical engineering play a part in transportation engineering.

A large portion of the material presented here is devoted to highway engineering. The increase in the number of roadways built in the last thirty years has had a parallel effect on the amount of literature in the highway engineering field. This increase is reflected in the number of sources selected to represent the area.

The second highest number of titles reflects the aviation and space programs. This material is growing rapidly and will continue to do so. The sources selected were chosen on two criteria: first, they must be current; and second, they must supply some form of bibliographic control over the literature. Not all items perfectly fit both criteria, but overall the section represents a fulfillment of these criteria.

GUIDES TO THE LITERATURE

1798. **Aerospace Periodical Index.** Boston: G. K. Hall, 1973-1982.

Devoted to one discipline, this readers' guide lists 137 U.S., worldwide, and house publications. Some areas outside the field of aerospace are covered, but these areas tend to deal with flight of some sort. This is a good source of information and is recommended for general through specific collections.

1799. **Rural Transport and Planning: A Bibliography with Abstracts.** Banister, David. London: Mansell, 1985. 448p.

This is a significant contribution to rural transportation and planning. The coverage includes North America and Europe with the majority of the material relating to Great Britain. The bibliography is very good, selecting the best of the literature. The abstracts are informative, but are descriptive only. This is a good bibliography in an area with little bibliographic control.

1800.   **Sources of Information in Transportation.** 3rd ed. Monticello, IL: Vance Bibliographies, 1985. 9v.

A basic reference to all modes of transportation which includes U.S. sources as well as major international references. The socioeconomic and technical aspects of each mode of transportation are included in this reference which is recommended for any collection in transportation.

ABSTRACTS, INDEXES, AND BIBLIOGRAPHIES

1801.   **Aeronautical Engineering.** Springfield, VA: NTIS, 1970- . monthly.

Contains reports and articles on aerodynamics and aeronautics culled from *STAR* (see entry 1808) and *IAA* (see entry 1805). Includes abstracts and subject, author, and contract number indexes. This is a derivative work, but useful for those who do not have access to the larger works.

1802.   **Aerospace Database.** New York: American Institute of Aeronautics and Astronautics, 1963- . monthly.

Provides references and abstracts, using a controlled vocabulary to key scientific and technical documents from over 40 countries. Available from DIALOG.

1803.   **HRIS Abstracts.** Washington, DC: Transportation Research Board, 1968- . quarterly.

This abstracting service provides information on highway and mass transit research, but excludes rail mass transportation. Journal articles, research reports, and conference papers are included. Though its broad subject arrangement slows subject access, this is an excellent source of information. It is also available online from DIALOG.

1804.   **Information Sources in Transportation, Material Management, and Physical Distribution: An Annotated Bibliography and Guide.** Davis, Bob J., ed. Westport, CT: Greenwood Press, 1976. 715p.

This bibliography covers a wide variety of material such as journals, monographs, and governmental publications. Brief annotations for most items are provided. It is included here for its background information, not for its currency.

1805.   **International Aerospace Abstracts.** New York: American Institute of Aeronautics and Astronautics, 1961- . semimonthly.

Between *STAR* (see entry 1808) and *IAA*, the two manage to cover the world's literature on aerospace engineering quite well. This service scans journal articles, books, proceedings, transactions, and translations to find material related in some way to aerospace. This is a major work and should be a part of any serious collection in aerospace engineering.

1806.   **Records of Achievement.** Springfield, VA: NTIS, 1983. 127p.

This contains a listing of all the Special Publications published since 1961. The index is by subject and lists the publication by number, not by title. It would be more helpful if a keyword index were provided. The listing includes a one- or two-line description as well as locations where the publication can be purchased.

1807.   **Satellites: Engineering Information Technical Bulletin.** New York: Engineering Information, Inc., 1984. 133p.

This contains abstracts from COMPENDEX (New York: Engineering Index, 1970-) from the period January 1982 through December 1983. It is well indexed by subject, author, and author affiliation, and provides citations so that the original source can be examined.

1808.   **Scientific and Technical Aerospace Reports.** Washington, DC: U.S. National Aeronautics and Space Administration, 1963- . semimonthly.

Commonly called *STAR*, this is the premier publication in the aerospace industry in terms of abstracting service. Together with *IAA* (see entry 1805), it covers the aerospace literature virtually completely. Even some dissertations and patents appear. The arrangement is by accession number with a series of indexes to the main body. This is a tool any aerospace collection cannot do without.

1809.   **Transportation Research Abstracts.** Washington, DC: National Academy of Science, 1974- . monthly.

This work covers all areas of transportation. Together with *HRIS* (see entry 1803), it effectively covers the transportation area in engineering. Like *HRIS*, it is a prerequisite for a transportation engineering collection.

1810.   **Transportation System Management: Bibliography of Technical Reports.** Oram, Richard L. Washington, DC: U.S. Department of Transportation, 1976. 152p.

Focuses on nine aspects of operational transportation improvements. Entries provide the following data: brief summary, report preparation information, date, and ordering details. Although dated, some of the techniques are still in use. It is recommended for research collections.

1811.   **TRIS.** Washington, DC: Transportation Research Board, 1968- . monthly.

This database on transportation research contains information on air, highway, rail, and maritime transport. Includes mass transit and other modes. The components of this database are *HRIS* (see entry 1803) and *Highway Safety Literature* (Washington, DC: Transportation Safety Board, 1968-). Available from DIALOG.

ENCYCLOPEDIAS

1812.   **Encyclopedia of Aircraft.** Taylor, Michael J. H., and John W. R. Taylor, eds. New York: Putnam, 1978. 253p.

Arranged alphabetically, this encyclopedia contains articles on the history of aircraft from the Wright brothers forward. Technical data, tables, and a glossary are provided. It is included here because of its completeness and is a good first-stop for information.

1813.   **Encyclopedia of Aviation.** New York: Scribner, 1977. 218p.

The coverage of this general purpose encyclopedia of aviation is broad, including such items as airlines and space exploration. A section covering records and flying feats is included. Recommended for its general approach to aviation.

1814. **Encyclopedia of U.S. Spacecraft.** Yenne, Bill. New York: Exeter Books, 1985. 192p.

This book does not successfully meet its goal of covering the entire U.S. space program. *Jane's All the World's Aircraft* (see entry 1817) provides much more information. The heavy use of illustrations and photographs overbalances the text. This was not designed for the knowledgeable layperson, engineer, technician, or scientist.

1815. **Illustrated Encyclopedia of General Aviation.** Garrison, Paul. Blue Ridge Summit, PA: TAB Books, 1979. 350p.

An alphabetic listing and explanation of concepts, expressions, phrases, and abbreviations. Included among other subjects are major manufacturers of aircraft and avionics and their more important products. Not included is information related strictly to military aviation or to the airlines.

1816. **Illustrated Encyclopedia of Space Technology: A Comprehensive History of Space Exploration.** New York: Crown, 1985. 301p.

Although at first glance this seems to be aimed at a juvenile audience, that impression is disproved upon closer examination. While it is not as detailed as *Jane's All the World's Aircraft* (see entry 1817), it is definitely better than *Encyclopedia of U.S. Spacecraft* (see entry 1814). It also includes a glossary which provides definitions of useful terms.

1817. **Jane's All the World's Aircraft 1986-87.** 77th ed. Taylor, John W. London: Jane's Publishing, 1986. annual.

This comprehensive listing of aircraft contains entries that are amply described and illustrated. It is considered to be the standard in terms of aviation description. If the collection is serious, *Jane's* should be included. All libraries, with the possible exception of school, should be interested in this title.

1818. **New Observer's Book of Aircraft.** Green, William, comp. London: F. Warne, 1952- . annual.

In essence, this is a state-of-the-art-aircraft-industry report which offers a guide to military, commercial, and private airplanes either in production or nearing production. It is not as comprehensive as *Jane's All the World's Aircraft* (see entry 1817), but is still of use to business and engineering personnel.

1819. **World Encyclopedia of Civil Aircraft, From Leonardo to the Present Day.** Angelucci, Enzo, ed. New York: Crown, 1984. 414p.

More than 400 civil aircraft are covered (early flying machines, airliners, freighters, research and experimental aircraft, competition and record breaking airplanes, and trainers) as well as certain military aircraft, from earliest attempts to today.

DICTIONARIES

1820. **Astronautical Multilingual Dictionary of the International Academy of Astronautics.** Prague, Czechoslovakia: Academia, 1970. 936p.

This is a massive work, listing terms in English, Russian, German, French, Italian, Spanish, and Czech. It is divided into two sections. The first is a section on basic aerospace terminology. This section should be used with care due to its age. The second section is the primary reason for its inclusion here. It deals with space law, and although this section has aged just as much as the terminology section, the international aspects of space law are now more germane than ever. It is recommended, but with some care.

1821. **Aviation Space Dictionary.** 6th ed. Fallbrook, CA: Aero Publishers, 1980- .

This dictionary attempts to bring together the terminology related to aviation and space flight. It is somewhat a derivative work, culling material from glossaries and dictionaries produced by the U.S. Air Force, Atomic Energy Commission, and the Federal Aviation Administration. Those definitions not coming from other sources were prepared by the editors. This is a good, general purpose dictionary.

1822. **Complete Multilingual Dictionary of Aviation and Aeronautical Terminology.** Demaison, Henri, comp. Lincolnwood, IL: Passport Books, 1984. 671p.

"Contains 13,000 terms you are likely to encounter in the fields of aviation and aeronautics. Each term is given in English, French, and Spanish" (preface). It has three main sections: trilingual lexicon, French index, and Spanish index. This is not a dictionary with definitions, but provides equivalent expressions in French and Spanish for a known English word. It is sometimes awkward to use and falls short of its title's claim of complete.

1823. **Dictionary for Automotive Engineering: English, French, German.** 2nd enl. ed. de Coster, Jean. Munich: K. G. Saur, 1986. 620p.

Entries are listed in dictionary form by word, first in English, then in French and German with definitions in these two languages. It is a "work of reference which systematically covers the most important areas of automotive engineering: the engine, chassis, transmission, steering, braking system, fuel system, lubricants, electrical system, and workshop equipment" (preface).

1824. **Dictionary of Aerospace Engineering in Three Languages: Russian, English, German.** Kotik, Mikhail Grigor'yevich, comp. New York: Elsevier Science Publishing, 1986. 879p.

This dictionary covers the three primary languages of aerospace engineering. The rapid changes in the industry together with the increase of jargon make this dictionary a necessity. The lead language here is Russian, not English, with English and German terms adjacent. This will be a valuable dictionary for those involved in translation or those who must deal with Russian aerospace materials.

1825. **Dictionary of Air Transport and Traffic Control.** Ocran, E. B. London: Granada, 1984. 243p.

As stated in the preface, this work was "designed for the benefit of the student of air transport and traffic control, the air traffic controller, the air pilot, the travel agent, the airline operator, the aviation writer, instructors, managers, aviation authorities, and the layman air passenger." It contains definitions obtained from the Civil Aeronautics Board, Federal Aviation Administration, Civil Aviation Authority, British Standards Institute, and the International Civil Aviation Organization.

1826. **Dictionary of Modern Engineering.** Oppermann, Alfred. Munich: K. G. Saur, 1986. 2v.

The preface indicates that this work "contains more than 450,000 terms and over one million translation possibilities for the fields of aviation, space travel, navigation, aerodynamics." This is an up-to-date German-English and English-German dictionary suitable for academic and technical collections.

1827. **Dictionary of Space Technology.** Angelo, Joseph A. New York: Facts on File, 1982. 380p.

Provides a thorough survey of most current U.S. programs involved in space technology, especially the current space shuttle program and the spacelab project. Useful to the student as well as the scientist.

1828. **Jane's Aerospace Dictionary.** 2nd ed. Gunston, Bill. London: Jane's Publishing, 1986. 565p.

Another excellent Jane's publication, this dictionary contains over 15,000 entries from astronautics, civil and military aeronautics, electronics, meteorology, and material science. Many acronyms are included, as are many of the field's obscure terms and phrases. This is a very up-to-date dictionary containing over 3,000 recently coined acronyms. The definitions are clear, concise (some may be too concise), and understandable. The assumption is made that the user has some knowledge of the field, thus some very elementary words are omitted. Besides the dictionary, there are several ready reference lists in the back, including Greek symbols, NATO reporting names, and military aircraft designations.

1829. **Language of Space: A Dictionary of Astronautics.** Turnhill, Reginald. New York: John Day, 1971. 165p.

This is a brief introduction to the language of space. The main reason for its inclusion here is the fact that it is predominantly a dictionary of terms that have evolved (or devolved) from space jargon. It can be a very valuable source, but should be used with care due to its age.

1830. **Multilingual Aeronautical Dictionary in Ten Languages: English-French-Dutch-German-Greek-Italian-Portuguese-Turkish-Spanish and Russian.** Neuilly sur Seine, France: NATO, 1980.

Entries provide the English word and a short definition of the word followed by a translation into its equivalent in nine other languages (no definition). It is a bit cumbersome, but considering the amount of information there probably is not a better way to facilitate its use. Part 2 contains nine alphabetical listings of terms (non-English) with a reference number referring back to the English definition. Part 3 is a list of English acronyms, abbreviations, and symbols. Prepared by nine panels of scientists and engineers from NATO member nations, this dictionary is much more multilingual than *Complete Multilingual Dictionary of Aviation and Aeronautical Terminology* (see entry 1822). This one contains ten languages.

1831. **NASA Thesaurus.** Springfield, VA: NTIS, 1985. 2v.

This is the authorized subject term listing used to analyze NASA documents. The first volume is an alphabetical listing of all subject terms, and volume 2 contains all thesaurus terms and permutations. This is a necessity in any aerospace engineering collection of whatever size or description.

1832. **Road and Track Illustrated Dictionary.** Dinkel, John. New York: W. W. Norton, 1981.

This dictionary of automotive terms contains definitions which are geared toward the novice or the nonexpert. The focus is on the internal combustion engine. It is an excellent source for basic information and should be useful in public and technical collections.

1833. **SAE Motor Vehicle, Safety, and Environmental Terminology.** Society of Automotive Engineers. Warrendale, PA: Society of Automotive Engineers, 1977. 179p.

An alphabetical listing of terms relating to motor vehicle safety which also includes safety guidelines. This is an authoritative list that should be found in both academic and technical collections.

1834. **Technical Dictionary for Automotive Engineering.** Bosch, Robert. Dusseldorf, West Germany: VDI, 1976- . 2v.

This two-volume, German-English, English-German dictionary contains about 15,000 terms from automotive engineering. It features cross-references for spelling variants, chemical formulas, synonyms, sources, and classification symbols. A must for engineering and technical schools; helpful to translators.

HANDBOOKS

1835. **CRC Handbook of Space Technology: Status and Projections.** Hord, Michael. Boca Raton, FL: CRC Press, 1985. 287p.

A compact volume that defines in quantitative terms the opportunities and limits for future space system capabilities. Figures are accompanied by descriptive narrative. This is a well-done source for virtually any collection.

1836. **Diesel Engine Reference Book.** Lilly, L. London: Butterworths, 1984. 1v. (various paging).

This in-depth handbook and reference work covers all types of diesel engines, including diesel engineering. As such, it is highly recommended for engineers, those involved in research and development, and for academic collections.

TL515
M274
1978
Sci
Ref

1837. **Guinness Aircraft Facts and Feats.** Taylor, John W. R., Michael J. H. Taylor, and David Mondey. Enfield, England: Guinness Superlatives, 1984. 256p.

This is a complete reworking of the 1977 *Guinness Air Facts and Feats*. A compendium of facts on aeronautical events, it contains appendices that list speed, height, distance, and disasters. Illustrations are good, as are the bibliography and index. The selection of items is curious, and no criteria for inclusion are provided. This is recommended with some caution.

TL685.7
H53
1986
Sci
(Checked out)

1838. **High Speed Commercial Flight: The Coming Era.** Loomis, James P. Columbus, OH: Battelle, 1987. 288p.

Technically not so much a handbook as a treatise, this work pulls together the state-of-the-art thinking on high speed commercial flight. Issues include operational concepts, pooling, international partnerships, technology alternatives, and market factors. Recommended for research collections in transportation engineering.

1839. **Jane's World Aircraft Recognition Handbook.** 3rd ed. Wood, Derek. London: Jane's Publishing Co., 1985. 572p.

According to the preface, this is "intended as a primer for students of the subject." It provides an introduction to the subject and a glossary, illustrations of the essential elements of the airframe, and an explanation of the layout of the book into fixed wing aircraft and rotary wing aircraft (helicopters) of various distinctive types. This is potentially an indispensable source for particular information.

1840. **National Transportation Statistics.** Washington, DC: U.S. Government Printing Office, 1977- . annual.

This compilation of transportation and energy statistics uses four formats: tree displays, modal profiles, performance indicators, and transportation trends. A glossary of terms and a bibliography are included. This would serve best in reference libraries with transportation collections.

1841. **1986 Space Satellite Handbook.** Curtis, A. R., ed. Woodsboro, MD: ARCsoft *TL796* Publishers, 1986. 80p. *.S42*
This is a listing of 15,891 objects launched between 1958 and 1985. Data were supplied *1986* by NASA, the Goddard Space Flight Center, NORAD, and the Smithsonian Astrophysi- *Sci* cal Observatory. The information is chronologically presented in list form. Distinctions are made between payload, platforms, and rocket. A good, quick reference source, it contains *Ref* a "current listing of all those satellites still in orbit and those which previously orbited the Earth, the moon, and the sun. This list includes everything large enough to be detected from Earth," as stated in the preface. There are some discrepancies between this work and the *R.A.E. Table of Earth Satellites* (see entry 1842). The internal evidence suggests the *R.A.E. Table* may be more reliable.

1842. **R.A.E. Table of Earth Satellites 1957 to 1986.** 3rd ed. King-Hele, D. G., et al. New *TL796.6* York: Stockton, 1987. *E2*
This is a chronological listing of launches from 1957-1986. The information is essen- *R253* tially the same as that found in the *Space Satellite Handbook* (see entry 1841), though discrepancies exist between the two. The *Space Satellite Handbook*'s reporting of apogee *1987* and perigee does not agree with the information in this volume. Based upon the introduc- *Sci Ref* tion and explanations of both, this work would be the most credible.

1843. **S.A.E. Handbook.** New York: Society of Automotive Engineers, 1924- . annual. *TL151* This is a classic handbook dealing predominantly with technical reports and standards *S62* as they pertain to the automotive industry, though it also covers a broader area. Volume 1 *Sci* of the 1987 handbook deals with materials and would be of interest to those in materials *Ref* engineering. The prime focus of the work is transportation engineering. This is a necessity for any collection in transportation engineering.

1844. **Transportation & Traffic Engineering Handbook.** 2nd ed. Homburger, Wolfgang, ed. Englewood Cliffs, NJ: Prentice-Hall, 1982. 883p.
The emphasis of this handbook is on traffic engineering. Mass transportation is mentioned, but the focus is generally narrower. This is a good source of specific information.

DIRECTORIES

1845. **Aerospace Consultant's Directory.** Warrendale, PA: Society of Automotive Engineers, 1984- . annual.
This is a service publication. If you have an idea for something, this book will direct you to the people who can make your idea a reality. The information in this directory changes rapidly; therefore, it should be used with some care.

1846. **Aerospace Facts and Figures.** Washington, DC: Aerospace Industries Association *TL501* of America, 1945- . annual. *.A818*
This is a summary of the financial aspect of the industry as a whole and would be quite *Sci Ref* handy as a quick reference tool. It is full of charts and tables, but contains very little text.

1847. **Aerospace Research Index: A Guide to World Research in Aeronautics, Meteorology, Astronomy, and Space Science.** Willmore, A. P., and S. R. Willmore, eds. Essex, England: Hodgson, 1981. 597p.
Arranged by country, then alphabetically by institution, this is a country-by-country listing of who is doing what research and where. Both a title/keyword index and a subject

index are provided. Within the latter, a notation is made to refer to specific countries. The physical layout is, at times, confusing. Since the names are bound to change, that aspect of the book is questionable. It is valuable in that it indicates major research centers, major areas of research emphasis, and major researchers. As stated in the preface, it is a "comprehensive source of reference on government establishments, industrial laboratories, and colleges and universities which engage in research of aeronautics, meteorology, astronomy, and space science."

1848. Berger-Burr's Ultralight and Microlight Aircraft of the World. 2nd ed. Berger, Alain-Yves, and Norman Burr. Somerset, England: Haynes, 1985. 504p.

Provides a glossary, history, and within country, a description of each aircraft which includes an illustration, the basic format of the aircraft, the design of wings, and the control system. Also included are manufacturers.

1849. Complete Illustrated Encyclopedia of the World's Aircraft. Mondey, David, ed. New York: A&W Publishers, 1978. 320p.

This is largely a directory, rather than an encyclopedia. Manufacturers are the prime interest here. It does a good job of listing all the manufacturers of production aircraft and is recommended for its strength in supply directory information.

1850. Directory of Transportation Libraries in the United States and Canada. Transportation Division, Special Libraries Association. New York: Special Libraries Association, 1973. 122p.

This is a listing of the major transportation libraries in the U.S. and Canada. General directory information is provided for each entry. Overall, the list has not changed substantially since 1973 in terms of major collections. Certain sections of the directory need to be used with care, such as personnel. This is recommended, but with care.

1851. Interavia ABC Aerospace Directory, 1986. Geneva, Switzerland: Interavia, 1986. 1751p.

This directory systematically lists all companies, organizations, and institutes that are directly and indirectly related to the aeronautics industry. The 40,000 entries are arranged geographically by continent and country.

1852. Jane's Avionics. Wilson, Michael, ed. London: Jane's Publishing, Inc., 1982/83- . annual.

The information from the field of aviation electronics is arranged alphabetically by country under each topic, and then alphabetically by manufacturer within that country. This is intended to be an annual or biannual publication.

1853. Jane's Spaceflight Directory. Turnill, Reginald. London: Jane's Publishing, 1984- . annual.

This is an excellent, comprehensive compilation of data on space operations. The use of photographs and illustrations is used to enhance the text rather than to hide deficiencies. The body of the text is subdivided into categories of space programs, military space, launches, solar system, world space centers, spacemen, and space contractors. The author expects and assumes that the reader has a basic knowledge of the subject. Besides providing ready answers to reference questions, this is an enjoyable book to read. It lists space programs by country and international programs by name, and includes dates, places, and names of those who manned the launchings.

1854. **Observer's Spaceflight Directory.** Turnill, Reginald. London: F. Warne, 1978. 384p.

This is a comprehensive, authoritative survey of space flights through 1977. Following a short, introductory section, space programs are listed alphabetically by sponsoring country or international agency, then subarranged by name of program or vehicle. The descriptions range from two or three lines to four or five pages.

1855. **Satellite Directory.** Potomac, MD: Phillips Publishing, 1979- . annual.

This contains information of interest to commercial satellite operators. The company index in the beginning is invaluable and is the only thing that provides access to the directory. The information is supplied by the listed companies. It has a good breakdown of receive-only and transmit-only satellites, and transmission and reception sites.

TL796.
US
S3
Sci Ref

1856. **Who's Who in Aviation and Aerospace.** Boston: National Aeronautical Institute, 1983- . annual.

Approximately 15,000 individuals are profiled including those from the fields of aviation and aerospace manufacturing; officials from government and the military; and leading aeronautical engineers, designers, and technical specialists. These were selected based on superior professional achievement in the aviation/aerospace fields.

TL539
.W55
Sci
Ref

1857. **World Aviation Directory.** Washington, DC: Ziff-Davis, 1940- . 2/year.

This is a directory covering the span of aviation in its broadest sense. Airlines, airports, aviation schools, manufacturers, publications, and governmental agencies are all listed. This is a treasure trove of information for anyone interested or involved in aviation.

TL512
A63
Sci
Ref

17 Biomedical Sciences

The biomedical sciences are an interdisciplinary field using engineering, physics, and chemistry for the most part in studying and treating living organisms. As a recognized field, it is very young. As practiced, however, it is a science as old as medicine and technology.

The emergence of biomedicine is so new that some universities still have difficulty in placing the unit within traditional disciplines. In most settings it is placed either in the medical school or in the engineering school. The administrative placement normally depends on the focus or strength of the biomedical department. This can pose a problem for the information provider depending upon the administrative placement of the information center itself.

One of the major areas of biomedical sciences is the modeling of human movements and the creation of prosthetic devices. In order to do such work, a significant amount of information must be acquired on electrical and electronic controls.

Without question, the social benefits and the scientific and layperson's interests will continue to keep biomedical science a viable and expanding area. The expansion and the multidisciplinary nature of the field may, however, cause difficulties for the traditional library and librarian.

GUIDES TO THE LITERATURE

1858. **Encyclopedia of Health Information Sources: A Bibliographic Guide to Approximately 13,000 Citations for Publications, Organizations, and Other Sources....** Wasserman, Paul, and Suzanne Grefsheim, eds. Detroit, MI: Gale, 1987. 483p.

This is a useful reference text, difficult to classify. On the one hand, it is a directory; on the other hand, it is a bibliographic guide to the literature dealing with biomedical issues. Under each heading is information on abstract services, indexes, annual reviews, yearbooks, associations, professional societies, organizations, bibliographies, encyclopedias and dictionaries, handbooks, manuals, and the like. This is an interesting reference work which can be used in a variety of ways. It is recommended for virtually any biomedical collection.

1859. **Guide to the Literature of Pharmacy and the Pharmaceutical Sciences.** Andrews, Theodora. Littleton, CO: Libraries Unlimited, 1986. 383p.

This comprehensive guide to the literature of pharmacology contains descriptive annotations on a wide range of subjects within the general field, making this an excellent choice for medical and medically oriented collections. It covers textbooks, monographs, reference works, periodicals, and databases.

1860. **Immunology: An Information Profile.** Nicholas, Robin, and David Nicholas. New York: Mansell, 1985. 216p.

This book is aimed at immunologists and students in the area. It gives a history of the field and an organization of the literature within the field. The information is volatile, but it is an excellent attempt at describing the literature of immunology and making the structure known to students. This will be an excellent addition to both working collections and research/educational collections.

1861. **Information Sources in the Medical Sciences.** 3rd ed. Morton, L. T., and S. Godbolt, eds. London: Butterworths, 1984. 534p.

This is a reworked edition of a very good guide to information sources. The second edition was titled *Use of Medical Literature* (London: Butterworths, 1977). The primary emphasis is still the British library user, though a sufficiently broad range of information is contained in the book to make it useful on a larger scale. Highly recommended.

1862. **Introduction to Reference Sources in the Health Sciences.** 2nd ed. Roper, Fred W., and Jo Anne Boorkman. Chicago, IL: Medical Library Association, 1984. 302p.

Written primarily for library school students, this work discusses the various fields of medical librarianship. It is written by two experts in the field and is highly recommended.

ABSTRACTS, INDEXES, AND BIBLIOGRAPHIES

1863. **Abridged Index Medicus.** Bethesda, MD: National Library of Medicine, 1970- . monthly.

This is a shortened version of the full *Index Medicus* (see entry 1891). Even though it is abbreviated, it is still an excellent source for medical and biomedical information. It contains the same information as found in *Index Medicus*, but the list of sources is much smaller. This is highly recommended for nonresearch collections.

1864. **AIDS Information Sourcebook.** Malinowsky, H. Robert, and Gerald J. Perry. Phoenix, AZ: Oryx Press, 1987. 112p.

The strong point of this work is its bibliography of books, journals, pamphlets, and other materials related to AIDS. There is a section on AIDS "hotlines" which may be of use. Because these "hotlines" tend to be somewhat volatile in their longevity, this section should be used with care. Overall, this is a welcome addition to a general purpose reference collection.

1865. **Alcohol and Sexuality: An Annotated Bibliography on Alcohol Use, Alcoholism, and Human Sexual Behavior.** O'Farrell, Timothy J., and Carolyn A. Weysnd. Phoenix, AZ: Oryx Press, 1983. 131p.

This book is arranged by a table of contents using subjects such as "Nature and Treatment of Sexual Problems among Alcoholics." There is an introduction to each of the four sections, with subheadings under these sections. Each entry has an abstract number. There are four appendices dealing with resources for alcohol information and sexuality, plus representative alcoholism and sexuality journals. An author index gives the abstract number. This is a good reference tool for the librarian working with physicians, psychologists, psychiatrists, nurses, social workers, and counselors who are involved in research, education, or treatment in this area. The user must know the specific subject area of alcohol and sexuality in order to use this source. No subject index is provided, but the specific areas are made accessible through the table of contents.

1866. **Alternative Medicine: A Bibliography of Books in English**. West, Ruth, and Joanna E. Trevelyan. London: Mansell, 1985. 210p.

The subject matter of the bibliography limits the audience, but this will still find a good usage in certain collections. Whatever one may believe about alternative medicine, this bibliography clearly points to a substantial body of literature in the area. It is recommended for collections which already have or plan to have materials in the area of alternative medicine.

1867. **American Medical Imprints, 1820-1910: A Checklist of Publications....** Cordasco, Francesco. Totowa, NJ: Rowman & Littlefield, 1985. 2v.

For retrospective or historical information in medical sciences, this is one of the best and most useful bibliographies in print. The only major drawback is that most of the entries are not annotated. Most journal literature is not covered, nor are annual reports listed. Despite any potential drawbacks, this is an excellent source for historical information in the medical sciences.

1868. **Bibliography of Bioethics**. Walters, Leroy. Detroit, MI: Gale Research, 1975- . annual.

The coverage includes journals, monographs, portions of monographs, court decisions, newspaper articles, and ephemera. The scope is sometimes overly broad, but the annual manages to give an unbiased view of the entire field of bioethics. It is highly recommended for any collection in biotechnology.

1869. **Bibliography of Drug Abuse, Including Alcohol and Tobacco: Supplement 1977-1980.** Andrews, Theodora. Littleton, CO: Libraries Unlimited, 1981. 312p.

This is a supplement to the highly recommended title *Bibliography of Drug Abuse* (Littleton, CO: Libraries Unlimited, 1977). The majority of the material in the supplement consists of reference material and treatises. This is an excellent source, but a new edition is needed.

1870. **Bibliography on Herbs, Herbal Medicine, "Natural" Foods, and Unconventional Medical Treatment.** Andrews, Theodora. Littleton, CO: Libraries Unlimited, 1982. 339p.

This is an annotated reference arranged by subject area. Given the interest in unconventional medicine, this will fill a prominent gap. Highly recommended for any collection with even a passing interest in unconventional medicine.

1871. **Clinical Toxicology of Commercial Products.** 5th ed. Gosselin, Robert E., Roger P. Smith, and Harold C. Hodge. Baltimore, MD: Williams & Wilkins, 1984. 1v. (various paging).

An excellent source outlining the toxicology of commercial products and the antidotes or procedures necessary to counteract exposure or ingestion. It is highly recommended for virtually any library or collection dealing with toxicology.

1872. **Compendium of Current Source Materials for Drugs.** Londos, Eutychia G. Metuchen, NJ: Scarecrow Press, 1982. 140p.

Gives complete bibliographical citations and detailed annotations under 12 applicable sections. A combined author/title index with page number reference is provided for each item. The following types of resources are covered: dictionaries, encyclopedias, journals, reports, online databases, treatment centers, etc. An index is included. This is a comprehensive, up-to-date quick reference tool helpful to the librarian needing to locate available sources in the field of drugs and alcoholism. The database section is particularly useful.

(handwritten: Z6675.R9 466 1982 Main)

1873. **Consumer Health Information Source Book.** 2nd ed. Rees, Alan M., and Jodith Janes. New York: Bowker, 1984. 530p.

This is a completely revised edition of the 1981 work by the same title. The majority of the new listings in this edition are new editions. The criteria for inclusion are very clearly stated and increase the authority of the book. This is an extremely important tool for the general reader seeking information. It is an essential tool for any medically related collection. To use the authors' terminology, it is "highly recommended."

(handwritten: RA776 .R4 1984 Sci Ref)

1874. **Critical Reviews in Biomedical Engineering.** Boca Raton, FL: CRC Press, 1981- . irregular.

This title supersedes *Critical Reviews in Bioengineering* (Boca Raton, FL: CRC Press, 1971-1980). This is a critical evaluation of the literature of biomedical engineering. Each issue is both a state-of-the-art review and a bibliography of the most important work in a specific area. An excellent tool, it is highly recommended for any research or academically oriented collection in biomedical engineering.

1875. **Cumulative Index to Nursing and Allied Health Literature.** Glendale, CA: Glendale Adventist Medical Center Publications Service, 1961- . quarterly with annual cumulations.

Formerly *Cumulative Index to Nursing Literature* until 1977, this is a subject-author index to worldwide journals of professional nursing. It is a master index to the nursing literature and a necessity for collections with nursing interests.

1876. **Dental Abstracts.** Chicago, IL: American Dental Association, 1956- . monthly.

Covers the field of dentistry and some allied areas. The work is divided into broad subject classifications. Abstracts are descriptive only. This is a specialized tool for use in special and research collections in dentistry.

1877. **Diabetes Literature Index.** Washington, DC: National Institute of Arthritis, Metabolism, and Digestive Diseases, 1966- . monthly.

Produced from the MEDLINE database (see entry 1898), this is a spinoff index. As a result, it contains the same information as found in MEDLINE. Because of the size of the MEDLINE database, an index such as this is very useful. It is recommended for specialized and research collections.

1878. **Drug Abuse Bibliography.** Advena, Jean Cameron. Troy, NY: Whitston, 1970- . annual.

Once a supplement to *Drugs of Addiction and Non-Addiction* (Troy, NY: Whitston, 1970), this annual has taken the lead in covering the literature of drug abuse. That coverage is very comprehensive, listing items which may appear to have little utility. Some may find this objectionable. It is recommended for medical and particular collections.

1879. **EMBASE.** Amsterdam, Netherlands: Excerpta Medica Foundation, 1974- . approximately every 2 weeks.

Database corresponding to *Excerpta Medica* (see entry 1883) consisting of abstracts and citation of articles from biomedical journals published worldwide. It covers the field of human medicine and related disciplines. Available from DIALOG.

1880. **Environmental Hazards to Young Children.** Kane, Dorothy Noyes. Phoenix, AZ: Oryx Press, 1985. 246p.

The bibliography contains over three thousand items on threats to the health and safety of young children. This will be a valuable reference for professionals in medicine and public health. It is included here because its major use will be as a bibliography, as opposed to the wishes of the publisher that it be used as a textbook.

1881. **Ergonomics: The Science of Productivity and Health: Capsule Reviews of the Principal Literature in Present-Day Ergonomics & Human Factors Engineering.** Burch, John L., comp. Lawrence, KS: Report Store, 1984. 125p.

This bibliography contains 62 titles published between 1965 and 1984. Monographs, technical reports, proceedings, and journals are included. The titles were selected by a team of experts. There are two appendices: the first is a list of recommended textbooks in the area, and the second is a core collection list. Considering the currency of the ergonomics issue, this will find a great deal of use.

1882. **Ethics and Cancer: An Annotated Bibliography.** Weiss, Gary B., and Harold Y. Vanderpool. Galveston, TX: University of Texas Medical Branch, 1984. 248p.

The currency of cancer and ethics should have produced a larger pool of material than presented here. The material on monographs simply is not present for the authors to annotate. The journal material is considerably richer. This is an excellent bibliography both for its completeness and for what it says about the dearth of monographs on this important topic. It is highly recommended for any serious biomedical collection.

1883. **Excerpta Medica.** Amsterdam, Netherlands: Excerpta Medica Foundation, 1947- .

This is the prime international abstracting service in the medical and health sciences. Divided into several sections, the abstracts are in English and are mainly descriptive. Some sections are no longer being published, resulting in a gap in numbering. The entire file became available as an online database, EMBASE (see entry 1879), beginning in 1974, and is updated approximately every two weeks.

    1)   *Anatomy, Anthropology, Embryology, and Histology*, 1947- . irregular.

    2A)   *Physiology*, 1948- . irregular.

    3)   *Endocrinology*, 1947- . irregular.

    4)   *Microbiology*, 1947- . irregular. Formerly *Microbiology: Bacteriology, Mycology and Parasitology.*

    5)   *General Pathology and Pathological Anatomy*, 1948- . biweekly.

    6)   *Internal Medicine*, 1947- . irregular.

    7)   *Pediatrics and Pediatric Surgery*, 1947- . irregular.

    8)   *Neurology and Neurosurgery*, 1948- . irregular.

    9)   *Surgery*, 1947- . semimonthly.

    10)   *Obstetrics and Gynecology*, 1948- . irregular.

11) *Oto-, Rhino-, Laryngology*, 1948- . irregular.

12) *Ophthalmology*, 1947- . irregular.

13) *Dermatology and Venereology*, 1947- . irregular.

14) *Radiology*, 1947- . irregular.

15) *Chest Diseases, Thoracic Surgery, and Tuberculosis*, 1948- . irregular.

16) *Cancer*, 1953- . irregular.

17) *Public Health, Social Medicine, and Hygiene*, 1955- . irregular.

18) *Cardiovascular Diseases and Cardiovascular Surgery*, 1957- . irregular.

19) *Rehabilitation and Physical Medicine*, 1958- . irregular.

20) *Gerontology and Geriatrics*, 1958- . irregular.

21) *Developmental Biology and Teratology*, 1961- . irregular.

22) *Human Genetics*, 1963- . irregular.

23) *Nuclear Medicine*, 1964- . irregular.

24) *Anesthesiology*, 1966- . irregular.

25) *Hematology*, 1967- . irregular.

26) *Immunology, Serology, and Transplantation*, 1967- . semimonthly.

27) *Biophysics, Bio-Engineering and Medical Instrumentation*, 1967- . irregular.

28) *Urology and Nephrology*, 1969- . irregular.

29) *Clinical Biochemistry*, 1947- . irregular.

30) *Pharmacology*, 1965- . irregular.

32) *Psychiatry*, 1948- . irregular.

35) *Occupational Health and Industrial Medicine*, 1971- . irregular.

36) *Health Economics and Hospital Management*, 1971- . irregular.

37) *Drug Literature Index*, 1969- . biweekly.

40) *Drug Dependence*, 1972- . bimonthly.

46) *Environmental Health and Pollution Control*, 1971- . irregular.

47) *Virology*, 1971- . monthly.

48) *Gastroenterology*, 1971- . irregular.

49) *Forensic Science Abstracts*, 1975- . bimonthly.

52) *Toxicology*, 1973- . irregular.

61) *Transplant Immunology Literature Index*, 1975- . monthly.

64) *Diabetes Mellitus Literature Index*, 1975- . monthly.

65) *Cancer Immunology Literature Index*, 1975- . monthly.

1884. **Female Reproductive Cycle: An Annotated Bibliography.** Paige, Karen Erickson, et al. Boston: G. K. Hall, 1985. 599p.

The literature contained here was published between 1965 and 1982. The materials are all English-language and usually pulled from major publications which can be easily obtained. Each entry is annotated with full descriptive information. Rarely is there an evaluative annotation. Additional references are included for some topics, but none are annotated. This is an excellent bibliography for a wide range of users, from laypersons to the researcher. It is highly recommended for virtually any collection.

R129
.S53
1985
Sci
Ref

1885. **Finding the Source of Medical Information: A Thesaurus-Index to the Reference Collection.** Shearer, Barbara Smith, and Geneva L. Bush. Westport, CT: Greenwood Press, 1985. 225p.

This subject index to medical reference books is based on keyword(s) found in reference materials. The only drawback to the publication is that it presupposes a reasonably large-sized reference collection. Where this condition can be met, it is an excellent tool.

1886. **First Statistical Compendium on Alcohol and Health.** Rockville, MD: National Institute on Alcohol Abuse and Alcoholism, 1981.

The subject index gives statistics on deaths, accidents, studies, treatment, crime, and economic costs associated with alcoholism. It provides relevant alcohol and associated health statistics. This is an easy-to-use reference with graphs and tables.

1887. **Guide to the Literature of Pharmacy and the Pharmaceutical Sciences.** Andrews, Theodora. Littleton, CO: Libraries Unlimited, 1986. 383p.

This is an annotated bibliography intended for librarians. It attempts to cover all pharmaceutical areas, and is not a textbook on "how to do research." The items are annotated with a descriptive abstract. This should be considered by any collection in the health sciences.

1888. **Hastings Center's Bibliography of Ethics, Biomedicine, and Professional Responsibility.** Frederick, MD: University Publications of America, 1984. 109p.

This work takes a broad view of the field of biomedical ethics. The majority of the material falls into the field of bioethics, the remainder deals with law, business, journalism, and the military. There are no cross-references, which limits the utility of the work. A larger bibliography to consult would be the *Bibliography of Bioethics* (see entry 1868).

1889. **Health, Medicine, and Bioethics: A Bibliography Selected from the ALTA Religion Database.** 3rd ed. rev. Peterson, Paul D., and Ruth F. Frazer, eds. Chicago, IL: American Theological Library Association, 1984. 574p.

The material on biomedical ethics is growing extremely fast. This bibliography lists monographs, journals, and Doctor of Ministry projects that relate to biomedical ethics. This work competes with BIOETHICS on LINE (Cambridge, MA: Kennedy Institute of Ethics, 1973-) and *Bibliography of Bioethics* (see entry 1868). The material here is predominantly religious in nature, and it is because of this slant that the work is included here. Note should be made that all citations here are available online via the ALTA database.

1890. **Hospital Literature Index.** Chicago, IL: American Hospital Association, 1945- . quarterly.

This is an index to the literature of hospitals focusing on the administration and management of health care facilities. Some non-hospital material is included, but it covers medical administration. Because of the narrow focus, it will have limited use except in specialized collections.

1891. **Index Medicus.** Bethesda, MD: National Library of Medicine, 1960- . monthly with annual cumulations.

This is the premier English-language index to medical and medical-related literature. It should be noted that the subject analysis is done by specialists in the field. The range of literature covered is huge. This is an index which must be owned by any serious medical collection. It is also available online from a variety of vendors, including the National Library of Medicine.

1892. **Index Medicus, or Quarterly Classified Record of the Current Medical Literature of the World.** Washington, DC: Carnegie Institution, 1879-1927. 3 series.

This was the first *Index Medicus.* Arranged by subject, it covered journals, books, and parts of books, much like the current title does. Used now for retrospective searching, this is an excellent piece of work given the time period. No volumes were published between 1899 and 1903.

1893. **Index of NLM Serial Titles.** 5th ed. Bethesda, MD: National Library of Medicine, 1984. 2v.

A KWOC index produced from SERLINE, NAL's online serials database. Approximately 41,500 titles cover all serials and congresses received by NLM plus many ceased titles in the NLM collection. This would be of particular interest to collections in the medical area dealing with nonstandard publications or foreign publications.

1894. **Index to Dental Literature.** Chicago, IL: American Dental Association, 1962- . quarterly.

This is a derivative list taken from the MEDLINE database of the National Library of Medicine. The arrangement is both by subject and by name. This is a good index for specialists which can also be an aid if the MEDLINE database (see entry 1898) or *Index Medicus* (see entry 1891) is not available.

1895. **International Nursing Index.** New York: American Journal of Nursing, 1966- . quarterly.

This index is based on and draws from the MEDLINE database of the National Library of Medicine (see entry 1898). The main portion of the work is the listing of publications. There is a list of serials indexed, publications of organizations and agencies, new nursing books, and dissertations. Recommended for nursing collections.

1896. **International Pharmaceutical Abstracts.** Bethesda, MD: American Society of Hospital Pharmacists, 1964- . semimonthly.

This is a premier abstracting service in the pharmaceutical sciences. For each entry there is a full bibliographic description followed by a descriptive abstract. The coverage is broad and international. It indexes the literature focusing on the development and use of drugs in practice and education. This is an excellent service, particularly noted for its strong indexing. It is available as an online database by the same name beginning with 1970 and is updated monthly.

1897. **Medical and Scientific Authors' Guide: An International Guide for Authors to More Than 500 Medical and Scientific Journals.** Banes, Joan, comp. New York: LeJacq Publishing, 1984. 1082p.

Reproduces the "Instruction to Authors" page(s) from a number of journals in the medical and health-related fields. In special instances, this could be a very worthwhile source.

1898. **MEDLINE.** Bethesda, MD: National Library of Medicine, 1966- . monthly.

This is the online version of MEDLARS. It corresponds to three printed indexes: *Index Medicus* (see entry 1891), *Index to Dental Literature* (see entry 1894), and *International Nursing Index* (see entry 1895). There are, however, other materials found in MEDLINE. This is a first rate database and a necessity in most medical collections.

1899. **National Library of Medicine Current Catalog.** Bethesda, MD: National Library of Medicine, 1966- . quarterly.

This is a listing of publications cataloged by the National Library of Medicine. It is divided into sections: (1) monographs subject, (2) monographs name, (3) serials subject, and (4) serials name. The items found here will also be found in the MEDLINE database produced by the National Library of Medicine (see entry 1898). An excellent source of bibliographic information on medical titles.

1900. **Nutrition Abstracts and Reviews.** Farnham Royal, England: Commonwealth Agricultural Bureau, 1931- . monthly.

This service has short and indicative abstracts to the literature of nutrition. Specifically, it covers the chemical composition of food, vitamins, the physiology of nutrition, and the feeding of animals. The service divided into two series in 1977: (A) *Human and Experimental*, and (B) *Livestock Feeds and Feeding*. This is a good source, but one with an obviously British slant.

1901. **Sexually Transmitted Diseases: An Annotated, Selective Bibliography.** Margolis, Stephen. New York: Garland, 1985. 162p.

As the title indicates, this is a selective list. Most of the monograph material listed is patient-oriented. The work appears to be nontechnical in its approach and is a good starting point for nonresearchers seeking to gain additional insight and material on this important topic. Recommended for general biomedical collections.

1902. **Substance Abuse Materials for School Libraries: An Annotated Bibliography.** Andrews, Theodora. Littleton, CO: Libraries Unlimited, 1985. 215p.

Almost 500 titles make up this title. Each item is annotated and provides descriptive information. Given the current interest in drug use in schools, this will find a large audience and will be well used by both school librarians and concerned laypersons. An excellent tool for school librarians.

1903. **Toxicity Bibliography.** Bethesda, MD: National Library of Medicine, 1968- . quarterly.

The material here is a derivative of *Index Medicus* (see entry 1891). The focus of the bibliography is to list documents having to do with toxic or adverse reactions to drugs in persons or animals. This is a good bibliography with a relatively wide range of uses.

1904. **Underwater Medicine and Related Sciences: A Guide to the Literature: An Annotated Bibliography, Key Word Index, and Microthesaurus.** Shilling, Charles W., and Margaret F. Werts. New York: IFI/Plenum, 1973- . irregular.

The majority of the abstracts found in this series were written by the authors of the series. The selection of materials and scope are somewhat limiting, but the series does manage to cover the area well. This should be a serious consideration for purchase by major collections in medicine.

ENCYCLOPEDIAS

1905. **Encyclopedia and Dictionary of Medicine, Nursing, and Allied Health.** 4th ed. Miller, Benjamin F., and Claire Brackman Keane. Philadelphia: W. B. Saunders, 1987. 1427p.

Contains definitions of a large number of terms with cross-references and indications of pronunciation. The definitions are brief but adequate. There are no literature references, and eponymic syndromes are not identified. This is a useful source for nurses, paramedical professionals, and laypersons.

1906. Encyclopedia of Alcoholism. O'Brien, Robert, and Morris Chafitz, eds. New York: Facts on File, 1982. 378p.

A simple-to-use desk reference in dictionary form, this encyclopedia contains more than 500 entries providing information on alcohol. Information provided includes substance, social institutions, customs, socioeconomic interrelations, and physical and psychological manifestations of alcoholism. Two small chapters at the beginning of the book give a history of alcohol and an introduction to the substance. Some of the entries have bibliographies and cross-references are provided. For the use of both the professional and interested layperson.

1907. Encyclopedia of Bioethics. Reich, Warren T., ed. New York: The Free Press, 1978. 4v.

QH332
.E52
Sci
Ref

This is included here not only because of the topic, but because it contains signed articles by authoritative experts in the field. The intent of the work is that it be used by laypersons. The type of topics covered include: ethical and legal problems; basic concepts and principles; ethical theories; religious traditions; historical perspectives; and disciplines bearing on bioethics. This should be a part of any collection which deals with ethics in science and technology.

1908. Encyclopedia of Medical History. McGrew, Roderick E. New York: McGraw-Hill, 1985. 400p.

Written in nontechnical language, this encyclopedia contains essays on historically important medical topics. Each entry includes a bibliography. This is highly recommended for any collection.

1909. Encyclopedia of Neuroscience. Adelman, George, ed. Cambridge, MA: Birkhauser Boston, 1987. 2v.

This work intends to cover the broad field of neuroscience. A large number of authors have contributed to the entries, the majority of whom are recognized authorities in their fields. The large number of contributors gives the work a somewhat uneven quality, but the overall effect is an authoritative ready reference on neuroscience. Highly recommended for major collections in medicine and biomedical engineering.

1910. Encyclopedic Dictionary of Sports Medicine. Tver, David F., and Howard F. Hunt. New York: Chapman & Hall, 1986. 232p.

This is a short entry encyclopedia which contains no bibliography. The main section is followed by a glossary, though it would have been better to include glossary words in the main section. This is a quick answer reference source only. Within this restriction, it works well.

1911. Merck Index: An Encyclopedia of Chemicals, Drugs, and Biologicals. 10th ed. Rahway, NJ: Merck, 1983. 1v. (various paging).

RS51
m4
1989
Sci
Ref

This has become a world-renowned index on chemicals and drugs, and the information relating to both. Each entry in the index consists of variant names, trademarks, formulas, and usage. The particular drug or chemical is listed only once, forcing use of the index. This is a "must have" title for most scientific and technical collections.

1912. **Potter's New Cyclopaedia of Botanical Drugs and Preparations.** rev. ed. Wren, R. C. Saffron Walden, England: C. W. Daniel, 1975. 400p.

This is a classic source for medically used herbal compounds. Provided is a description of the plants from which the herbs are derived. This is not a high use item, but is still a one-of-a-kind reference tool.

1913. **Understanding Medical Terminology.** 7th ed. Frenay, Agnes Clare, and Rose Maureen Mahoney. St. Louis, MO: Catholic Health Association, 1984. 618p.

This is a student or layperson's text to medical terminology. The book is divided into sections, each dealing with a type of medical disorder. There is a section on terminology used in the allied fields of medicine. This is a good basic book on terminology. It should be highly useful in general and nonresearch collections.

DICTIONARIES

1914. **Bailliere's Nurses Dictionary.** 19th ed. Jeffries, Pamela M. London: Bailliere Tindall, 1979. 480p.

This well-known dictionary in the nursing field is included here because it is a classic and is still used by a large number of people in the field. It needs updating, but for general definitions, is more than adequate.

1915. **Black's Medical Dictionary.** 35th ed. Harvard, C. W. H., ed. Totowa, NJ: Barnes & Noble, 1987. 1006p.

This is a classic dictionary in medicine. It is a quick reference tool, not an in-depth source. A clear choice for any collection with interests in medicine.

1916. **Black's Veterinary Dictionary.** 15th ed. West, Geoffrey P. Totowa, NJ: Barnes & Noble, 1985. 896p.

A standard reference tool for any veterinary library, this is constantly updated, reliable, and very complete. It is also clear enough for the pet owner to use in recognizing symptoms or beginning first aid. Illustrated with line drawings and photographs.

1917. **Dictionary of Alcohol Use and Abuse: Slang, Terms, and Terminology.** Abel, Ernest L., comp. Westport, CT: Greenwood Press, 1985. 189p.

Contains approximately 4,000 very short and simple definitions of slang terms. This is an extensive bibliography of sources that includes primarily slang words, as well as the more common technical terms relating to the effects of alcohol and the treatment of alcohol related problems. Easy to understand.

1918. **Dictionary of Biomedical Acronyms and Abbreviations.** Dupayrat, Jacques. New York: Wiley, 1984. 131p.

The main areas covered in this dictionary are medicine, biology, and biochemistry. It is intended for use by researchers in the field who already have some background in the terminology. This is an excellent dictionary in a fast growing area and is highly recommended for any medical or biomedical collection used by researchers.

1919. **Dictionary of Immunology.** Herbert, W. J., P. C. Wilkinson, and D. I. Stott, eds. Oxford: Blackwell Scientific Publications, 1985. 240p.

This is an undergraduate level dictionary. It can meet the basic needs of the clinician in areas other than his or her specialty. Provided are short descriptions of diseases with immunological features, vaccines, and some obsolete terms. This is a good choice for general collections.

1920. **Dictionary of Medical Acronyms & Abbreviations.** Jablonski, Stanley. St. Louis, MO: Mosby, 1987. 205p.

The entries here were obtained by scanning literature at the National Library of Medicine. Brief descriptions, usually no more than one line, follow each entry. The major contribution of this work is that it is current. It is recommended for most collections.

1921. **Dictionary of Medical Ethics.** rev. ed. Duncan, A. S., G. R. Dunstan, and R. B. Wellbourn, eds. New York: Crossroad Publishing, 1981. 459p.

This is both a dictionary and, in effect, a survey of medical ethics. There appears to be no bias in terms of religious viewpoints. This is an excellent source of information which provides both short answers and, with considerably more work, a compendium of views on medical ethics. This work belongs in almost any collection.

1922. **Dictionary of Medical Syndromes.** 2nd ed. Magalini, Sergio I., and Euclide Scrascia. Philadelphia: Lippincott, 1981. 944p.

Defines a plethora of symptoms from across the spectrum of medicine. The entries contain very complete information. In addition to the definition, etiology, diagnostic procedures, therapy, prognosis, and a short bibliography are provided. This is an excellent source for its completeness and should be in virtually every collection.

1923. **Dictionary of Traditional Chinese Medicine.** Zhufon, Xie, et al. Hong Kong: Commercial Press, 1984. 428p.

This dictionary contains 3,325 common terms of traditional Chinese medicine and pharmacy, and includes entries for famous doctors and medical texts. It is indexed by Latin name and by Chinese characters. Recommended for specialized collections.

1924. **Dictionary of Words about Alcohol.** 2nd ed. Keller, Mark, Mark McCormick, and Vera Efron. New Brunswick, NJ: Rutgers Center of Alcohol Studies, 1982. 291p.

Contains some very lengthy and some very short definitions written in paragraph form. A bibliography is included. This is an easy-to-use reference tool that seems to give a select number of definitions; therefore, the coverage is limited and basic.

1925. **Dorland's Illustrated Medical Dictionary.** 26th ed. Philadelphia: W. B. Saunders, 1981. 1485p.

This is a standard dictionary, well known in the health sciences. The definitions are sometimes brief, but they are always adequate. Illustrations are provided. This is highly recommended for medical collections at any level.

1926. **Dorland's Pocket Medical Dictionary.** 23rd ed. Philadelphia: W. B. Saunders, 1982. 754p.

This is the "pocket" edition of *Dorland's Illustrated Medical Dictionary* (see entry 1925). Meant as a quick reference, the definitions are sometimes too brief. The brevity of the work requires some prior knowledge in order to utilize it to its fullest. Recommended for professional use or specialized collections.

1927. **Ffrangcon Roberts' Medical Terms: Their Origin and Construction.** 6th ed. rev. and enl. Lennox, Bernard, ed. London: Heinemann Medical Books, 1980. 132p.

In two parts, the first part is a listing of words and their origin. The second part lists synonyms and antonyms for the purposes of comparison and contrast. This is an excellent means to obtain definitions and is highly recommended for virtually any medical collection from the public library through research collections.

1928. **Industrial Medicine Desk Reference.** Tver, David F., and Kenneth A. Anderson. New York: Chapman & Hall, 1986. 307p.

A dictionary in which entries for chemicals cite the current official worker exposure limits. This makes the dictionary a very specialized tool and perhaps mistitled. There is no bibliography for entries. This is recommended for specialized collections only.

1929. **International Dictionary of Medicine and Biology.** Landau, Sidney C., ed. New York: Wiley, 1986. 3v.

The subheadings of the dictionary are printed in slightly smaller type than the main headings and are indented one space. This makes it somewhat difficult to locate terms. Once past the layout irregularity, this is a good dictionary. It is recommended for both specialized and general collections.

1930. **MASA: Medical Acronyms, Symbols, & Abbreviations.** Hamilton, Betty, and Barbara Guidos. New York: Neal-Schuman, 1984. 186p.

The proliferation of symbols and abbreviations in almost any field is problematic. This work attempts to give the reader some help in the medical area. The terms are drawn from all major medical specialties and include multiple definitions where warranted. This is a highly recommended work for virtually any collection in the medical sciences.

1931. **Medical Abbreviations: 4,200 Conveniences at the Expense of Communications and Safety.** Davis, Neil M. Huntington Valley, PA: Davis Associates, 1987. 102p.

This is a listing of abbreviations intended to break the jargon of medicine. The subtitle indicates the tenor of the book. It will be of interest to public libraries and to the layperson.

1932. **Medical and Health Sciences Word Book.** 2nd ed. Hafer, Ann, comp. Boston: Houghton Mifflin, 1982. 363p.

One primary intent of this work is to induce the reader to pronounce and spell the terms correctly. Terms have been gathered from a variety of sources, including *Index Medicus* (see entry 1891). This would be of greatest interest to public libraries and the layperson.

1933. **Medical Terminology from Greek and Latin.** Patterson, Sandra R., and Lawrence S. Thompson. Troy, NY: Whitston Publishing, 1982. 275p.

This work deals with Greek and Latin prefixes, suffixes, root words, and plurals. The intent is to allow the user to build definitions of medical terminology based on Greek and Latin stems and attendant parts. This is a novel approach and will be useful for some. Recommended for any collection in medicine.

1934. **Melloni's Illustrated Medical Dictionary.** 2nd ed. Dox, Ida, Biagio John Melloni, and Gilbert M. Eisner. Baltimore, MD: Williams & Wilkins, 1985. 533p.

This is an excellent source of illustrations dealing with medical terminology. The strength of this dictionary is found in its use of illustrations. An excellent attempt is made to avoid "circular" definitions that send the user to all parts of the dictionary. As a result this work is not as comprehensive as some, but the tradeoff is definitely worth the price. Highly recommended for any medical collection.

1935. **Merck Manual: Of Diagnosis and Therapy.** 14th ed. Berkow, Robert, ed. Rahway, NJ: Merck, Sharp and Dome Research Laboratories, 1982. 2578p.

RC55
M4
Sci
Ref

This is a standard work found in any good collection in medicine. Divided into broad subject areas, it covers the breadth of medicine. An excellent subject index is included. This is a "must" for any serious collection in this area.

1936. **Pharmacological and Chemical Synonyms: A Collection of Names of Drugs, Pesticides, and Other Compounds Drawn from the Medical Literature of the World.** 8th ed. Marler, E. E. J. New York: Elsevier, 1985. 545p.

The subtitle is a virtual annotation to this work. It lists common names, proprietary terms, and research code numbers for chemicals and compounds as they are listed in the literature. This is an excellent tool for specialized collections and research collections.

1937. **Psychiatric Dictionary.** 5th ed. Campbell, Robert Jean. New York: Oxford University Press, 1981. 693p.

This is a broad based approach to definitions in psychiatry. The major hypotheses of psychiatry were taken into account when the definitions were written. What results is an unsatisfactory dictionary for the specialist, but a good dictionary for the layperson or the novice. It is recommended with some care for general collections.

1938. **Slang and Jargon of Drugs and Drink.** Spears, Richard A. Metuchen, NJ: Scarecrow Press, 1986. 585p.

Covers the period from 1700 to the present, both in retrospect and as augmented by the author. It is a collection of about 5,000 terms used for drugs, alcohol, and tobacco, giving the source of the word and short definitions. It is an excellent, extensive resource of slang or "street language" but difficult to use. The guide to using this dictionary is essential in order to understand the information given with each entry because of the numerous cross-references.

1939. **Stedman's Medical Dictionary.** 24th ed. Baltimore, MD: Williams & Wilkins, 1982. 1678p.

This dictionary groups definitions into categories, a practice which mandates the use of the main cross-reference section. The dictionary is difficult to use for definitions, but serves well if the purpose is to examine related terms. It is recommended with caution.

1940. **Taber's Cyclopedic Medical Dictionary.** 15th ed. Thomas, Clayton L., ed. Philadelphia: F. A. Davis, 1985. 2170p.

This is intended for those with some grounding in medicine or the allied health areas. Phonetic spellings and abbreviations are normally found. This is a good, general purpose dictionary for medicine and is highly recommended for any medical collection.

1941. **Webster's New World Medical Word Finder.** 4th ed. Willeford, George, comp. Englewood Cliffs, NJ: Prentice-Hall, 1987. 433p.

This is a standard dictionary, modelled on the Webster dictionary model. It provides spelling, syllabification, pronunciation, and definitions for most common medical terms. The major focus of the dictionary is on medical and paramedical terms, though dental and associated terminology is also covered to a lesser extent. Highly recommended for almost any collection.

HANDBOOKS AND LABORATORY GUIDES

1942. **AHFS American Hospital Formulary Drug Information 87.** McEvoy, Gerald K., ed. Bethesda, MD: American Society of Hospital Pharmacists, 1987. 2091p.

This is a collection of reports by experts with the intent of distributing unbiased, evaluative drug information to the medical community. The reports are usually two to three pages long. Updated quarterly, this is an excellent work and is highly recommended for any medical or biomedical collection.

RS355
.A48
Sci
Ref

1943. **American Drug Index.** Philadelphia: Lippincott, 1956- . annual.

This is a listing of the pharmaceuticals available for dispensation. Each item is listed by brand name, generic name, and chemical name. A secondary component of the work is a listing of manufacturers and distributors. This is an excellent work for specific collections.

1944. **American Medical Association Family Medical Guide.** rev. ed. Kunz, Jefferey R., and Asher J. Finkel, eds. New York: Random House, 1987. 832p.

Intended for use in the home, this may be too complex for some. The book is comprised of four sections: the "healthy body," symptoms and self-diagnosis, explanations of simple diseases, and health care in the home. The overall level is uneven with some descriptions and definitions being overly simplistic and some being overly technical and complicated. However, the work is to be commended for the excellent charts on diagnosis in the second section. A better choice for home use would be *Complete Guide to Symptoms, Illness & Surgery* (see entry 1953) because of the evenness of its treatment. This title is still recommended as a good second choice for general collections.

1945. **Biomedical Signal Processing.** Cohen, Aron. Boca Raton, FL: CRC Press, 1986. 2v.

Provides physiologists, engineers, and computer scientists with methods for analysis, representation, and classification of complex signals. Theory and practice of random digital and analog signal theory are discussed. An appendix lists signal processing computer programs. This is a researcher's handbook, recommended only for clear research collections.

Blood compatible materials+ their testing

R857
P6
B66
1986
Sci

1946. **Blood Compatibility.** Williams, D. F., ed. Boca Raton, FL: CRC Press, 1987. 2v.

Includes information on the interaction between the blood and biomaterials, specifically implants and assist devices. The focus is on the basic physiology of blood in relation to homeostasis and thrombosis. This is a mammoth work which will be used by serious researchers in the biomedical community. It is highly recommended for research collections.

1947. **Cancer, Diet, and Nutrition: A Comprehensive Sourcebook.** Greenwald, Peter, Abby G. Ershow, and William D. Novelli, eds. Chicago, IL: Marquis Who's Who, 1985. 673p.

This sourcebook is divided into three main sections: (1) scientific evidence linking cancer to diet and nutrition; (2) epidemiologic support for the link between cancer and diet; and (3) social marketing and cancer prevention. This is a technical sourcebook not aimed at the general public. It will find good utility in a medical research collection.

1948. **Carcinogenesis and Aging.** Anisimov, Vladimir N., ed. Boca Raton, FL: CRC Press, 1987. 2v.

This set pulls together much of the literature and research on the increase of cancer in aging animals and humans. Current concepts such as the role of age-related shifts in the production of enzymes as well as DNA repair are discussed. This is a highly technical work for those doing research in the field. Highly recommended, but only for research collections.

1949. **Clinical Toxicology of Commercial Products: Acute Poisoning.** 5th ed. Gosselin, Robert E., et al. Baltimore, MD: Williams & Wilkins, 1984. 2009p.

This is designed for use by physicians treating chemical poisonings. Emergency care for acute poisonings is the focal point. Indexes covering ingredients, treatments, trade names, and manufacturers' names and telephone numbers are provided. This will be an excellent tool in any acute care facility.

1950. **Common Symptom Guide: A Guide to the Evaluation of 100 Common Adult and Pediatric Symptoms.** 2nd ed. Wasson, John, et al. New York: McGraw-Hill, 1984. 391p.

Serves as both a textbook and a handbook for medical students and others in the health care profession. The pertinent information on symptoms is arranged under the heading "complaints." This is a good choice for most medical school libraries and professional collections. It will find some limited use in public libraries.

1951. **Complete Book of Medical Tests.** Moskowitz, Mark A., and Michael E. Osband. New York: W. W. Norton, 1984. 386p.

This work deals not only with questions about tests but contains discussions on purposes of certain tests, normal ranges, and cost data. This is a valuable reference tool for those who wish to be informed consumers. It is a very good balance between supplying information to the patient and clearly indicating the need for professional care. Recommended for general use collections.

1952. **Complete Guide to Prescription and Nonprescription Drugs.** rev. ed. Griffith, H. Winter. Tucson, AZ: HP Books, 1987. 888p.

This is now a classic guide for the informed patient. The revised edition continues what the first began and provides a supplementary guide for patient education. The work consists of instruction sheets detailing for the layperson the uses and indications of prescription and nonprescription drugs. This is an excellent tool in any general purpose collection.

1953. **Complete Guide to Symptoms, Illness & Surgery.** Griffith, H. Winter. Tucson, AZ: HP Books, 1985. 896p.

This is a supplementary guide to medical treatment. More technical information is found in other titles; however, this book promotes full participation with a physician in treatment of diseases and ailments. This is, in effect, a medical reference book for patients and should be in the collection of any general or public library.

1954. **Complete Handbook of Approved New Animal Drug Applications in the United States.** Shotwell, Thomas K., Paul W. Carr, and Guy E. Cooper. Dallas, TX: Shotwell & Carr, 1980- . annual. looseleaf.

Arranged by the animal class of dog, cat, or swine, this work is suitable for large libraries with teaching and research orientation. The format makes this a timely source for the latest information on drug application for animals.

1955. **CRC Handbook of Engineering in Medicine and Biology.** Boca Raton, FL: CRC Press, 1976- . irregular. [currently in 2 volumes].

This is now a standard work in the use of engineering techniques in medicine and biology. This was one of the first handbooks dealing with the biomedical engineering area. As such, it has an engineering thrust which should be kept in mind when using the tool. It is still excellent in its synthesis of technology with science and is highly recommended to the point that it is a necessity in any serious collection in biomedical engineering.

1956. **CRC Handbook of Physiology in Aging.** Masoro, Edward J., ed. Boca Raton, FL: CRC Press, 1981. 502p.

This handbook provides an encyclopedic coverage of currently available data and knowledge regarding physiologic changes occurring with age from young adulthood through senescence. Extensive references to the primary literature are provided. This is an excellent choice for specialized collections.

1957. **Current Diagnosis.** Conn, Rex B., ed. Philadelphia: Saunders, 1966- . biennial.

The intent is to cover in detail the diagnostic methods for particular diseases. It specifically omits the treatment of the disease. Highly recommended for medical collections.

1958. **Current Drug Handbook 1984-1986.** Patterson, H. Robert, Elinor Sidor Sheridan, and Edward A. Gustafson. Philadelphia: W. B. Saunders, 1984. 283p.

Contains information on drugs in table form. The information provided in each table includes names, sources, synonyms, preparations, dosage, administration, usage, contraindications, and notes. Highly recommended for any medical collection.

1959. **Current Veterinary Therapy IX — Small Animal Practice.** Kirk, Robert W., ed. Philadelphia: W. B. Saunders, 1986. 1346p.

This is a very up-to-date source that is well indexed and includes bibliographies. Some illustrations are provided. This is definitely a "must-have" for libraries with educational orientation.

1960. **Drug Evaluations.** 6th ed. Chicago, IL: American Medical Association, 1986. 102p.

The aim is to provide physicians and other health-care professionals with up-to-date, unbiased information on the clinical use of drugs. Highly recommended for medical collections and an authoritative source.

1961. **Drug Facts and Comparisons.** St. Louis, MO: Facts and Comparisons Division, Lippincott, 1987. 2226p.

Published in both looseleaf and microfiche editions, this work provides a comparison on the therapeutic value of similar products. There is also a cost index figure for like drugs. This is highly recommended for all types of collections with a medical focus.

1962. **Essential Guide to Prescription Drugs.** Long, James W. New York: Harper & Row, 1987. 933p.

This is a comprehensive guide to prescription drugs for the layperson or patient. The drugs listed are those marketed in the United States and Canada. This is highly recommended for any collection in medicine with the layperson in mind.

1963. **Formulation of Veterinary Dosage Forms.** Blodinger, Jack, ed. New York: Dekker, 1983. 316p.

SF917
F67
1983
Sci

The emphasis is appropriate for the manufacturer of veterinary drugs. It includes formulations, dose dispensing equipment, and regulations. The author and subject indexes are well done.

1964. **French's Index of Differential Diagnosis.** 12th ed. Hart, F. Dudley, ed. Bristol, England: Wright, 1985. 1032p.

A classic in the field of differential diagnosis. Symptoms are listed under the disease to which they belong. This makes the work somewhat difficult for anyone but the expert to use. The range of diseases and symptoms covers the common to the very rare. This is a specialty item for experts in the field.

1965. **Grant's Atlas of Anatomy.** 8th ed. Anderson, James E. Baltimore, MD: Williams & Wilkins, 1983. 1v. (various paging).

Detailed cross-sections are provided for each part of the body. The atlas is arranged in the order that the student would find the parts of the body in a dissecting class. Textual comment is kept to a minimum.

1966. **Handbook of Abusable Drugs.** Blum, Kenneth. New York: Gardner, 1984. 721p.

The overall intent of the book is to demonstrate the social links inherent in drug abuse. The work is biased in its approach and views problems from more a social than medical standpoint. Nonetheless, it contains material of interest to the biomedical and scientific community such as the tabular information correlating drugs to side effects. It is recommended for most medical collections.

1967. **Handbook of Bioengineering.** Skalak, Richard, and Shu Chien, eds. New York: McGraw-Hill, 1987. 1v. (various paging).

The editors have pulled together the contributions of a range of experts in bioengineering to produce a mathematically oriented handbook for researchers. A decision was made by the editors not to deal with agricultural and food technology. The result is a volume with enough engineering detail to satisfy engineers, and enough nonengineering material to satisfy biologists and physicians. This handbook is excellent in its balanced approach to bioengineering. It is highly recommended for research collections in the biomedical sciences and biomedical engineering.

1968. **Handbook of Clinical Dietetics.** American Dietetic Association. New Haven, CT: Yale University Press, 1981. 517p.

The purpose is to define required dietetic diet content and terminology. Extensive bibliographies are a distinct feature. This is a specific handbook with a specific audience. It covers the field well.

1969. **Handbook of Clinical Neurology.** Vinken, Pierre J., and George W. Bruyn, eds. New York: Elsevier, 1968- . irregular.

Covers all aspects of clinical neurology. This has become a classic work, approaching the status of a treatise. It is an excellent choice for any medical collection emphasizing research.

1970. **Handbook of Medical Library Practice.** 4th ed. Darling, Louise, ed. Chicago, IL: Medical Library Association, 1983. 2v.

A good survey of medical library practice, this handbook covers such areas as the emergence of the modern medical library; the medical librarian; administration; technical processing; readers' services; automation in medical libraries; audiovisual materials; research; rare books, archives, and history of medicine; library planning, furniture and equipment; the National Library of Medicine; the library and its public; identification and communication; professional associations; and British medical libraries. It is recommended for medical libraries and library science collections.

1971. **Handbook of Medical Treatment.** 17th ed. Watts, H. David. Greenbrae, CA: Jones Medical Publications, 1983. 478p.

This is an excellent starting point for the day-to-day care of patients. The coverage of diseases and treatments is broad and not too deep. More specialized sources should be used for in-depth coverage. This has become a classic desk reference and a well used tool in medical collections.

1972. **Handbook of Neurochemistry.** 2nd ed. Lajtha, Abel, ed. New York: Plenum, 1982-1985. 10v.

This is very close to a treatise in the depth of coverage in neurochemistry. Written by experts in the field, each section is complete within itself. This is highly recommended for any medical research collection.

1973. **Handbook of Non-Prescription Drugs.** 8th ed. Washington, DC: American Pharmaceutical Association, 1986. 741p.

This is an excellent handbook for both specialists and laypersons. It lists a wide variety of nonprescription drugs and their indications. Appropriate use of the specific drug is also indicated. Very useful in virtually any collection with some medical material.

1974. **Handbook of Obstetrics & Gynecology.** 8th ed. Benson, Ralph C. Los Altos, CA: Lange Medical Publications, 1983. 804p.

A practical handbook along the lines of a refresher manual for physicians and medical students. The clinical procedures and applications of medical theory are stressed. This is, however, not a medical textbook. It presupposes some medical grounding and is recommended for the medical collection of practitioners and medical libraries.

1975. **Handbook of Pediatrics.** 15th ed. Silver, Henry K., et al. Norwalk, CT: Appleton & Lange, 1987. 924p.

The focus is on diagnosis and treatment of pediatric disorders. Recent advances in clinical treatment are noted. The intended audience is the medical student and the physician. Recommended for medical library collections and professional collections.

1976. **Handbook of Poisoning: Prevention, Diagnosis & Treatment.** 12th ed. Dreisbach, Robert H., and William O. Robertson. Norwalk, CT: Appleton & Lange, 1987. 589p.

A compendium of poisons and the diagnosis and treatment of the specific poison. Some hazardous materials which are nonpoisonous are also included. Agricultural, industrial, medical, and household poisons are covered. This is an excellent source for information on the treatment of poisons and is highly recommended for any collection with a medical component.

1977. **Handbook of Toxic and Hazardous Chemicals and Carcinogens.** 2nd ed. Sittig, Marshall. Park Ridge, NJ: Noyes Publications, 1985. 950p.

More general than *Handbook of Poisoning* (see entry 1976), this handbook lists almost 800 toxic and hazardous chemicals. The information for each entry covers chemical, health, and safety information as appropriate. It is highly recommended for any collection with a segment dealing with poisons.

1978. **Handbook of Veterinary Procedures & Emergency Treatment.** 4th ed. Kirk, Robert Warren, and Stephen I. Bister. Philadelphia: W. B. Saunders, 1985. 1000p.

The entire text has been updated to include interpretation of symptoms, systems examination, diagnostic procedures, therapy, lab tests, tables, and charts. It contains an excellent emergency section and is indexed. Available in Spanish, French, Italian, and Japanese, it is an authoritative and familiar reference to professionals.

1979. **Injury Fact Book.** Baker, Susan P., Brian O'Neill, and Ronald S. Karpf. Lexington, MA: Lexington Books, 1984. 313p.

A statistical analysis of the patterns of injury. The concentration is on fatal injuries, and the data are gathered from governmental, medical, and insurance sources. This is an excellent analysis in terms of statistics and the textual discussion of the findings. It is highly recommended for any biomedical collection used by researchers.

1980. **Krusen's Handbook of Physical Medicine and Rehabilitation.** 3rd ed. Kottke, Frederick J., G. Keith Stillwell, and Justus F. Lehman. Philadelphia: W. B. Saunders, 1982. 1023p.

Covers the techniques of physical medicine. The emphasis is on management and evaluation of specific disorders together with rehabilitation. This is a specialized handbook for specialized collections.

1981. **Med Tech: The Layperson's Guide to Today's Medical Miracles.** Galton, Lawrence. New York: Harper & Row, 1985. 381p.

This is a scientifically sound medical handbook written for the layperson. The book contains 98 topics arranged alphabetically. There is a lack of references and a bibliography, but the tone and quality of the book make it an excellent choice for public and general collections in medicine.

1982. **Medical Mycology Manual.** 4th ed. Beneke, E. S., and A. L. Rogers. Minneapolis, MN: Burgess, 1980. 173p.

This is a professional handbook for use by researchers and laboratory technicians in medical mycology. Each fungus listed is described, followed by a list of occurrences, etiological agents, and references to the primary literature. This is highly specific and recommended only for specialized collections.

1983. **Merck Veterinary Manual: A Handbook of Diagnosis, Therapy, and Disease Prevention and Control for the Veterinarian.** 6th ed. Fraser, Clarence M., ed. Rahway, NJ: Merck & Co., 1986. 1677p.

Sections are titled: "Disease and Body Systems," "Toxicology," "Nutrition," "Behavior," "Prescribing," "Poultry," "Exotics," and "Laboratory Animals." There is a quick reference section as well. This is a good ready reference tool for the practitioner and is a basic source of information. It is highly recommended for specific collections.

1984. **Nuclear Medical Physics.** Williams, Lawrence E., ed. Boco Raton, FL: CRC Press, 1987. 3v.

This set covers the physical basis of nuclear medicine and is intended as a complete source of data for scientists and physicians. It begins with quantum theory and leads to the production and attenuation of ionizing radiation. This is a massive compendium of facts and tables with text. It should be a part of any collection which supports nuclear medicine.

1985. **Nurse's Drug Handbook.** 4th ed. Loebl, Suzanne, and George R. Spratto. New York: Wiley, 1986. 977p.

This handbook is intended for nursing students and nursing practitioners. It concentrates on drugs by grouping them into classes. Some in-depth descriptions of more important drugs are also given. This is a very useful reference in medical collections and nursing libraries.

1986. **Nursing ... Drug Handbook.** Horsham, PA: Intermed Communications, 1981- . annual.

This title supersedes *Nurse's Guide to Drugs* (Horsham, PA: Intermed Communications, 1979-1981). Because it is an annual it tends to be more up-to-date than *Nurse's Drug Handbook* (see entry 1985). Both are excellent guides to drugs, their dosage, indications, and contents. Useful in medical collections and nursing libraries.

1987. **Oxford Textbook of Medicine.** 2nd ed. Weatherall, D. J., J. G. G. Ledingham, and D. A. Warrell, eds. New York: Oxford University Press, 1987. 2v.

This work reflects the current British practice of internal medicine. There is an index at the back of each volume which acts as a master index for both volumes. The major problem with this work is its lack of a uniform approach to diseases. Material found under one heading for one disease is found under a different heading for another entry. Recommended for research collections only and for those with an interest in British medical practice.

1988. **Parasitology for Veterinarians.** 4th ed. Georgi, Jay R. Philadelphia: W. B. Saunders, 1985. 344p.

This work is composed of three main parts: (1) Identification, Life-cycle, and Pathogenesis of Parasites; (2) Livestock and Domestic Pets and Chemicals in Use for Control; and (3) Diagnosis. Illustrations are redone well in this edition and the photomicrographs are excellent. Appeals to both the student and the practitioner.

1989. **Photomedicine.** Ben-Hur, Ehud, ed. Boca Raton, FL: CRC Press, 1987. 3v.

This set examines the place of photomedicine by describing the basics of the field followed by a series of its potential applications. This is both a handbook and a state-of-the-art review. It is highly recommended for biomedical and biomedical education collections.

1990. **Physicians Desk Reference.** Ordell, NJ: Medical Economics, 1974- . annual.

Supersedes *Physicians Desk Reference to Pharmaceutical Specialties and Biologicals* (Ordell, NJ: Medical Economics, 1947-1973). This is the primary desk reference for the working physician. It deals with the pharmaceutical issues of indications, dosage, side effects, and interactions of prescription drugs. This is a necessary part of any medical collection in any type of library.

1991. **Physicians Desk Reference for Non-Prescription Drugs.** Ordell, NJ: Medical Economics, 1980- . annual.

This is a guide to nonprescription drugs which lists their ingredients, actions, dosage, and adverse reactions. It is a companion to *Physicians Desk Reference* (see entry 1990) and is just as important.

1992. **Physician's Handbook.** 21st ed. Krupp, Marcus A., et al. Los Altos, CA: Lange Medical, 1985. 800p.

This is a smaller handbook stressing diagnosis. It is of interest to practicing physicians and medical students because it contains diagnostic and therapeutic information gleaned from texts, laboratory examinations, and new procedures. It is recommended for medical collections with an interest in medical education.

1993. **Prescription Drugs and Their Side Effects.** 5th ed. Stern, Edward L. New York: Perigee Books, 1987. 204p.

This is a good handbook for those on the periphery of the medical profession. It is too basic for practicing physicians. Information on drugs, side effects, manufacturer, dosage, and means of administration are given. The primary use for particular drugs is listed. This is recommended for medical collections with an informed, but not expert clientele.

1994. **Simulation and Control of the Cardiac System.** Sideman, Samuel, and Rafael Beyar, eds. Boca Raton, FL: CRC Press, 1987. 3v.

This set presents an integrated approach to the cardiac system and its control. It reviews various aspects of control in the cardiac system, including cardiac mechanics, coronary hemodynamics, and metabolic pathways. Of particular interest is the fact that it meets head-on some controversial issues such as the solution to the inverse problem. It is highly recommended for research collections in biomedicine.

1995. **U.S. Dispensatory.** 27th ed. Osol, Arthur, Robertson Pratt, and Alfonso R. Gennaro, eds. Philadelphia: Lippincott, 1973. 1292p.

This is predominantly a collection of articles on specific drugs or classes of drugs. The intent of the articles is to supply information on various pharmaceuticals in terms of dosage, therapeutic actions, preparation, interactions, and nomenclature. This is a necessary tool in pharmacology and is highly recommended for any collection dealing in any way with pharmacology.

1996. **United States Pharmacopeia Drug Information for the Consumer.** Mt. Vernon, NY: Consumers Union, 1987. 1202p.

Many experts feel this is the best consumer-oriented work available in its field. The arrangement of the work is by the generic name of the drug. The index contains both the generic name and the brand name. Each entry includes information on the part of the body affected, brand names, prior precautions before usage, proper use, and side effects. This is a required tool for most general purpose medical collections.

1997. **United States Pharmacopeia, Twenty-First Revision: The National Formulary, Sixteenth Edition.** Rockville, MD: United States Pharmacopoeial Convention, 1985. 1683p.

The first *United States Pharmacopoeia* was published in 1820. It and the *National Formulary* represent a composite listing of what were two publications. The composite work is a listing of standards which have been developed in the medical profession for drugs, identification, purity, strength, and formulas. This is, in effect, the master listing of all drugs recognized in the U.S. and is an absolute necessity for most medical and the majority of medical research collections.

1998. **Upson's Handbook of Clinical Veterinary Pharmacology.** Upson, Dan W. Lenexa, KS: Veterinary Medicine Publishing Co., 1985. 660p.

Provides actions, responses, and mechanisms by which each drug operates along with the adverse or toxic reactions. Arranged by body system (central nervous system) or function (muscle relaxants), it contains a good introduction with definitions, background, and regulations of pharmacology. Aimed at the general practitioner, it fills the need for office reference works because of its emphasis on clinical applications.

1999. Veterinary Drug Index. Lewis, Benjamin, and Leon O. Wilkin. Philadelphia: W. B. Saunders, 1982. 327p.

This is very good as a ready reference or quick reference for the veterinary practitioner. It gives dosage, indications, and contraindications for each drug and contains a list of sources for supply. Useful appendices are included, along with separate sections of generic, trade, and drug classification for pharmaceuticals and biologicals.

2000. Veterinary Pharmaceuticals and Biologicals 1987/1988. 5th ed. Lenexa, KS: Veterinary Medicine Publishing Co., 1986. 586p.

Basically a "physicians desk reference" for veterinarians, this work contains current product information gathered from the manufacturers only. It is divided into four main sections: an alphabetical list of products, products listed by manufacturer, product identification (color plates of each), and a cross index of generic and proprietary names. This is a good basic source as long as one keeps the bias of the manufacturers in mind.

2001. Women's Drugstore. Silverman, Harold M. New York: Dell, 1985. 403p.

This is a guide to drugs, prescription and nonprescription, and medical devices commonly used by women. The arrangement is by broad topics such as pregnancy, contraception, and hormone replacement. The material on drug interactions and side effects is very useful. Because of its use of medical terminology, some prior knowledge is necessary. This will be a useful addition not so much for medical reference, but for general reference collections with an informed but nonexpert clientele.

2002. Yearbook of Agriculture 1984: Animal Health: Livestock and Pets. Washington, DC: U.S. Department of Agriculture, 1984. 646p.

Aimed at the pet owner and livestock producer, this provides good, basic background information on animal health in general. Tables on norms, laws, and vaccinations are included along with a glossary and index. Contains very practical information on care, feeding, reproduction, and housing. Any library could use this reference.

POPULAR MEDICAL GUIDES

The following are some popular guides which might be of interest in public, special, and medical libraries.

2003. Advocate Guide to Gay Health. rev. ed. Fenwick, R. D. Boston: Alyson Publications, 1982. 236p.

This is a good guide to wellness in the gay community. It discusses particular medical problems of the gay community as well as common medical problems.

2004. Compleat Herbal: Being a Description of the Origins, the Lore, the Characteristics, the Types, and the Prescribed Uses of Medicinal Herbs, Including an Alphabetical Guide to All Common Medicinal Plants. Harris, Ben Charles. Barre, MA: Barre Publishers, 1972. 243p.

This is a guide to herbs and the powers ascribed to them. It is a useful reference source for some questions.

2005. **Complete Medical Guide.** 4th ed. Miller, Benjamin F., with Lawrence Galton. New York: Simon & Schuster, 1978. 639p.

This is not a complete medical guide, but a short description of diseases and medical terminology.

2006. **Dictionary of Drugs: The Medicines You Use.** rev. ed. Fisher, Richard B., and George A. Christie. New York: Schocken Books, 1976. 256p.

A layperson's guide to drugs and their components. This is particularly interesting for the information on interactions of various drugs with other drugs and common substances.

2007. **Patients' Guide to Medicine: From the Drugstore through the Hospital.** 9th ed. Brown, Warren J. Largo, FL: Aero-Medical Consultants, 1981. 259p.

A guidebook to the medical profession and allied health fields. The intent is to make the patient a wise consumer of medical practice. This is a good overview and recommended for public library collections.

DIRECTORIES

2008. **Alcohol, Drug Abuse, and Mental Health Research Grant Awards (ADAMHA).** Rockville, MD: Public Health Service, 1984.

Gives reference to over 209 million dollars in research and training awards to individuals and organizations in 49 states; Washington, DC; Puerto Rico; and seven foreign countries. Recipients are 368 colleges, universities, hospitals and professional organizations, and not-for-profit organizations. Arranged by area, organization, principal investigators, awardee, fellowship awards, research training awards, organization or program director, project title, and grant number index. This is an essential tool for hospital or medical school researchers in determining information regarding past grants and awards. It is quick and easy to use.

2009. **American Dental Directory.** Chicago, IL: American Dental Association, 1947- . annual.

Arranged by geographical location, alphabet, and membership classification, with a geographical list of dentists describing their type of practice. This is a good source of information for those in the dental profession. Standard directory information is all that is given. This is recommended for dental collections and some medical collections.

2010. **American Medical Directory.** Chicago, IL: American Medical Association, 1906- . irregular.

This is the master listing of physicians in the U.S. It lists all legally qualified physicians in alphabetical order, and by state and city within each state. It also includes physicians from the Canal Zone, Puerto Rico, Virgin Islands, certain Pacific Islands, and U.S. physicians temporarily located in foreign countries. It is indispensable for directory information in the medical community.

R 712.A
A6
Sci
(up to
1979)

2011. **American Veterinary Medical Association Directory.** Schaumburg, IL: American Veterinary Medical Association, 1956. biennial.

This was issued irregularly until 1974 when it became biennial. It is an excellent source of information about the veterinary world consisting of the United States, Canada, "Other Countries," and nonmembers. "Others" include Antigua to Zimbabwe. It is divided into three main sections: alphabetical by member name; geographical by state and town or country with who's who-type entry; AVMA information, including policies, guidelines, ethics, history, other associations, federal and state agencies, and veterinary schools. Also included are films and video, practice arts, and specialty boards. This will be very useful to practitioners and to veterinary medicine libraries.

2012.   **Bioscan.** Phoenix, AZ: Oryx Press, 1987- . bimonthly. looseleaf.
This is a new publication giving up-to-date information on companies, investments, and research and development. It covers the "biotechnology revolution" by focusing on the corporate growth in biotechnology. Information includes address, employees, history, facilities, stock/financial history, investments, investors, strategy, agreements with other organizations, research and development, products on the market, and products in development. This is a clearly indexed and well done source recommended for business, technology, and biomedical collections.

2013.   **Dictionary of American Medical Biography.** Kaufman, Martin, Stuart Galishoff, and Todd L. Savitt. Westport, CT: Greenwood Press, 1984. 2v.
An individual must be deceased prior to January 1, 1977, in order to be included. A half-page biography and bibliography comprises each entry. This work contains more recent figures than many other medical biography collections. It is an excellent addition to any collection dealing with medical history.

2014.   **Directory of Biomedical and Health Care Grants.** Phoenix, AZ: Oryx Press, 1988. 480p.
This is a derivative work drawn from the GRANTS (Phoenix, AZ: Oryx, current) database and *Directory of Research Grants* (Phoenix, AZ: Oryx, 1975-). It lists over one thousand funding programs and will prove to be a time-saving compilation for some researchers. Recommended for research collections.

2015.   **Directory of Health, Education, and Research Journals.** Pratt, Lee. Rutherford, NJ: Fairleigh Dickinson University Presses, 1984. 137p.
A directory of over 400 health related serials. The information provided includes publisher, circulation, author payment, photo policy, and scope of journal. This is a good collection development tool for any medical or health related collection.

2016.   **Directory of Medical Specialists.** 22nd ed. Chicago, IL: Marquis Who's Who, 1985. 3v.
This is the authorized publication of the American Specialty Boards, which certify physicians as medical specialists. A section on the requirements for certification is included. The listing is by member, then by geographic location. This is an excellent listing of physicians and contains considerably more information for each entry than does the *American Medical Directory* (see entry 2010). It will find use in any library where the clientele has any interest in medicine and physicians.

2017.   **Directory of Pathology Training Programs.** Bethesda, MD: Intersociety Committee on Pathology Information, 1969/70- . annual.
This is an aid for top physicians seeking pathology training programs. It covers hospitals, medical schools, and laboratories, and is extremely useful in medical school collections.

2018.   **Directory of Physicians in the United States, Puerto Rico, Virgin Islands, Certain Pacific Islands and U.S. Physicians Temporarily Located in Foreign Countries.** 29th ed. Chicago, IL: American Medical Association, 1985. 4v.

Included in the listing for each name is directory-type information supplemented with the name of the medical school, the year of first license at the present address, professional activities, and any board certification. The first volume is an index to the last three which are arranged geographically by state, territory, or foreign country. This is highly recommended for directory information in medical collections.

2019. Encyclopedia of Medical Organizations and Agencies: A Subject Guide.... 2nd ed. Kruzas, Anthony T., Kay Gill, and Robert Wilson, eds. Detroit, MI: Gale, 1987. 975p.

This source lists and describes organizations related to biomedical and health sciences. The organizations are first divided into 78 chapters then subdivided into types of organizations. Entries include information on contact person, address, a brief description, and other information as applicable. The U.S. bias is evident. This is a good tool for organizational information, but should be used with care in terms of contact persons, as they change rapidly. It is recommended for large collections in the biomedical and health sciences.

2020. Health Care U.S.A. Carper, Jean. New York: Prentice-Hall, 1987. 653p.

This is a directory of organizations, agencies, treatment centers, specialists, and hot lines for medical problems. The problems addressed range from AIDS to Sudden Infant Death Syndrome. Public libraries will find this tool to be invaluable for its directory information. Each medical problem is described as to cause, symptoms, diagnosis, and treatment. Highly recommended for all but research collections.

2021. Health Information Resources in the Federal Government 1984. Washington, DC: National Health Information Clearinghouse, 1984. 128p.

The arrangement of the directory is alphabetical by keyword in the agency's name. Covering 113 entries, sufficient information is given to contact the agency, together with a brief description of its services and activities. This is a very good source for governmental information in the health sciences and is recommended for all medical or biomedical collections.

2022. International Directory of Contract Laboratories. Jackson, Edward M., comp. New York: Dekker, 1985. 157p.

The focus of this work is on commercial and contract laboratories. It is directed toward those in industry and governmental agencies. The internal arrangement is alphabetical, with standard directory information on each entry, including the types of testing done. This should be useful to a wide variety of individuals and organizations involved in the testing of substances. It is highly recommended for all research collections.

2023. International Medical Who's Who: A Biographical Guide in the Biomedical Sciences. 2nd ed. Harlow, England: Longman, 1985. 2v.

This is a much needed update to the 1980 edition. Approximately 12,000 persons are included in this edition. The work is divided into two parts: individual profiles in alphabetical order make up the first part; the second is a listing of experts in different subject areas for different parts of the world. In a biographical guide such as this, with an international scope, there will always be some omissions; however, this work will still be a very useful addition to any medical or biomedical collection.

2024. IPA Drug Name Cross Reference List: X Ref-86. Tousignaut, Dwight R., and Susan K. Moss, eds. Bethesda, MD: American Society of Hospital Pharmacists, 1986. 613p.

This work makes it possible to search for a particular drug regardless of the nomenclature used to describe it. It is a derivative of *International Pharmaceutical Abstracts* (see entry 1896). Proprietary names, generic names, chemical abstracts registry numbers, trade names, chemical names, and investigational numbers are all included in the volume. The information is international in scope, including many foreign drugs not licensed for marketing in the U.S. This is a highly recommended title for any research oriented collection in biomedical science.

2025. **Medical and Health Information Directory: A Guide to Associations, Agencies, Companies, Institutions, Research Centers, Hospitals, Clinics, Treatment Centers, Education Programs, Publications, Audiovisuals, Data Bases, Libraries, and Information Services in Clinical Medicine....** 3rd ed. Kruzas, Anthony, Kay Gill, and Karen Backus, eds. Detroit, MI: Gale, 1985. 2v.

This title annotates itself. Volume one deals with organizations, agencies, and institutions. Volume two contains directory information on libraries, publications, audiovisuals, and database services. A massive amount of information is contained in these two volumes. The second volume appears easier to use, but this may be a familiarity bias. This will be a good choice for medical and biomedical collections needing wide ranging directory information.

2026. **National Directory of Drug Abuse and Alcoholism Treatment and Prevention Programs.** Rockville, MD: U.S. Department of Health and Human Services, 1984. 429p.

This listing of alcoholism and drug abuse agencies was compiled as a result of a survey. Federal, state, local, and privately funded agencies are collected in this resource. Most of the book deals with treatment units, but there are three small sections listing state authorities, drug and alcohol programs, and V.A. medical centers. Treatment units are listed alphabetically by state, city, and then by program name. Address, phone number, and focus are included. The term *focus* refers to treatment, prevention, and service units for either or both alcoholism or drug abuse. This is a quick reference tool for the location of agencies or treatment programs. It gives one-word descriptions of the agencies listed.

2027. **Pharmaceutical Manufacturers of the United States.** 4th ed. DeRenzo, D. J., ed. Park Ridge, NJ: Noyes Data, 1987. 300p.

A guide to the health care product manufacturers in the U.S. Standard directory information is usually found for each entry. Additional information such as annual sales, number of employees, listing of products, and location of facilities is given where it is known. The range of entries and the amount of information is very broad. This is an excellent tool for use in medical and general collections.

Author/Title Index

Reference is to entry number. The letter "n" indicates an item that is mentioned in an annotation.

Subject Index

Reference is to entry number.